Recte

with thanks for
your continuing interest
in and support of my
work

— Ralph

CAMBRIDGE STUDIES
IN ENGLISH LEGAL HISTORY

Edited by
D.E.C. YALE
Fellow of Christ's College
and Reader in English Legal History at the University of Cambridge

The English Judiciary in the Age of Glanvill and Bracton presents a study of the evolution of a professional judiciary in medieval England through the careers of forty-nine royal justices from the last decade of Henry II until 1239. Those years were crucial for the growth of the common law, producing the two legal treatises *Glanvill* and *Bracton*. The period also represents a critical phase in the growth of a professional civil service for England. Turner's study plots the shifts from unspecialised multipurpose royal servants to corps of specialists, each concentrating on one sphere.

By using the method known as prosopography, Turner succeeds in bringing vague outlines of the early royal justices into sharper focus. Although they played a major role in the shaping of English common law, little biographical material has been available. This study, by looking at the judges collectively, succeeds in overcoming the scarcity of sources for individuals and presents a composite picture.

The resulting picture reveals much about the bench in the late twelfth and early thirteenth centuries, and also about the body of royal servants in England. The forty-nine men who contributed so greatly to English law came equally from the laity and clergy. Laymen brought to the bench practical experience in the courts of shire and hundred, while clerics brought varying degrees of knowledge of the written law. Most came from the middle or lower ranks of the knightly class, and all were eager to climb to higher rank. Over half came from families with a tradition of service to the king, yet tracing patterns of patronage shows that they were more likely to owe appointment to the justiciar than to the king directly. Although contemporaries accused them of ambition, greed, and sycophancy, most had only modest success in rising a notch or two on the social scale. Those who rose most spectacularly were those who stood closest to the king.

This study, bringing together legal history, social history, and biography, will interest students of all aspects of medieval English life.

THE ENGLISH JUDICIARY IN THE AGE OF GLANVILL AND BRACTON, c. 1176–1239

RALPH V. TURNER
The Florida State University

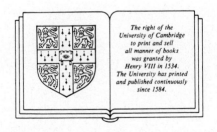

The right of the
University of Cambridge
to print and sell
all manner of books
was granted by
Henry VIII in 1534.
The University has printed
and published continuously
since 1584.

CAMBRIDGE UNIVERSITY PRESS

CAMBRIDGE

LONDON   NEW YORK   NEW ROCHELLE
MELBOURNE   SYDNEY

For my fellow-students in
the 'Painter School' of Medieval English History
The Johns Hopkins University,
1958–1962

Published by the Press Syndicate of the University of Cambridge
The Pitt Building, Trumpington Street, Cambridge CB2 1RP
32 East 57th Street, New York, NY 10022, USA
10 Stamford Road, Oakleigh, Melbourne 3166, Australia

First published 1985

Printed in Great Britain at the University Press, Cambridge

Library of Congress catalogue card number: 84-20058

British Library cataloguing in publication data
Turner, Ralph V.
The English judiciary in the age of Glanvill
and Bracton, c 1176–1239. – (Cambridge studies
in English legal history)
1. Judges – England – History – 12th century
2. Judges – England – History – 13th century
I. Title
344.207′14′09   KD7285

ISBN 0 521 26510 X

CONTENTS

ACKNOWLEDGEMENTS

Students of the Middle Ages call to mind readily the metaphor of 'dwarfs standing on the shoulders of giants', and if I have seen the early common law justices clearly, it is because of the broad shoulders of the giants who preceded me. Most noteworthy is the contribution of two scholars, whose studies made me aware of the possibilities of judicial biographies: Doris M. Stenton and C. A. F. Meekings. Innumerable references to their works in this book make clear the debt I owe to their studies. When I began this study, Meekings offered valuable advice; and after his death, Mrs Meekings generously allowed me to use his unpublished papers. Other British scholars offered advice and encouragement during my visits to England for research. J. C. Holt read an early draft of the entire manuscript, David Crook shared his work with me, and Paul Brand, Christopher Cheney, Michael Clanchy, S. C. F. Milsom and Neil Stacy made valuable suggestions. Many American scholars also contributed to the making of this book, most notably Samuel E. Thorne, whose magisterial work on *Bracton* has so changed the chronology of the common law. I owe a special debt to my companions in the medieval seminar at the Johns Hopkins University, whose friendship has remained constant over the years since we took our degrees and to whom this book is dedicated.

Financial support came from several sources. The department of history at the Florida State University was generous in providing time for research and funds for secretarial assistance and typing. The Council for Faculty Research of the Florida State University, the Penrose Fund of the American Philosophical Society, and the Project in Legal History of the American Bar Foundation provided funds for research trips to England. I am indebted to the Master and Fellows of St Edmund's House, University of Cambridge, for their hospitality during my stays with them, first in 1977 and again in 1980–1, when they elected me a visiting fellow. My friends in London who offered hospitality and encouragement during my visits there also merit my thanks: Frank and Alice Prochaska, Ian Graham, and James Dick.

The staffs of the many libraries and archives in Britain where I undertook research did much to make this book possible: among them the British Library, Cambridge University Library, the Institute for Historical Research, University of London, Public Record Office, Lambeth Palace Library, and the Westminster Abbey Muniments Room. Among American libraries, I am indebted to the Strozier Library at the Florida State University, especially to the inter-library loan staff, and to the libraries of Duke University and Emory University.

Tallahassee, 27 October 1983   R.V.T.

ABBREVIATIONS

A.H.R.	*American Historical Review*
A.J.L.H.	*American Journal of Legal History*
Annales Mon.	*Annales Monastici,* ed. H.R. Luard, 5 vols., Rolls Series (1864–9)
B.I.H.R.	*Bulletin of the Institute of Historical Research,* University of London
Bio. Reg. Univ. Oxf.	A.B. Emden, *A Biographical Register of the University of Oxford to A.D. 1500,* 3 vols. (Oxford, 1957–9)
B.L.	British Library
Book of Fees	*The Book of Fees,* Public Record Office, 3 vols. (1921–31)
Br. Note Book	*Bracton's Note Book,* 3 vols. (London, 1887)
Cal. Chtr. Rolls	*Calendar of Charter Rolls,* Public Record Office, 6 vols. (1903–27)
Cal. Docs. relating to Ireland	*Calendar of Documents relating to Ireland* ed. H.S. Sweetman, 1: *1171–1251,* Public Record Office
Cal. Inq. Post Mort.	*Calendar of Inquisitions Post Mortem,* Public Record Office (1904–)
Cal. Lib. Rolls	*Calendar of Liberate Rolls, Henry III,* Public Record Office (1917–64), 6 vols.
Cal. Pat. Rolls	*Calendar of Patent Rolls, Henry III* [1232–72], Public Record Office (1906–13)
Cartae Antiq. Rolls	*Cartae Antique Rolls 1–10,*

	ed. Lionel Landon, Pipe Roll Society, new ser., 17 (1939); *11–20*, ed. J. Conway Davies, Pipe Roll Society, new ser., 33 (1960)
Cat. Anc. Deeds	*Descriptive Catalogue of Ancient Deeds*, 6 vols., Public Record Office (1890–1915)
Chron. Maj.	*Matthaei Parisiensis Chronica Majora*, 7 vols., ed. H.R. Luard, Rolls Series (1872–84)
Close Rolls	*Close Rolls, Henry III*, 14 vols., Public Record Office (1902–38)
Complete Peerage	G.E. Cokayne, *Complete Peerage of England, Scotland, Ireland, Great Britain, and United Kingdom*, 12 vols., new edn (London, 1910–59)
C.R.R.	*Curia Regis Rolls*, 16 vols., Public Record Office (1923–)
C.U.L.	Cambridge University Library
Delisle, *Recueil*	*Recueil des actes de Henri II*, Introduction and 3 vols., ed. Léopold Delisle and Elie Berger (Paris, 1909–27)
Dial. de Scac.	*Dialogus de Scaccario, the Course of the Exchequer*, ed. and trans. Charles Johnson, Medieval Classics (London and New York, 1950)
D.N.B.	*Dictionary of National Biography*, ed. Leslie Stephen and Sidney Lee, 63 vols. (London, 1885–1900)
Docs. preserved in France	*Documents preserved in France, illustrative of the history of Great Britain and Ireland, 918–1206*, ed. J.H. Round, Public Record Office (1899)
Eng. Hist. Docs.	*English Historical Documents*,

	gen. ed., David C. Douglas; 2, *1042–1189*, ed. David C. Douglas and George W. Greenaway (London, 1955); 3, *1189–1327*, ed. Harry Rothwell (London, 1975)
E.H.R.	*English Historical Review*
English Justice	Doris M. Stenton, *English Justice between the Norman Conquest and the Great Charter*, American Phil. Soc. Proc. (Philadelphia, 1964)
Exc. è Rot. Fin.	*Excerpta è Rotulis Finium*, ed. C. Roberts, 2 vols., Record Commission (London, 1835–6).
Fasti, Lincoln, *Fasti, Mon. Cath.,* *Fasti, St Paul's*	*Le Neve, Fasti ecclesiae anglicanae, 1066–1300*, ed. Diana E. Greenway, Institute of Historical Research (London, 1968–)
Foedera	*Foedera, Conventiones, Litterae, etc.*, new edn, Record Commission (London, 1816–30, 1869)
Gerald of Wales	*Giraldi Cambrensis Opera*, 7 vols., ed. J.S. Brewer and J.F. Dimock, Rolls Series (1861–91)
Gesta Hen. Secundi	*Gesta Regis Henrici secundi Benedicti Abbatis*, 2 vols., ed. William Stubbs, Rolls Series (1867)
Glanvill	*Tractatus de legibus et consuetudinibus regni Anglie qui Glanvilla vocatur*, ed. and trans. G.D.G. Hall, Medieval Texts (London, 1965).
Governance	H.G. Richardson and G.O. Sayles, *The Governance of mediaeval England from the Conquest to Magna Carta* (Edinburgh, 1963)

H.M.C.	*Royal Commission on Historical Manuscripts*
Honors and Knights' Fees	William Farrer, *Honors and Knights' Fees*, 3 vols., (London and Manchester, 1923–5)
Itin. Hen. II	Robert W. Eyton, *Court, Household and Itinerary of Henry II* (London, 1878)
Itin. Ric. I	*Itinerary of Richard I*, ed. Lionel Landon, Pipe Roll Society, new ser., 13 (1935)
Intro. to C.R.R.	C.T. Flower, *Introduction to the Curia Regis Rolls*, Selden Society, 62 (London, 1943)
Jl. Br. Studies	*Journal of British Studies*
Justiciarship	Francis J. West, *The Justiciarship in England, 1066–1232*, Cambridge Studies in Medieval Life and Thought (Cambridge, 1961)
List of Sheriffs	*Public Record Office Lists and Indexes, List of Sheriffs for England and Wales from the earliest times to A.D. 1831* (London, 1898)
M.T.B.	*Materials for the History of Thomas Becket*, 7 vols., ed. J.C. Robertson and J.B. Sheppard, Rolls Series (1875–85)
Meekings, *Studies*	C.A.F. Meekings, *Studies in thirteenth century justice and administration* (London, 1981)
Mem. Roll	*Memoranda Roll 1 John*, ed. R.A. Brown, Pipe Roll Society, new ser., 31 (1957)
Monasticon	William Dugdale, *Monasticon Anglicanum*, new edn by John Caley, Henry Ellis, and Bulkeley Bandinel, 6 vols. (London reprint, 1846)

Pat. Rolls	*Patent Rolls Henry III*, 2 vols., Public Record Office (1901–03)
Pat. Lat.	*Patrologiae cursus completus. Patres . . . latinae*, ed. Jacques Paul Migne, 217 vols. (Paris, 1844–55)
Pipe Roll	*Great Roll of the Pipe* 5 Henry II . . ., Pipe Roll Society, orig. ser. 1–38 (London, 1884–1925); new ser., 1– (London, 1925–)
P.B.K.J.	*Pleas before the King or his Justices (1198–1212)*, ed. Doris M. Stenton, 4 vols., Selden Society, 67–8 (1948–9), 83–4 (1966–7)
Pollock and Maitland	Frederick Pollock and F.W. Maitland, *History of English Law before the time of Edward I*, 2 vols. (London, 2nd edn, 1898)
P.R.O.	Public Record Office, London
Ralph de Diceto	*Radulphi de Diceto Opera Historica*, ed. William Stubbs, 2 vols., Rolls Series (1876)
Red Book Exch.	*Red Book of the Exchequer*, ed. Hubert Hall, 2 vols., Rolls Series (1897)
Roger Howden	*Chronica Rogeri de Houedene*, ed. William Stubbs, 4 vols., Rolls Series (1868–71)
Rot. Chart.	*Rotuli Chartarum*, ed. T. Duffus Hardy, Record Commission (London, 1837)
Rot. Cur. Reg.	*Rotuli Curiae Regis*, ed. Francis Palgrave, 2 vols., Record Commission (London, 1835)
Rot. de Dominabus	*Rotuli de Dominabus et Pueris et*

	Puellis [1185], ed. J.H. Round, Pipe Roll Society, 35 (1913)
Rot. de Lib. ac de Mis.	*Rotuli de Liberate ac de Misis et Praestitis, regnante Johanne,* ed. T. Duffus Hardy, Record Commission (London, 1844)
Rot. de Obl. et Fin.	*Rotuli de Oblatis et Finibus,* ed. T. Duffus Hardy, Record Commission (London, 1835)
Rot. Lit. Claus.	*Rotuli Litterarum Clausarum,* ed. T. Duffus Hardy, 2 vols., Record Commission (London, 1833, 1844)
Rot. Lit. Pat.	*Rotuli Litterarum Patentium,* ed. T. Duffus Hardy, Record Commission (London, 1835)
Sanders, *Baronies*	I.J. Sanders, *English Baronies: a study of their origin and descent 1086–1327* (Oxford, 1960)
Sayles, *Select Cases*	*Select Cases in the Court of King's Bench, Edward I – Henry V*, ed. G.O. Sayles, 7 vols., Selden Society, 55 (1936), 57–8 (1938–9), 74 (1955), 76 (1957), 82 (1965), 88 (1971)
T.R.H.S.	*Transactions of the Royal Historical Society*
V.C.H.	*Victoria History of the Counties of England* eds. H. Arthur Doubleday, William Page, Louis F. Salzman, Ralph B. Pugh (London and Westminster, 1900–34; then Inst. Historical Research, London, 1935–)
Westminster Domesday	Westminster Abbey, Muniments Book 11

THE REPUTATION OF THE ROYAL JUSTICES

A monk in the mid twelfth century took note of the progress of his day; among the advances he observed was the growth of 'so many kinds of professions . . . varieties of positions and posts'.[1] Certainly the appearance of professional civil servants was a noteworthy change in the later twelfth and early thirteenth centuries. A significant group of English civil servants are the royal justices in those crucial years for the growth of the common law, the time between the writing of the two great legal treatises: *Glanvill*, written c. 1187–9, and *Bracton*, once thought to have been written in the late 1250s, but now known to date in its earliest version from the 1220s and 1230s. Those years saw the appearance of professional judges in England's royal courts.

Great barons, bishops and abbots served Henry II, his sons Richard I and John, and his grandson Henry III as judges from time to time, particularly as itinerant justices in their own counties. Others who might be termed the king's 'men-of-all-work', serving him in the chancery, at the Exchequer, or as sheriffs also sat occasionally on the bench. By the last ten years of Henry II, however, we can make out some royal servants who were beginning to concentrate on the work of justice and who must be regarded as forerunners of a professional judiciary. By the time of Richard I a small group of these men must be regarded as a corps of professional judges, performing few other tasks. In the reign of John and in his son's early years, this corps stands out more clearly as a body of professionals.

The royal justices were unashamedly the king's servants, confident that in serving his interest they were contributing to the common good. Yet they had something of the bureaucrats' concern for regular procedures, for 'due process'. Today when the principle of the rule of law seems threatened from so many

[1] William of St Thierry's 'Golden Epistle', c. 1144–8, *Pat. Lat.* 184: col. 318, where it is attributed to St Bernard.

directions, it is useful to recall the planting of that principle in the Anglo-American legal tradition. The roots of 'due process' lie in the twelfth and thirteenth centuries, planted there by professional royal servants whose energies made the *curia regis* a court for complaints of all freemen, creating a common law for all England.

The time of *Glanvill* and *Bracton* was the golden age of medieval justice, yet the early justices were frequently obscure men who have left few traces in the surviving records. Little is known of their lives, although they are credited with work that has influenced civilization for seven centuries and on continents unknown to them. They were sometimes objects of scorn for chroniclers, preachers, and satirists of their own time. Later historians have not had much success in coming to know the early common law judges. Edward Foss made perhaps a premature stab at reconstructing their lives in the mid nineteenth century.[2] He did the best he could with the sources available to him, but some of his biographical sketches are far from the facts as they are known today. More recent historians have been content to heap praise on the early royal justices without knowing much about their lives. Even the great F.W. Maitland, for example, assumed that the judiciary of the Angevin kings was heavily clerical in composition when in fact only half were in ecclesiastical orders. According to him, under Henry II and Richard I, 'English law was administered by the ablest, the best educated men in the realm . . .' Historians since Maitland have held a similarly high opinion of these judges. F.M. Powicke wrote that the judiciary of Henry III was 'probably the most stable and helpful, as it was the most intelligent, element in the State at this time'.[3] Sir Cyril Flower, first editor of the *curia regis* rolls, wrote:

they showed qualities which have been held to be typical of the English people. They were humane and kindly disposed to those who were brought before them, especially to the poor and afflicted. While they had a healthy respect for the traditions of the past, they were always ready to explore more direct paths to justice and to make experiments that might shorten the delays of the law.[4]

[2] Edward Foss, *The Judges of England*, 9 vols. (London, 1848–64).
[3] Pollock and Maitland, 1: 132, cf. pp. 160–1, 169–70; F.M. Powicke, *King Henry III and the Lord Edward* (Oxford, 1947), p. 143. See also *English Justice*, pp. 82–5. [4] *Intro. to C.R.R.*, p. 498.

The justices' contemporaries are not much more helpful in allowing us to come to know them. Royal officials, including judges, proved popular targets for the pens of the twelfth-century moralists and satirists, some of whom wrote out of personal bitterness, having failed in the contest for royal patronage and high office.[5] Capable of condemning *curiales* in classical Latin style was John of Salisbury. He knew many of Henry II's courtiers, and he came to despise them, especially those in clerical orders. Indeed, the theme of his *Policraticus* can be said to be 'the incompatibility of the type of character required for the royal administration with the religious and ecclesiastical duties of a churchman'.[6] Throughout his book, John of Salisbury complained of the venality, avarice, and sycophancy of royal officials. He recognized that these sins were all linked to ambition, a desire to rise above others. John made harsh remarks about royal justices, writing that they seemed 'rather extortioners than judges'.[7] He blamed Henry II for his selection of judges, finding him either ignorant of the law or contemptuous of it by choosing such greedy men. John had especially sharp comments about itinerant justices: 'What I have said concerning governors and other judges should apply also to proconsuls, whom our countrymen commonly call itinerant or "wandering" justices. The name is erroneous, but still it fits, because, following their own desire in pursuit of avarice, they "wander" from the path of equity and plunder the people.'[8]

John condemned the venality of all Henry II's officers. He pointed out that 'money is the sole driving force' for expediting

---

[5] Examples are Peter of Blois, Ralph Niger and Gerald of Wales. See Egbert Türk, *Nugae Curialium: Le règne d'Henri II Plantagenet (1145–1189) et l'éthique politique*, Centre de Recherches d'hist. et de philologie, Hautes Etudes médiévales et modernes, 28 (Geneva, 1977): 188.

[6] Hans Liebeschutz, *Medieval Humanism in the Life and Writings of John of Salisbury*, Studies of the Warburg Inst., 17 (London, 1950): 17. Cf. Ralph V. Turner, 'Clerical judges in English secular courts: the ideal vs. the reality', *Medievalia et Humanistica*, new ser., 3(1972): 83–4.

[7] *Policraticus*, v, 10, 11, 15; vi, 1, trans. John Dickinson, *The Statesman's Book of John of Salisbury* (New York, 1927), pp. 114–45, 174–9. John accused royal judges of being ignorant of law and lacking in goodwill, 'as is proved by their love of gifts and rewards, exercising the power which they have in the service of avarice or advancing the fortunes of their own flesh and blood ...' v, 11, p. 125.

[8] *Policraticus*, v, 15, p. 145. The Latin allows a play on the word *errantes*.

any business at the royal court.[9] He added that not only must money be paid for action but for inaction as well: 'Not merely is there no act, no word to be had without payment, but they will not even keep silent unless paid a price, silence itself is a thing for sale.' John recognized, however, that royal servants depended at least partly on payments from petitioners. He wrote, 'I am willing to concede that court officials may accept gifts so long as they do not shamelessly extort them.'[10]

A correspondent of John of Salisbury, Ralph Niger, denounced Henry II bitterly in one of his chronicles. He complained that the king had brought to England to install as officials 'shameful slaves, common foot soldiers of the household'.[11] He accused Henry of quibbling overmuch in contending causes so that he might sell justice. Ralph Niger was not alone in his accusation that the king was a delayer and seller of justice. Later Gerald of Wales made the same charges against Henry II.[12]

Walter Map, one of Henry II's clerks and occasionally an itinerant justice, composed *De nugis curialium*, a collection of court gossip. A typical courtier, Map saw clearly the sycophancy that prevailed at Henry's court, something almost inevitable in a feudal society which made dependence upon superiors its basis.[13] He flattered the king for his legal ability, but he also commented satirically on the quality of royal justice. He complained of such delays in settling cases that many died or spent all their money before their suits were settled, and he pointed out that money was the source of all pardons. In his view, judges were only champions of justice in cases in which 'Mother Purse' (*mater bursa*) failed to open her lips.[14] He blamed corruption on

---

[9] *Policraticus*, v, 10, p. 114.

[10] *Policraticus*, v, 10, pp. 116–17.

[11] Robert Anstruther, ed., *The Chronicles of Ralph Niger*, Caxton Soc., 13 (London, 1851): 167–9, Chron. II.

[12] *Gerald of Wales*, 5: 201; 8: 160; also 8: 183–6, where he recorded the dream of a Lincolnshire knight, directed by St Peter to warn Henry II of his misdeeds. One of the knight's admonitions was 'concerning the rendering of justice freely and without cost'.

[13] M.R. James, ed., *De nugis curialium*, Anecdota Oxoniensia, Medieval and Modern ser. (Oxford, 1914). For a description of the work, see Antonia Gransden, *Historical Writing in England c. 550 to c. 1307* (Ithaca, N.Y., 1974), pp. 243–4. See also Alexander Murray, *Reason and Society in the Middle Ages* (Oxford, 1978), pp. 107–8.

[14] *De nugis cur.*, v, 6, p. 241; v, 7, pp. 252–3.

the base birth of the judges, whom he claimed to be often the sons of serfs, seeking through clerical careers to rise above their station. He cited the Roman poet Claudian, 'Nothing is harder than the lowly whenever he riseth to high degree.'[15]

A disappointed courtier, Peter of Blois, also denounced the lives of lawyers and *curiales* in his letters.[16] He gave perhaps the most detailed criticism of Henry II's royal justices in a letter addressed to the king some time after early 1182.[17] Peter sought to warn Henry II of the abuses of his itinerant justices, foresters, sheriffs, and other officials in a letter which would at the same time demonstrate his own learning, studding it with strings of quotations from Scripture, the classics, and Roman law. He complained that the people had to bear the burden of multitudes of royal ministers, who were like locusts in that as soon as some left others arrived. He gave a detailed picture of the faults of Henry's judges, writing that the justices on eyre 'frequently err themselves, while they search out the errors of others'. He quoted the Sermon on the Mount (Matt. 5: 6), 'How blest are those who hunger and thirst to see right prevail . .' Then he went on to say, 'Those who judge your poor hunger and thirst only for money, ignoring justice and prudence.' Like Walter Map, he complained of the low origin of many of the justices, pointing out that royal officials chose unsuitable men for selfish reasons, and that nobles (*viri nobiles et discreti*) resented judges of inferior station with no claim to their offices other than their connection with the king's *familiares*.

Peter's chief complaint was that justice was so costly to the poor. He called the king's attention to justices who sought gifts, who would not grant writs (*litterae*) unless promised money. He warned, 'Whoever sells writs in this way puts on sale the justice of God . . . which he is bound to exhibit freely.' He concluded

---

[15] Map also tells of an abbot who became an itinerant justice, and 'spurred on spoiling of the poor, hoping perchance to win a bishopric through the favour gained from his spoils', i, 10; trans., Frederick Tupper and Marbury Bladen Ogle (London, 1924), p. 8.

[16] *Pat. Lat.*, 207: col. 43, no. 14. Peter complained of courtiers' vain hopes for worldly gain, writing that the courtier's life is 'death to the soul', and quoting *Ecclesiasticus* (7: 1–7), 'seek not of the Lord preeminence, neither of the king the seat of honor . . . Seek not to be judge . . .' For Peter's denunciation of lawyers, see no. 26, cols. 91–2.

[17] *Pat. Lat.*, 207: cols. 298–302, no. 95.

his letter by warning Henry II of his responsibility for his servants' sins and urging him to 'judge most strictly the judges of
your kingdom'.

Complaints about curialists continued in the thirteenth century. Two scholar-bishops, Robert Grosseteste and St Edmund
of Abingdon, denounced clerics in the royal service who neglected
their care of souls to pursue the king's interests. The bishop of
Lincoln was scandalized by the appointment of the abbot of
Ramsey as an itinerant justice, and he complained to St
Edmund.[18] The scholarly archbishop of Canterbury denounced
courtiers in a sermon. Applying an allegorical interpretation to
the Old Testament account of King Ahab's death (1. Kings 22)
he equated the false prophets who had caused his disaster with
royal counsellors: '. . . false counsellors, grasping persons, flat-
terers, the hard of heart, and oppressors of the poor. With such
people the court of every prince and great man is filled.
Whoever, therefore, wishes to lead a good life, let him depart
from court.'[19]

Near the end of the thirteenth century, the corruption of
royal justices and their punishment by Edward I inspired the
Narratio de Passione justiciariorum. The king, following his return
from Gascony in 1289, removed from office ten judges, including the chief justices of King's Bench and Common Pleas. The
'Passion' describes the justices' fall, satirizing their sufferings in
a 'ribald travesty of biblical texts'. Its author writes of their misdeeds before their dismissal, noting that 'they sat with the rich
in secret places to murder the innocent and their right hand was
full of bribes'.[20]

Moral and satirical writers, then, made three chief criticisms
of courtiers: excessive ambition, sycophancy, and greed. In
their view, royal judges were guilty of these three faults, and

[18] H.R. Luard, ed., *Letters of Robert Grosseteste*, Rolls Series (1861), pp. 105–8, *epis-
tola*, xxvii. Later he sought removal of the prior of Crowland from the
itinerant justices, p. 262, no. lxxxii.

[19] Clifford H. Lawrence, *St Edmund of Abingdon* (London, 1960), p. 131, citing
B.L. Harl. MS. 325, f. 163 v.

[20] T.F. Tout and Hilda Johnstone, eds., *State Trials of the Reign of Edward I*, Royal
Hist. Soc., Camden 3rd ser., 8 (1906): 93–9. *Eng. Hist. Docs.*, 3: 922–4, gives a
translation of the *Passio*. For another poem on the venality of judges, only
slightly later, see Thomas Wright, ed., *Political Songs of England*, Camden Soc.,
6 (1839): 224–30. For comment see F.M. Powicke, *The Thirteenth Century
1216–1307*, Oxford History of England, 4 (Oxford, 1953): 361–6.

especially of the third one, greed. The three sins were closely connected in writers' minds. A theme in much writing on avarice is the way in which money disturbs the social order, enabling some men to rise above their rightful station. Sycophancy was a necessary part of a search for patronage by the ambitious.[21]

Comments on individual judges are usually lacking, but when they are encountered, they are so lapidary that they offer little real evidence for the careers of justices.[22] An exception is the dramatic condemnation of the life of a royal justice found in the 'Vision of Thurkill.' It is a description of the punishments in hell awaiting sinners from all levels of society, written in 1206 by the monk Ralph of Coggeshall. Such 'vision' literature usually portrays only 'types', composite pictures of classes, professions, or other categories, but among these sinners is a royal justice, who can be identified. The description is so specific that the author must have had in mind Osbert fitz Hervey, a judge with long experience on the bench under Richard I and John. Ralph described him as 'one most expert in worldly law', and 'famous throughout England among high and low for his overflowing eloquence and experience in the law'.[23] Most of what was written about the judge is less complimentary, however. He was accused of greedily gaining wealth by taking gifts from litigants on both sides of lawsuits; and worse still, he died without making a will in which he could dispose of his ill-gotten gain with pious gifts. As punishment, the demons in hell invented new tortures, forcing him to gulp down burning coins, then running an iron wheel up and down his back, forcing him to vomit up the coins.[24]

---

[21] Murray, *Reason and Society in M.A.*, pp. 81–3, 107–8.

[22] E.g. *Gerald of Wales* labelled William de Sainte-Mère-Eglise, one of Henry II's aides and Richard I's judges: *curia sequela est et domini regis familiaris*, 1: 260.

[23] H.L.D. Ward, ed., *Jl. of the Br. Archaeol. Assoc.*, 31 (1875): 420–59. For a new edition see Paul G. Schmidt, ed., *Visio Thurkilli, relatore, ut videtur, Radulpho de Coggeshall*, Akademie der Wissenschaften der DDR, Zentral institut für alte Geschichte und Archaologie, Bibliotheca Scriptorum Graecorum et Romanorum Teubneriana (Leipzig, 1978); also Schmidt, 'The vision of Thurkill', *Jl. of Warburg and Courtauld Inst.*, 41 (1978): 50–64. Ralph did not mention the justice's name, but the identification seems clear. The date of death mentioned in the 'Vision' – 1206 – corresponds with Osbert's death. Also Ralph, monk at an Essex house, would have known of Osbert, a knight of East Anglian origin and with landholdings there.

[24] *Jl. Br. Archaeol. Assoc.*, 31: 452–3.

Occasionally chroniclers made brief comments on judges, such as Matthew Paris' remarks on William of Raleigh's consecration as bishop of Norwich in 1239. William was a longtime royal judge, chief justice of the court *coram rege*, and the authority most cited in *Bracton*. The chronicler quoted Luke (15: 10), 'There is joy among the angels of God over one sinner who repents;' and he expressed the hope that Raleigh, like St Matthew, who had fled from taxation to the apostolate would fly from curial occupations to a summit of great sanctity.[25] Matthew Paris had a practice of penning scathing obituaries for those royal justices he believed had injured his house of St Albans. He wished to point out that punishment caught up with them. He claimed that Henry of Bath had enriched himself with rents, manors, gold and silver second to none of the justices, and that on a single eyre he had accumulated over 200 librates of land.[26] Matthew Paris' resentment of a number of other judges of Henry III led him to compose similar obituaries.[27]

The chroniclers, even when denouncing royal justices for their misdeeds, usually admitted their knowledge of the law. Gervase of Canterbury and Roger of Howden both accepted without question Hubert Walter's right to be recognized as the master of English law and custom, but they joined other chroniclers in criticizing his hunger for riches and his thirst for lavish living, which led him to neglect his priestly duties.[28] Matthew Paris had only praise for Simon of Pattishall, an experienced judge of Richard I and King John; he described Simon as a faithful and honest man, 'who at one time guided the reins of the justices of the whole kingdom'.[29] Matthew Paris' obituary of Thomas of Moulton, justice for Henry III, described

---

[25] *Chron. Maj.*, 3: 617–18.   [26] *Chron. Maj.*, 5: 213.

[27] Adam fitz William is described as 'a man of the shrewdest sort in worldly affairs and the riches which come from them', H. T. Riley, ed., *Gesta Monasterii Sancti Albani*, Rolls Series (1867–9), 4: 329–30. Roger of Whitchester is described as a judge who 'strove wholly to please the royal will', *Chron. Maj.*, 5: 716. And he uses similar language to characterize Master Ralph of Norwich, *Chron. Maj.*, 5: 560.

[28] For favourable comments on Hubert's legal knowledge, William Stubbs, ed., *Gervase of Canterbury: Historical Works*, Rolls Series (1879–80), 2: 406; *Roger Howden*, 4: 12. For criticisms, see *Gervase of Canterbury*, 2: 410–11; *Roger Howden*, 4: 12–13; *Gerald of Wales*, 1: 426–7; J. Stevenson, ed., *Radulphi de Coggeshall Chronicon Anglicanun*, Rolls Series (1875), pp. 159–60.

[29] *Chron. Maj.*, 3: 296, 542.

him as 'learned in the law, but coveting too much to enlarge his possessions'. Matthew acknowledged that Henry of Bath was a *miles literatus, legum terrae peritissimus.* He described another of Henry III's justices, John of Lexington, as *vir magnae auctoritate et scientiae.*[30] Another chronicler gave a more detailed description of John's legal training, calling him 'learned in both laws, namely canon and civil law'.[31]

Medieval English monarchs rarely commissioned 'official' histories to combat the anti-government bias of monastic chroniclers.[32] Yet Henry II had learned courtiers who were capable of writings which challenged the usual charges against his judges. Some of the writers were royal justices themselves, one of whom was the author of the treatise on English law known as *Glanvill,* shortly before the king's death. Not surprisingly, *Glanvill* praises Henry's *curia regis:*

no judge there is so audacious as to presume to turn aside at all from the path of justice or to digress in any respect from the way of truth. For there, indeed, a poor man is not oppressed by the power of his adversary, nor does favour or partiality drive any man away from the threshold of judgement... the king is ever guided by those of his subjects most learned in the laws and customs of the realm who he knows to excell all others in sobriety, wisdom and eloquence, and whom he has found to be most prompt and clear-sighted in deciding cases on the basis of justice and in settling disputes, acting now with severity and now with leniency as seems most expedient to them.[33]

Richard fitz Neal, author of the *Dialogus de Scaccario,* served Henry II and his successors not only at the Exchequer but also as judge of common pleas and on eyre in the counties. His book represents the civil servant's rising self-confidence, his pride in his craft. In the *Dialogus,* Richard took care to assure his readers that the Exchequer did not function arbitrarily, but followed established rules. He wrote in the Dedication: 'To be sure, the Exchequer has evolved its own rules, not by hazard, but by the deliberation and decisions of great men; and if those rules be observed in every particular, the right of individuals will be maintained, and the reverence due to the Treasury will come to

---

[30] *Chron. Maj.,* 4: 49; 5: 213, 384. [31] *Annales Mon.,* 1: 345, annals of Burton.
[32] Antonia Gransden, 'Propaganda in English medieval historiography', *Jl. of Medieval History,* 1 (1975): 363–81.
[33] *Glanvill,* Prologue, p. 2.

the King in full . . .'[34] Walter Map shared Richard fitz Neal's
favourable view of the Exchequer, finding it 'one place in which
money can do no miracles, for the glance of the King seems ever
fresh there'.[35] Fitz Neal's view of the itinerant justices, however,
veered far from that of Map. His account of their work was:
'They, giving audience in each county, and doing full justice to
those who considered themselves wronged, saved the poor both
money and labour'.[36]

Peter of Blois, who condemned courtiers, had praise for them
elsewhere. In 1180, he wrote a letter to the clerks of the royal
household, expressing the view that civil servants ought not to
be condemned but rather praised: '. . . even if they cannot have
leisure for prayer and contemplation, they are nevertheless
occupied in the public good and often perform works of salvation. . . I think it is not only laudable but glorious to assist the
king, to hold office in the State, not to think of oneself, but to be
all for all.'[37]

In his work as secretary to two archbishops of Canterbury,
Peter wrote letters in defence of clerics employed as royal justices. He drafted a letter to the pope for Richard of Dover,
defending three bishops whom Henry II had named royal justices in 1179. The letter pointed out that it was useful for
bishops to serve on the bench, where they could protect the
Church's liberties, monastic property, and the needs of widows,
orphans, and the poor.[38] Later Peter wrote a letter for Hubert
Walter, seeking exemption from the rules of residence for a
cathedral canon who was a royal justice. His argument was that
since the cleric was occupied in 'the public business of the king',
he was devoting himself to the welfare of all.[39]

The chronicler Master Ralph de Diceto knew many prominent persons at the court of Henry II. He had great respect for
the king, and in his history he wrote favourably of royal legal

---

[34] *Dial. de Scac.*, p. 3; cf. pp. 7, 13. This translation is not from the Johnson edn
but from *Eng. Hist. Docs.*, 2: 492.
[35] He concluded, 'I heard judgement there given in favour of a poor man against
a rich one', *De nugis cur.*, v, 7, p. 253 of the James edn.
[36] *Dial. de Scac.*, p. 77.
[37] *Pat. Lat.*, 207: col. 440, no. 150, partial translation in R.W. Southern, *The
Making of the Middle Ages* (London, 1953), pp. 212–13.
[38] *Pat. Lat.*, 200: cols. 1459–61, no. 96.
[39] Master Thomas of Hurstbourne, *Pat. Lat.*, 207: cols. 403–4, no. 135.

reforms.[40] Ralph praised Henry II for turning to the episcopate, 'the sanctuary of God', in 1179 to seek judges who would not oppress the poor or favour the rich. Ralph excused their involvement in worldly matters in violation of canon law, offering as an excuse, 'the importunity of the King, his good intentions, and his actions pleasing to God and meet for the praise of men'.[41] Yet the three bishops – Geoffrey Ridel, John of Oxford, and Richard of Ilchester – were longtime *familiares regis*, notorious as Henry II's counsellors in his conflict with Becket.

The critics of the judges seem to outnumber their supporters. How then are we to evaluate these comments by contemporary writers? Were they justified in their condemnation of royal justices for their ambition, sycophancy, and greed? It is important to know these men who gave shape to the common law, swayed neither by the sharp comments of contemporary chroniclers, preachers, and satirists, nor by the sometimes uncritical and uninformed praise of modern lawyers and legal scholars.

It is difficult to know men who, as individuals, left little mark on the histories of their own day beyond a few cryptic comments, mostly about their corruption. The judges of the Angevin kings wrote little that casts any light on their personalities. The earliest surviving letters of royal justices date only from the early years of Henry III. Three works written by justices – the legal treatises *Glanvill*, *Bracton*, and the *Dialogus de Scaccario* – illuminate only slightly their thinking about their responsibilities. Yet these shadowy figures can be brought into the light by focusing on a number of them collectively: seeing the individual as a member of a group may make him stand out more clearly, or at least make it possible to paint a composite picture, lining up the shadows to create sharper outlines.

This is the task of prosopography, a new approach to medieval biography. Many scholars at work on prosopographical studies view it as the proper way to approach political history. They stress ties of family, friendship, and patronage in building political alliances, in creating an effective ruling party, and in making government operate smoothly. But prosopography is

---

[40] *Ralph de Diceto*, 1: 434.
[41] *Ralph de Diceto*, 1: 435; translation *Eng. Hist. Docs.*, 2: 481–2.

also social history, perhaps mainly so. It can locate the position of this group of royal servants among the *curiales* and local officials of the Angevin kings, indicate the degree of social mobility operating for them and their families, and recognize trends in the status of the group as a whole. Prosopography stresses the importance of family ties and personal relationships in advancement to high office; it assumes that such links – especially patronage – are significant for explaining political behaviour.

English royal government in the Middle Ages offers a fruitful field for the prosopographer to cultivate. The powerful influence of Stubbs, Maitland, and Tout long confined students to constitutional and institutional approaches. Impersonal studies of numerous government offices already exist. Our understanding of them can gain a new dimension, however, with studies that bring to life the men who operated them. An acquaintance with the lives of members of the judiciary can aid in understanding the operations of the *curia regis* and the common law they were creating. Lawrence Stone has suggested that this method 'could be a means to bind together constitutional and institutional history on the one hand and personal biography on the other'.[42]

The history of medieval England lies in 'a morass of administrative detail', and the lives of the early royal justices can only be uncovered by plunging into that morass.[43] Lady Stenton pored over the pipe rolls, feet of fines, cartularies and chronicles to rescue the earliest royal judges from anonymity. Her work was made more difficult by the fact that few official copies of nonfinancial royal records survive before the justiciarship of Hubert Walter, 1193–8.[44] The plea rolls provide surprisingly little information about the personnel of the royal courts. The earliest rolls of court cases to survive are from 1194, although hints of

[42] See George Beech, 'Prosopography', in James M. Powell, ed., *Medieval Studies: An Introduction* (Syracuse, N.Y., 1976), pp. 151–84; Lawrence Stone, 'Prosopography', in Felix Gilbert and Stephen R. Grabaud, eds., *Historical Studies Today* (New York, 1972), pp. 107–40.

[43] The phrase of J.E.A. Jolliffe, 'The *camera regis* under Henry II', *E.H.R.*, 68 (1953): 358.

[44] For an admirable survey of the types of surviving medieval English records, see M.T. Clanchy, *From Memory to Written Record, England 1066–1307* (Cambridge, Mass., 1979), chap. 3, pp. 60–87.

their existence in other records led to a supposition that plea rolls were kept earlier. Even after 1194, however, little effort was made to preserve the plea rolls until about 1232.[45] The feet of fines – official enrolments of final concords, compromise settlements of pleas in the royal courts – are always carefully dated and name the judges present; but they began to be kept only in 1195, although some stray copies of final concords in the possession of the parties to the plea – chirographs – survive from as early as 1163. Nonetheless, Lady Stenton was able to compile lists of the royal justices from 1100 to 1215, using pipe roll evidence for justices on eyre before 1195. C.A.F. Meekings, who performed the same task for the judges of Henry III, found his work easier because of the greater abundance of royal records in the thirteenth century.[46] For example, the patent and close rolls began to record writs of appointment of justices to the Bench at Westminster and to the King's Bench, and the liberate rolls began in the 1240s to record writs authorizing payments of justices' salaries.[47]

---

[45] *Dial. de Scac.*, pp. 70, 77, tells of the itinerant justices returning their rolls to the treasurer. Clanchy, p. 74, is confident that enrolments only began in 1194, and that any earlier references to judicial rolls such as those in the *Dial. de Scac.* refer to lists of amercements only. Cf. Sayles, *Select Cases*, 2: xv–xvi, and Doris M. Stenton, *The Earliest Lincolnshire assize rolls A.D. 1202–1209*, Linc. Rec. Soc., 22 (1926): xxi–xxii, who are convinced that justices required rolls. See also H.G. Richardson, ed., *Mem. Roll 1 John*, p. xxiii, where he states that from 1166, 'There were methodically kept plea rolls which the justices were required to deliver to the exchequer'. Later Richardson with G.O. Sayles, *Governance*, p. 185, n. 6, and p. 214. In the account of a lawsuit by a monk of Ford Abbey, c.1193–9, he describes a plea that had come before Glanvill and the *justiciarii Scacarii* in 34 Hen. II, and he states *loquela in rotulo domini Regis inbreviata hiis verbis* . . ., Brian Kemp, 'Exchequer and Bench in the late twelfth century – separate or identical tribunals?' *E.H.R.*, 88 (1973): 575, from Ford Cartulary MS., pp. 418–19. Parties to a plea at Lincoln in 1219 vouched to warranty the rolls of itinerant justices from the time of Henry II, and the judges ordered the rolls produced, as if they assumed that such rolls existed, Doris M. Stenton, ed., *Rolls of the Justices in Eyre for Lincs 1218–19 and Worcs. 1221*, Selden Soc., 53 (1934): 411, no. 853.

[46] *P.B.K.J.*, 3: xlvii–ccxciv, App. I, 'The development of the judiciary 1100–1215'. Meekings, 'General eyres 1218–1272', typescript at P.R.O. Some of his lists of justices have been published in introductions to recent volumes of the *curia regis* rolls (1955–79), e.g. *C.R.R.*, 11: xii–xiv; 12: xi–xiv; 13: xi–xxii; 14: x–xviii; 15: xiv–xxi, lxi–lxiv; 16: xiv–xviii, xlvii–lii. His lists for justices Hilary 1218 to Michaelmas 1222 remain unpublished. David Crook of the P.R.O. has completed revised lists of general eyres, 1194–1272, which correct Stenton's and Meekings' work, now being prepared for publication.

[47] *Select Cases*, 4: x–xii.

The work of these scholars made it possible for me to identify the men serving most frequently as royal justices simply by counting the number of eyres they went on and the number of terms of court they sat at Westminster or in the court *coram rege*. Before about 1179, however, not enough chirographs survive to form any strong impression of the regularity with which individual justices were sitting on the bench. I have selected thirteen men from the last ten years of Henry II, fourteen from Richard I's reign, seventeen from King John's time, and thirteen from the early years of Henry III who served on the judicial bench often enough to be singled out for study. Since several served for periods extending into more than one reign and are thus counted twice, the number of individual justices to be examined is only forty-nine. Certainly by about 1200 a truly professional judiciary can be said to have appeared in England. While many earlier royal justices were men-of-all-work for the king, we begin to note more who concentrate mainly on judicial matters. What was exceptional with Godfrey de Lucy under Henry II begins to be normal for a corps of at least a half-dozen or so men by the middle years of Richard Lionheart's reign. A small and stable band of professionals with Simon of Pattishall at their head becomes even easier to see in King John's time.

An appropriate date to mark the completion of the process is William of Raleigh's appointment to the bench following the death of his master Martin of Pattishall in November 1229, or certainly Raleigh's retirement from the court *coram rege* in 1239. By the time of Pattishall and Raleigh, justices and their clerks formed a 'school' of legal studies at Westminster, excerpting the plea rolls and writing the *tractates* that together form the great treatise attributed to Henry de Bracton.[48] Clearly by the 1230s we can see members of the professional judiciary, learned in both laws, who regarded English law as a suitable subject for scholarly study. Fulltime professionals were the mainstays of the judicial bench throughout the reigns of John and Henry III, although some multipurpose royal servants would occasionally serve as justices, even as late as the time of Edward I.[49]

Few biographical sketches of medieval English justices have

---

[48] On this see Thorne's comments in his introduction to vol. 3, *Bracton*, pp. xxxv–xxxvi. [49] *Select Cases*, 1: lxiii–lxvi.

been written since Foss's *Judges of England* was begun in 1848. His work, written before the mass of medieval English royal records became available in printed editions, 'has long outlived its usefulness', although much of his guesswork continues to be accepted as fact today.[50] Some brief biographical studies have been published in the twentieth century as introductions to editions of feet of fines and plea rolls.[51] While this work builds on these earlier studies, it is not a biographical dictionary, but a broader study of the evolution of a professional judiciary in medieval England.

Clearly, study of earlier royal justices in a collective fashion rather than as a series of individual biographical sketches can aid in painting a composite picture of the bench of judges, men difficult to know as individuals given the paucity of sources. This study can also contribute to our understanding of the circumstances surrounding the birth of the common law. An awareness of the personal relationships of justices with their patrons, with other office-holders, and with the king will help us to connect the content of the law to the environment and mentality of the time. Although the evidence is scattered in many small scraps, we can piece it together with patience to see something of the judges' own outlook. We can even seek to measure the distance between the ideal set for them by chroniclers and other critics and their actual achievement. Not only can a look

---

[50] *Select Cases*, 4: ix–x.

[51] For C.A.F. Meekings' biographies of Adam fitz William, Alan of Wassand, Martin of Pattishall, Robert of Nottingham, Roger of Whitchester, William of Raleigh, and William of York, see Meekings, *Studies* for reprints of articles from *Archaeologia Aeliana* (no. xiv), *Yorks Archaeol. Jl.* (no. xiii), *E.H.R.* (no. v), and *B.I.H.R.* (nos. viii, x, xi, xii, xiii). See also *The 1235 Surrey Eyre*, 1, Surrey Rec. Soc., 31 (1979): App. II, *Biographica*, pp. 161–260; *C.R.R.*, 16 (for 1237–42): xx–xxviii, containing material from an unpublished paper, '*Coram rege* justices, 1240–1258'.

For biographical material on earlier justices, see Barbara Dodwell, ed., *Feet of Fines for Norfolk 1198–1202*, Pipe Roll Soc., new ser., 27 (1952): xiv–xvi; Doris M. Stenton, ed., *The earliest Northamptonshire assize rolls A.D. 1202, 1203*, Northants Rec. Soc., 5 (1930): xvii–xix; *Earliest Lincs assize rolls*, pp. xxiii–xxviii; Ralph V. Turner, 'The Judges of King John: their background and training', *Speculum*, 51 (1976): 447–61; 'Simon of Pattishall, pioneer professional judge', *Albion*, 9 (1977): 116–27; Margaret S. Walker, ed., *Feet of Fines for the county of Lincolnshire, 1199–1216*, Pipe Roll Soc., new ser., 29 (1954): xxviii–xxxviii; F.J. West, 'The *curia regis* in the late twelfth and early thirteenth centuries', *Historical Studies (Australia and New Zealand)*, 6 (1954): 175–81.

at the careers of the justices contribute to legal history, but it can also contribute to social history, indicating ties of family and patronage, social mobility, and answering questions about the power structure of late twelfth-century and early thirteenth-century England. In medieval terms, this group may serve as the 'type' of a larger reality, the medieval English civil servant.

2

GLANVILL AND HIS COLLEAGUES, c. 1176–89

1 ELABORATION OF THE EYRE SYSTEM

The late twelfth and early thirteenth centuries were a time of great growth for more rational procedures, centralization, and professionalization in government. Nowhere in Europe can this process be seen more clearly than in England under Henry II, who created new machinery of justice for his subjects. He made the new procedures available in his own court, the *curia regis*, operated by his own servants. Henry's innovation set in motion a growing centralization, as more and more cases came into the *curia regis* instead of into the traditional courts. Some means of carrying royal justice to the people was needed, and in the late twelfth century Henry II revived the practice of his grandfather in sending itinerant commissioners to the counties. As Lady Stenton said, 'In the last ten years of Henry II's reign there was a rapid coming and going of itinerant justices to hear an ever increasing volume of pleas.'[1] Yet the eyre system took shape slowly. In the first eleven years of Henry's reign, there had been only 'occasional desultory visitations of *curiales*;' but then began the series of assizes, which by expanding the scope of royal justice made necessary new circuits of itinerant justices.[2]

The great council at Clarendon in February 1166 resulted in the Assize of Clarendon, which created the jury of presentment, bringing more accused criminals to trial. About the same time came the assize of novel disseisin, which placed many actions concerning possession of land under royal jurisdiction. These new procedures created pressure for more judges to hear the new pleas for which the king was taking responsibility, and

---

[1] *English Justice*, p. 76.
[2] *Governance*, p. 196. Lady Stenton in *English Justice*, p. 71 stated, 'There is little evidence that between 1160 and 1166 the king made any attempt to maintain judicial eyres.'

within a few months of the council came the first general eyre of Henry II's reign. Earl Geoffrey de Mandeville and Richard de Lucy, the justiciar, set out on an eyre covering the eastern half of the kingdom that ended in October 1166 with the earl's death at Chester. Enforcement of the assize then fell to the sheriffs in the shires left unvisited. At the same time, Alan de Neville led a forest eyre, which continued in 1167, and he may also have undertaken the task of enforcing the Assize of Clarendon.[3] The aims of these circuits were to ensure that the Assize of Clarendon was administered properly, to conduct the trials of those accused by presenting juries, and possibly to see that wrongful disseisins were remedied.[4] These were not the only aims, however, for the itinerant justices' work was never solely judicial; they had administrative, financial, information-gathering, and supervisory work as well. Chroniclers regarded the eyres as more concerned with increasing royal revenues than with rendering justice; and indeed, the justices frequently doubled as financial agents, assessing aids and tallages in the counties.[5]

During the years 1168–70 a new visitation took place on a more elaborate plan with several teams of justices named and with each one visiting a different corner of the country. It was 'certainly the most thorough and exhaustive eyre that had yet been carried out'.[6] It required the creation of a 'bench of judges', a body of men who would continue to go out on cir-

---

[3] *P.B.K.J.*, 3: liii–liv, 'The development of the judiciary 1100–1215.'

[4] *Governance*, pp. 198–9, argues that implementing the Assize of Clarendon was only a small part of the justices' work, that the juries of presentment made their indictments before local officials, but Lady Stenton maintains that judgment of those indicted had to be made before the justices, *P.B.K.J.*, 3: liii. The text of the assize in *Roger Howden*, 2: cii, criticized by Richardson and Sayles as untrustworthy, clearly states that accused criminals were to stand trial before the justices. J.C. Holt, 'The Assizes of Henry II: the texts', in Dr. A. Bullough and R.L. Storey, eds., *The Study of medieval records, Essays in Honour of Kathleen Major* (Oxford, 1971), pp. 104–6, and David Corner, 'The Texts of Henry II's Assizes', in *Law-Making and Law-makers in British History*, ed. Alan Harding, Royal Hist. Soc. Studies in History, 22 (London, 1980): 7–20, prove conclusively the reliability of Howden's texts.

[5] *Roger Howden* complained of the cost of the 1198 eyre under Richard I 'By these and other vexations, whether just or unjust, the whole of England from sea to sea was reduced to poverty', 4: 62. He said of a visit by itinerant justices to Boston fair in 1202, that they 'gained money for the king's use, to the injury of many', 4: 172.

[6] *Governance*, p. 203; W.L. Warren, *Henry II*, (Berkeley and Los Angeles, 1973), p. 286.

cuits.[7] Still, it is difficult to identify the men responsible for the work of justice before 1176, when the feet of fines began to survive in some numbers. Before then, we must depend upon the pipe rolls' lists of judges responsible for judicial debts incurred on the eyres. These lists begin in 1166, but they are often incomplete, listing only one justice's name plus the phrase *et socii*.

In the last ten years of Henry's reign – from the great eyre of the spring of 1179 until his death in July 1189 – about fifty-five names are listed as justices at Westminster or on eyres to the counties. Twenty or so names appear only once or twice among those witnessing fines at Westminster or in the counties. I have selected for study thirteen men shown to have been most often on the judicial bench by a count of the number of times their names appear on Lady Stenton's lists. They include five high-ranking royal officers: Ranulf de Glanvill, the justiciar from 1180 to Henry II's death; Richard fitz Neal, the treasurer; and three bishops, Geoffrey Ridel, bishop of Ely; Richard of Ilchester, bishop of Winchester; and John of Oxford, bishop of Norwich. They also include eight men of lesser dignity: two clerics, Jocelin, archdeacon of Chichester; and Master Godfrey de Lucy, future bishop of Winchester; and six laymen, including William Basset, Michael Belet, Alan de Furnellis (or Fourneaux), Roger fitz Reinfrid, William Ruffus, and Robert of Wheatfield. Three other names – Hugh Bardolf, Hubert Walter, and Master Thomas of Hurstbourne – appear on final concords regularly from 1185 on. Their work on the bench continued throughout the time of Richard I, and they will be grouped with the justices of the next reign.

It is possible in spite of limited evidence, at least from 1179 on, to bring these men into the light and to see them more clearly than as faceless *familiares regis* or *curiales*. The regularity with which these men's names appear makes clear that they formed a corps of royal officers responsible for justice, although those who staffed the eyres and sat at the Exchequer hearing pleas were by no means lawyers or professional judges. They were members of a network of royal servants who held multiple offices, both local and at court.

From 1171 to 1175, there were no new judicial eyres. Instead,

---

[7] *English Justice*, p. 73.

the men who went about the kingdom on the king's business were busy with administrative tasks. In 1170 the Inquest of Sheriffs began, and in 1172 the collection of a scutage for the Irish campaign probably occupied the justices. In 1173–4 the great rebellion disrupted the normal operations of government, and collecting tallages would have taken up the justices' time.[8]

Three circuits covered a good part of the country in 1175. Heading one of the eyres was Ranulf de Glanvill, the future justiciar, serving for the first time as an itinerant justice. Another eyre was the king's own itinerant court, composed of three men who heard pleas as Henry II travelled about the kingdom: William fitz Ralph, Bertram de Verdun, and William Basset.[9] William Basset's judicial work had begun in 1168 when he first went on eyre, and it continued both in the counties and at Westminster until the spring of 1185. At the same time that these three were hearing pleas, a corps of royal officers at the Exchequer in Westminster – whether called *barones* or *justiciarii* – continued to hear pleas.

The next significant step in the growth of the courts came with the Assize of Northampton in January 1176, a date some scholars see as more important for the judicial eyres than 1166. J.E.A. Jolliffe wrote, 'It is in 1176 that we are first conscious that experiment is over and the time come for the parcelling of the kingdom into areas for regular judicial visitation.'[10] Following the council at Northampton, Henry II named eighteen *justicias errantes* – six groups of three men – sent to different parts of the country.[11] The party of justices that visited the North was headed by Ranulf de Glanvill. Among others named to the commissions were three men who would remain prominent on the bench throughout the rest of Henry II's reign and into the reign of Richard I: Michael Belet, William Ruffus, and Roger fitz Reinfrid. The latter two died by the middle of Richard's reign, but Michael Belet continued his judicial work for a quarter-century, until his death in 1201. These justices continued their eyres in 1177, but some were given the additional duty of levy-

---

[8] *P.B.K.J.*, 3: lvi. [9] *English Justice*, p. 75; *P.B.K.J.*, 3: lvi.
[10] Jolliffe, *The Constitutional History of Medieval England* (3rd edn, London, 1954), p. 212; Pollock and Maitland, 1: 156, maintains a similar view.
[11] *Ralph de Diceto*, 1: 404; *Gesta Hen. Secundi*, 1: 106.

ing a tallage. They became so overburdened that much work had to be concluded at Westminster. Two groups of justices, most of whom were sheriffs, continued at work to complete cases until the king's return from Normandy in July 1178.[12]

When Henry II returned to England in July 1178, he examined the justices to learn whether they had done their work 'discreetly and well'. He decided that eighteen justices were too many, that 'the land and its people had been overmuch burdened by the great multitude of judges'.[13] Instead, he commissioned five members of his *privata familia* – two clerks and three laymen – to follow him on his travels about the kingdom hearing 'the complaints of the people' and only consulting him about cases too difficult to decide themselves.[14] Not enough royal charters or final concords survive to reveal the names of the five judges, but one of them must have been Geoffrey Ridel, bishop of Ely, who was often in the king's company in late 1176.[15] Maitland's view was that when the king returned to the Continent, this group of five justices continued its work at Westminster sitting at the house of the Exchequer. He traced to this reform of Henry II's the origin of the court of Common Pleas, but many of today's scholars attach less significance to it, seeing it as 'only one of a series of similar experiments'.[16] Whatever the circumstances, the *curia regis ad scaccarium* was hearing increasing numbers of pleas in Henry II's last years. The justiciar was obliged to give some time to hearing pleas when the king was abroad because of Henry II's practice of granting writs of protection from being impleaded *nisi coram me vel capitali justicia mea*. Many religious houses and some individuals possessed this privilege.

More legal innovations came at the Easter Council of 1179. One result was the grand assize; another was the appointment of

---

[12] *P.B.K.J.*, 3: lviii–lx; *Governance*, p. 212; and Warren, *Henry II*, p. 295.
[13] *Gesta Hen. Secundi*, 1: 207.
[14] The Latin phrase is *clamores hominum*. Some authorities maintain that the five justices did not follow the king, but established themselves at the Exchequer, *Governance*, p. 211; Warren, *Henry II*, p. 296.
[15] *Itin. Hen. II*, pp. 223–5.
[16] Pollock and Maitland, 1: 153–5; S.B. Chrimes, *Introduction to the Administrative History of Medieval England* (3rd edn, Oxford, 1966), p. 50, n. 1. Similarly, A.L. Poole, *From Domesday Book to Magna Carta*, Oxford History of England (2nd edn, 1955), 3: 413; and *English Justice*, pp. 75–6.

new groups of justices, the most extensive eyre yet, with twenty-one judges on four circuits. No doubt, the resignation of Richard de Lucy from the justiciarship at the Easter Council offered an occasion for still another judicial experiment. The new appointments attracted a chronicler's attention because Henry II in an attempt to find judges who would 'neither oppress the poor in the judgments nor favor the causes of the rich by taking bribes' turned to 'the sanctuary of God', the episcopate.[17] The king appointed three bishops: Richard of Winchester, Geoffrey of Ely, and John of Norwich. Among the twenty-one were several others serving for the first time who would remain on the bench for the rest of Henry II's lifetime; they include Robert of Wheatfield, Godfrey de Lucy, Alan de Furnellis, and Richard fitz Neal, the treasurer. Alan died about the same time as Henry II. Robert of Wheatfield lived until 1193–4, and he continued to serve as a justice as late as August 1193. Both Godfrey de Lucy and the treasurer remained on the bench throughout the reign of Richard Lionheart, even though they became bishops in late 1189.

These twenty-one itinerant justices were not the entire judicial element of the kingdom. Some justices remained behind at the Exchequer to hear cases, as final concords indicate.[18] After the late summer eyres of 1179, lesser men continued the four circuits of the counties, carrying on the work until 1181. The three bishops remained at Westminster, and they continued for several years to hear pleas regularly at the Easter and Michaelmas Exchequer sessions.

The six justices on the northern circuit were successors to those justices of 1175 and 1178 who had travelled with the king 'to hear the complaints of the realm'. They followed the king in the spring and early summer of 1179.[19] Among them was Ranulf de Glanvill, heading the northern circuit; two others appointed to the same circuit who would continue to serve Henry II frequently on the bench were Godfrey de Lucy and Alan de Furnellis. Glanvill was named justiciar at the time of Henry II's departure for the Continent in April 1180, and this fourth group of justices then became the justiciar's court, accompanying him

---

[17] *Ralph de Diceto*, 1: 434–7.   [18] *P.B.K.J.*, 3: lxiv.
[19] *English Justice*, p. 75; *P.B.K.J.*, 3: lxi–lxii.

to the northern counties in the winter of 1180–1.[20] With 1179–80, then, we are approaching the threefold pattern of royal courts that will prevail in the thirteenth century: groups of justices on eyre throughout the kingdom, one group of justices *coram rege*, and others stationary with the Exchequer at Westminster.

Ranulf de Glanvill, the new justiciar, was 'immensely active' on the eyres; he went out on circuit himself nearly every year.[21] There was a wide-sweeping eyre in early autumn of 1182 and continuing into the summer of 1183.[22] Another eyre with four main circuits began in autumn 1184 and continued in January and February 1185. Besides these four main groups, another group accompanied the justiciar as he moved about the country.[23] In the last four years of Henry II – 1186–9 – groups of justices went out so frequently that it is difficult to sort them out. One can see some justices at work somewhere in England every year. Indeed, five parties were at work in spring 1189 shortly before the king's death in midsummer.[24] What H. G. Richardson wrote about the eyres before 1183 was still true in the last four years of Henry, '. . . that there were no fixed circuits, and that while the order observed in one year might be loosely founded on the proceedings in the previous year, everything was provisional and subject to alteration and revision, even while an eyre was in progress'.[25] Nonetheless, the eyre was becoming a permanent feature of English government, a useful instrument for bringing royal justice to the shires, one that would flourish for about a century.

No pattern for the assignment of justices to circuits makes itself apparent. The seven laymen among the judges were also sheriffs, and they occasionally went to the counties of which they were sheriffs. No consistent pattern appears of either sending them or not sending them to the counties they held. The criterion seems to have been their knowledge of the region. Glanvill, after he became justiciar, chose to lead circuits to the North, where his earlier experience as sheriff made him familiar with conditions. Michael Belet, although sheriff of Worcester-

[20] *P.B.K.J.*, 3: lxv.   [21] *Justiciarship*, p. 59; Warren, *Henry II*, p. 294.
[22] *P.B.K.J.*, 3: lxv, lxvii.   [23] *P.B.K.J.*, 3: lxix.   [24] *P.B.K.J.*, 3: lxxvii–lxxviii.
[25] H.G. Richardson, 'Richard fitz Neal and the *Dialogus de Scaccario*', *E.H.R.*, 43 (1928): 170–1.

shire, was a royal *pincerna* rarely resident in his shire; and he more often went on eyre to the eastern counties, where he held property through his wife. On the other hand, William Basset was primarily a local official, only coming to Westminster for the twice-yearly Exchequer sessions, and he was often a justice in Warwickshire and Leicestershire or Lincolnshire, where he was sheriff at one time or another.

Justice was also available to Henry II's subjects in the 1180s at Westminster in the spring and autumn, when royal officials gathered for the Easter and Michaelmas sessions of the Exchequer. Leaders of the eyres often returned to Westminster for these twice-yearly sessions, for their names occur most frequently as witnesses to the final concords made at the Exchequer. The eyres had an effect of forcing more judicial business on royal officials at Westminster, for once they ended, complainants who had not succeeded in getting a hearing in their own localities followed the justices there. Surviving final concords indicate an increasing number of suits settled at the Exchequer sessions. Whether there was any specialization at the Exchequer at this time, with some staff concentrating on financial audits and others on judgments, cannot be known with certainty. Such men as Richard of Ilchester or Richard fitz Neal seem to have been equally at home at both tasks.[26] Contemporaries seem to have used such terms as *justiciarii*, *barones de scaccario*, and *curia regis* with maddening imprecision.[27]

In any event, justice was clearly becoming more readily available to Henry II's subjects through the work of a corps of identifiable royal officials. These were men who had proven their ability and their loyalty through previous service to the king. Glanvill did not bring a group of his own retainers into the royal courts in 1180; instead, he relied on men he found already in the

[26] John E. Lally, 'The Court and Household of Henry II', Ph.D. Thesis (Liverpool, 1969), table 2, pp. 302–3, listed the men present at the making of 37 final concords or charters at Westminster, 1165–89: among them, Glanvill, 27; Richard fitz Neal, 24; Geoffrey Ridel, 18; John of Oxford, 18; William Basset, 17; Richard of Ilchester, 16; Roger fitz Reinfrid, 13; Michael Belet, 10; Godfrey de Lucy, 9; Robert of Wheatfield, 8; William Ruffus, 6; Alan de Furnellis, 5; Jocelin, archdeacon of Chichester, 4.

[27] For a discussion of the problem surrounding 'Exchequer' and 'Bench' see my article, 'The origins of Common Pleas and King's Bench', *A.J.L.H.*, 21 (1977): 240–5.

king's service. Only gradually between 1185 and the end of Henry II's reign, did Glanvill bring his *familiares* into the work of justice, and they would continue in the courts under Richard I.

2 THE JUSTICES' ORIGINS

Walter Map, one of Henry II's courtiers, in conversation with Ranulf de Glanvill complained of the base birth of royal justices. He claimed that they were often sons of serfs, seeking to rise above their station through clerical careers. Peter of Blois also complained in a letter to the king about the low origin of the justices. Complaints about the base birth of royal servants are a commonplace not only of twelfth-century writers but throughout the Middle Ages. Did such complaints have any basis in the case of the thirteen men who served Henry II on the judicial bench in his last years?

Although the genealogical evidence is only sketchy, it seems safe to assume that all thirteen of these royal servants came from Norman families. The lowest level of evidence – their Christian names – reveals none named for an Anglo-Saxon saint. Eight came from what we might call 'administrative families', that is, with a tradition of service to the king. The best known example is Richard fitz Neal, son of Nigel bishop of Ely, who was the nephew of Roger of Salisbury, Henry I's chancellor and chief justiciar. Richard's family had a tradition of financial expertise.[1] Another member of an administrative family was William Basset, whose forebears had served Henry I. His grandfather, Ralph Basset, had been one of the viceregal group that governed England during Henry I's visits to Normandy. Ralph and his son Richard, William's father, are both described by chroniclers as *capitales justiciarii* or *justiciarii totius Anglie*[2]. Geoffrey Ridel was related to the Basset family; he was either a grandson or great-nephew of Richard Basset. An earlier Geoffrey Ridel,

---

[1] *Dial. de Scac.*, pp. xiv–xv.

[2] T. Arnold, ed., *Henrici Huntendunensis Historia Anglorum*, Rolls Series (1879), pp. 245, 290, 318; Joseph Stevenson, ed., *Chronicon Monasterii de Abingdon*, Rolls Series (1858), 2: 170; Marjorie Chibnall, ed. and trans., Ordericus Vitalis, *Historia Ecclesiastica*, Oxford Medieval Texts (Oxford, 1972–), 6: 468. For a discussion of the Bassets' responsibility for justice in relation to that of Roger of Salisbury, see *Justiciarship*, pp. 21–3.

his maternal grandfather, was prominent in the government of Henry I until he drowned in the 1120 wreck of the 'White Ship'.[3] It was natural that Godfrey de Lucy should have followed his father Richard de Lucy, justiciar until 1179, into the king's service. Michael Belet's family had gained the hereditary serjeanty of *pincerna* or royal butler in the time of Henry I. This serjeanty was a working office, not an honorific one, as were some hereditary household offices.[4] Little can be learned about the origins of William Ruffus, whose name is so common that it is almost impossible to disentangle him from other men of the same name recorded on charters and pipe rolls. Probably he was related to other royal servants surnamed Ruffus or 'le Rous' at Henry II's court. Herbert Ruffus is described as *serviens meus* in a royal grant of 1159. Herbert's son, Richard Ruffus, served as one of Henry II's chamberlains from 1168 on.[5] The fathers of two justices – John of Oxford and Alan de Furnellis – were sheriffs.[6]

Four of the justices had fathers or uncles of baronial rank, if we count bishops as barons. This category would then include Richard fitz Neal, son of the bishop of Ely, and Master Jocelin of Chichester, nephew of Bishop Hilary of Chichester, one of Henry II's supporters in his struggle against his archbishop of Canterbury.[7] Richard Basset, William's father, had risen to baronial rank when Henry I granted him the barony of Great Weldon, Northamptonshire, sometime after 1122.[8] Richard de Lucy, father of Godfrey, originally held only knightly rank but by 1166 his service to the king had raised him to baronial standing. The baronial families, then, are almost identical with the administrative families. They were not descended from com-

[3] *D.N.B.*, s.v. 'Ridel, Geoffrey'.
[4] *Book of Fees*, 1: 70. J.E.A. Jolliffe, *Angevin Kingship* (London, 1956), maintains that Belet's *pincernaria* was purely honourific, but other hereditary household officials were working officers. See Emma Mason, 'The Mauduits and their chamberlainship of the Exchequer', *B.I.H.R.*, 49 (1976): 1–23.
[5] *V.C.H., Staffs*, 17: 169. Foss, *Judges of England*, 1: 303, assigned William Ruffus' parentage to Ralph de Rufus, one of the Conqueror's knights, but he failed to give any source for this.
[6] Henry of Oxford, sheriff of Berks and Oxon., 1154; Geoffrey de Furnellis, sheriff of Devon and Cornwall, 1129. *List of Sheriffs*, pp. 6, 21, 107.
[7] Henry Mayr-Harting, 'Hilary, Bishop of Chichester (1147–69) and Henry II', *E.H.R.*, 78 (1963): 210.
[8] A fee of 15 knights, Sanders, *Baronies*, p. 49.

panions of William the Conqueror, but had achieved higher status through service to Henry I, or in one or two cases through service to his grandson.

The remaining judges had families of knightly or lesser status. The families of two sheriffs' sons – John of Oxford and Alan de Furnellis – might be classed as both administrative and knightly, as might those of Michael Belet and William Ruffus. John of Oxford's father was sheriff of Oxfordshire, 1154–5, and as late as 1163 he was in charge of royal building operations at Oxford. John inherited some property in the town of Oxford, while his brother William inherited their father's manor of Ibston.[9] Alan de Furnellis' father, Geoffrey, was sheriff of Devon and Cornwall under Henry I.[10] Michael Belet was the son of Hervey Belet, a knight with lands in Lincolnshire, Northamptonshire, and Oxfordshire.[11] Roger fitz Reinfrid was probably of knightly rank, for he paid scutage on land in Dorset as early as 1161, which must have represented his inheritance.[12] Ranulf de Glanvill was the second son of a Suffolk knight who held of the honour of Eye; his father, Hervey, was not unknown. He had won respect as a participant in the crusaders' conquest of Lisbon in 1147 and as a suitor at the Suffolk shire court. Ranulf improved his position through a good marriage. Bertha, his wife, brought as *maritagium* some Suffolk lands of her father, Theobald de Valoignes, lord of Parham.[13] Robert of Wheatfield came from a knightly family enfeoffed following the Conquest. He was descended from Geoffrey, who held two hides of land at Wheatfield, Oxfordshire, part of the honour of Wallingford.[14]

The origins of one of the thirteen justices are so obscure that it is possible that he rose from humble stock, though still from among free landholders. The background of Richard of Ilchester is completely shrouded except for the region of his birth: the

[9] *Bio. Reg. Univ. Oxf.*, 2:1414. H.E. Salter, *Facsimiles of Charters in Oxford Muniment Rooms* (Oxford, 1929), no. 43, and notes to nos. 42 and 92.

[10] *List of Sheriffs*, p. 21.

[11] *D.N.B.*, s.v. 'Belet, Michael'; *V.C.H., Oxon.*, 9: 175–6; and unpublished notes of the late C.A.F. Meekings.

[12] *Pipe Roll 7 Hen. II*, p. 47; *8 Hen. II*, p. 24.

[13] S.J. Bailey, 'Ranulf de Glanvill and his children', *Camb. Law Jl.* (1957) p. 166; Richard Mortimer, 'The family of Ranulf de Glanville', *B.I.H.R.*, 54 (1981): 3, 7–8.

[14] *Red Book Exch.*, p. 309; *V.C.H., Oxon.*, 8: 101, 263.

diocese of Bath. The only light to fall on his family is the fact
that Gilbert Foliot, bishop first of Hereford and later of London,
claimed him as a kinsman (*cognatus*).[15] Richard's career is another
indication that the Church did enable ambitious young men of
no particular background to climb to places of power and
prestige.

Patronage was as important an aspect of social mobility in
twelfth-century England as it would be in the better-documented
later centuries. Ambitious young men sought to attach themselves to a noble or episcopal household, to win the attention of
powerful men, gaining profitable posts, and perhaps moving
into royal government, the centre of power, where their
influence could purchase them social status and added wealth.
At the same time, barons and bishops were eager to place members of their households in posts in royal government in order to
have clients strategically located to look out for their interests.
Some royal servants remained in the *familia* of another while
working in government posts. Royal clerks, for example, were
often cathedral canons, members of episcopal households,
although usually absentees. It has been estimated that about a
quarter of cathedral prebendaries were regularly absent in the
king's service, and in some instances the number could rise
higher.[16] Royal clerks, shifted back and forth from ecclesiastical
to royal duties, must have had a blurred sense of the distinction
between the two spheres. Other royal justices were more members of the justiciar's household than of the king's, although this
may not have been the case with any significant number before
about 1185, by which time Ranulf de Glanvill had recruited
several associates. It is impossible to see clearly the links in the
chain of patronage, but we can speculate on the identity of patrons
who might have provided an introduction to the royal service
for some of the thirteen justices.

Sometimes life imitated chivalric legend, and men made such
an impression on the king through acts of courage that they
owed their promotion directly to him. The most notable example

[15] Charles Duggan, 'Richard of Ilchester, royal servant and bishop', *T.R.H.S.*,
    5th ser., 16 (1961): 3; Adrian Morey and C.N.L. Brooke, eds., *The Letters and
    Charters of Gilbert Foliot* (Cambridge, 1967), pp. 268, 299.
[16] C.N.L. Brooke, 'The composition of the chapter of St Paul's 1068–1168',
    Camb. Hist. Jl., 10 (1951): 120.

among the thirteen justices is Glanvill, whose spectacular military success in the 1173–4 rebellion won him Henry II's favour. His rigorous enforcement of the Assize of Clarendon in Yorkshire, where he was sheriff in 1166, may have already attracted the king's favourable attention.[17] Sometimes ties of patronage are clear because they are also family ties. The most obvious instance is Richard fitz Neal, whose father purchased his post of treasurer for him about 1158.[18] Also Godfrey de Lucy was assured of entry into the royal government through his father, the justiciar. Richard de Lucy saw that his son had a valuable benefice – the deanery of St Martin-le-Grand – to support him while in the schools of London.[19] He entered the service of Henry II about the time of his father's retirement in 1179, when he was one of the justices named for the great eyre of that year.[20] Master Jocelin, archdeacon of Lewes, had as patron his uncle Hilary, bishop of Chichester, who was close to Henry II early in his reign, serving as sheriff and as itinerant justice. The bishop had made his nephew chancellor of the cathedral by 1167.[21] The post of archdeacon was practically reserved for near-kinsmen of bishops in the mid twelfth century, although Jocelin may not have won his post until after his uncle's death in 1169. By then, Master Jocelin was already in the king's service, for in 1167 he was excommunicated for carrying a message from royalist bishops to Thomas Becket.[22]

The patrons of other justices present problems. William Basset would have needed a patron, for his father died in 1146 in the midst of the Anarchy, too early to aid him in establishing himself. William was a younger son, not the heir to his father's

---

[17] *Justiciarship*, p. 54; Holt, 'The Assizes of Henry II', p. 106.
[18] *Dial. de Scac.*, pp. xiv–xv. *D.N.B.*, s.v. 'Fitzneale, Richard', gives 1169 as the date. H.G. Richardson states that 'it is generally accepted that his father purchased the office in 1158 and that by 1160 Richard had obtained possession', in 'Richard fitz Neal and the *Dial. de Scac.*', *E.H.R.*, 430 (1928): 162.
[19] In 1171, *Bio. Reg. Univ. Oxf.*, 3: 2192. By 1176 the king had given him the church at Wye also, Eleanor Searle, ed. and trans., *The Chronicle of Battle Abbey*, Oxford Medieval Texts (Oxford, 1980), pp. 268–70.
[20] *Ralph de Diceto*, 1: 434–7.
[21] Mayr-Harting, 'Hilary of Chichester', pp. 209–16; Delisle, *Recueil*, Introduction, p. 401; Marjorie Chibnall, ed., *Select documents of the English lands of the Abbey of Bec*, Camden 3rd ser., 73 (1951): 3–4, no. 5.
[22] *M.T.B.*, 6: 273, 275–8.

barony, but he apparently came into possession of a portion of his father's land at Sapcote, Leicestershire.[23] It is likely that his sponsor in introducing him to the royal service was Robert, earl of Leicester, joint-justiciar with Richard de Lucy. One of William's earliest recorded appearances is in 1158–9, when he witnessed one of the earl's charters.[24] Another link was the fact that Basset was a Leicestershire landholder, and that he succeeded his brother Ralph as sheriff of that shire in 1163.[25]

Henry II's other co-justiciar was the patron of Roger fitz Reinfrid. Roger was a member of the household of Richard de Lucy from the time Richard became sole justiciar in 1168 until his resignation in 1179. During those ten years he witnessed a number of the justiciar's private charters.[26] Roger felt enough devotion to the justiciar to make a gift of an advowson to the abbey which Richard founded on his retirement.[27] Another possible sponsor of Roger fitz Reinfrid was Simon de St Liz, earl of Huntingdon and Northampton (d. 1184). In July 1175, Earl Simon gave Roger his soke, or franchisal jurisdiction, in the city of London to hold in heredity for one bezant yearly.[28] At some unknown date, Roger became the earl's man through an exchange of land.[29]

The three bishops on the bench all seem to have begun their careers in the service of the royal chancellor, Thomas Becket. John of Oxford witnessed one of Henry II's writs as early as 1162–3.[30] Geoffrey Ridel was at the chancery at the time of Becket's appointment as archbishop of Canterbury, and after Becket's resignation, Henry II gave Geoffrey the duties of the chancellor without assigning him the actual title.[31] Another of

---

[23] William Dugdale, *The Baronage of England*, (London, 1675–6), 1: 382. His elder brother was Ralph Basset of Drayton, Staffs.

[24] *Docs. preserved in France*, pp. 376–7, no. 1062. As early as 1151/2 Basset witnessed a charter for the bishop of Lincoln, David M. Smith, ed., *English Episcopal acta*, 1, *Lincoln 1067–1185* (London, 1980), p. 88, no. 141.

[25] He first accounted for the shrievalty as his brother's deputy, *Pipe Roll 9 Hen. II*, p. 31, then in his own right, 1164–70, *List of Sheriffs*, pp. 75, 144.

[26] Lally, 'Court and household of Henry II', pp. 75–6, 357.

[27] Gift of the church at Ramsden Bellhouse, Essex, to Lesne Abbey, *Monasticon*, 6: 457.

[28] B.L. MS. Harl. Chtr. 43 c. 26; *Foedera*, 1: 46.

[29] *C.R.R.*, 4: 42–3.

[30] All Souls College, Oxford, MS. DD.c.218, no. 8. I owe this reference to Prof. J.C. Holt.

[31] *D.N.B.*, s.v. 'Ridel, Geoffrey'; Delisle, *Recueil*, Introduction, pp. 92–3.

Becket's clerks was Richard of Ilchester, described as *scriptor Curiae* in the earliest of Henry II's pipe rolls. His name appears on witness lists for royal charters as early as 1159.[32] Becket's friendship with the bishop of Poitiers, a former companion in the household of Theobald of Canterbury, won Richard his appointment as archdeacon of Poitiers, 1162–3.[33] But Richard may have had another powerful patron before he entered the royal chancery. He seems to have been a clerk in the household of Robert of Gloucester, Henry Plantagenet's uncle, during the Anarchy.[34]

Several potential patrons appear in the case of Alan de Furnellis. According to the *Cartae Baronum* of 1166, he held land in Dorset and Devonshire of five men of baronial rank, among them Bartholomew, bishop of Exeter, and Robert fitz Roy, baron of Okehampton, Devon, and a natural son of Henry I.[35] Another candidate for Alan's patron is Reginald fitz Roy, earl of Cornwall and another illegitimate son of Henry I, who was prominent in the early years of Henry II. Since Alan was chiefly active in local administration in Devon and Cornwall until 1179, he would have worked closely with the earl.[36]

What training had the thirteen justices received which prepared them for their judicial activity? Their biographies reveal them to be mainly men of practical experience in other branches of royal government, not 'learned' men in the academic sense. Whether clerics or laymen, Henry II's judges acquired their knowledge of the law largely through practical lessons. Some of them, no doubt, had experience in pleading before the shire courts, *curia regis*, or church courts as attorneys or advocates for their patrons. For those who felt a need for

---

[32] *Pipe Roll 2, 3, 4, Hen. II*, Record Commission (London, 1844), pp. 30, 31, 47, 121, 122. Lambeth MS.241, f. 59ᵛ, cited by Morey and Brooke, p. 539.

[33] *D.N.B.*, s.v. 'Richard of Ilchester'; Duggan, 'Richard of Ilchester', p. 2. *M.T.B.*, 3: 120.

[34] Duggan, 'Richard of Ilchester', pp. 3–4.

[35] Gerbert de Percy, baron of Poorstock, Dorset, *Red Book Exch.*, p. 217; Bartholomew, bishop of Exeter, p. 248; Robert fitz Roy, baron of Okehampton, Devon, pp. 248, 253; William de Tracy, baron of Bradninch, Devon, p. 254.

[36] In 1174, Alan and Payn the Chaplain accounted at the Exchequer for Devon as Earl Reginald's deputies, *List of Sheriffs*, p. 21. Alan was royal farmer of the stannaries from 1169 on, *Pipe Roll 15 Hen. II*, p. 47; *32 Hen. II*, p. 152. On Reginald, see Warren, *Henry II*, pp. 372–3.

further legal learning, their response must have resembled that of Abbot Samson of Bury St Edmunds, 1182–1211. His monastic biographer states that when the abbot found himself appointed a papal judge-delegate, 'He called in two clerks learned in the law and associated them with himself, using their advice in ecclesiastical business, and he studied the decrees and decretals when he had an hour to spare.' The biographer continues, 'Soon, with reading and experience of cases, he gained the reputation of a wise judge, who administered justice according to the rules of law.' When Samson had to preside over secular courts as lord of the liberty of St Edmunds, he learned through experience aided by 'his native power of reasoning'.[37] Clearly, a degree in canon or civil law was not considered a necessary preparation.

The source of the legal knowledge of the seven laymen who were judges is problematical. Hardly any books of English law existed before the treatise known as *Glanvill*. Yet increasing reliance upon written records in government makes it unlikely that these laymen were completely unlettered in Latin. The steadily growing number of documents with which had to deal – writs, pipe rolls, chirographs – implies at least their 'pragmatic literacy'. Opportunities for the sons of knights to receive an elementary education in Latin letters were wider in twelfth-century England than is generally recognized. Although not much is known of the education of laymen in the later twelfth century, the *miles literatus* was not as rare as he is assumed to have been. Younger sons of knights or ambitious sons of humbler freemen saw education as a path to employment with abbots, bishops, sheriffs, or other royal officials as clerks or accountants.[38]

No evidence exists concerning the education of any of the laymen among Henry II's justices. It can no longer be presumed, however, that the military aristocracy of England looked at bookish learning with complete contempt and that their education consisted only of hunting, horseback riding,

---

[37] H.E. Butler, ed., *The Chronicle of Jocelin of Brakelond*, Medieval Texts (London, 1949), pp. 33–4.

[38] For a fuller discussion, see Ralph V. Turner, 'The *Miles Literatus* in twelfth and thirteenth-century England: How rare a phenomenon?', *A.H.R.*, 83 (1978): 928–45.

and swordplay. Most sons of knights learned some rudimentary Latin from their parish priest, from the chaplain of some baronial household, from their mother, or perhaps at school. Medieval usage limited the term *literatus* to one learned in Latin, but laymen who did not master Latin may well have been 'literate' in today's usage. It is likely that those knights who had no instruction in Latin could read Anglo-Norman, their everyday spoken language and the language most often spoken in the courts. Although this language was not a subject for formal study in the schools, French literature was flourishing in the noble households of twelfth-century England. Many members of the Anglo-Norman and Angevin aristocracy – both men and women – were patrons of French literature, sponsoring authors, translators, and copyists, and collecting books. Among the earliest works was the *Leis Willelme*, chiefly a compilation of Anglo-Saxon laws made sometime before 1135. Official documents were written solely in Latin, however, until quite late in the twelfth century, when a few Anglo-Norman versions began to appear.[39]

There has been speculation that the justiciar, Ranulf de Glanvill, attained a high level of learning. He had such a reputation for legal learning that the *Tractatus de legibus et consuetudinibus regni Anglie* has borne his name from the thirteenth century until today. Some authorities reject his authorship, not on grounds of his inability to write such a work, but on grounds of his lack of leisure to complete it.[40] Glanvill has been suggested as the author of two other works: a crusading chronicle of the 1147 conquest of Lisbon and an account of an East Anglian shire-moot from c. 1150.[41]

Glanvill did not have to draw his knowledge of English law from books at school. There was a tradition of legal expertise in hundred and shire courts among the knightly class, which was

---

[39] On literacy in the Anglo-Norman language, see Dominica Legge, *Anglo-Norman Literature and its Background* (Oxford, 1963), and Clanchy, *From Memory to Written Record*, pp. 154–74.

[40] *Glanvill*, pp. xxxi–xxxii.

[41] Josiah C. Russell, 'Ranulf de Glanville', *Speculum*, 45 (1970): 69–70; reprinted in his *Twelfth Century Studies* (New York, 1980), pp. 126–41. For recent criticism of Russell's view, see J.S. Falls, 'Ranulf de Glanville's formative years, c. 1120–1179: the family background and his ascent to the justiciarship', *Medieval Studies*, 40 (1978): 315–17.

entirely an oral tradition in the twelfth century. The warrior-aristocrats of the Middle Ages – from the Vikings to the crusaders – had admired eloquence in pleading. Attending the courts was both a duty and a diversion for men of knightly rank, a feudal obligation and an alternative to military activity. English knights sharpened their skills in pleading through years of attendance at courts, first as youthful observers of suits and later as suitors, attorneys, and jurors. Glanvill's father, Hervey, declared that he had attended courts of shire and hundred for fifty years, first in company with his father.[42] Besides attending the public courts, many knights, as lords of their own lands and as stewards for other landholders, had to preside over private courts themselves.

Legal procedure in all secular courts before Henry II introduced the writ system operated almost completely through the spoken word, not through written documents. It was not until the early thirteenth century that legal treatises and registers of writs were written primarily for the instruction of laymen.[43] The laymen on the bench under Henry II came from such an oral tradition, and they found their practical experience just as useful as the clerks found their school books. The law of Henry II – the common law – grew chiefly out of earlier administrative devices, not from the learned law of the schools.[44] Certainly the laymen cited by the author of *Glanvill* as legal authorities came to their knowledge through years of experience in the courts. Early manuscripts of the treatise attributed to Glanvill give opinions on points of law of seven justices, among them only one cleric, but including four of Henry's lay judges: the two justiciars, Richard de Lucy and Glanvill, William Basset, and Robert of Wheatfield.[45]

The clerical colleagues of the laymen on the bench would not have felt that the laymen's primarily practical and oral instruction was inferior to their own schooling. At an early date,

---

[42] Clanchy, *From Memory to Written Record*, pp. 199–201. For Hervey de Glanvill, see Helen Cam, 'An East Anglian shire-moot of Stephen's reign, 1148–1153', *E.H.R.*, 39 (1924): 570–1.

[43] Clanchy, *From Memory to Written Record*, pp. 220–6; Turner, 'The *Miles Literatus*', pp. 940–1.

[44] E.g. the jury. See Ralph V. Turner, 'The origins of the medieval English jury, Frankish, or Scandinavian?' *Jl. Br. Studies*, 7 (1968): 1–10; 'Roman Law in England before the time of Bracton', *Jl. Br. Studies*, 15 (1975): 1–25.

[45] *Glanvill*, pp. xliv–xlv. William Basset is cited only by the initials, 'W.B'.

knights won reputations for their skill in pleading and served as pleaders for others in return for grants of land.[46] Monasteries made a practice of employing one of their knights as an advocate in suits coming before secular courts. The chronicler of St Albans praised a knight who acted as the abbot's legal adviser in a plea at Westminster in the early thirteenth century. The knight is described as *miles eloquentissimus et sapientissimus* and *in placitis civilibus providus et circumspectus* and in similar phrases with no hint of condescension because his eloquence was not that of the schools.[47] No doubt, lay lords imitated the abbot in employing one of their knights, skilled in speaking, as a pleader in the courts. The art of speaking well was highly regarded by both clergy and laity in the twelfth and thirteenth centuries. Not only did lay education depend heavily upon oral instruction, but the cathedral schools with their lectures and debates stressed strongly oral presentation.[48] To call someone *vir eloquentiae* was a great compliment.

Concrete evidence for the education of the clerics among Henry II's justices is only a little easier to find than for the laymen. Only three – Geoffrey Ridel, Godfrey de Lucy, and Jocelin of Chichester – bore the title *Magister*, which indicated advanced studies at a cathedral school or university.[49] By the mid twelfth century, however, advanced study seems not to have been uncommon among royal clerks and accountants. The distinction between academic and practical subjects was not as sharp in the twelfth-century schools as it would become later in the thirteenth century, by which time schools teaching practical skills such as the *ars dictaminis*, accounting, or some elementary law had grown up outside the university curriculum.[50] Monas-

---

[46] Robert C. Palmer, 'The origins of the legal profession in England', *Irish Jurist*, 11 (1976): 126–35.

[47] *Gesta Abb. Mon. S. Albani*, 1: 221, 225–6, a dispute with Robert fitz Walter in 1200. Cf. Searle, *Chron. Battle Abbey*, p. 214, where one of the monks and a knight are the abbot's spokesmen in a suit of the 1160s.

[48] Eleanor Rathbone, 'The influence of Bishops and members of cathedral bodies in the intellectual life of England, 1066–1216', Ph.D. Thesis (London, 1935), pp. 85–6. Cf. Clanchy, *From Memory to Written Record*, 'Listening to the Word', pp. 214–20.

[49] Geoffrey is given the title in only one charter, Delisle, *Recueil*, 1: 297.

[50] Michael T. Clanchy, '*Moderni* in education and government in England', *Speculum*, 50 (1975): 685. On the business schools, see Turner, 'The *Miles Literatus*', pp. 943–5.

teries in the twelfth century still provided instruction for some boys not destined for the monastic life, and Richard fitz Neal received a good education from the monks of Ely. John of Oxford probably attended the schools at Oxford, where he grew up and began his ecclesiastical careers.[51] No light can be cast on the education of Richard of Ilchester, whom Gerald of Wales describes as 'a man of more natural sense than scholarship, and more clever in worldly business than in the liberal arts.'[52] When he was a young man, Richard was present at the court of Earl Robert of Gloucester, which was a brilliant intellectual centre. More light falls on the schooling of Master Godfrey de Lucy. He went to school at London in the early 1170s, studying under Master Henry of Northampton. By 1176 Godfrey had gone abroad to continue his studies, possibly at Bologna, for his attorney in a lawsuit explained his absence, saying that 'he is studying at the schools far away beyond this realm'.[53]

Whatever their formal education, this group of clerics shared the intellectual curiosity that characterized Henry II's courtiers. Richard fitz Neal's *Dialogus de Scaccario* is evidence enough for his intellectual power. John of Oxford was the friend and patron of Daniel of Morley, a student of Arabic science; Daniel wrote for him the *Philosophia*, an account of what he had learned at Toledo.[54] Such men felt fully at home at the royal court, where 'it is school every day, constant conversation with the best scholars and discussion of intellectual problems'.[55]

Canon law studies were flourishing in late twelfth-century England, with the *Decretum* in use by the late 1150s. English scholars were soon active in making collections of decretals, and some became teachers at continental centres for canon law

[51] *Dial. de Scac.*, p. xiv; Salter, *Facs. of Oxford Chtrs.*, no. 42.
[52] *Gerald of Wales*, 7: 70.
[53] R.W. Hunt, 'The Disputation of Peter of Cornwall against Symon the Jew', in *Studies in Medieval History Presented to F.M. Powicke*, eds. R.W. Hunt, W.A. Pantin, and R.W. Southern (Oxford, 1948), p. 142 and note; *Chron. Battle Abbey*, p. 326.
[54] Richard W. Hunt, 'English learning in the late twelfth century', *T.R.H.S.*, 4th ser., 19 (1936): 24. John may have kept a journal on his voyage to Sicily in 1176, which supplied Ralph de Diceto with information for his chronicle, Gransden, *Historical Writing in England*, p. 228, n. 66.
[55] Peter of Blois, *Pat. Lat.*, 207: col. 197, epist. 66.

studies.[56] Roman law studies were also advancing, with civilian manuscripts becoming widespread, and we can see signs of some familiarity with Roman legal principles 'in a fairly wide stratum of the educated class in England about 1180'.[57] Although Master Vacarius established no lasting school of legal studies, there is some evidence for the study of Roman law at a number of cathedrals and other centres in England by the mid twelfth century. Studies at these schools, however, cannot have reached a level equal to that reached at Oxford by the end of the century. By the 1190s a law school was functioning at Oxford, using Vacarius' *Liber pauperum* as a text. It may have begun chiefly as a centre of canon law, although both laws were taught there.[58]

Were any of Henry II's justices learned in Roman and canon law? There is no proof that any of the thirteen ever studied at Bologna or any other continental centre of legal studies, although it has long been assumed that a number of Henry II's servants did receive some academic training in Roman law either on an elementary level in England or on a higher level on the Continent. It was not uncommon in the mid twelfth century for bishops to send bright young clerks from their chapters to study abroad.

The fact that five of the six clerics among the judges were archdeacons is not direct evidence for legal training, for their duties could have been carried out by deputies. Certainly Richard of Ilchester never performed in person his responsibilities as archdeacon of Poitiers, for he only visited the city once in the whole period that he held the post.[59] Master Jocelin,

---

[56] Jane E. Sayers, *Papal Judges-Delegate in the Province of Canterbury, 1198–1254* (Oxford, 1971), p. 35; Stephan Kuttner and Eleanor Rathbone, 'Anglo-Norman canonists of the twelfth century', *Traditio*, 7 (1949–51): 279–358.

[57] Eleanor Rathbone, 'Roman law in the Anglo-Norman realm', *Studia Gratiana*, 11 (1967): 263; see also, Turner, 'Roman law in England before Bracton'.

[58] On legal studies at Oxford, see R.W. Southern, 'Master Vacarius and the Beginning of an English Academic Tradition', in J.G. Alexander and M.T. Gibson eds., *Medieval Learning and Literature, Essays presented to Richard William Hunt* (Oxford, 1976), pp. 257–86; Peter Stein, 'Vacarius and the Civil Law', *Church and Government in the Middle Ages, Essays presented to C.R. Cheney on his Seventieth Birthday* (Cambridge, 1976), pp. 121–36. Leonard E. Boyle suggests that legal studies at Oxford centred about canon law, although both laws were taught there until 1234, 'The Beginnings of Legal Studies at Oxford', paper given at Medieval Academy of America meeting, Nashville, Tenn., 6 Apr. 1978.   [59] *D.N.B.*, s.v., 'Richard of Ilchester.'

archdeacon of Chichester, may well have studied canon law under his uncle, for Bishop Hilary of Chicester was 'pre-eminently a canon lawyer who had made his name as an advocate at the papal *curia*'.[60] A papal letter describes Godfrey de Lucy, bishop of Winchester, and a fellow-bishop together as *vos, qui iuri sapientes estis et in talibus exercitati*. Godfrey de Lucy had been a canon of Exeter when Bartholomew (d. 1184), a noted canonist, was bishop. If Godfrey actually resided for any time with the chapter at Exeter, he could have acquired some familiarity with canon law.[61]

Yet higher studies in rhetoric would have acquainted some of the justices with principles of Roman law, for rhetorical studies from the time of Cicero had included some legal teaching, and the early Italian law schools had grown out of schools of rhetoric. The early English schools did not teach directly from the Digest or the Institutes, but from various compendia and such condensations as Master Vacarius' handbook. The *Dialogus de Scaccario* reveals that Richard fitz Neal had read the Institutes, although he seems to have known the Digest only indirectly. The author of *Glanvill* – whether he be Ranulf de Glanvill, Godfrey de Lucy, or some other royal servant – had some knowledge of Roman law, although not to any great breadth or depth.[62] The probability that the clerical group of Henry II's justices had some knowledge of the law of Rome, then, is strong, although the degree of their learning remains in doubt. However deep or shallow their knowledge, the law reflected in *Glanvill* shows little trace of Roman influences. Chronology is the crucial factor: the legal innovations of Henry II had begun in the 1160s before Romano-canonical procedure had developed sufficiently to serve as a model. The Romano-canonical system, relying upon examination of individual witnesses supplemented by written instruments, arose as the church courts' method of proof only about 1200. Henry and his advisers had to hammer native

---

[60] Warren, *Henry II*, p. 477.
[61] Cited by C.R. Cheney, *From Becket to Langton: English Church Government 1170–1213* (Manchester, 1956), p. 29. For Bishop Bartholomew, see Adrian Morey, *Bartholomew of Exeter, Bishop and Canonist* (Cambridge, 1937), p. 38. Since Godfrey's name never appears on any Exeter deeds, it is possible that he was an absentee canon, p. 86.
[62] *Dial. de Scac.*, introduction, p. xvii; Turner, 'Roman law in England before Bracton', pp. 15–19.

materials – the writ and the jury – into the shape of the English system of justice, the common law.[63]

In spite of the perception of some of their contemporaries, these royal servants of Henry II were not really 'raised from the dust'. Perhaps their ambition – their desire for rapid advancement – led chroniclers, preachers, and satirists to perceive them as more lowly-born than they actually were. However humble their origins, these were men with great practical aptitude for government, and with two sources of legal learning to draw upon: the laymen could look back to the oral tradition of the courts of shire and hundred, and the clerics among them could turn to the written law of canonists and civilians. The great textbook of the common law, *Glanvill*, is proof of the impact of the two traditions. To such men fell the task of implementing the legal reforms of Henry II, and they did not fail.

3 JUSTICES' ACTIVITY IN OTHER ASPECTS OF ROYAL GOVERNMENT

The thirteen men who staffed Henry II's judicial bench were not yet professional lawyers or judges. Although they must have had a reputation for knowledge of the law, it was not a full-time occupation for them. Nearly all Henry's servants had a number of responsibilities simultaneously, the justices no less than others except in two instances. Less than half of them, however, can be considered members of the *privata familia regis*, constantly in the king's company and witnessing his charters in Normandy as well as in England. The thirteen formed strands in an intricate network of multiple offices, local, at Westminster, and with the roving royal household, ranging from sheriffs and chamber servants to bishops, justiciar, and treasurer. They had held a wide range of royal offices before they came to serve the king in the work of justice, and most continued to hold other posts while serving on eyres and at Westminster. Hearing pleas was becoming more and more a part of the work of the Exchequer sessions, and most of the thirteen witnessed final concords at the Easter

---

[63] Turner, ibid., pp. 21–2; R.C. van Caenegem, 'L'Histoire du droit et la chronologie. Réflexions sur la formation du 'Common law' et la procédure Romano-canonique', *Etudes d'Histoire de droit canonique dédiés à Gabriel le Bras* (Paris, 1965), 2: 1465.

and Michaelmas sessions. Does their presence mean that they can be counted as *barones de scaccario*? Unfortunately, little can be learned about the division of labour at the Exchequer at this early date.

Seven of Henry II's royal justices were laymen, and six were in clerical orders. Three were bishops at the time that they served on the bench, all former counsellors of the king in his quarrel with his archbishop: Richard of Ilchester, Geoffrey Ridel, and John of Oxford. Three were archdeacons: Master Jocelin, archdeacon of Chichester (or Lewes); Richard fitz Neal, archdeacon of Ely; Godfrey de Lucy, archdeacon of Derby and of Richmond. The office of archdeacon was, of course, a common source of income for royal officials. Obviously, these men's careers stood in opposition to the Church's ideal that the clergy should stand apart from worldly concerns. Yet Richard fitz Neal, in his *Dialogus de Scaccario* sought to defend his own and other clerics' service in secular government. He wrote:

> For all power is of God the Lord. It is not therefore unreasonable or improper for ecclesiastics to take service under kings, as supreme, and under other powers, and to preserve their rights, especially in matters not inconsistent with truth and honour. But they should be served for the preservation, not only of those honours through which the glory of regal majesty shines forth, but also of the worldly wealth which pertains to them by virtue of their office.[1]

Other writers also were apologists for clerics in royal government. Peter of Blois and Ralph de Diceto recognized that if the Church wished to lead society toward Christian goals, the clergy had to assume some positions of leadership in secular government.[2]

Most of the justices found their way to the bench through earlier service in the royal household, the chancery, or the Exchequer. But four – William Basset, Alan de Furnellis, Roger fitz Reinfrid, and Ranulf de Glanvill – were primarily local officials before their appointment as justices, not *familiares regis* at court. The office of sheriff under Henry II can be described as 'a general-purpose regional governor, who might control several

---

[1] *Dial. de Scac.*, p. 1, translation from *Eng. Hist. Docs.*, 2: 491.
[2] For a fuller discussion of this problem, see Turner, 'Clerical judges in English secular courts', pp. 75–98.

counties together with their castles, manors and escheats'.[3] Such an important post often went to a trusted intimate of the king, but in these cases local office provided the introduction to court and to service in central government. The work of sheriffs gave them practical judicial experience in presiding over the shire courts, which were the basic courts for most Englishmen until Henry II's assizes created a need for a system of central courts. William Basset had little connection with King Henry II or the royal household, except in 1175 when he accompanied the king about England.[4] Before his first appearance as an itinerant justice in 1168, he had been active as a sheriff, however. Basset first appeared in the king's service at the 1163 Exchequer audits, when he accounted for Warwick and Leicestershire as his brother's deputy. The following year William Basset accounted for Leicester only, but from 1164 until 1170 he was sheriff of the two shires. He was dismissed from his post following the Inquest of Sheriffs in 1170, and he had to offer Henry II a fine of 100 marks. Basset was again named sheriff in 1177, holding the shrievalty of Lincolnshire apparently until his death in 1185.[5]

Alan de Furnellis began his career as a local official in Devon and Cornwall, where he had financial responsibilities long before he first acted as a royal justice in 1179. His first eyre was to the North in company with Glanvill, not to the South West where he had a close acquaintance with conditions. Beginning in 1169 he was the royal farmer of the stannaries, collecting a tax on tin mined in Devon and Cornwall.[6] Alan served as one of the undersheriffs of Cornwall in 1174 for Reginald fitz Roy, earl of Cornwall, who held the county in place of a royal sheriff responsible to the Exchequer; Alan was also sheriff of Devon, 1178–84.[7] But before then, he had many of a sheriff's responsibilities there. He was responsible for royal properties at Exeter,

---

[3] David A. Carpenter, 'The decline of the curial sheriff in England 1194–1258', *E.H.R.*, 91 (1976): 5.

[4] He witnessed three charters at that time, *Itin. Hen. II*, pp. 193, 196, 200.

[5] *Pipe Roll 9 Hen. II*, p. 31; *List of Sheriffs*, pp. 75, 144. For his fine, see *Pipe Roll 19 Hen. II*, p. 182; *20 Hen. II*, p. 142; *21 Hen. II*, p. 91. For Lincs see *List of Sheriffs*, p. 68.

[6] *Pipe Roll 15 Hen. II*, p. 47; *6 Ric. I*, p. 166; George R. Lewis, *The Stannaries: a study of the English tin mines* (Cambridge, Mass., 1908), pp. 132–3.

[7] *List of Sheriffs*, p. 21; Warren, *Henry II*, pp. 372–3.

where he supervised repairs to the royal castle and the king's houses, 1169–73. He accounted at the Exchequer in 1176 for the Devonshire forest amercements, and in 1180 he supervised the transfer of 1000 marks from Exeter to Winchester on its way to London.[8]

Roger fitz Reinfrid seems to have entered the royal service through the household of Richard de Lucy, justiciar until 1179.[9] He assisted the justiciar in the supervision of Windsor and its surrounding lands. In 1172 he accounted for rents from the cattle farm (*census vaccarie*) of Windsor; the next year he had custody of Windsor Castle, and he retained responsibility for it and for the royal lands of Windsor until 1193, long after Richard de Lucy's retirement.[10] The pace of Roger's activity picked up in 1176, the year he first served as an itinerant justice. That year he also became sheriff of Sussex, an office he occupied until 1187. From 1186 until Henry II's death he was also sheriff of Berkshire.[11]

After the death of Henry II and in the absence of the new king, Richard I, Roger moved closer to the centre of English government. This was because his brother Walter of Coutances, archbishop of Rouen, was practically ruler of England while Richard I was away on crusade, 1191–3.[12] Roger had duties which took him away from judicial work, mainly the custody of royal castles. He continued to hold Windsor Castle until 1193, and he was also given charge of Wallingford Castle, the Tower of London, and Bristol Castle.[13] Roger's role in legal and political affairs came to an end after Hubert replaced the archbishop of Rouen in the viceregal office at the end of 1193.

The most important of the thirteen justices, Ranulf de Glanvill, the justiciar, rose from local affairs to his high rank. Before he began his judicial work after 1174, Glanvill served Henry II

[8] *Pipe Roll 16 Hen. II*, p. 100; *17 Hen. II*, p. 27; *18 Hen. II*, p. 100; *19 Hen. II*, p. 146; *22 Hen. II*, p. 147; *23 Hen. II*, p. 6; *27 Hen. II*, p. 153.
[9] Lally, 'Court and household of Henry II', pp. 75–6, 357.
[10] *Pipe Roll 18 Hen. II*, p. 17; *19 Hen. II*, p. 63; *20 Hen. II*, p. 9; *23 Hen. II*, p. 51; *25 Hen. II*, p. 87; *28 Hen. II*, p. 106; *30 Hen. II*, p. 57; *34 Hen. II*, p. 148; *4 Ric. I*, p. 165.
[11] *List of Sheriffs*, pp. 6, 141.
[12] Delisle, *Recueil*, Introduction, pp. 106–13; *D.N.B.*, s.v. 'Coutances, Walter de.'
[13] *Pipe Roll 2 Ric. I*, p. 159; *3 Ric. I*, p. 149; *4 Ric. I*, p. 301; *5 Ric. I*, pp. 313, 149, 159.

chiefly as sheriff, mainly in northern shires far from his native Suffolk. It may be, however, that he had spent his early years – before 1163 – in military life, campaigning with the king on the Continent.[14] Glanvill was sheriff of Warwick and Leicestershire for a year in 1163–4, and about the same time he was named sheriff of Yorkshire, a post he held until 1170. The Inquest of Sheriffs resulted in his removal and the later requirement that he repay over £1570 in coin plus other treasure he had looted from the shire.[15] But the king pardoned him, and in 1171 Glanvill accompanied him on the expedition to Ireland. Also in 1171, Glanvill was named custodian of the honour of Richmond, Yorkshire.[16] In 1173, Henry II appointed him sheriff of Lancashire; in 1174, sheriff of Westmorland; and in 1175, sheriff of Yorkshire once again.[17] Glanvill's position in the North made him a key figure for the protection of England from Scottish threats.

The turning point in Glanvill's career came during the rebellion of 1173–4 with the battle near Alnwick Castle on 13 July 1174, which resulted in the capture of the king of Scotland. It was a sensational victory for a sheriff with only local levies and neighbouring lords to rout the Scots and take their king prisoner.[18] Glanvill took his place at court soon after this. Sometime in 1174 he sat in judgment alongside such prominent royal officials as the justiciar, Richard of Ilchester, Geoffrey Ridel, and other high officers.[19] In 1175 Glanvill headed a party of justices on eyre in the East and North of the kingdom. The next year he headed one of the six groups of justices that spread across the kingdom to carry out the Assize of Northampton. The years 1176 and 1177 found Glanvill in Flanders as an ambassador at the count's court.[20] In 1179 Glanvill headed the

---

[14] Russell, 'Glanville', pp. 77–8. He did, however, witness some charters in England in the 1150s. For a full account of Glanvill's early career, see Falls, 'Ranulf de Glanville's formative years', pp. 312–27.

[15] *List of Sheriffs*, p. 161; *Pipe Roll 16 Hen. II*, p. 63; *23 Hen. II*, pp. xxvi, 81.

[16] Charles R. Young, *Hubert Walter, Lord of Canterbury and Lord of England* (Durham, N. Car., 1968), p. 6; *Pipe Roll 17 Hen. II*, p. 117; *18 Hen. II*, p. 5; *21 Hen. II*, p. 4; *29 Hen. II*, p. 57.

[17] *List of Sheriffs*, pp. 72, 150; *Pipe Roll 22 Hen. II*, p. 99.

[18] Jordan Fantosme's metrical chronicle in R. Howlett, ed., *Chronicles of the Reigns of Stephen, Henry II, and Richard I*, Rolls Series (1884–90), 3: 353–63.

[19] *Justiciarship*, p. 55, citing B.L. MS. Lansdowne 415, f. 22^V.

[20] *Pipe Roll 22 Hen. II*, p. 211.

group of justices on the northern circuit, which accompanied
the king after the Easter council until his return to the Continent in April 1180. Henry II left Glanvill behind as regent in
England, and his justiciarship can be said truly to have begun,
although his actual appointment may have been earlier, sometime following the resignation of Richard de Lucy at Easter
1179.[21]

An equal number of justices entered the king's service
through the chancery. These four were, not surprisingly, all
clerics. While three of the four rose to episcopal dignity, Master
Jocelin had to be content with the rank of archdeacon of
Chichester (or Lewes). Like the three bishops, he won the king's
notice during the Becket controversy. He was excommunicated
for having been a messenger from the English bishops to the
exiled Becket in December 1167, but Henry II ordered his
absolution by another bishop.[22] Jocelin next surfaces in the
royal records in September 1178, when he went on a mission to
the pope, for the king.[23] There is little evidence of Jocelin's
activity between that embassy and his first appearance as a justice on eyre in 1185, although he was with the king from time to
time. The archdeacon witnessed a few royal charters including
one in Normandy, probably in 1183.[24] He was not active in royal
government after an eyre in July 1190, except for an appearance
at Salisbury, 16 August 1195, on eyre with Hubert Walter,
although he lived until 1204–5.[25]

The three bishops named as justices in 1179 had won Henry
II's favour for their support of his cause against Thomas Becket.
Although they had both ecclesiastical and royal responsibilities,
they involved themselves deeply in the Becket conflict until its
conclusion. They were perhaps the three main shapers of royal

---

[21] *Justiciarship*, pp. 55–7.

[22] *M.T.B.*, 6: 273, 277; W.J. Millor, H.E. Butler, and C.N.L. Brooke, eds., *The
Letters of John of Salisbury*, Oxford Medieval Texts (Oxford, 1955–79), 2:
no. 236.

[23] *Pipe Roll 24 Hen. II*, p. 106. His fellow envoys were Osbert de Camera and
Walter Map.

[24] Delisle, *Recueil*, 2: 181, 188, 199; *Itin. Hen. II*, pp. 235, 242, 244. Henry Mayr-
Harting, ed., *The Acts of the Bishops of Chichester, 1075–1207*, Canterbury and
York Soc., pt. cxxx (1946): 50, suggests 1182 as the correct date for the Nor-
man charter.

[25] *Rot. Lit. Pat.*, p. 48, Nov. 1205. Master R. of Chichester has letters patent for
the prebend that had belonged to Jocelin, archdeacon of Chichester.

policies in the long quarrel with the archbishop. They were 'shrewd and able politicians', who drafted royal letters which were not polished pieces of rhetoric but were 'businesslike, blunt and even rude in tone'.[26] The effectiveness of the three can be measured by the bitterness of the invective hurled at them by the archbishop and his sympathizers.[27] All three were definitely *curiales*, often witnessing the king's charters both in England and on the Continent.

Two of them – Geoffrey Ridel and Richard of Ilchester – began their careers as royal servants in the chancery under Thomas Becket.[28] By 1163, when Richard of Ilchester was named archdeacon of Poitiers, he was one of the courtiers in the king's closest confidence. Geoffrey Ridel was also a chancery clerk in Henry II's earliest years; he accompanied the king to Normandy in 1156–7.[29] Once Becket resigned the chancellorship after his consecration as archbishop in 1162, the king assigned direction of the chancery to Geoffrey, though without the title. Geoffrey Ridel remained chancellor in all but name until his election as bishop of Ely in 1173.[30] To make clear that Geoffrey was Becket's replacement, Henry II insisted on appointing him to the archdeaconry of Canterbury, the benefice that had supported Becket while chancellor.[31]

John of Oxford's name appears on a royal charter as early as 1161 in Normandy, and the next year or so he drew up one of Henry II's writs. But the course of his career remains clouded until January 1164, when he is said to have presided over the Council of Clarendon.[32] He, like the archdeacons of Poitiers and Canterbury, was active as a royal agent in the Becket conflict from that time until the archbishop's murder. The king won for

---

[26] Poole, *From Domesday Book to Magna Carta*, p. 210; Beryl Smalley, *The Becket Conflict and the Schools* (Oxford, 1972), p. 163.

[27] E.g. Beckett called Geoffrey Ridel *archidiabolus* and *ille schismaticus, M.T.B.*, 6: 141; 7: 20, 59; and he referred to John of Oxford as 'that notorious schismatic', *M.T.B.*, 5: 388. John of Salisbury referred to John of Oxford as *ille jurator, Letters*, 2: 298, no. 213.

[28] *D.N.B.*, s.v. 'Richard of Ilchester'; Delisle, *Recueil*, Introduction, pp. 92–3.

[29] Delisle, *Recueil*, 1: 264, 267, 286, 297, *Itin. Hen. II*, p. 22.

[30] Delisle, *Recueil*, Introduction, pp. 92–3; *Itin. Hen. II*, pp. 151, 174, 316.

[31] *Fasti, Mon. Cath.*, p. 13; Warren, *Henry II*, p. 457.

[32] Delisle, *Recueil*, Introduction, p. 397; H.G. Hewlett, ed., *Chronica Rogeri de Wendover*, Rolls Series (1886–9), 1: 26. Sole witness to an 1162–3 writ, All Souls College, Oxford MS. DD.c.218, no. 8.

him in 1165 appointment as dean of Salisbury Cathedral, an
action which infuriated Becket.[33] John of Salisbury noted with
irony in a letter complaining to the pope about the appointment that the new dean, 'that man of proved religion and happy
report . . . has not set his mind to learning the Church's rites –
no, not for a single month'.[34]

The three were active on the king's behalf as ambassadors to
the pope and to other powers, so that they were often on continental journeys in the years 1164–70. Their activity earned
them the opprobrium of Becket and his partisans, even to the
point of their excommunication. John of Oxford and Richard of
Ilchester were both excommunicated for having allegedly taken
an oath to Frederick I's anti-pope, when they were envoys to the
emperor at the Diet of Wurzburg in May 1165.[35] Richard of
Ilchester was excommunicated a second time on Ascension Day
1169. Geoffrey Ridel was also excommunicated at that time,
and he too had the distinction of enduring a second excommunication, in October 1169.[36] It was John of Oxford, hated by
Becket above all Henry II's agents, who escorted the archbishop
to England when he ended his long exile on 1 December
1170.[37]

All the while that the three were involved in the Becket controversy as counsellors and envoys, they also found time to
serve Henry II in other capacities. They continued to serve the
king after the crisis ended, often in the capacity of justices on
eyre or at Westminster. Their elevation to the episcopate did
not diminish their role in royal government. Geoffrey Ridel was
with the king in Normandy during most of the period between
Becket's death and his own nomination to the see of Ely in 1173.
Although Geoffrey was replaced at the chancery after his elevation to the episcopate, the king still called on him for
diplomatic duties. He accompanied the king's daughter Joan as
far as the Mediterranean Sea on her way to Sicily in 1176 for her
marriage to King William II, and the next year he was an
ambassador to the court of the French king.[38] Geoffrey Ridel

---

[33] *M.T.B.*, 3: 392; 5: 199, 275, 397–9. [34] *Letters of John of Salisbury*, 2: no. 213.
[35] *M.T.B.*, 1: 53; 5: 182–5.
[36] *M.T.B.*, 6: 572, 594, 601; 7: 113, 115–16, 358–9.
[37] *M.T.B.*, 3: 115–16; 7: 400.
[38] *Gesta Hen. Secundi*, 1: 119–20, 127; *Itin. Hen. II*, pp. 206, 215.

may have been one of the five members of the royal household selected in 1178 to hear pleas brought before the king as he travelled about England. The bishop of Ely first served as an itinerant justice in 1179, when he – along with other bishops – headed one of the four eyres of that year. After that, he was at Westminster for almost every session of the Exchequer through January 1189. He headed an eyre once more in 1188 that visited the East and North.

Richard of Ilchester was with the king frequently from the time he entered his service until 1185, three years before his death, witnessing over seventy royal charters both in England and on the Continent.[39] He could be found sitting at the Exchequer as early as 1169, where he was head of the chancellor's staff. Henry II decreed that he should sit alongside the justiciar, 'in order to be next to the treasurer and to give careful attention to the writing of the roll'.[40] Richard fitz Neal was an admirer of the bishop of Winchester, who seemed to him to epitomize the capable civil servant. He wrote of him:

He is without doubt a great man and intent on great matters... Before the time of his promotion, when he was serving in a subordinate capacity in the king's court, he seemed from his loyalty and industry to be indispensable to the king's business, being prompt and efficient in the reckoning of accounts, in the writing of the rolls and the drawing up of writs. Wherefore a place was found for him at the treasurer's side...[41]

Richard had such expertise in financial matters that Henry II sent him to Normandy in the autumn of 1176 to head the government of the duchy, with such wide powers that he is described in one Norman charter as *post regem iudex et major justitia.* His task was to reorganize the Norman system of finance and taxation, repairing damage done during the rebellion of 1173–4 and bringing Norman administration into line with that of England. He remained across the Channel for about eighteen months, until the spring of 1178.[42] Richard of Ilchester had first served as an itinerant justice to the region around London in

[39] Duggan, 'Richard of Ilchester', *T.R.H.S.*, 5th ser., 16: 4.
[40] *Dial. de Scac.*, p. 17; translation from *Eng. Hist. Docs.*, 2: 500.
[41] *Dial. de Scac.*, p. 27; translation from *Eng. Hist. Docs.*, 2: 506–7.
[42] Lucien Valin, *Le Duc de Normandie et sa cour (912–1204), étude d'histoire juridique* (Paris, 1910), pp. 159, 272, no. 18.

1168. After that, he sometimes heard pleas at Westminster, as did most barons of the Exchequer. He did not go on eyre again until 1179, when he led the group that made a circuit of the South West. From the completion of that circuit until autumn 1184, the bishop of Winchester was active on the bench at Westminster almost continuously.

Until he was elected bishop of Norwich in 1175, John of Oxford was frequently away from England either with the king in Normandy or on missions to the pope, the emperor, or other foreign potentates. In the summer of 1176 he went on new travels for Henry II, journeying to Sicily to negotiate a marriage-treaty with the Sicilian king and returning in the autumn to escort the English princess there.[43] He was an envoy once again in 1184, sent to France to effect a reconciliation between Philip-Augustus and the count of Flanders.[44] John of Oxford first served as a royal justice at Westminster in 1177. Then in 1179, joining his two episcopal colleagues in leading eyres, he travelled to the South East. John next went on eyre in the autumn and winter of 1188–9, visiting once again the South East, although he was at Oxford in January 1189 with the justiciar. Between these two eyres – 1179 and 1189 – John sat regularly with the justices at the Exchequer. His last appearance there was on 28 June 1189. He set forth on the Third Crusade, but misfortune prevented his reaching the Holy Land, and he returned to England with papal permission.[45] Although he lived until 1200, he retired from secular government after Henry II's death, except for joining the itinerant justices at York in November 1192 and at Norwich for the 1194 eyre.

Two of Henry II's justices came to the bench by way of the domestic side of the royal household. Michael Belet and William Ruffus were officers of the chamber. As early as ten years before Michael Belet first served as a justice, he appears on the pipe rolls carrying out the work of his serjeanty, transporting wine from Oxford to the royal lodge at Woodstock. He may have been a royal servant even earlier, for he was pardoned of

---

[43] *Gesta Hen. Secundi*, 2: 115–17; *Ralph de Diceto*, 1: 416–17; *Itin. Hen. II*, p. 202.

[44] *Gesta Hen. Secundi*, 1: 334.

[45] John Appleby, ed. and trans., *Chronicon Ricardi Divisensis De tempore regis Ricardi primi*, Medieval Texts (London, 1963), pp. 5, 11.

scutage as early as 1161. By 1172, the pipe rolls begin to term him *pincerna*, an hereditary post he continued to hold under the sons of Henry II.[46] Several entries in the financial records reveal Michael in his role as royal butler, supplying wine for the court and purchasing firewood.[47] Although he was with the royal household at least as early as 1166, Belet did not witness a royal charter until 1175, and he witnessed a total of less than twenty.[48] In addition to Belet's work as butler, he was sheriff of Worcestershire, 1175–85, a post he held until the death of Henry II.[49]

A second chamber officer among the thirteen justices is William Ruffus. It is difficult to distinguish William Ruffus the royal justice from other men of the same name, although he can be identified as the chamber officer whose name first surfaces in the records in 1168, when he and another royal servant were accounting for £10 for the queen's maintenance.[50] Two years later William Ruffus was charged with spending £20 for the maintenance of Henry the young king, and in 1172 he was among those handling funds for the young king's coronation. He had greater responsibility in 1174, when he was concerned with garrisoning Leicester Castle; and shortly afterwards, he became *custos* of Berkhampstead Castle, Hertfordshire.[51] By 1182 William Ruffus had gained the higher rank of *dapifer Regis*, a title he bore for the rest of Henry II's reign.[52] William Ruffus witnessed about ten of Henry II's charters, the earliest dated 7 October 1171.[53] Like six other of the justices, he served as sheriff: Devonshire, 1175–7; Bedfordshire and Buckinghamshire, 1179–87; Sussex, 1187–9; and Bedford and Buckingham again under Richard I, 1189–95.[54] William Ruffus' first eyre was to the

---

[46] *Pipe Roll 7 Hen. II*, p. 96; *12 Hen. II*, p. 116; *18 Hen. II*, p. 37; *21 Hen. II*, p. 187. Belet offered Richard a fine of £100 for confirmation as *pincerna*, *Pipe Roll 2 Ric. I*, p. 102. His son succeeded him as *pincerna* by 1206, *Pipe Roll 6 John*, p. 123; *Rot. de Obl. et Fin.*, p. 358.

[47] *Pipe Roll 12 Hen. II*, p. 116; *21 Hen. II*, pp. 15, 187, 203; *31 Hen. II*, p. 120; *32 Hen. II*, p. 38.

[48] Delisle, *Recueil*, 2: 122, 210, 248, 307; *Itin. Hen. II*, pp. 196, 241, 242, 244, 246, 272, 274, 277, 290.

[49] *List of Sheriffs*, pp. 144, 157.   [50] *Pipe Roll 14 Hen. II.*, p. 191.

[51] *Pipe Roll 16 Hen. II*, p. 128; *18 Hen. II*, p. 87; *20 Hen. II*, p. 140; *26 Hen. II*, p. 8.

[52] *Itin. Hen. II*, p. 246; *P.B.K.J.*, 3: lxxvii.

[53] *Cal. Chtr. Rolls*, 2: 351–2.   [54] *List of Sheriffs*, pp. 1, 34, 141.

southwestern counties in 1176–7, perhaps because he was sheriff of Devon at the time. His next eyre was to the eastern counties in 1183, possibly visiting Bedfordshire and Buckinghamshire where he was then sheriff. In 1185 William Ruffus was with three different parties of itinerant justices, and in 1187 he went to the West Country. He occasionally witnessed final concords at Westminster as well.

Only one justice, neither a *familiaris regis* nor a local official, seems to have come to the judiciary by way of work at the Exchequer alone. Obviously, this is Richard fitz Neal who rarely strayed from Westminster, where he occupied the post of treasurer which his father had purchased for him around 1158.[55] Richard was possibly already chief writing clerk at the Exchequer at the time Nigel of Ely secured the higher office for him. The treasurer did not join Henry II when the king came from Normandy to make a circuit about his kingdom, though he did leave Westminster in 1173 to assist in levying aids and tallages.[56] Richard went on eyre for Henry II only twice, in 1179 and 1180, and he also went twice on eyre in the reign of Richard I. Fitz Neal travelled to Normandy in 1176 in company with Richard of Ilchester to aid in the reorganization of the Norman Exchequer. Otherwise, he remained at the Exchequer concentrating on his twin duties of treasurer and royal justice.

Two justices seem to have begun their service to the king on the bench. Little evidence survives of Robert of Wheatfield's career beyond his name listed among the royal justices witnessing final concords from the spring of 1179 until 1193. He can be considered one of the lesser *curiales*, for he was sometimes in the king's company, witnessing eight royal instruments in the period from December 1181 to February 1187.[57] He was neither a chancery clerk nor a chamber officer, as were other royal justices. As far as the records reveal, his appointment as a royal justice on the 1179 eyre marks his first post in the king's service. He may have had some minor office at the Exchequer earlier, however. Robert did hold one significant office in addition to

---

[55] *Dial. de Scac.*, p. xv.   [56] Delisle, *Recueil*, 1: 427–8.
[57] He witnessed eight royal instruments, Dec. 1181 to Feb. 1187, *Itin. Hen. II*, pp. 245, 246, 261, 273, 274, 277; *Cal. Chtr. Rolls*, 3: 270.

his service as justice on eyre and at Westminster: sheriff of Oxfordshire, 1182–5.[58]

The second justice for whom no evidence of earlier royal service explains his appointment as a justice is Master Godfrey de Lucy, son of the justiciar. He was in the schools until a year or two before his father's retirement in 1179. Possibly he had some experience in government service through his father's household, but his first work for the king was his participation in the northern eyre of 1179. After his judicial career began, he served Henry II occasionally in other capacities, chiefly on diplomatic missions. He was one of the ambassadors sent to Normandy in 1184 to arrange terms between the king of France and the count of Flanders.[59] Also that year he was one of the royal commissioners sent to Canterbury to order an archiepiscopal election.[60] He and an associate were responsible in 1184 for provisions for Henry the Lion, exiled duke of Saxony, who was living at his father-in-law's court.[61] In 1186, Godfrey de Lucy was one of three royal envoys sent overseas, although neither their destination nor their mission is known.[62]

Even though these thirteen men were the core of Henry II's judiciary, they can hardly be termed professional justices, although two of them – Master Godfrey de Lucy and Robert of Wheatfield – seem to have had few other responsibilities. The other eleven performed other tasks for the king, in most instances, varied tasks. Judicial work occupied the justices only for periods of weeks, probably less than half the year: possibly six to eight weeks at Westminster twice a year for the Easter and Michaelmas sessions of the Exchequer, and an additional six to eight weeks on eyre. Clearly, they were men-of-all-work for the monarch, and we must look to a later period before a truly professional judiciary is to be found in England.

4 THE REWARDS OF OFFICE

Writers such as Walter Map and Peter of Blois criticized Henry II's judges for their ambition, their desire to rise above their

---

[58] *List of Sheriffs*, p. 107.   [59] *Gesta Hen. Secundi*, I: 334.
[60] *Itin. Hen. II*, p. 256, 25 July 1184.
[61] *Pipe Roll 30 Hen. II*, p. 138.   [62] *Pipe Roll 32 Hen. II*, p. 179.

inherited rank.[1] These criticisms may reflect uneasiness at changing social conditions in late twelfth-century England as competition for land and office intensified. Advancement was no longer as easy as it had been in the years following the Conquest, when land had been plentiful. The old landed families were beginning to close their ranks to newcomers with the doctrine of 'disparagement' and growing anti-foreign feeling. New men rising through the civil service presented a threat to the hierarchical and static social structure which conservative critics of royal justices found comfortable. The literary doctrine of three social orders was the invention of those in the first order, those who prayed, as propaganda to keep those below them in their places.[2] The men who served Henry II on the bench were clearly ambitious. Six of them seem to have been the first of their family to enter the king's service, and they sought to make their posts a pathway to higher social standing.

To be at the *curia regis* or the Exchequer where many powerful people were gathered together presented opportunities. Not only were valuable favours to be won from the king, but courtiers could cultivate friendships with others who had favours to offer. Only at these meeting places of the influential could one hope to hear of valuable appointments or to meet potential patrons. The medieval concept of friendship differed from the modern Anglo-American attitude and resembled more closely that still prevailing in Latin countries. Friendship in an age when personal ties were felt very strongly was expected to bring definite advantage to friends. A friend, particularly one in high position, looked out for his friends' interests and won them favours whenever opportunity arose. Those without friends in high places did not question such a situation, but simply regretted their misfortune in lacking influential friends. Members of the royal household and the various officers of state formed a mutual aid group, binding themselves to one another with feudal ties. An example is the bishop of Ely's grant of two

---

[1] *De Nugis Cur.*, pp. 252–3; Peter of Blois, *Pat. Lat.*, 207: col. 300, epist. 95.
[2] Murray, *Reason and Society in the Middle Ages*, p. 97.

knight's fees to Ranulf de Glanvill in 1182, binding the justiciar to Bishop Geoffrey in a tenurial relationship.[3]

The justices sought to increase their wealth, and they succeeded in doing so, although provision would not be made for regular payments of salaries to royal officials until the thirteenth century. Older household offices, such as Michael Belet's post of *pincerna*, provided serjeanty tenures. The position was profitable enough for Belet to offer King Richard I a fine of £100 in order to keep it.[4] Some officers, such as sheriffs, 'farmed' their offices, paying the king a fixed portion of the revenues they raised and keeping the rest for themselves as profit. That the office was profitable is proven by the fines offered for appointment as sheriff. When William Ruffus left his shrievalty of Bedford and Buckinghamshire in 1187, he still owed the king thirty-eight falcons in payment for his appointment.[5] Glanvill, when sheriff of York, so plundered the shire that Henry II compelled him to restore over £1570 cash, silver plate, palfreys, and other goods.[6] Other officers depended upon the king's occasional gifts, infrequent grants of lands or ecclesiastical benefices. The king did not hesitate to provide for his servants by pressuring others into making grants to them. It was particularly easy for him to cajole religious foundations into finding benefices for royal clerks.

Reward for royal servants came not so much directly from the king as it did from other opportunities which royal office presented to them. A number of Henry II's judges were in the business of profiting from custodies. Richard of Ilchester[7] was custodian of several vacant abbacies and bishoprics which

---

[3] Vivienne Killingsworth, 'An edition of the writs and charters of Henry II relating to Norfolk, Suffolk, Cambridge and Huntingdon with studies of his measures and practices as revealed by these documents' B. Litt. Thesis (Oxford, 1975), citing B.L. MS. Add. 9822, f. 42ᵛ.

[4] The post brought Michael serjeanty tenures at Sheen and Bagshot, Surrey, *Red Book Exch.*, pp. 456, 561. Fine for two purposes – to retain the *pincernaria* and for justice in a lawsuit – *Pipe Roll 2 Ric. I*, p. 102.

[5] *Pipe Roll 34 Hen. II*, p. 120.

[6] *Pipe Roll 23 Hen. II*, pp. 81–2.

[7] Richard had custody of the see of Lincoln, 1166/7–73, *Pipe Roll 13 Hen. II*, pp. 57–8; *14 Hen. II*, p. 76; *15 Hen. II*, p. 44; *16 Hen. II*, p. 111; *18 Hen. II*, p. 95; *19 Hen. II*, p. 140; Winchester, 1171–2, *Pipe Roll 18 Hen. II*, p. 85; *19 Hen. II*, p. 57; and Glastonbury Abbey, *Pipe Roll 18 Hen. II*, p. 75; *19 Hen. II*, p. 197. He also had a lay custody, the honour of Mortain, 1166–78/9, *Pipe Roll 13 Hen. II*, pp. 148–9; *24 Hen. II*, p. 39.

brought him considerable income, among them his future
bishopric of Winchester. Geoffrey Ridel had custody of the
bishopric of Ely before he was named bishop, and other justices
had custody of vast baronial estates.[8] The business could be
followed on a smaller scale too. Jocelin, archdeacon of Chichester,
offered a fine of 100 shillings for custody of a widow and her
daughters.[9]

Grants of expense money to royal servants, chiefly for travel,
are recorded on the pipe rolls from time to time. Robert of
Wheatfield received twenty marks in 1187 from Henry II *ad se
sustentandum in servitio regis*, perhaps for expenses on his eyre of
that year. Glanvill received a larger sum to sustain himself in the
king's service: freedom from accounting for his farm of the
county of Westmorland.[10] The king also pardoned his servants
sitting at the Exchequer from payment of scutages, tallages, and
other levies on their lands, and from payment of customs on
their household purchases.[11]

Positions in the royal service brought other, indirect benefits.
The special protection that the king extended to certain
favoured servants and their families gave them demesne status,
sicut propria mea domenica.[12] They were excused from court
appearances while occupied on the king's business; this protected
them for appointment to juries and from having pleas brought
against them. By the early thirteenth century, itinerant justices
had protection from all pleas except the assize of novel
disseisin.[13]

Royal officials – including the justices – exploited their opportunities for getting gifts from petitioners. The favour of royal
justices was worth cultivating. It could be a crucial factor in suits
in Henry II's day, when proceedings were not yet fixed in a formal
pattern and the conclusion was often a compromise between

[8]   *Pipe Roll 16 Hen. II*, p. 95; *18 Hen. II*, p. 117. William Ruffus had custody of
      the lands of William d'Aubigny, 1187–8, 84½ knight's fees, *Pipe Roll 33 Hen.
      II*, p. 111; *34 Hen. II*, pp. 2, 3; Sanders, *Baronies*, p 2. William Basset in 1168
      had custody of the honour of Belvoir, 36 knight's fees, *Pipe Roll 14 Hen. II*, p.
      59; *15 Hen. II*, p. 30; Sanders, *Baronies*, p. 12.
[9]   *Pipe Roll 32 Hen. II*, p. 47.
[10] *Pipe Roll 26 Hen. II*, p. 76; *33 Hen. II*, p. 45. Robert received £19 from Richard
      I in 1191, *Pipe Roll 3 Ric. I*, p. 160.
[11] *Dial. de Scac.*, pp. 46–8.   [12] Jolliffe, *Angevin Kingship*, pp. 90–4.
[13] Doris M. Stenton, ed., *Rolls of Justices for Lincs and Worcs.*, pp. 338–9, no.
      699.

the two parties. Or perhaps a powerful friend at court could divert or halt entirely the course of justice. Informal approaches to justices about suits coming before them were not unknown. Evidence for such contacts is a letter from Gilbert Foliot, bishop of London, to Geoffrey Ridel, seeking his influence in a kinsman's suit to secure his inheritance.[14]

Because of their influence, royal justices had opportunities to benefit financially, as the account of expenses for gifts left by a twelfth-century litigant, Richard de Anesty, reveals.[15] Magnates and monastic houses granted royal officials lands and ecclesiastical livings, perhaps pressured by a king seeking to provide for his servants, or perhaps to purchase favours and influence at court. Or an important royal officer could exert his own pressure. Richard of Ilchester wrote to the monks of Battle Abbey asking to be named parson of a church in their gift, 'very sure of his demand since he was so powerful'. Nonetheless, the monks refused his request, explaining that they wanted a priest who would be resident in the parish.[16] Richard of Ilchester had more success with the abbots of Mont-Saint-Michel, St. Albans, and Westminster, all of whom presented him to churches.[17] An account of Richard de Lucy's request to the monks of Battle Abbey illustrates the application of pressure by a father on his son's behalf. Richard wrote to the monks of Battle Abbey asking them to grant Godfrey de Lucy a church that had fallen vacant.

[14] *Letters and Charters of Gilbert Foliot*, pp. 303–4, no. 230. Roger of Durnford was seeking his inheritance against the abbot of Westminster in a lawsuit. Cf. John E. Lally, 'Secular patronage at the court of Henry II', *B.I.H.R.*, 49 (1976): 171, for William of Curzon's request for Richard of Ilchester's intervention in his suit against the monks of Bury St Edmunds.

[15] He spent 'in gifts, in gold and silver and in horses 17½ marks', *Eng. Hist. Docs.*, 2: 457.

[16] Searle, *Chron. Battle Abbey*, p. 312, parish church of St Mary at Battle. He had more success with the monks of Westminster, who granted his petition to grant the vicarage at Datchworth to a certain clerk, Westminster Domesday, ff. 227, 380b. When Geoffrey Ridel asked the abbot of Bury St Edmunds for timber for buildings on his Ely lands, the abbot agreed, 'not daring to offend him . . . but against his will', *Chron. Jocelin of Brakelond*, p. 71.

[17] Church of 'Mertoc', dioc. of Ely, held of Mont-St Michel, *Chronique de Robert de Torigni*, ed. Leopold Delisle, Soc. de l'hist. de Normandie (Rouen, 1872–3), 2: 309–10; two-thirds of the churches of Luton and Houghton, held of St Albans, *Gesta Abb. S. Albani*, 1: 124; church of Datchworth, Herts., held of Westminster Abbey, Westminster Domesday, f. 227. The abbot of Westminster also granted him a house at Fishmarket, London, to hold for a pound of pepper yearly, Westminster Domesday, f. 368.

The monks wished to oblige the justiciar, 'for they realized that he was their willing patron in all of their affairs', and they unanimously agreed to his request.[18]

What rewards did our thirteen royal servants reap? In order to evaluate their success, it is useful to divide them into two groups: first, those who were prominent in great affairs of state, held high office, and won spectacular rewards; second, those who had little part in political events, who held no office higher than sheriff, and whose gains do not seem so great. The lack of records such as wills or inquisitions *post mortem* prevents any precise estimate of the wealth accumulated by the justices. But twelfth-century sources do permit us to form some impression, at least, of the more spectacular successes. Glanvill, the justiciar, accumulated such a fortune that Richard Lionheart, according to one account, required of him a fine of £15,000.[19] This chronicler exaggerated shamelessly, but his figure indicates the impression that contemporaries had of Glanvill's wealth. Certainly the pipe roll record of his exploitation of Yorkshire makes believable the thought that he could have raised £15,000. Michael Belet, a less influential figure falling into our second category, had to offer Richard I only a £100 fine to keep his post of *pincerna*. The three bishops who served on the bench had earned their episcopacies through diplomatic and propagandistic efforts during the Becket conflict. Richard of Ilchester was rewarded with Winchester, the richest episcopal see after Canterbury and earlier he had held profitable plural livings.[20] Geoffrey Ridel, elected to another rich episcopate, Ely, reputedly left at his death treasure in coin worth 3,200 marks plus gold and silver plate, palfreys and other riches.[21] Fees collected when he was acting chancellor earned him substantial sums, at least two shillings for each document drawn up at the

---

[18] *Chron. Battle Abbey*, pp. 268–70, church of Wye.

[19] *Chron. Richard of Devizes*, p. 5. The pipe rolls record no such enormous fine.

[20] Archdeacon of Poitiers, *M.T.B.*, 3: 120; canon of Lincoln, *Fasti, Lincoln*, pp. 137–8; church of Morden, Cantab., *C.R.R.*, 2: 29; collegiate church of St Necton, Hartland, Devon, *Monasticon*, 6: 436; and 12s. return from the church of St Mildrith, London, B.L. Cotton Chtr. XI. 52. See above, note 17.

[21] *Ralph de Diceto*, 2: 68.

chancery.[22] Richard fitz Neal also earned a bishopric through his service to the king, though long after the other three. Henry II possibly named him to London shortly before his death, but the election process was not completed until Richard's nomination had been confirmed by the new king in September 1189.[23]

A listing of the ecclesiastical preferments that one judge, Godfrey de Lucy, held before becoming bishop of Winchester in autumn 1189 shows how profitable it was to be a prominent royal servant. Of course, being the justiciar's son was no handicap to one's career! Godfrey was dean of St Martin-le-Grand, London; archdeacon of Derby, and later of Richmond as well; canon of Exeter, Lincoln, York, and St Paul's cathedrals; and vicar of two parish churches.[24] He was custodian of his late father's estates for a nephew from 1181 to 1185 or later; and he secured possession of the honour of Ongar, Essex, for himself until 1194. But Godfrey lost Ongar to his niece, when she made Richard I an offering of £700 for half her grandfather's lands.[25]

The fortunes of lesser men on the bench rose less dramatically. The value of their landholdings is difficult to estimate, for their lands consisted of small, scattered holdings, a knight's fee here and there, portions of knight's fees as small as one-twelfth, a few virgates here, a librate there, plus some burgage tenures. For example, Robert of Wheatfield held two hides at his birthplace in Oxfordshire and a hide at Moorcourt manor through inheritance. At his death, he held in addition half a knight's fee plus eight virgates, some smaller rural holdings, and four marks' worth of rents in Oxford.[26] His heir was charged a relief of 60 marks for the inheritance in 1193-4. To give this figure some meaning, we can recall that a 'reasonable' relief for a baron was

---

[22] See the schedule of chancery fees drawn up following King John's accession, supposedly a restoration of old rates prevailing under Henry II, *Foedera*, 1: 75–6.

[23] *Gesta Hen. Secundi*, 2: 85. *D.N.B.*, s.v. 'Fitzneale, Richard', suggests that Richard I was only ratifying an earlier nomination of Henry II.

[24] *D.N.B.*, s.v. 'Lucy, Godfrey de'; *Bio. Reg. Univ. Oxf.*, 3: 2192.

[25] *Pipe Roll 2 Ric. I*, p. 104; *6 Ric. I*, pp. xxi, xxii, 24, 28, 250; *Red Book Exch.*, pp. 78, 733 lists Godfrey as holder of 6½ knight's fees in Essex and Herts, presumably referring to his father's honour of Ongar.

[26] H.E. Salter, ed., *The Feet of Fines for Oxfordshire, 1194–1291*, Oxon. Rec. Soc., 41 (1930): 2, no. 4; *V.C.H., Oxon.*, 8: 101, 263.

£100, although the Angevin kings arbitrarily exacted whatever amount they could get.[27] Such holdings cannot be called substantial, but Robert had increased their size, and he had placed himself well within the ranks of the 'gentry' of south Oxfordshire. Similar is the story of Michael Belet. He inherited four knight's fees, adding to them a manor in Norfolk through his marriage to the daughter and coheir of John de Cheney, and he held two Surrey manors as serjeanty tenures.[28] Again the increase in size is hardly meteoric; nonetheless, there was some increase. Robert and Michael did not accept their place in society passively in the way that conservative critics felt they should.

The justices' ambition can be seen more clearly if we turn to their families. Medieval ethics did not condemn what today would be called nepotism. Instead, a concern for placing *consanguines* and *familiares* in profitable posts was considered normal, even justifiable. Clergy and laity alike could quote Scripture to justify such action: 'If any provide not for his own, and especially for those of his own house, he hath denied the faith and is worse than an infidel' (I Timothy, 5: 8). What rank did sons attain through the efforts of their fathers? As we have seen, Richard de Lucy did very well for his son Godfrey, showering him with benefices and establishing him in the king's service. Glanvill did not leave a son, only three daughters, among whom he divided his possessions before setting off for the Holy Land. One of his sons-in-law, Ralph of Arden, was an itinerant justice and sheriff of Hereford and Yorkshire. He shared in the disgrace of a number of sheriffs on the accession of Richard Lionheart and had to offer 1000 marks to win the king's goodwill.[29] He was restored fully to favour by Hubert Walter, Glanvill's nephew, once he succeeded to the justiciarship in 1193. Hubert Walter had been reared in the household of Ranulf, and the justiciar made him one of his clerks by 1181. Hubert began to accumulate ecclesiastical livings, becoming dean of York in July 1186.[30]

---

[27] *Pipe Roll 6 Ric. I*, p. 93; *7 Ric. I*, p. 145. A.L. Poole, *Obligations of Society in the Twelfth and Thirteenth Centuries* (Oxford, 1946), pp. 95–6.

[28] *Red Book Exch.*, pp. 331, 456, 561; *C.R.R.*, 2: 208, 266.

[29] *Chron. Richard of Devizes*, p. 5; *Pipe Roll 2 Ric. I*, p. 47. See also Bailey, 'Glanvill and his children', pp. 171–8.

Some of the ecclesiastics among the justices had illegitimate sons for whom they needed to provide. Richard of Ilchester had an illegitimate son, Herbert le Poer, who became a canon of Lincoln Cathedral in 1167–8, archdeacon of Canterbury in 1175, and bishop of Salisbury in 1194. His father probably employed him at the Exchequer, and under Richard I he was sometimes a royal justice at Westminster.[31] Herbert's successor at Salisbury, Richard Poore, was probably his brother, another bastard of the bishop of Winchester. Richard was sent to the schools of Paris, where he became a teacher of theology. Richard Poore proved to be a mobile bishop: elected to Chichester in 1214, he was translated first to Salisbury in 1217, then to Durham in 1228.[32] Godfrey de Lucy also had an illegitimate son, though he fared less well. His father did give him some property in the Strand, London.[33]

More striking is the success of members of our second group – lesser laymen – in providing for their families. Four had sons who followed them into the public service. William Basset's son, Simon Basset, assisted in the tallaging of Nottinghamshire in 1198. Later he was associated with William de Humez, constable of Normandy, acting as his attorney at Westminster.[34] Michael Belet chose one of his younger sons for a clerical career, and Michael Belet junior earned the title *magister*. He followed his father into the king's service, becoming a royal clerk by 1199. He had succeeded his father as *pincerna* by 1206, after offering King John a fine of £100.[35] Roger fitz Reinfrid's eldest son Gilbert was evidently illegitimate, since he did not succeed to his father's lands. He did, however, follow his father in the king's service; he became Henry II's *dapifer*, and he witnessed

---

[30] Young, *Hubert Walter*, pp. 3–12; C.R. Cheney, *Hubert Walter* (London, 1967), pp. 17–18, 21–2; John T. Appleby, *England without Richard 1189–1199* (Ithaca, N.Y., 1965), pp. 20, 164.

[31] *Fasti, Mon. Cath.*, p. 14; *Fasti, Lincoln*, pp. 127–8; Charles Duggan, 'Bishop John and Archdeacon Richard of Poitiers', in Raymonde Foreville, ed., *Thomas Becket, Actes du Colloque international de Sédières* (Paris, 1975), p. 35. He witnessed a final concord at Westminster on 22 Mar. 1185, *P.B.K.J.*, 3: lxx.

[32] *D.N.B.*, s.v. 'Poor, Poore, or le Poor, Richard'; J.C. Russell, *Dictionary of Writers of Thirteenth Century England* (London, 1936), pp. 118–19.

[33] *H.M.C., Reports*, 14, Appendix 8: 194.

[34] *Pipe Roll 9 Ric. I*, p. 150; *C.R.R.*, 2: 214; *Rot. de Obl. et Fin.*, p. 249.

[35] *Pipe Roll 1 John*, pp. 145, 185, 196, 228, 240; *6 John*, p. 123; *Rot. Chart.*, 1: 100b; *Rot. de Obl. et Fin.*, p. 358.

many royal charters in France, 1180–9.[36] Gilbert fitz Reinfrid remained in the royal service, holding shrievalties and significant custodies from King John; but he ran foul of the king during the baronial rebellion and suffered a severe punishment in 1216, when he had to offer a fine of 12,000 marks.[37] Alan de Furnellis had a son and heir, Geoffrey, who assisted him as sheriff of Oxfordshire in 1187–8 and shared the farming of the stannaries in 1189, and who succeeded his father in their charge by 1194.[38] Henry de Furnellis, perhaps another son, was named sheriff of Devonshire in 1194, an undersheriff for Geoffrey fitz Peter in Shropshire, 1202, and an itinerant justice in 1199 and 1200.[39]

These men were eager to arrange advantageous marriages for their sons, which could bring them additional land. William Basset's son Simon gained a knight's fee in Derbyshire through his marriage.[40] Michael Belet had seven sons, one of whom entered the church, as we have seen. His eldest son was married to a daughter of Fulk de Oiry, a tenant of Lincolnshire fenland estates and steward for his lady, the countess of Aumale.[41] Possibly the best marriage was made by Gilbert fitz Reinfrid, Roger's son. Richard I gave him in marriage the heiress to the barony of Kendal, Westmorland.[42]

A strong sense of family motivated the justices not only to look out for the fortunes of their sons, but of other relatives as well. Clerics could aid their kinsmen in clerical orders in finding posts in the royal secretariat. Richard fitz Neal had a kinsman of unknown degree (*consanguinei nostri*), William of Ely, who suc-

---

[36] Delisle, *Recueil*, 2: 134, 142, 203, 240, 268, 293, 307, 359, 371, 372, 413, 421.

[37] J.C. Holt, *The Northerners* (Oxford, 1961), pp. 65, 137, 229; Sidney Painter, *The Reign of King John* (Baltimore, 1949), pp. 208, 255, 274, 370.

[38] A grant by Alan to Wells was made with the assent of 'Geoffrey his heir', *H.M.C., D & C. Wells*, 1: 42. See also *Pipe Roll 33 Hen. II*, p. 46; *34 Hen. II*, p. 130; *1 Ric. I*, p. 166.

[39] *List of Sheriffs*, pp. 21, 34, 117; *Pipe Roll 9 Ric. I*, pp. 1, 4, undersheriff for Richard Revel and Geoffrey fitz Peter. *P.B.K.J.*, 3: cliv, autumn eyre; clxvii, summer vacation court. Henry held the manor of Kilve and land at Oar, Somerset, and land of the manor of Brundon. He was dead by 1221, *C.R.R.*, 10: 106–7; *Pipe Roll 9 Ric. I*, p. 143.

[40] He married the heiress of Richard de Vernon, *Pipe Roll 6 Ric. I*, p. 209; *6 John*, p. 171.   [41] *Rot. Lit. Claus.*, 1: 12b.

[42] William Farrer, ed., *Lancashire Pipe Roll, also early Lancashire Charters* (Liverpool, 1902), p. 75.

ceeded him at the treasury in 1196. Probably William had been
employed at the Exchequer before Richard was elected bishop
of London; after the election, William was one of the bishop's
clerks, 1190–2, and a canon of St Paul's after 1192.[43] Richard
granted to his relative a tenement which he held at Westminster
of the abbey shortly before his death. Richard had grand accom-
modations in Westminster, consisting of houses, a court with
adjoining stable, and a chapel.[44] Stephen Ridel, chancellor of
John count of Mortain and later archdeacon of Ely and canon of
Lincoln, may have been aided in launching his career by his kinsman Geoffrey Ridel.[45] Master Philip de Lucy, a relative, perhaps
a nephew of Godfrey de Lucy, had an active career in both
Church and secular government. He was clerk of the chamber
about the time of Godfrey's death, then after 1207 or so, chiefly
concerned with Hampshire affairs where he had several
livings.[46]

Lay kin could benefit from their relatives' positions. During
the years of Glanvill's justiciarship, five of his *consanguines* held
shrievalties, which means that they were one-fifth of all the
sheriffs in England.[47] A striking illustration of concern for
kinsmen is Robert of Wheatfield's oblation to Richard I of £100
to purchase an heiress to provide his brother with land and a
wife. This is a hefty sum if we remember that the average annual
income of a knight was £10 to £20.[48] Similar evidence of family
ties is Geoffrey Ridel's gift of land to his cousin's new husband
on the occasion of her marriage in 1173.[49] Perhaps she had no

---

[43] H.G. Richardson, 'William of Ely, the King's treasurer, 1195–1215',
    T.R.H.S., 4th ser., 15 (1932): 47–9; *Fasti, St. Paul's*, p. 35.
[44] Westminster Domesday, ff. 341b, 342, Richard's charter, c. 1196, and King
    John's confirmation, 20 April 1200. For a description of the property at the
    time it passed to Hubert de Burgh, c. 1222–4, see f. 347b.
[45] *Fasti, Lincoln*, p. 145; *Fasti, Mon. Cath.*, p. 51.
[46] C.A.F. Meekings and Philip Shearman, eds., *Fitznell's Cartulary*, Surrey Rec.
    Soc., 26 (1968): lix. He witnessed one of Godrey's charters, 25 Aug. 1204,
    B.L. MS. Add. 29, 436, f. 30ᵛ.
[47] Mortimer, 'Family of Glanvill', pp. 13–14. Because some counties were nor-
    mally grouped together, the total of sheriffs at one time was only 25.
[48] For the daughter of William de Monasteriis, *Pipe Roll 2 Ric. I*, p. 45; *5 Ric. I*, p.
    123. Sidney Painter, *Studies in the History of the English Feudal Barony*,
    (Baltimore, 1943), p. 172.
[49] Delisle, *Recueil*, 2: 10. Galliena daughter of William Blund married Robert de
    Insula, early 1173. Glanvill purchased land as *maritagium* for his sister when
    she married William de Stuteville, *Rot. Chart.*, p. 54.

father living to give a *maritagium* to her. Most amazing is Roger
fitz Reinfrid's offer of ten marks for custody of an heir in order
to concede the custody to his daughter, Bonanata. Did he have a
strong-willed daughter, unwilling either to marry or to enter a
nunnery, for whose support he sought to provide? It seems
strange that she did not enter the convent of St Mary Clerkenwell with which Roger had strong ties.[50] John of Oxford granted
his sister's son a stone house he had built at the port of Lynn.
The nephew did not have a freehold, however; he had to pay
rent to the cathedral church of Norwich and to the bishop, and
John reserved for himself and his successors use of the large
wine-cellar in front of the house.[51]

The relatives of Roger fitz Reinfrid illustrate vividly the
family ties linking together Church and civil service in the time
of Henry II and his sons. Roger came from an extraordinary
family of churchmen: Master John of Coutances, bishop of
Worcester 1196–8, was either his brother or nephew; Master
Walter of Coutances, bishop of Lincoln 1183–4, archbishop of
Rouen 1184–1207, and practically ruler of England during
Richard I's absence on crusade, was his brother or perhaps
brother-in-law; and a possible third brother was Master Odo of
Coutances, a canon at Rouen Cathedral.[52] Since Roger entered
the king's service by 1169, five years before Walter joined the
chancery, it seems that Roger smoothed the way for his
brother's entry into the royal service. If that was so, then Walter
was able to return the favour by providing for one of Roger's
sons. He named Roger's son William a canon of Lincoln Cathedral
and archdeacon of Rouen.[53]

One reward which the royal justices and other prominent servants of Henry II received might be termed 'psychic reward'.
Power has often been its own reward for certain kinds of personalities. The excitement of being near the king, the thrill of

---

[50] *Pipe Roll 3 Ric. I*, p. 60. Roger witnessed Clerkenwell's charters, made gifts to
it, and provided for his wife's and his own burial there, W.A. Hassell, ed., *Cartulary of St. Mary Clerkenwell, R.H.S.*, Camden 3rd ser., 71 (1949), *passim*.

[51] Barbara Dowell, ed., *Norwich Cathedral Priory, Episcopal Charters*, Pipe Roll
Soc., new ser., 40 (1975): 76–7, no. 137. John's nephew was Peter son of
Geoffrey, son of Durand, who still held the house in 1205, pp. 97–8, no.
175.

[52] The family was Cornish despite the name, *Gerald of Wales*, 7: 38–9.

[53] *Fasti, Lincoln*, p. 148.

exercising power, the flattery of petitioners must have been intoxicating to some of these men. Their influence caused those seeking favours to address them in flattering terms, as Bishop Gilbert Foliot did Geoffrey Ridel in a letter seeking his influence in a relative's lawsuit. The bishop praised Geoffrey's talent as something God-given, a talent he was using righteously.[54] For Henry's servants power was something that made material rewards possible, not only for themselves but for their friends as well. They all had dependents for whom they needed to secure favours and offices, and they used their positions to such an end. For example, Richard fitz Neal rewarded two of his chaplains with prebends at St Paul's after he became bishop of London.[55] By winning favours for their friends, royal officers' friendship became valuable, and they recruited a larger circle of clients.[56] As their prestige increased, perhaps they gained some sought-after feeling of respectability.

To summarize, we have seen that the justices of Henry II came chiefly from the knightly class, or from families only recently elevated to the baronage. Seven of the thirteen came from families with an administrative background. They were assuredly not of rustic origin, as some critics claimed. They fall into two groups: first, those with the most spectacular success, who were clearly *familiares regis*, who held high offices, and who gained great rewards. A group of six, they include Glanvill and the three bishops who had been Henry's close companions since the Becket conflict. Two fall into this group, even though they do not qualify on every count. Godfrey de Lucy, although active at the Exchequer and on the bench, did not hold higher office until Richard I named him a bishop. Richard fitz Neal, although treasurer, cannot be called a member of Henry's *privata familia*. The second group consists of seven men who were not so close to the king, who did not rise so fast or so far, but who did further their own and their families' fortunes. This group includes only one cleric, Master Jocelin of Chichester, and six laymen: William Basset, Michael Belet, Roger fitz Reinfrid, Alan de Furnellis, William Ruffus, and Robert of Wheatfield.

---

[54] *Letters and Charters of Gilbert Foliot*, pp. 303–4, no. 230.
[55] Alan, 1196; Roger, c. 1192, *Fasti, St. Paul's*, pp. 62, 68; *H.M.C., Various Collections*, 7: 28 (MSS of St George's Chapel, Windsor).
[56] Lally, 'Patronage at the court of Henry II', pp. 168–74.

Although these men were ambitious, seeking to use their posts as stepping stones to higher social position, wealth, and power, some were doubtless disappointed. Master Jocelin perhaps dreamed of a bishopric for himself! Others, if their ambitions were more modest, saw them fulfilled. Michael Belet, for example, lived to see his son Master Michael Belet secure in a post as royal clerk, provided with an ecclesiastical living.[57] Roger fitz Reinfrid and Alan de Furnellis also saw their sons assuming posts in the royal administration.

'New men' could fall from power more quickly than they rose, once they lost royal favour. The sudden fall of Roger of Salisbury and his circle earlier in the century could be repeated! None of Henry II's justices seems to have suffered such a dramatic loss of favour, with the possible exception of Ranulf de Glanvill. The circumstances of his surrender of the justiciarship early in Richard I's reign are obscure. Chroniclers give conflicting stories of his dismissal in disgrace with the king's demands for an enormous fine and of his voluntary resignation from office in order to go on crusade. No official record of Glanvill's amercement or fine survives, although some of his assistants were subjected to 1000 mark fines.[58] Yet after a gap of only three years, Richard I named Glanvill's nephew Hubert Walter to the justiciarship.

Clearly, the concern of royal servants for their families was not allowed to threaten seriously the king's free choice of his own officials. The Angevin monarchs tolerated heritability of certain ceremonial offices or of household offices that they could watch closely, but they did not permit working posts away from their presence to become hereditary.

---

[57] King John presented him to the church of Hinclesham, diocese of Norwich, Sept. 1200, *Rot. Chart.*, p. 75b.

[58] For a survey of the evidence, see Mortimer, 'Family of Glanvill', pp. 12–13. Ralph of Arden, Glanvill's son-in-law, and Reiner de Waxham, undersheriff for Yorks, owed 1000 marks each, and Roger de Glanvill, sheriff of Northumberland, owed 400 marks *ne fiat super eum inquisitio, Pipe Roll 2 Ric. I*, pp. 47, 67, 101, 111.

3

THE ORIGINS OF A PROFESSIONAL JUDICIARY
IN THE REIGN OF RICHARD I

1 THE TWO ROYAL COURTS: JUSTICES ON EYRE AND BENCH AT WESTMINSTER

The pattern of justice in Henry II's last years consisted of frequent circuits of the counties by itinerant justices supplemented with judicial sessions at Westminster during the Easter and Michaelmas Exchequer terms. This pattern was stretched almost out of shape by the strains of Richard I's absence, first on crusade and then in captivity in Germany. Ranulf de Glanvill gave up the justiciarship in September 1189. Richard's changing schemes for government during his absence brought several other changes in justiciars, none of whom had any experience on the bench until Hubert Walter took office in late 1193. Neither of the joint-justiciars named to replace Glanvill came from the ranks of royal administrators; nor did their successor in March 1190, William Longchamp, newly named bishop of Ely.[1] Longchamp was forced from office in October 1191 and replaced by Walter of Coutances, archbishop of Rouen. Walter had long experience under Henry II in the chancery and chamber, but not on the bench.[2] Even had these men brought with them a thorough grounding in English law, they still could not have given full attention to the work of justice in the face of more pressing problems. Walter of Coutances, for example, had little opportunity to send out itinerant justices because most royal officials were busy raising the king's ransom and suppressing Count John's rebellion.[3]

Some attention to justice was required, however, due to disorders and disturbances throughout England. The people

---

[1] See *Justiciarship*, pp. 65–74, on Richard's early arrangements for government during his absence.
[2] *Justiciarship*, pp. 74–8.   [3] *P.B.K.J.*, 3: xciv.

needed to see the justiciar and the royal justices doing justice in the different parts of the kingdom, carrying the king's authority to its four corners. Because of the justices' frequent movements about the land, it is impossible to separate neatly Bench and eyre activity before Richard I's return to England in 1194. William Longchamp covered all England with judicial visitations during the first two years of his justiciarship, 1190–1; and his successor the archbishop of Rouen similarly sent out six groups of justices in the summer of 1192.[4] In 1193, however, all royal officials were too busy with other tasks to give much time to judicial work. No itinerant justices visited the shires, and the Bench at Westminster held only sporadic sessions.[5]

A clear picture of what came to be the normal pattern of four terms of court each year at Westminster supplemented by visits of justices to the counties and a general eyre over all England every four years does not take shape until 1194. Hubert Walter as justiciar brought his enormous energy and organizing skill to the task of strengthening the royal courts. The archbishop's administration renewed the movement for legal innovation which had marked the reign of Henry II. Our picture of the courts' work may be distorted, however, by the quantity of new evidence that sharpens their image after 1194. Hubert Walter's revolution in record-keeping resulted in the first surviving plea rolls, which date from the autumn eyre of 1194, and in the feet of fines, official copies of chirographs kept at the Treasury from 1195.[6]

Hubert Walter organized a general eyre – *iter ad omnia placita* – in the autumn of 1194, part of his programme for restoring order to England after Count John's rebellion. It consisted of eight circuits which got underway in less than two months. One group of justices was back at Westminster by 27 October, concluding its work there. Only the Bedfordshire–Buckinghamshire

---

[4] *P.B.K.J.*, 3: lxxxi–lxxxix; xcii–xciv; *Justiciarship*, p. 71.
[5] Lady Stenton found two fines for the period between Easter and Trinity, one at Oxford in August, and three for Michaelmas. *P.B.K.J.*, 3: xciv–xcv.
[6] The earliest surviving eyre roll is for the Wilts eyre of 1194, P.R.O. KB 26/3, published in *Placitorum abbrevatio*, Rec. Com. (London, 1811), pp. 10–20; F.W. Maitland, ed., *Three Rolls of the King's Court in the Reign of King Richard I, 1194–1195*, Pipe Roll Soc., 14 (1891): 65–115. Numerous publications of early feet of fines, e.g. Joseph Hunter, ed., *Fines sives pedes finium (1195–1214)*, Rec. Com. (London, 1835–44).

group continued its work in the summer of 1195.[7] While the eyre was underway, judicial sessions went on at Westminster; the Michaelmas term of 1194 lasted from 13 October until 18 December.

The 1194 eyre took place at a time when the justiciar and the barons of the Exchequer were preoccupied with raising enormous sums for Richard I's ransom. One of the tasks assigned to the itinerant justices was the tallaging of the cities, boroughs, and royal demesne. Entries on the pipe rolls hint at an effort to increase the profits of justice. The lists of amercements and fines are longer than ever, and counties fearing heavy-handed assessing of amercements promised fines *ut bene tractetur.*[8]

A general eyre was 'a great county occasion', which comprehended all other public courts of the shire within which the justices were sitting.[9] Not only did the itinerant justices hear pleas normally coming before the county and hundred courts, but any from that county pending at Westminster were also adjourned for their hearing. An eyre brought the court of Common Pleas to the counties both in the persons of the justices and in their jurisdiction.[10] If the business of an eyre was not completed on time, its cases came to Westminster for hearing. The eyre was the tribunal where most of a county's civil litigation and conveyancing by royal writ were carried out. The articles of the eyre – *capitula itineris* – were sets of instructions to the justices, the first of which survive from 1194. The justices heard all pleas of writs – that is, mainly disputes about possession of land – plus pleas of the crown, acting on presentments of juries and on private appeals. The articles of the eyre reveal that the justices had numerous administrative tasks in addition to their judicial work. Besides empowering the justices to hear pleas, the articles commanded them to make inquiries about many

---

[7] *Justiciarship*, p. 81; David Crook, unpublished list of general eyres, P.R.O. See also *Rot. Cur. Reg.*, 1: contents, for dates of Michaelmas sessions at Westminster.

[8] *Pipe Roll 7 Ric. I*, pp. xxiii–xxv. See fines by the barons of Cumberland, p. 265, the knights of Lancs, p. 150, and the county of Northumberland 'for a kindly hearing of the jurors' verdict', and fines of Devon and Cornwall, pp. 130, 134, that they be treated kindly.

[9] C.A.F. Meekings, ed., *The 1235 Surrey Eyre*, Surrey Rec. Soc., 31 (1979): 90–4.

[10] *1235 Surrey Eyre*, p. 23.

local matters of interest to the king.[11] The *capitula* of the 1194 eyre reveal 'a great effort by the central authority to control local administration, realize all available assets in the country, and deal with the accumulated business of the courts expeditiously after a period of disorder'.[12]

In the years between eyres *ad omnia placita*, justices sometimes made circuits which were limited either in geographic terms or in types of suits heard. The justiciar and a group of his justices might hear pleas as he journeyed to the Welsh border or to some other outlying region during vacations. Or a party of justices might make a circuit around the Home Counties during the summer recess. Some eyres dealt only with pleas of the crown, others with possessory assizes, or sometimes with both. Two circuits, limited in geographic scope, went to East Anglia and to the North of England in 1196.

The last general eyre of Richard's reign set out in the autumn of 1198 on five circuits, led by the new justiciar Geoffrey fitz Peter. These groups continued their circuits in 1199 after a Christmas vacation, and some of them did not conclude their work until early autumn 1199, after the accession of King John. The West Midlands circuit did not even begin until after John's coronation in the summer of 1199.[13] The coming of a new king to the throne, then, did not cause any sudden shift in the organization of the judiciary.

The justiciarship of Hubert Walter marks a crucial period in the growth of the court of Common Pleas, or Bench at Westminster. Its origins are dim, overshadowed by the Exchequer and by the itinerant judicature. It makes itself clearly visible, however, by the time of the archbishop's justiciarship. While the eyres had earlier been the chief resort for freemen wishing to take advantage of Henry II's new procedures, now a court sitting in Westminster at the house of the Exchequer was becoming regularly available as an alternative. Anyone willing to take the trouble and to bear the costs of travel to Wesminster

---

[11] *Roger Howden*, 3: 264; William Stubbs, ed., *Select Charters* (9th ed., Oxford, 1913), pp. 251–7. English translation in *Eng. Hist. Docs.*, 3: 303–6.

[12] Cheney, *Hubert Walter*, pp. 92–3.

[13] *P.B.K.J.*, 3: Appendix I, 'Development of the Judiciary 1100–1215'; corrected by David Crook, unpublished list of general eyres, P.R.O.

could avoid waiting until the itinerant justices' visit to his county. The court at Westminster was 'a court of luxury', providing a speedy hearing for those able to afford the added costs of pleading there. At the same time, growing numbers of cases in the counties meant that itinerant justices were often unable to keep to their time-tables and had to complete suits at Westminster.[14] Lawsuits had long formed part of the work performed at the twice-yearly sessions of the Exchequer at Westminster, with the amount of legal business increasing steadily in Henry II's last years. Unfortunately, the sparse supply of evidence – lack of any plea rolls and limited surviving final concords – clouds our picture of this process.

It became necessary to add two terms of court to the legal calendar, doubling the time available for hearing pleas at Westminster. Royal justices, in addition to acting on suits during the Easter and Michaelmas Exchequer sessions, began to hear pleas during Hilary term (beginning 20 January) and Trinity term (beginning late May or early June, depending on the date of Easter). Lack of enough final concords makes it impossible to pinpoint the first Hilary and Trinity sessions, but they were no earlier than 1188 or 1189. The first surviving Trinity term fines in any numbers date from 15–25 July 1195. Doubtless they indicate a need to conclude cases adjourned to Westminster from the 1194 eyres. Hilary fines survive in large numbers from 1196, when justices continued their work until two weeks before Easter.[15] Creating new terms of court may have had some connection with the extension of Exchequer sessions beyond their accustomed closing dates. It is impossible to tell how long Exchequer sessions lasted in those days, but pressure of dealing with Richard's ransom may have forced them to continue throughout a good part of the year. In that case, men

---

[14] G.J. Turner, ed., *Brevia Placitata*, Selden Soc., 66 (London, 1951): p. li; *English Justice*, pp. 92–3.

[15] Lady Stenton labels a fine of 20 Feb. 1190 as Hilary term and two of 28 May and 6 June 1190 as Trinity term, *P.B.K.J.*, 3: lxxxix–lxxx. But the courts were not keeping to regular terms during Longchamp's justiciarship. She groups fines under the heading Trinity term 1195, *P.B.K.J.*, 3: ci. They also mark the first tripartite fines, with the 'feet' handed over to the treasurer. Hilary term 1196: 2 (rightly 20?) Jan.–6 Apr., *P.B.K.J.*, 3: cviii–cix. For Trinity term 1196, 18 June–8 July, see *P.B.K.J.*, 3: cxii.

already at Westminster for the extended Easter Exchequer session could have taken on the additional duty of hearing pleas in the summer of 1195.

The beginnings of the Bench are intertwined with the Exchequer, the first sedentary branch of royal government, which is usually labelled an accounting office; but it essentially comprised the justiciar's staff whatever their tasks might be. As we have seen, several of Henry II's justices were also *barones de scaccario*. Historians have long debated the birth of the *curia regis* or *justiciarii de banco*, or in modern language the Bench at Westminster or court of Common Pleas. Scholarly discussions can be confusing, causing us to echo Walter Map, 'I speak of the court (*curia*), and I do not know, God knows, what is the court.'[16] Several scholars, notably H.G. Richardson and G.O. Sayles, argue that the court of Common Pleas grew out of the *curia regis ad scaccarium* – the barons of the Exchequer sitting in judgment – but others disagree about the meaning of this phrase, taken from *Glanvill*.[17] A problem is that what such terms as *curia regis, bancus, justiciarii*, and *scaccarium* mean to modern scholars may not be what they meant to twelfth-century writers, who could be maddeningly imprecise in their language. For example, *Glanvill* enumerates the royal courts as *curia regis ad scaccarium et coram justitiis ubicumque fuerint*.[18] But is he enumerating two or three groups of judges here? Brian Kemp has pointed out the many ways in which Richard fitz Neal employed the term *curia regis* in the *Dialogus de Scaccario*, and he noted the lack of precision in the

[16] *De nugis cur.*, chap. 1, p. 1.
[17] Modern discussion of the question goes back to Maitland, who held that the Bench arose when Henry II's five justices following him in 1178 settled at Westminster once the king returned to the Continent, Pollock and Maitland, 1: 153–5. H.G. Richardson in the introduction to *Mem. Roll 1 John*, xiii–xiv, argues that the Bench had its origin in an omnicompetent Exchequer, and that only by the time of King John did the Exchequer staff split into two groups, one for financial and another for judicial work. He and G.O. Sayles repeat these findings in *Governance*, pp. 210–11. Brian Kemp, 'Exchequer and Bench in the late twelfth century – separate or identical tribunals?' *E.H.R.*, 88 (1973): 563, finds specialization earlier, by the mid-1190s.
[18] G.E. Woodbine, ed., *Tractatus de Legibus et Consuetudinibus Regni Angliae* (New Haven, 1932), pp. 183–4, placed a comma after *curia regis*, indicating three courts. The most recent editor, G.D.G. Hall, *Glanvill*, p. xii, omitted the comma, making *curia regis ad scaccarium* denote a single court.

language of pipe rolls and final concords.[19] Exchequer clerks could even use the term in a physical sense, as in a pipe roll reference to repairs on the quay of the *curia regis* at Westminster.[20]

Kemp follows Richardson's and Sayles' view that the court of Common Pleas had its origin in an omnicompetent Exchequer, and that only slowly did pressure of increasing pleas cause a body of judges to separate from the financial officials. He offers as evidence testimony of the treasurer of Salisbury in a document concerning conveyance of land to Ford Abbey, c. 1193–9, which used such terms as *justiciarii scaccarii, justiciarii domini regis apud Westmonasterium, barones scaccarii,* and *curia domini regis* as if synonymous.[21] Kemp's view 'that in the early 1190s there was as yet no separation into distinct institutions of the financial and general judicial aspects of the *curia regis* at Westminster' is not accepted by all, however. A problem lies in the difficulty in identifying the barons of the Exchequer, whose names are rarely recorded in the careful way that justices' names were listed on final concords.[22] Logic leads us to suppose that some barons must have begun giving their chief attention to the judicial side of the Exchequer, others to traditional financial accounts before the death of Henry II. Some documents from Henry's last years do hint at a separation between two groups at Westminster.[23] A cartulary copy of the witness-list for a deed made sometime between 1182 and 1185 recognized royal jus-

---

[19] Kemp, 'Exchequer and Bench', pp. 563, 565–6.
[20] *Pipe Roll 20 Hen. II*, p. 137.
[21] Kemp, 'Exchequer and Bench', p. 577, from Forde Abbey Cartulary, unpublished ms. in private possession, pp. 418–19.
[22] Thomas Madox, *The History and Antiquities of the Exchequer of the Kings of England*, (2nd edn., London, 1769), 2: 312–19, made some sketchy lists, even though they are named only rarely in charters or final concords.
[23] *Pipe Roll 28 Hen. II*, p. 107, describes witnesses to a final concord as *baronibus et justiciariis domini regis*, leaving it uncertain whether they were one or two groups. R.C. van Caenegem, *Royal Writs in England from the Conquest to Glanvill*, Selden Soc., 72 (London, 1959): 31, cites an 1188 pipe roll entry which records a litigant offering one fine for having a plea *in curia regis*, then a second fine for having it *in curia regis ad scaccarium*, Van Caenegem concludes that 'the difference between the *curia regis* as the highest law court, to become soon the common bench, and the exchequer as an accounting office for royal debtors was clearly realized in the late twelfth century'.

tices and barons of the Exchequer as two distinct groups even when jointly witnessing a document.[24]

Exactly what does *Glanvill*'s phrase *curia regis ad scaccarium* mean? It could simply mean the place at which the royal justices sat, 'the king's court at the house of the Exchequer'. This translation makes sense in practically every instance, and the idea of the Exchequer as a place can be detected in late twelfth-century references. Records of proceedings before the royal justices certainly convey such a sense, when they describe a final concord as made *in curia regis apud Westmonasterium ad Scaccarium.*[25] Yet this does not tell us much about the division of labour within 'the house of the Exchequer'.

Since the language of the treatise, the pipe rolls, and final concords fails to tell us when Exchequer and *curia regis* personnel separated, we must seek answers elsewhere. Does not the addition of two terms of court – Hilary and Trinity – to the Easter or Michaelmas terms, traditional times for Exchequer audits, have some significance for the separation of the two staffs? Only in the middle years of Richard I do four annual terms of court become common. At the same time, we can see growing specialization within the financial sphere of the Exchequer, with a special branch set up in 1193 to deal with King Richard's ransom and with two escheators named in 1194.[26] Clearly, the added judicial sessions indicate a greater degree of specialization and professionalization among the king's servants at the Exchequer.

A look at the names of the justices witnessing final concords provides further proof. Francis West examined a number of

[24] C.U.L. MS. Mm 19.4 f. 201, printed in David Douglas, ed., *Feudal Documents from the Abbey of Bury St. Edmunds*, Br. Acad. Records of Soc. and Econ. Hist. (London, 1932), p. 181, no. 200: *coram justiciis domini regis Henrici secundi vidilicet Ricardo episc. Winton. et Ranulfo de Glanvilla Wmo. Basset et Rogero Fil. Reinfrei et coram Ricardo thesaurario et baronibus de scaccario apud Westmonasterium.*

[25] P.R.O. MS. D.L. 42/5, f. 39v, final concord dated 9 Oct. 1174. See also the finding of a recognition taken in 1187 *apud Westmonasterium ad Scaccarium*, MS. 'Warkton Book,' f. 7v, Rodney Thomson, ed., 'Twelfth-century documents from Bury St Edmunds Abbey', *E.H.R.*, 92 (1977): 818, no. 29. William fitz Stephen's life of Becket, written 1173–5, *M.T.B.*, 3: 51, describes the Exchequer as 'where the pleas of the king's crown are heard', Thomas Hearne, ed., *Adami de Domerham Historia de rebus gestis Glastoniensibus* (London, 1727), 2: 377–9, describing a disputed abbatial election in 1198, notes that the monks sent representatives to London *ad regis justiciarios*, and that the representatives then elected an abbot *in scaccario regis.*

[26] *Justiciarship*, pp. 80–1.

final concords, noting names of judges under Richard I and John, and his study led him to see a change in 1196. According to him, the men who composed the *curia regis* before then 'were not professional justices, but well-known figures in the financial administration, or even in politics'; after 1196 they were a smaller, more stable group, 'who look like professional justices, whose main duties were judicial ... in sharp contrast to the larger and more diffuse group of the previous reigns'.[27]

A close look at more complete lists than West could compile indicates a less dramatic transition to a professional or at least proto-professional judiciary. The process was a slow one, perhaps starting late in Henry II's reign, with Master Godfrey de Lucy and Robert of Wheatfield, who were joined a little later by Hubert Walter and Master Thomas of Hurstbourne. Their regular appearances as witnesses to final concords and the absence of any record of their other activity make plausible the possibility that they were specializing. Simon of Pattishall first came to the *curia regis* in 1190, and he remained there until the outbreak of civil war at the end of John's reign. Osbert fitz Hervey joined Pattishall at Westminster in 1191, his judicial career continued until his death in 1206. Such men were concentrating their energies at the Bench, even though they may have occasionally carried out other tasks, chiefly financial.

West is right, however, to associate the rise of a professional judiciary with Hubert Walter's justiciarship. The archbishop recruited a group of men to hear pleas who could relieve the barons of the Exchequer of some of their burden.[28] Actually, the crucial date is not 1196, as West wrote, but 1194 when Hubert Walter introduced a number of administrative reforms. One of his reforms was the revival of the general eyre, which required recruitment of a number of new justices. In 1194, five 'professionals' began to sit regularly at the Bench: Richard Barre, Ralph Foliot, William de Sainte-Mère-Eglise, Richard of Herriard, and William de Warenee. These five professional justices cannot be considered barons of the Exchequer. The first two came from the chancery. While the remaining three had some earlier involvement in financial work, it was away from the

---

[27] West, 'The *Curia regis* in the late twelfth and early thirteenth centuries', pp. 174–5; *Justiciarship*, pp. 83–4.   [28] *Justiciarship*, pp. 82–3.

Exchequer in the counties, or in William de Sainte-Mère-Eglise's case mainly in Normandy with the chamber.

Of course, some men regularly on the bench cannot be considered professionals in the same specialized sense; six were also powerful political figures, holders of important offices, or *familiares regis*. For example, Geoffrey fitz Peter, one of those left *in fiscum* or *in regimine regis* while Richard I was away on crusade, Hubert Walter, Hugh Bardolf, and of course Richard fitz Neal can be considered barons of the Exchequer as well as justices of Common Pleas. Some had less exalted rank than others, but stood close to the centre of power, as much political figures as civil servants, still multi-purpose royal agents in the traditional mould. Nonetheless, by the 1190s we can see two distinct groups of royal servants working in the house of the Exchequer at Westminster, barons of the Exchequer and justices of the Bench (*de banco*). The justices kept their own rolls known as *rotuli curie domini regis de Westmonasterio*, clearly differentiated from the Exchequer's pipe rolls.[29] Yet the continued presence of Richard fitz Neal, the treasurer, on the bench provides a warning that separation of the two groups was not total.

2 THE EMERGENCE OF A PROFESSIONAL JUDICIARY

A group of proto-professionals, if not fully professional justices guiding the work of the *curia regis* became visible by the middle years of Richard I. Several members of this group had first joined the Bench under Henry II. The death of Henry II and his son's accession caused no dramatic change in the personnel of the judiciary except at the top. Glanvill was dismissed from the justiciarship and left England to die on Richard Lionheart's crusade, but none of the royal justices shared his disgrace. Death had already removed four justices who had been among Henry II's stalwarts: William Basset (d. 1185), Alan de Furnellis (d. 1189 at latest), Geoffrey Ridel, bishop of Ely (d. 1189), and Richard of Ilchester, bishop of Winchester (d. 1188). Five others survived to serve Richard I only occasionally. Jocelin, archdeacon of Chichester (d. 1202–3), and John of Oxford, bishop of Norwich (d. 1200), rarely engaged in judicial activity.

[29] *C.R.R.*, 1: 57, 123, 181, 408.

Roger fitz Reinfrid (d. 1196) and Robert of Wheatfield (d. 1193–4) were among the five associates *in regimine regni* named to share in governing the kingdom during Richard's absence,[1] but neither took much part in governmental affairs after Walter of Coutances gave up the justiciarship. William Ruffus (d. 1194–5) survived long enough to serve on the 1194 eyre to East Anglia. Nine other royal justices who had begun their work under Henry II continued in the new reign with such regularity that they must be counted among the corps of professional royal servants becoming specialists in the work of justice.

Approximately 100 men served Richard I as judges at one time or another, but 62 sat on the bench only once or twice, perhaps one term at Westminster or a single eyre. A quarter of these were earls, bishops and abbots, or high ranking *curiales*, some of whom were present for a great council or some state occasion and witnessed a few final concords by chance. Others appeared once or twice as leaders of eyres to their native regions, appointed to add a degree of dignity to the team of justices and to bring to the career civil servants the benefit of their knowledge of local conditions.

Excluding the episcopal justiciars William Longchamp of Ely, Walter, archbishop of Rouen and Hubert Walter of Canterbury, four abbots and eleven bishops sat on the bench under Richard I, but only four sat with any frequency. Godfrey de Lucy, bishop of Winchester, and Richard fitz Neal, bishop of London, were both justices of Henry II, elevated to the episcopate early in the new reign, who remained active throughout Richard's time. Gilbert de Glanvill, bishop of Rochester, had been a judge in 1187 and 1188, and under Richard I he was mainly active from spring 1194 to summer 1196. Herbert le Poer, archdeacon of Canterbury and then from June 1194 bishop of Salisbury, joined the justices at Westminster in infrequent appearances between 1190 and 1197.

Laymen of highest rank were not normally to be found at the Bench. Three earl's names appear among the justices, but only one – Roger Bigod, earl of Norfolk – for more than a single term. Two men below the rank of earl, yet influential *curiales*, can be found among the justices a few times: William Marshal, later to

---

[1] *Roger Howden*, 3: 16; *Gesta Hen. Secundi*, 2: 87.

win an earldom, and William Briwerre, a *curialis* who would
serve on the bench more often in the time of King John. Two
less prominent royal servants – Oger fitz Oger and John of
Guestling – sat on the bench with some regularity, but not often
enough to be counted among the corps of professionals. John of
Guestling's chief service as a justice would come in King John's
reign, and would continue into the minority of Henry III.

Hubert Walter's practical genius produced a number of
innovations to perfect Henry II's legal reforms. Among
Hubert's contributions was his revival of the general eyre in the
autumn of 1194. His recruitment of personnel for it proved to
be a step toward a professional judiciary. The eyre covering all
England with eight groups of justices required a larger number
of men – forty-seven – than the panel of royal justices sitting at
Westminster could provide. The lists of justices for the different
circuits are loaded with names of prominent local men, clerks or
serjeants from other branches of royal government, and members of bishops' staffs recruited for temporary service on the
bench. Hubert Walter recruited members of his archiepiscopal
familia, his brother, and other relatives to fill the ranks of royal
justices for this eyre.[2]

Hubert Walter combined the highest secular office in the
kingdom with the highest ecclesiastical office in a way not seen
in England again until the time of Cardinal Wolsey. Clerks of the
archiepiscopal *familia* sometimes took part in work of the Chancery or Exchequer but rarely of the Bench. Although some
occasionally joined the judicial bench, most notably on the
1194 eyre, none of the archbishop's clerks became regular
members of the panel of justices at Westminster.[3] The two
clerks of Hubert Walter who acted most often as royal justices
did so in the time of King John, after the archbishop had
resigned the justiciarship: Master Godfrey de Insula and Master
Geoffrey of Buckland. Those Canterbury clerks known to have

---

[2] Hubert Walter's brother, Theobald of Valoignes; his kinsmen, sons-in-law of
Glanvill, Ralph of Arden and William de Auberville; clerks of the archiepis-
copal household, Henry de Castellun, Master Godfrey de Insula, and Master
Simon of Scales.

[3] For names of some of Hubert Walter's canonists and clerks, see C.R. Cheney.
English Bishops' Chanceries 1100–1250 (Manchester, 1950), pp. 17–18; *Hubert
Walter*, pp. 164–6, 170.

had some mastery of canon law were not among those summoned to the Bench.

Recruitment in 1194 was rendered more difficult for the
archbishop by a new regulation that sheriffs could not act as justices in their own shires, although they could join the groups of
justices visiting neighbouring counties. In the eyre of 1192
seven sheriffs had served as itinerant justices in their own shires,
and one justice served in a shire from which he had recently
retired as sheriff.[4] The articles of the 1194 eyre, however, stated
that no sheriff could act as justice for pleas of the crown in his
own county.[5] This marked a return to the old principle that
pleas of the crown were to be heard only by specially appointed
royal agents. The rule was to be often overlooked in the future;
between 1194 and 1209 sheriffs or undersheriffs sat as justices at
least twenty times.[6] Some of the sheriffs were men active in the
royal household or at the Exchequer, who rarely visited their
counties and who had deputies to carry out their duties.

Counting names on final concords from Richard I produces
fourteen names which recur most often. The names appear frequently enough to indicate that the fourteen formed an inner
core of the 100 occasional justices. They were capable of offering direction to the temporary appointees who joined them in
the *curiae regis* at Westminster and in the counties. Among the
names are so many familiar from the reign of Richard's father
that in some measure the group of men recruited during Glanvill's
justiciarship remained responsible for justice under the new
king. Eight whose careers in the judiciary had begun under
Henry II continued their work for Richard I. Three who had served
Henry II remained on the bench throughout the new king's
reign: Michael Belet, who continued his activity until 1201 in
King John's reign; Godfrey de Lucy (d. 1204), who last served on
the eyre of 1198–9; and Richard fitz Neal, who was at the Bench
regularly until 1196, then occasionally until his death in
1198.

Others who would become familiar names in the new reign
had earned some experience on the bench under Henry II.
Three of them had witnessed fines from 1185 on, so that they

---

[4] *Pipe Roll 12 John*, p. xvi.
[5] *Roger Howden*, 3: 264; also Stubbs, *Select Charters*, pp. 251–7.
[6] *Pipe Roll 12 John*, p. xviii.

might almost have been grouped with the judges of Henry II. Hubert Walter first appeared among the justices at Westminster with his uncle Ranulf de Glanvill as early as 1184.[7] From 1185 until Glanvill's dismissal from the justiciarship, Hubert Walter was seated at his uncle's side on the bench. Then he set out on the Third Crusade. During the first years of Richard's reign, then, Hubert was making a name for himself in the Holy Land, and he did not return to England until the spring of 1193. His first appearance at the *curia regis* at Westminster under Richard I was as justiciar in the spring of 1194, and he would preside over the courts until his resignation from the justiciarship in the summer of 1198.

Two others were men whom the justiciar knew from his apprenticeship under his uncle. Master Thomas of Hurstbourne's first recorded appearance as a royal justice was in March 1185 at Westminster. A short time later, on 2 April, he witnessed fines while on an eyre to the eastern counties looking into royal custodies.[8] Thomas continued to go on eyres throughout Richard I's reign, and he was normally at Westminster for the terms of court from 1186 until November 1199, almost to the end of his life (d. 1200–1).[9] Earliest evidence for Hugh Bardolf's work as a royal justice dates from January 1185. Later that year he went to the southwestern counties, and in November he was at Westminster. His judicial work continued in 1186 and in 1188–9. In the reign of Richard I, Hugh Bardolf was an itinerant justice practically every year except 1190, when he was with the king *en route* to the Mediterranean. He returned to England from Sicily in the autumn, carrying messages from the king to Longchamp.[10] Although Hugh was often a justice in the counties, he was less frequently at Westminster. His work as a judge continued under King John, when he joined the Bench mainly for vacation courts and joined the justices *coram rege* on John's first two visits to England. Bardolf's last judicial activity was with the summer vacation court in August 1203, not long before his death in the autumn.[11]

[7] Cheney, *Hubert Walter*, p. 21; Salter, *Facs. of Oxford Chtrs.*, no. 43.
[8] *Rot. de Dominabus*, p. 65.   [9] *Fasti, St. Paul's*, p. 81.
[10] *Itin. Ric. I*, p. 43. *Pipe Roll 2 Ric. I*, p. 112, indicates that Hugh had brought letters from Richard: *per preceptum Regis de ultra mare per Hugonem Bard.*
[11] *Pipe Roll 5 John*, p. 103; *6 John*, p. 212.

Two other justices among the fourteen who served Richard I regularly began their service under his father, although they had gained only slight experience on the bench before Henry II's death. Ralph Foliot, archdeacon of Hereford, first joined the *curia regis* at various times and locations, 1186–8, but he was chiefly working as a chancery clerk. Evidence for his judicial work increases under Richard I. He first went on eyre in the summer of 1190, then again in 1192. The significant date for Ralph's recruitment as one of the 'professional' justices is 1194. In June of that year he first joined the Bench at Westminster, and in the fall he was an itinerant justice. The archdeacon of Hereford continued to serve through Michaelmas 1197, a year or two before his death, which was probably 20 December 1199.[12]

Geoffrey fitz Peter, successor to Hubert Walter as justiciar, first did temporary duty as a justice both at Westminster and in the countryside in 1188–9; then in Richard I's reign, he became more active. He went on the first eyre of the new reign under William Longchamp's supervision in 1190–1 and on others: in 1192, on Hubert Walter's general eyre of 1194, and on one he led as justiciar in 1198–9. Geoffrey fitz Peter also made appearances at the Bench every year before he succeeded Hubert Walter in the justiciarship on 11 July 1198.

Six new names began to appear in the 1190s among the justices, men who had no experience in Henry II's *curia regis*. Two of them – Simon of Pattishall and Richard Barre – joined the judiciary around the time of William Longchamp's general visitation in the summer of 1190. Simon of Pattishall would have a long and distinguished career on the bench, covering most of two reigns, until the outbreak of civil war in 1215. Richard Barre came to England as the new archdeacon of Ely in the company of the chancellor, William Longchamp and he went on the chancellor's eyre in the summer of 1190 as did two other clerks who had come from Normandy.[13] Richard's association with Longchamp meant that after the chancellor's

---

[12] Z.N. Brooke and C.N.L. Brooke, 'Hereford Cathedral Dignitaries in the twelfth century', *Camb. Hist. Jl.*, 8 (1944): 16.

[13] Hubert archdeacon of Evreux and Warin precentor of Evreux. Unlike Richard Barre, they never became career royal judges, *P.B.K.J.*, 3: lxxxi, lxxxii, lxxxiii, lxxix, lxxx.

fall from power he was not summoned to the courts again until 1194, when Hubert Walter recruited him for the autumn eyre. After that, the archdeacon was almost continuously in the law courts until 1200. A third man, Osbert fitz Hervey, was an itinerant justice in 1191 to his native East Anglia, and he continued to go on circuits chiefly to that area until 1202. As one scholar has written, 'Of all the justices his knowledge of East Anglian disputes was probably the greatest.'[14] In the autumn of 1191, Osbert joined the court at Westminster, and he remained there almost continuously until Easter term 1206. He had died by late summer of that year.[15]

The other three men did not join the *curia regis* until 1194: Richard of Herriard, William de Sainte-Mère-Eglise, and William de Warenne of Wormegay. Richard of Herriard would remain in the judiciary for ten years, until Michaelmas 1204. He retired from the Bench four years before his death about 6 April 1208.[16] William de Sainte-Mère-Eglise, although a longtime royal *familiaris*, first sat at the Bench in June 1194, then led one of the eyres the following autumn, returning to Westminster by 2 December. He acted as a judge from time to time until Michaelmas 1198. William did not join the justices again until April 1201 during King John's visit to England. By then he had become bishop of London and was too busy with ecclesiastical affairs to take an active part in secular administration.[17] William de Warenne's work as a royal justice began in Michaelmas term 1193 and continued at Westminster the following spring. He went on the 1194 eyre and on the 1198–9 eyre, and in the interval he was often at Westminster. He continued to serve at the Bench in the first two years of John's reign, last serving there in Easter term 1200.

Hubert Walter's appointment to the justiciarship has importance for the *curia regis* not only because of reforms in record-

---

[14] Barbara Dodwell in introduction to *Feet of Fines, Norfolk, Ric. I-John*, Pipe Roll Soc., new ser., 27 (1952): xv. Another Osbert fitz Hervey, Glanvill's brother, had served as a justice occasionally in the 1180s, Mortimer, 'Family of Glanville', *B.I.H.R.*, 54 (1981): 5–10.

[15] *Rot. Lit. Pat.*, p. 66b, writ of 26 Aug. 1206 indicates that he had died. *Rot. Lit. Claus.*, 1: 52, obviously misdated 10 April 1205, commands the sheriffs of Norfolk and Suffolk and of Essex to turn his lands over to a custodian.

[16] *Rot. Lit. Claus.*, 1: 109b. The priory of Witney kept his orbit on 6 April, *V.C.H., Hants*, 2: 149.   [17] *D.N.B.*, s.v. 'William of Sainte-Mère-Eglise'.

keeping or revival of the *iter ad omnia placita*. The archbishop may take credit for the recruitment of a corps of professional royal servants specializing in the work of justice, even if they cannot yet be termed a 'professional' judiciary in the complete sense of the term. The twin pressures of raising enormous sums of money and of coping with a larger volume of lawsuits forced a greater degree of specialization on the justiciar's staff. Clearly, changes in justiciars have more importance for the personnel of the courts than do changes in monarchs. Several of the justices who first took their places at the Bench under Richard I continued to serve there in the reign of his successor.

Among the fourteen justices were six who, while sitting frequently on the bench, had other responsibilities that took much of their time. Some held high office which gave them political power. The most obvious example is Hubert Walter, who combined in himself the highest offices in both the English Church and the royal government. This combination, coupled with the king's absence and inattention, made Hubert the most powerful of the justiciars and perhaps the most powerful of any medieval English monarch's chief ministers. Much of his energy had to go into the raising of money.[18] Yet the archbishop found time to attend to the judicial sphere: he usually sat at Westminster with his judges, and he won a wide reputation for knowledge of the law.[19] Roger of Howden wrote of Hubert, 'There was to be found no one like him who stored up the laws and customs of the kingdom', and other chroniclers echoed his view.[20]

Five other justices wielded less power, but were still multipurpose royal servants of the old school. Their existence is a reminder that the growth of professional offices was a gradual process, or perhaps that the work of justice was too important to be left entirely to specialists. This group included in addition to the archbishop two other bishops, named to the episcopate by Richard I in September 1189. Godfrey de Lucy, bishop of Winchester, also combined spiritual and temporal power. His

---

[18] *Justiciarship*, pp. 80–3.

[19] His name always appears as presiding over the justices witnessing final concords at Westminster, but this is not absolute proof of his presence. It can be shown that on some dates when he is listed at the head of the justices he was actually elsewhere in the kingdom, Cheney, *Hubert Walter*, p. 95, n. 3; *Justiciarship*, p. 88.   [20] *Roger Howden*, 4: 12; cf. *Gervase of Canterbury*, 2: 406.

rich bishopric made him one of England's most powerful barons, and he seems to have been ambitious to wield political power in the old Anglo-Norman episcopal tradition. He purchased a shrievalty and custody of castles from the king, even though such activities were no longer considered fitting for bishops.[21] Godfrey was determined to play a leading part in the government during the king's absence on crusade, but his quarrel with William Longchamp imperilled his plan. Yet he remained active in the judiciary until the autumn of 1199. Richard fitz Neal, treasurer since 1158, was a financial expert who found time to sit regularly at the Bench until 1196, when failing health forced his retirement. He continued to make occasional appearances on the bench, however, until April 1198. Three not in the episcopate include Geoffrey fitz Peter and two longtime *familiares* of Henry II, Hugh Bardolf and William de Sainte-Mère-Eglise.

Geoffrey fitz Peter does not appear as the holder of any royal office before the last decade of Henry II's reign. By 1185 he had become chief royal forester, leading a group of forest justices to eight counties on the great forest eyre.[22] He retained his title of royal forester until he exchanged it for that of justiciar in 1198. Geoffrey's role in royal government increased under Richard Lionheart. The king had received papal permission to release from their crusading vows men needed at home for the government, and Geoffrey was one of those chosen to remain in England. He was one of a small corps of men left *in fiscum* or *in regimine regis* to aid the two justiciars in governing.[23] Geoffrey fitz Peter moved even nearer to the centre of power in the justiciarship of Hubert Walter. Geoffrey was associated so closely with the new justiciar that he has been called 'his most important colleague'.[24] Geoffrey was active all the time in the work of the courts, serving on eyres and at Westminster regularly before he became justiciar in 1198.

Hugh Bardolf was one of Henry II's *familiares* who remained close to the centre of power during the reigns of the king's two

---

[21] *Chron. Richard of Devizes*, p. 8; *Pipe Roll 2 Ric. I*, pp. 126, 151.
[22] *Justiciarship*, p. 98; Charles R. Young, *The Royal Forests of Medieval England* (Philadelphia, 1979), pp. 39–40.
[23] *Roger Howden*, 3: 16; *Richard of Devizes*, p. 6; Appleby, *England without Richard*, p. 20.   [24] *Justiciarship*, p. 108.

sons. He was *dapifer*, a title he held until the death of Henry II and possibly throughout the reign of Richard I.[25] Some chroniclers name Hugh as one of the group of justices left in England by the new king to assist the chancellor and the joint-justiciars, but it seems clear that he set out for the Holy Land with Richard and the crusaders. He began the journey in 1190, but in the autumn he returned in a great rush to England from Sicily to take an important part in the government.[26] When Walter of Coutances revealed royal letters – dated 9 and 23 February 1191 – making new arrangements for the government, Hugh Bardolf was among the *appares* to whom the king addressed the letters.[27] Later Richard Lionheart during his German captivity addressed a letter to the archbishop of Rouen and four justiciars – among them Hugh Bardolf – as his chief agents in England.[28] Throughout the reign of Richard I, Hugh had custody of castles, another indication of his influence in the upper spheres of authority.[29]

The change in justiciars at the end of 1193 did not affect Bardolf's position near the centre of government. He was a close associate of the new justiciar Hubert Walter. When the archbishop undertook reform of the administration in the autumn of 1194, Hugh acquired new responsibilities along with William de Sainte-Mère-Eglise. They were the two escheators for the kingdom, and Hugh held the post of escheator for the North until 1197.[30] About the same time that Bardolf and William were named escheators, they were given responsibility for the 'bail and custody' of the Jews, probably foreshadowing

---

[25] Delisle, *Recueil*, 2: 133, 159, 181, 216, 227, 237, 240; *Itin. Hen. II*, pp. 239, 252, 253. Charters of Richard I do not refer to him as *dapifer*, although a pipe roll entry for 1198 still applies that title to him, *Pipe Roll 10 Ric. I*, p. 139.

[26] *Gesta Hen. Secundi*, 2: 101; *Roger Howden*, 3: 28, names him as one of four colleagues of the two justiciars in Dec. 1189. *Itin. Ric. I*, pp. 29–36, Mar. 27–3 July; p. 43, 6 Oct. in Sicily. He had returned to Westminster by 6 Nov. 1190, *Itin. Ric. I*, p. 43. Landon notes that it was possible, given favourable conditions, to make the journey from Sicily in a month, p. 196, note. *P.B.K.J.*, 3: App. II, has Hugh at Westminster on 11 April and 16 June and at Stamford on 16 Sept. 1190.

[27] *Ralph de Diceto*, 2: 90; *Roger Howden*, 3: 96.

[28] *Itin. Ric. I*, p. 73, letter of 30 Mar. 1193.

[29] Mountsorel and Kenilworth in 1191, *Pipe Roll 3 Ric. I*, 123; Norham and Durham in 1195, *Rot. Lit. Pat.*, p. 35; *Howden*, 3: 153–4, 285; *Mem. Roll 1 John*, p. 61.   [30] *Pipe Roll 6 Ric. I*, pp. xx–xxi; *9 Ric. I*, p. xxv.

the office of justice of the Jews.[31] In the midst of all this activity, Hugh Bardolf found time to serve as a royal justice. He was named as an itinerant justice for practically every eyre in the reign of Richard I.

William de Sainte-Mère-Eglise was a longtime member of the households of Henry II and Richard I, described by Gerald of Wales as *curiae sequela est et domini regis familiaris*.[32] William served Henry II as *clericus de camera* on both sides of the Channel in the years 1180–9.[33] Apparently William continued for a time to serve as Richard Lionheart's chief chamber clerk, but by spring 1193 he had won the title of *protonotarius* or king's secretary.[34] When Hubert Walter made his administrative reforms in 1194, William de Sainte-Mère-Eglise was much involved in them. Along with Hugh Bardolf, he was charged with custody of royal escheats and with responsibility for collection of debts owed to Jewish moneylenders.[35] Also in 1194 William de Sainte-Mère-Eglise first joined the judicial bench, sitting at Westminster in June and leading one of the autumn eyres. He continued to serve in the courts until Michaelmas 1198. His judicial activity at Westminster was probably due to the convenience of his presence there performing financial tasks in any case.

These six men, then, had duties which could take them away from the courts frequently. Three were sheriffs, for Henry II and his two sons often chose sheriffs from among the *curiales* or high-ranking officials. But the appointees were non-resident sheriffs who employed deputies to carry out their duties. Since the office was profitable, men were willing to pay heavily for their appointment; Godfrey de Lucy offered Richard I 1000

---

[31] H.G. Richardson, *The English Jewry under the Angevin Kings* (London, 1960), pp. 119, 135; *Mem. Roll 1 John*, p. 72. See also Alice C. Crammer, 'The Jewish Exchequer: an inquiry into its fiscal functions', *A.H.R.*, 45 (1939–40): 327–7; 'The origins and functions of the Jewish Exchequer', *Speculum*, 16 (1941): 226–9. [32] *Gerald of Wales*, 1: 260–1.

[33] Delisle, *Recueil*, 2: 246, a grant to William describes him as *clerico nostro de camera nostro*, dates 1181–3; witness-lists, 2: 230, 268, 272, 281, 283, 305, 420, 421. J.E.A. Jolliffe identifies William de Sainte-Mère-Eglise with a *Willelmus de Camera*, a serjeant, a layman, of Bishop Nigel of Ely, '*Camera regis* under Henry II', p. 343.

[34] *Pipe Roll 1 Ric. I*, Rec. Com., pp. 11, 225; *Roger Howden*, 3: 209, letter of Richard I, dated 19 Apr. 1193.

[35] *Pipe Roll 6 Ric. I*, pp. xx–xxi; *7 Ric. I*, pp. 33–64, roll of escheats; Richardson, *English Jewry*, pp. 117–19.

marks for the shrievalty of Hampshire plus certain other privileges.[36] There is no evidence, however, that either Geoffrey fitz Peter or Hugh Bardolf obtained their shrievalties by offers of fines. Their appointment may have been a means of providing these royal servants with an income. Geoffrey fitz Peter had first held royal office in 1184 as sheriff of Northamptonshire, a post he held until Henry II's death. Under Richard I, he held multiple appointments. He was again sheriff of Northamptonshire, 1191–4, he was named undersheriff of Staffordshire, 1197–8, then sheriff 1198–1204, and sheriff of Yorkshire, 1198–1200.[37] Hugh Bardolf had first served as sheriff in 1184, when Cornwall was placed in his charge. In 1187 he exchanged Cornwall for Wiltshire, and the next year Henry II also named him sheriff of Somerset and Dorset; he held these counties until 1189.

Following the accession of Richard I, William Longchamp removed a number of sheriffs in 1190–1 and replaced them with men of his own choice. He took advantage of Godfrey de Lucy's absence in Normandy to take the county of Hampshire from him.[38] The chancellor gave Hugh Bardolf Staffordshire with Warwick and Leicestershire in 1190 and Westmorland in 1191, but following Longchamp's fall in autumn 1191, Bardolf had to give up Warwick and Leicester in exchange for Yorkshire. King Richard, on his return from captivity in 1194, made a number of changes in sheriffs. He took Yorkshire from Hugh, apparently for no other reason than to sell it to someone else at a higher price,[39] for he soon named Hugh sheriff of Northumberland. Bardolf continued to hold the county of Westmorland until 1199, and in 1198 he became sheriff of Cumberland. Then after King John's accession, Hugh was shifted to other counties: first to Cornwall and Devon for a year and then to Nottingham and Derby which he held until his death in 1203.[40]

The eight lower-ranking men whose activity was less political and more purely legal had fewer assignments that took their

---

[36] *Richard of Devizes*, pp. 7–9; *Roger Howden*, 3: xxviii, note 4.
[37] *D.N.B.*, s.v. 'Fitzpeter, Geoffrey'.
[38] Appleby, *England without Richard*, p. 51.
[39] *Roger Howden*, 3: 241; *Pipe Roll 6 Ric. I*, p. xix.
[40] *List of Sheriffs*, pp. 21, 26, 34, 102, 122, 127, 144, 150, 152, 161; corrected by Brian E. Harris, 'The English sheriffs in the reign of John', M.A. Thesis (Univ. of Nottingham, 1961), App. I.

attention away from the *curia regis*. Only one of them was a sheriff in the time of Richard I. Simon of Pattishall held office as sheriff during much of the period that he was on the bench. In 1193 and 1194 he was sheriff of Essex and Hertfordshire. When Richard I shifted a number of sheriffs on his return from Germany, he sent Simon to his native Northamptonshire, where he remained as sheriff after Richard's death, until 1203.[41] Pattishall is also exceptional among the lesser professionals in holding custody of a castle for a time.[42] He was custodian of Northampton Castle, which stood at the greatest road junction in the Midlands.

Close ties still linked Exchequer and Bench in the 1190s, and the justices concerned themselves sometimes with financial matters, as they would continue to do in the thirteenth century. It is possible, however, to admit this while denying that the justices of the Bench and the barons of the Exchequer were identical. The important point in signaling the rise of a professional judiciary is that practically the *only* other activity for this group of eight was occasional financial work – assessing aids, collecting tallages from the royal domain, or levying other taxes – which belonged traditionally to the itinerant justices. Richard Barre, for example levied amercements in Norfolk and Suffolk in 1197 on merchants who had sold grain to the king's enemies in Flanders.[43]

Another indication of connections between Bench and Exchequer staffs is the selection, from men sitting at the Bench, of the justices assigned to have custody of the Jews' debts. The first keepers or *custodes* of the Jews, or at least their forerunners, were Hugh Bardolf and William de Sainte-Mère-Eglise.[44] Riots in 1194 had resulted in the burning of many records concerning debts to the Jews, necessitating a new system of record-keeping. In February 1198 the king named Simon of Pattishall one of four justices of the Jews.[45] King John removed Simon in 1200 and replaced him with another justice of the Bench, William de

---

[41] *List of Sheriffs*, p. 43; *Pipe Roll 7 Ric. I*, p. 217, indicates that he was sheriff in 1194. See also Harris 'The English Sheriffs', App. I. p. 200.

[42] Northampton Castle, 28 July 1191, *Roger Howden*, 3: 136.

[43] *Pipe Roll 10 Ric. I*, pp. xix–xx, 92. For Richard of Herriard as tallager, see *Chancellor's Roll 8 Ric. I*, p. 46.   [44] Richardson, *English Jewry*, pp. 117–19.

[45] *Pipe Roll 10 Ric. I*, pp. 125, 165, 210.

Warenne. This marked William's departure from the Bench, although he continued to be one of the justices of the Jews until his death in 1209.[46]

Some royal justices were custodians of properties temporarily in the king's possession. Master Thomas of Hurstbourne practically made a career of holding vacant abbeys and bishoprics for Henry II,[47] and he continued this work for Richard I. After Hubert Walter's translation from Salisbury to Canterbury in 1193, Thomas took charge of the vacant bishopric; and when Geoffrey Plantagenet was suspended from his functions as archbishop of York in 1195, Thomas accounted for his lands.[48] Ralph Foliot, archdeacon of Hereford, had custody of escheats in Shropshire and Worcestershire in 1190.[49] William de Warenne received custody of considerable lands when Count John's honour of Gloucester was seized following his rebellion during his brother's captivity. William was custodian of the honour from 1194 through 1196.[50] Custody of such estates was a heavy responsibility; for example, Master Thomas accounted for revenues at Winchester amounting to over £600 for half a year. Yet the custodians undoubtedly left bailiffs or stewards on the spot in charge of day-to-day supervision of these lands, contenting themselves with occasional visits. Their custodies did not prevent them from remaining at Westminster most of the year.

Only occasionally can the eight lesser professionals be observed carrying out tasks unconnected with the Exchequer or Bench. Richard of Herriard crossed the Channel in 1195 to deliver seventeen horses to King Richard, a task that might fall more within the sphere of the Chamber than the Exchequer.[51]

[46] *Rot. Chart.*, p. 61; *Rot. de Obl. et Fin.*, pp. 92, 425; *Rot. Lit. Claus.*, 1: 107b, dated 1208.

[47] Bishopric of Chester, *Pipe Roll 30 Hen. II*, p. 24; *31 Hen. II*, pp. 141–2; abbey of St Werbaugh, Chester, *Annales Cestriensis*, ed. R.C. Christie, Lancs-Cheshire Rec. Soc. (1887), p. 31; *Pipe Roll 31 Hen. II*, p. 142; abbey of Abingdon, *Pipe Roll 31 Hen. II*, p. 29; *32 Hen. II*, pp. 116–17; bishopric of Winchester, *Pipe Roll 1 Ric. I*, Rec. Com., p. 5.

[48] *Pipe Roll 6 Ric. I*, p. 256; *7 Ric. I*, pp. 29–32; *Chancellor's Roll 8 Ric. I*, pp. 174, 184; *Pipe Roll 9 Ric. I*, pp. 118–20; *10 Ric. I*, p. 157. He accounted for the lands of York from 1195 to 1198.   [49] *Pipe Roll 2 Ric. I*, pp. 4–5.

[50] *Pipe Roll 6 Ric. I*, p. 240; *Chancellor's Roll 8 Ric. I*, p. 105; *Pipe Roll 9 Ric. I*, p. 129.

[51] *Pipe Roll 7 Ric. I*, p. 205. The next year he was still overseas with the king, *Chancellor's Roll 8 Ric. I*, p. 33.

In 1198 Herriard again went overseas in the king's service, help-
ing to transport treasure to Germany for the king's nephew
Otto.[52] Richard Lionheart was spending large sums in support of
Otto's bid for the imperial title.

A significant group within the fourteen most frequent justices
of Richard I, then, had few responsibilities off the bench beyond
occasional financial matters. No evidence at all survives of
Osbert fitz Hervey's holding any other post in the administration during the years that he was on the bench. Although
Michael Belet continued to hold his title of *pincerna* under
Richard I, no evidence permits us to see him actually carrying
out the duties of butler as he did for Henry II. With the corps of
royal justices serving Richard I, we can make out the approaching shadows of that modern mammoth, the bureaucracy. The
old undifferentiated group of clerks and *curiales* who took on any
duties assigned to them by the king or the justiciar is giving way
to something approaching government departments with
defined duties.

3 BACKGROUND AND EARLY CAREERS

The backgrounds of members of Richard I's judiciary indicate a
tendency toward turning the permanent machinery of government over to professionals. Men without the prestige of old
families, without independent means, and perhaps without
scruple in their search for advancement were dispensing justice
in the king's name. Clearly, more and more power was passing
into the hands of men from middling knightly families, men
whom the old nobility and conservative clerics might well mistrust. Critics preoccupied with social stability could without too
much exaggeration see a threat to the established order.
Especially could they see a threat if they had not bound one of
the justices to them through ties of patronage.

A basic classification of the fourteen justices most active
under Richard I is their clerical or lay status: seven in each
category. The traditional view is that the judicial bench was
chiefly clerical until the time of Edward I, a view that now must

---

[52] *Pipe Roll 10 Ric. I*, p. 198.

be revised.[1] The experience of laymen with the workings of the courts of shire and hundred or franchisal courts made them as useful for the *curia regis* as clerics with their knowledge of books on Roman and canon law. We must recognize the contribution that these laymen made to English common law. They were not passive spectators on the bench, but were active participants in proceedings, whose learning in Anglo-Norman legal traditions was respected.

A glance at the geographical origins of the justices shows, not surprisingly, that most came from the more populated and prosperous South and East of England. Several had East Anglian connections, which may account for their presence on the bench. Such connections acquainted them with Ranulf de Glanvill or with Hubert Walter. Henry II's great justiciar had a Suffolk origin, while his nephew was born in Norfolk. Only two justices came from as far north as the Midlands: Hugh Bardolf, son of a Lincolnshire knight, and Simon of Pattishall, from the Northamptonshire village of the same name.[2] Only one or possibly two of the fourteen came from across the Channel. William de Sainte-Mère-Eglise was a native Norman; he came from the ducal manor of Sainte-Mère-Eglise in the Cotentin.[3] It seems possible that Richard Barre grew up in Normandy, although he did have English kinsmen who were Berkshire knights.[4] Perhaps he took his surname from the village of La

---

[1] For statements of the orthodox view, see T.F.T. Plucknett, *Early English Legal Literature* (Cambridge, 1958), p. 82; Pollock and Maitland, 1: 133–5, 205.

[2] Sir Charles Clay, 'Hugh Bardolf the justiciar and his family', *Lincs History and Archaeology*, 1 (Lincs Local Hist. Soc., 1966): 5–7. Clay corrects earlier accounts – Dugdale, Foss, and *D.N.B.* – which had identified William Bardolf, sheriff of Norfolk and Suffolk, 1170–5, as Hugh's father. For Simon, *Complete Peerage*, 10: 311. *Honors and Knights' Fees*, 1: 92, citing a crown debt owed by Roger dean of Pattishall in 1201, suggested that Simon was descended from a family of hereditary rural deans. But *Complete Peerage*, 10: 311–12, n. 'f', points out that Roger was not dean of Pattishall, but merely held a benefice there, while his title was dean of Brackley.

[3] Delisle, *Recueil*, Introduction, p. 496; *D.N.B.*, s.v. 'William of Sainte-Mère-Eglise'.

[4] John G. Jenkins, ed., *The Cartulary of Missenden Abbey* (Bucks Archaeol. Soc., Records Branch, 1939–62), 2: 2, no. 267. Lewis Loyd, *The Origin of some Anglo-Norman Families*, Harl. Soc., 103 (1951): 98, points out that the Sifrewasts continued to hold fees near their ancestral centre at Chiffrevast, Normandy.

Barre, lying east of Lisieux on the old Roman road to Paris.[5] Whether Richard Barre was English or Norman by birth cannot be known, but he certainly passed much of his life before 1190 on the Continent.

The toponymics of several justices mark them as natives of obscure villages, and other evidence indicates rural origins for the rest. No native Londoner appears on the list until the time of King John. The obscurity in origin of Richard's justices points toward the growth of a professional group of royal officials. Eight of the thirteen judges we met under Henry II came from families with a tradition of service to the king. Three of these families were still represented on Richard I's bench with Michael Belet, Richard fitz Neal, and Godfrey de Lucy, but only four others can be said to have come from administrative families: Hubert Walter, nephew of the great Glanvill; Osbert fitz Hervey, Hubert's brother; William de Warenne, whose father had been active in Henry II's government; and Geoffrey fitz Peter, son of a forester, and possibly younger brother of Simon fitz Peter, a *familiaris regis* and sheriff for Henry II.[6] The others are the first of their families to enter the royal service.

Complaints about 'new men' filling the royal administration have some basis in the time of Richard I. Only one of the justices came from an old baronial family which had been powerful since the Conquest, yet his father had also been prominent in administrative work under Henry II. William de Warenne's father, Reginald, was the third son of William II de Warenne, earl of Surrey. Reginald then became a baron through his marriage to Alice, daughter and heir of William of Wormegay. The marriage brought Reginald the lordship of Wormegay,

---

[5] Canton Beaumesnil, dépt. Eure, August le Prévôst, *Mémoires et notes pour servir à l'histoire du départment de l'Eure*, eds., L. Delisle and L. Passy (Evreux, 1862–9), 1: 177.

[6] Cheney, *Hubert Walter*, pp. 17–18; Young, *Hubert Walter*, pp. 5–6. Reginald de Warenne (d. 1178) was often present at court during Henry II's early years, *Itin. Hen. II*, pp. 26, 43, 67, 77; he was a royal justice several times between 1164 and 1175, *P.B.K.J.*, 3: App. III; he was sheriff of Sussex, 1170–6, *List of Sheriffs*, p. 141. For Geoffrey fitz Peter's pedigree, see *Complete Peerage*, 5: 122–3, note 'c'; *D.N.B.*, s.v. 'Fitzpeter, Geoffrey'. For Simon, see *Itin. Hen. II*, pp. 33, 63, 68, 85; Killingsworth, 'An edition of writs and charters of Henry II relating to Norfolk, Suffolk, Cambridge and Huntingdon', nos. 22, 23, 55, 79, 80, 121, 210.

fourteen and a quarter knight's fees in Norfolk and Suffolk.[7]
William's inheritance, which came through his maternal
grandfather, was centred near Lynn in Norfolk with other
manors scattered over Norfolk and Suffolk. In addition, he
inherited some holdings of the honour of Warenne from his
father, including land in Kent, Sussex, and Yorkshire.[8] Godfrey
de Lucy, of course, was the son of a baron, although his father
had not been born into the baronage, but had won his rank
through administrative service.

Richard fitz Neal was the son of a bishop – literally a member
of an episcopal *familia* – and in rank perhaps to be classed among
the baronial families, yet more properly placed with the
administrative families. Another justice, Ralph Foliot, was a
member of a famous ecclesiastical family that included the
bishops Gilbert and Robert Foliot. Ralph might be classed,
then, as also related to a baronial family. He was the nephew of
Gilbert Foliot, although his parents and place of birth are
unknown.[9] One of Gilbert's charters, issued in 1144 when he
was still bishop of Hereford, describes Ralph, one of the witnesses, as *nepote episcopi*.[10] Gilbert Foliot was 'a man with a powerful sense of family', and at Hereford and later at London he
provided generously for his relatives. Members of his family
among the canons and other officers of the two cathedrals num-
bered thirteen or fourteen.[11] It was only natural, then, for Ralph
Foliot to have chosen an ecclesiastical career.

As with Henry II's justices, most of his sons' judges came from
families among the ranks of the knights. Michael Belet, as we
have seen, inherited land in Lincolnshire, Northamptonshire,
and Oxfordshire. Hugh Bardolf also came from the middle
ranges of the knightly class. He was the son of Hugh Bardolf the
elder (c. 1120–6), who held tenements in Lincolnshire of the earl
of Chester and of the brothers Ralph and Richard de la Haye,
and also had holdings in Nottinghamshire and Derby. Hugh the

---

[7] He offered a 700 mark fine, *Pipe Roll 12 Hen. II*, p. 19; Charles T. Clay, *Early
Yorkshire Charters*, 8: *The Honour of Warenne* (Yorks Archaeol. Soc., Record Ser.,
extra ser., 6, 1949), p. 32.
[8] *Early Yorks Chtrs.*, 8: 33; *Honors and Knights' Fees*, 3: 323.
[9] On Gilbert Foliot's family, see Adrian Morey and C.N.L. Brooke, *Gilbert
Foliot and his Letters* (Cambridge, 1965), App. II.
[10] Morey and Brooke, *Letters and Charters of Gilbert Foliot*, p. 374, no. 312.
[11] Morey and Brooke, *Gilbert Foliot and his Letters*, pp. 44–5, 49.

elder married Isabel, possibly a member of the Twist family of South Carlton, Lincolnshire.[12] Osbert fitz Hervey had landholdings centred in Norfolk and Suffolk, although he had some land in Essex as well.[13] He was the brother of Hubert Walter, and through his aunt's marriage to Glanvill, the great justiciar's nephew. He is easily confused with another Osbert fitz Hervey, Glanvill's brother, who was undersheriff of Norfolk and Suffolk in 1182 and a royal justice on occasion in the 1180s.[14]

Four others came from the lower ranks of the knights. When Richard of Herriard first surfaces in the records in 1184, he is mentioned as a knight of Robert III, Earl of Leicester, pardoned of twenty shillings' scutage from land in Wiltshire.[15] Yet he took his name from a Hampshire village, and he also inherited land at Southrope in the same shire. Richard was a knight of William I, earl of Salisbury, pardoned of thirty-five shillings' scutage from his Hampshire land in 1191.[16] Additional holdings came to Herriard through marriage, when sometime before 1183 he married Ela, coheir with her sister of land in Somerford, Wiltshire.[17] Simon of Pattishall took his name from the Northamptonshire village. The 1166 Inquest of Knight's Fees lists two men of that toponymic, each holding at Pattishall a fifth part of a fee belonging to the honour of Wahull.[18] The pipe roll for 1192 lists Simon as holder of a knight's fee of the honour

---

[12] Clay, 'Hugh Bardolf', pp. 5–7, and genealogical table on p. 29.

[13] Manor of Dagworth, Suffolk, *Cal. Inq. Post Mort.*, 1: 147–8, no. 521; *Book of Fees*, 2: 916. Land of the count of Perche in Suffolk and land of the fee of William of Mountchesney in Norfolk, *Pipe Roll 9 John*, p. 113; *Rot. Lit. Claus.*, 1: 79. A knight's fee of the abbey of Bury St Edmunds, Suffolk, B.L. MS. Harl. 645, f. 25. Land at Tibenham, Norfolk, held of St Benet Holme Abbey, J.R. West, ed., *Register of St. Benet of Holme 1020–1210* (Norf. Rec. Soc.), 1: 121, no. 218; 140–1, no. 260. 60 A. at Doddinghurst, Essex, *Cal. Inq. Post Mort.*, 1: 129, no. 466.

[14] Mortimer, 'Family of Glanville', pp. 5–6, 9–10. For a reference to him as undersheriff, see *Chron. of Jocelin of Brakelond*, p. 53.

[15] *Pipe Roll 30 Hen. II*, pp. 94–5.

[16] *C.R.R.*, 1: 390; *Pipe Roll 3 & 4 Ric. I*, p. 121.

[17] He offered Henry II 20 marks to have his wife's inheritance, *Pipe Roll 30 Hen. II*, p. 84; *32 Hen. II*, p. 171. But a division of the inheritance had to be made with Walter Mautravers, son of Ela's sister, which occasioned litigation, *C.R.R.*, 10: 17–18; *Br. Note Book*, 3: 389–90, no. 1437, oblations for a final concord, *Pipe Roll 32 Hen. II*, pp. 163, 173; *33 Hen. II*, p. 198; oblation by Richard of 80 marks to have Walter's land, *Pipe Roll 7 Ric. I*, p. 139; *9 Ric. I*, p. 210. [18] *Complete Peerage*, 10: 311.

of Wahull, which must have been the same land held by other Pattishalls – presumably his ancestors – in 1166.[19]

The careers of Hubert Walter and Geoffrey fitz Peter were the sort that inspired critical comments by chroniclers and moralists, for they climbed from modest levels of knighthood to the heights of power. Their lives illustrate the immodest ambition which critics of medieval courtiers always condemned. Hubert Walter came from a family of the 'lower ranks of the feudal class', whose seat was at West Dereham, Norfolk.[20] His paternal grandfather held a small fee of the honour of Lancaster with manors in Lancashire, Norfolk and Suffolk. His mother brought more Suffolk land to her husband. She was coheir of Theobald of Valoignes, lord of Parham; but more important for Hubert's future, she was sister-in-law to Ranulf de Glanvill.[21] Geoffrey fitz Peter was born on the royal manor of Ludgershall, Wiltshire, where a royal castle stood, sometimes a residence of Henry II. Geoffrey's parents were Peter the forester of Ludgershall, who died a monk at Winchester, and his wife Matilda, who later married Hugh of Buckland.[22] Geoffrey may have been the brother of Simon fitz Peter (d. 1182–3?), who was a marshal of the royal household in 1165 and later sheriff of several shires. Nothing definite can be known of Geoffrey fitz Peter, however, before his first appearance among the *curiales*, c. 1182.

Less is known about the origins of the remaining three justices. Richard Barre was a kinsman of the Sifrewasts, a Berkshire family of some substance, but nothing more is known of his family. William de Sainte-Mère-Eglise and Master Thomas of Hurstbourne, like Geoffrey fitz Peter, were born on manors of the royal domain which the king sometimes visited, William a native of a ducal manor in Normandy and Master Thomas coming from King's Hurstbourne or Hurstbourne Regis in the forest of Chute, Hampshire.[23] Nothing is known of the status of

---

[19] *Pipe Roll 3 & 4 Ric. I*, p. 201; *Honors and Knights' Fees*, 1: 92.
[20] Young, *Hubert Walter*, pp. 5, 165; according to Cheney, p. 16, Hubert was from a family 'not of the first rank, yet holding estates by knight-service'.
[21] Cheney, *Hubert Walter*, pp. 16–17.   [22] *Complete Peerage*, 5: 122–3, note 'c'.
[23] Delisle, *Recueil*, introduction, p. 496; *D.N.B.*, s.v. 'William of Sainte-Mère-Eglise'. Hurstbourne Regis, now Hurstbourne Tarant, was part of the royal domain until Henry III granted it to the nuns of Tarant, Dorset, *V.C.H., Hants*, 4: 319–24.

either man's parents, except that William's mother was still living at Sainte-Mère-Eglise in 1195 sharing a pension with her son.[24] Bright youths of less than knightly rank residing on royal manors may have had opportunities for schooling and careers in the king's service denied to others. This is little more than speculation; however, it was not uncommon for inhabitants of the royal domain on either side of the Channel to find employment in the king's service.[25]

Nothing is known of Thomas of Hurstbourne's schooling, although his title of *magister* indicates some advanced schooling at a cathedral school or university. Of Richard's regular staff of justices, Thomas is the only one addressed as 'Master'. William de Sainte-Mère-Eglise must have received some early formal education, but no clue remains to reveal where or what sort. Since he began witnessing Henry II's charters as a *clericus de camera* about 1180, he must have entered the royal household as a youth. The royal court itself could have been his chief school; Henry II's court was no mean intellectual centre. Neither can anything concrete be known of Ralph Foliot's education, although he most likely studied at Hereford, a centre of higher learning in the second half of the twelfth century.[26] Ralph seems to have remained at Hereford as a member of the episcopal household from the time of his uncle's translation to London in 1163 until about 1180.[27]

Certainly Ralph was a man of some intellectual and spiritual interests. He left his collection of about twenty books to Hereford Cathedral, whose titles indicate surprisingly spiritual interests for a professional royal servant. His library consisted chiefly of glossed manuscripts of books of the Bible, but it also contained Honorius of Autun's *Gemma Animae*, Peter Lombard's

---

[24] Thomas Stapleton, ed., *Magni Rotuli de scaccarii normanniae sub regibus angliae*, Soc. Antiq. of London (1840–41), 1: clxxvi, 276.

[25] T.F. Tout, *Chapters in the administrative history of medieval England* (Manchester, 1920–33), 1: 117, n. 3.

[26] Kathleen Edwards, *The English Secular Cathedral* (Manchester, 1967), pp. 189–91. J.C. Russell, 'Hereford and Arabic Science in England', *Isis*, 18 (1932): 14, 19–20.

[27] In Nov. 1177, Ralph was described as 'clerk of the bishop of Hereford', W.D. Macray, ed., *Charters and Documents illustrating the History of the Cathedral, City, and Diocese of Salisbury*, Rolls Series (London, 1891), pp. 40–1, no. 48. In Dec. 1178 he was described as 'canon of the church of Hereford', Morey and Brooke, *Letters and Charters of Gilbert Foliot*, p. 449, no. 410.

Four Books of Sentences, and an untitled treatise beginning: *Quicunque vult salvus esse, hanc fidem teneat.*[28] That Ralph had some intellectual interests is further indicated by his friendship with Gerald of Wales, who had several friends among the Hereford canons. The archdeacon wrote a letter in support of Gerald's claim to the church at Chesterton, Oxfordshire. Following Ralph's death Gerald wrote to his chaplains and clerks, urging their prayers for his soul; and he also sent a letter of condolence to Ralph's brother William Foliot, precentor of Hereford. In his letter, Gerald described Ralph as one of the 'twin gems of the clergy', and 'a brilliant man, a remarkable man, and a man among very few men'.[29]

It is possible to be more precise about the education of the remaining four clerics among the justices. We have already seen that Richard fitz Neal received his early education from the monks at Ely, and that Godfrey de Lucy studied first in the schools of London and later abroad. That they both had some acquaintance with the learned law has been shown. They cannot have been the only royal justices in the last quarter of the twelfth century to have had an awareness of the principles of civil and canon law. The author of *Glanvill* assuredly had some knowledge of Roman law. Although the author of this treatise bearing the great justiciar's name is unknown, it is likely that he was one of the royal justices of Richard I who had begun their careers on the bench during Glanvill's justiciarship, more likely one of the five clerics in this group.[30]

Study of civil or canon law was becoming a well-travelled route to a successful career in the late twelfth century, and English students were taking the road to Bologna in increasing numbers. Yet only one of Richard I's royal justices, Richard Barre, can definitely be shown to have gone there. A poem written by one of his companions at Bologna predicted that he would handle the suits of bishops and the business of kings, and

---

[28] Arthur T. Bannister, *A Descriptive Catalogue of the Manuscripts in the Hereford Cathedral Library* (Hereford, 1927), p. iii.

[29] *Gerald of Wales*, 1: 262–3, 270, 334–5. The other 'gem' was Peter de Leche, archdeacon of Worcester.

[30] On the question of authorship, see *Glanvill*, pp. xxxi–xxxiii. Hall concludes that it was not Glanvill, Hubert Walter, or Geoffrey fitz Peter, but an unknown royal clerk. Of the five clerics who joined the bench late in Glanvill's justiciarship, Godfrey de Lucy seems the strongest candidate.

that they would reward him with pleasure and riches. The poem was recalled by Stephen of Tournai in a letter to Richard congratulating him on his new post as archdeacon of Ely; the letter makes clear that they had been fellow students at Bologna, probably around 1150.[31] Stephen, an eminent canonist who lived at Orléans and Paris before he became bishop of Tournai in 1192, formed an important link between Bolognese decretists and the Anglo-Norman school of canon law.

Evidence survives which enables us to see the archdeacon of Ely as more than a careerist clerk. His friendship with Stephen of Tournai, lasting for years after they left Bologna, says something about his intellectual powers. Stephen's treatment of the problem of 'criminous clerks' closely resembled Henry II's views, and Anglo-Norman canonists borrowed from his *Summa decreti*. Richard Barre certainly knew his friend's work, and he would have found in it justification for his service with Henry II during the Becket conflict. Indeed, it is tempting to nominate him as author of an anonymous treatise, *Summa de multiplicis juris divisione*, which bases royal jurisdiction over clerics accused of civil crimes on the English tradition of the King's Peace.[32] Also, Richard's authorship of a biblical compendium reveals intellectual pretensions and perhaps some depth of Christian devotion. Richard Barre dedicated his *Compendium de veteris et novo testamento* to William Longchamp. Richard explained in the preface that he had selected the most important passages of each book of the Bible, arranging them according to topics, and placing subject-headings in the margins 'in the manner of Roman law-books' for the convenience of a busy statesman.[33]

According to Hubert Walter's own words, it was his uncle Ranulf de Glanvill and his wife Bertha who brought him up (*qui nos nutrierunt*).[34] The abbot of Reading who had long known and

---

[31] J. de Silve, ed. *Lettres d'Etienne de Tournai* (Paris, 1893), pp. 346–7, no. 275. For Stephen's career, see Kuttner and Rathbone, 'Anglo-Norman Canonists', pp. 293, 296.

[32] Pembroke College, Cambridge, MS.72. See Richard M. Fraher, 'The Becket Dispute and two decretist traditions: the Bolognese masters revisited and some new Anglo-Norman texts', *Jl. of Medieval Hist.*, 4(1978): 347–68.

[33] Two mss. survive: a fifteenth-century one, B.L. MS.Harl. 3255, and another, Lambeth Palace MS. 105.

[34] Foundation charter of West Dereham Abbey, B.L. MS.Add. 46,353, f. 8, printed in *Monasticon*, 6, pt. 2: 899. Cf. a grant to Reading Abbey, B.L. MS.Egerton 3031, ff. 52V–53, here the phrase is *qui nos educaverunt*.

admired the archbishop wrote in 1197 that he had been 'trained from the cradle in secular studies (*secularibus disciplinis*)', and while still a youth though one 'of astonishing wisdom', he had come to the courts where he won the gratitude of all for his protection of the poor and oppressed.[35] The archbishop, hesitating to involve himself in discussion with Abbot Samson of Bury St Edmunds, admitted his inferiority to the abbot in skill as a debater (*disputator*) and clerk (*clericus*).[36] This evidence suggests that Hubert Walter had spent little or no time in the schools. No doubt, he received some tutoring in the *trivium* from clerks on Glanvill's staff. His own intelligence combined with close observation of his uncle gave him an education in Exchequer procedures and English law through direct experience that made him an acknowledged expert.

No less an authority than Maitland nominated Hubert Walter as the possible author of *Glanvill*, and others have maintained that he had studied Roman law at Bologna.[37] Yet no strong evidence supports such speculation. The supposition rests on the slim evidence of an obituary calendar of benefactors for a chapel at Bologna honouring St Thomas Becket, built by English students there. The name of Hubert Walter, lord of Canterbury, does appear on the list, but he could have been a benefactor of the chapel without ever having enrolled in the Bolognese schools.[38]

Hubert Walter's reputation for legal learning may have rested on his mastery of English law, but he and other churchmen on the bench had some experience with canon law. In 1187, Hubert Walter could be observed acting as a papal judge-

---

[35] Giles Constable, 'An unpublished letter by Abbot Hugh II of Reading concerning Archbishop Hubert Walter', in *Essays in Medieval History presented to Bertie Wilkinson*, eds. T.A. Sandquist and M.R. Powicke (Toronto, 1969), text of letter, pp. 29–31, from MS.Douai, Bibliothèque Municipale, 887, f. 106.

[36] *Chron. of Jocelin of Brakelond*, p. 84. *Gerald of Wales*, 3: 30, told an anecdote about Richard Lionheart correcting Hubert's grammar once when the archbishop was speaking Latin.

[37] Pollock and Maitland, 1: 164; Hall in *Glanvill*, p. xxxii, finds Maitland's argument 'not convincing'.

[38] Cheney, *Hubert Walter*, p. 18, argues this way. See also Cheney's 'Hubert Walter and Bologna', *Bull. of Medieval Canon Law*, new ser. 2 (1972): 81–4. For an opposing view, see H.G. Richardson's introduction to *Mem. Roll 1 John*, p. lxii, and with G.O. Sayles, *Law and Legislation from Aethelberht to Magna Carta* (Edinburgh, 1966), p. 74.

delegate in a case heard at St Katherine's Chapel in Westminster Abbey, conveniently near the house of the Exchequer.[39] As papal legate from 1195 to 1198, he was the pope's highest legal official in the kingdom, and he had to give some attention to the Church courts as well as to the *curia regis*. As Hubert Walter himself said, he had 'the two swords committed to his custody'. Abbot Samson of Bury St Edmunds and St Hugh of Lincoln accused the archbishop of confusing his spiritual and temporal responsibilities on some occasions, and the chronicle of Glastonbury Abbey pictures the justiciar, Richard fitz Neal, William de Sainte-Mère-Eglise, and the bishop of Salisbury hearing an ecclesiastical case *ad scaccarium regis*.[40] Clerical members of the judiciary could not avoid some contact with the Church's legal system. After all, three of them were bishops and five were archdeacons at one time or another. Even though they were frequently absent from their posts, they did gain some experience as ecclesiastical judges.[41]

Evidence for the education of the seven laymen on the bench is much sketchier than that for clerics, but lack of evidence for their schooling can no longer be considered proof of their illiteracy. The old identification of *clericus* with *literatus* and *laicus* with *illiteratus* is no longer tenable, as recent scholarship has shown.[42] Indeed, it would be difficult to doubt the literacy of Geoffrey fitz Peter, whom Lady Stenton supported as a candidate for author of *Glanvill*. Other scholars have suggested that

---

[39] Cheney, *Hubert Walter*, p. 26.

[40] *Chron. of Jocelin of Brakelond*, pp. 82–5. Abbot Samson accused Hubert Walter of both hearing secular lawsuits and inspecting religious houses on a visit to Norfolk and Suffolk. Decima L. Douie and Hugh Farmer, eds., *Magna Vita Sancti Hugonis*, Medieval Texts (London, 1961–2), 2: 28–9. Hugh of Lincoln wanted to know by virtue of which sword the archbishop forbade him from punishing a clerk who had insisted on impleading a man in secular court in a case involving corporal punishment, despite the bishop's prohibition. See below chap. 6, pt. 2. For the justices acting as ecclesiastical judges, see Hearne ed., *Adami de Domerham Historia*, 3: 364, date c. 18 Oct. 1196.

[41] E.g. Richard Barre in 1184 witnessed papal judges-delegates' arbitration of a case concerning Missenden Abbey, *Cart. Missenden Abbey*, 1: 220, no. 247. He was a papal judge-delegate himself in a dispute between the rector of Manchester and the monks of Lenton, c. 1198–1213, pp. 330–1. William de Sainte-Mère-Eglise, after he became bishop was called by Innocent III frequently to be a papal judge-delegate, *Magna Vita Sancti Hugonis*, 1: xxxiii.

[42] Turner, 'The *Miles Literatus*', *A.H.R.*, 83: 928–45; Clanchy, *From Memory to Written Record*; Murray, *Reason and Society in M.A.*, pp. 263–70.

he began his career as a clerk for Thomas fitz Bernard, chief royal forester, or for one of the chief justiciars, Richard de Lucy or Ranulf de Glanvill.[43] In no surviving documents, however, is Geoffrey fitz Peter ever called *clericus*. No one would suggest that he was a *clericus* in the religious sense, that is, in holy orders or at least tonsured. Of course, he could well have been a *clericus* in the bookish sense of a scribe, secretary, or accountant. The meaning of the word is as imprecise in medieval Latin as is 'clerk' in modern English.[44] It seems more plausible that Geoffrey's career began as an estate steward or bailiff for Thomas fitz Bernard. Whatever the details of his early employment, he almost certainly picked up a knowledge of Latin along the way.

There were no schools and hardly any textbooks for the study of English law before the appearance of *Glanvill* between 1187 and 1189. Only a few antiquarian collections of laws – sometimes incorporating forgeries – were available earlier.[45] Not until the first decade of the thirteenth century would the English equivalent of schools of *ars notaria* or 'business schools' come into being.[46] Before the opening of these schools, any advanced training was purely practical, based on novices' observation of experienced officials at work. Everyday experience under the supervision of an expert was preferred to a university degree as the proper preparation for a life of government service. Richard fitz Neal expressed doubt about the value of Scholastic studies in the schools. He claimed that his *Dialogus de Scaccario* was more valuable than the books of philosophers, providing information that was *non subtilia sed utilia*.[47] Richard's *Dialogus* itself illustrates such a practical apprenticeship, as the master-clerk initiates a novice into the mysteries of the Exchequer. The same situation prevailed for those seeking careers

---

[43] *P.B.K.F.*, 1: 9–10; also Stenton, *Rolls of Justices for Lincs and Worcs.*, p. xxl, suggests that Geoffrey was a clerk of the *curia regis* for the justiciar. Painter, *Reign of King John*, p. 11, says that Geoffrey started his career as Glanvill's clerk. *Justiciarship*, p. 99, suggests that he was the clerk of Thomas fitz Bernard.

[44] On medieval usage of the word *clericus*, see Turner, 'The *Miles Literatus*', pp. 930–1, and Murray, *Reason and Society in M.A.*, pp. 263–4.

[45] Plucknett, *Early Eng. Legal Lit.*, pp. 19–33; Richardson and Sayles, *Law and Legislation*, pp. 120–31.

[46] Turner, 'The *Miles Literatus*', p. 943.

[47] *Dial. de Scac.*, p. 5. See also M.T. Clanchy, '*Moderni* in education and government in England', *Speculum*, 50 (1975).

in the courts. Most twelfth-century knights gained knowledge of English law through years of attending the courts, local and royal. After all, 'suit to court' had long been a basic feudal obligation. Since English common law grew chiefly out of native traditions, with only limited influence from the learned law of the schools, such a practical training was more useful than academic study.[48] A university degree, then, was not the only ticket to a successful career in the royal government.

Without powerful friends in high places no one could even begin a career. A patron was essential, or perhaps a series of patrons leading up to the justiciar or the king himself, if one were truly ambitious. It is easy to identify the patrons of the three members of the episcopate on the bench: Hubert Walter, Godfrey de Lucy, and Richard fitz Neal. They all had close relatives in high office to sponsor their entry into the royal government and to secure ecclesiastical benefices for their financial support.

Five others seem to have been longtime *familiares regis*, members of Henry II's household who moved to the service of the justiciar. Michael Belet, as has been shown, was a member of Henry II's household from 1166, holding the post of *pincerna*. His years as a justice beginning in 1176 acquainted him with the future justiciars Ranulf de Glanvill, Hubert Walter, and Geoffrey fitz Peter. Belet became a substantial property holder in Norfolk through his marriage to the daughter and coheir of John de Cheney, and this must have strengthened his ties with Glanvill and Hubert Walter, fellow East Anglians at Westminster.[49] Hugh Bardolf began his career as *dapifer* or *senescallus regis* in the household of Henry II around 1180.[50] By about 1185, however, Hugh was moving from the royal household into the sphere of the justiciar, working as a royal justice and Exchequer officer.[51]

---

[48] Turner, 'Roman law before Bracton', pp. 19–21; Palmer, 'Origins of the legal profession in England', pp. 134–5.

[49] *C.R.R.*, 2: 208, 266; *Cal. Chtr. Rolls*, 2: 302, where their son gave the manor of Rudham to the canons of Coxford.

[50] He witnessed a number of royal charters in Normandy and Maine, 1180–3: Delisle, *Recueil*, 2: 135, 159, 181, 216, 227, 237, 240; *Itin. Hen. II*, pp. 239, 252, 253.

[51] Glanvill entrusted him with transport of money for the defence of the Welsh marches, *Pipe Roll 31 Hen. II*, p. 7. Hugh was at Winchester, Dec. 1186, counting, weighting, and sacking the royal treasure, *Pipe Roll 33 Hen. II*, p. xxxix; *Itin. Hen. II*, p. 275. He assessed scutages and tallages in the Southwest, 1187, *Pipe Roll 33 Hen. II*, pp. 147, 156.

Hugh did not return to the Continent with Henry II after 1184 except early in 1187 when he and Glanvill were with the king until Easter.[52] A third knight, Geoffrey fitz Peter first appears among the *familiares regis* c. 1182–3, when he accompanied Henry II and Glanvill to the Continent. The Norman Exchequer rolls for 1184 record the king's gift of fifteen pounds to him.[53]

Two clerics on the bench began their careers in the royal service as clerks for Henry II. Ralph Foliot, archdeacon of Hereford, is described as *regis sigillarius* in a charter witness-list from 1183–4, although he sometimes left Henry II's side to serve on diplomatic missions.[54] Two or three years later he began to witness fines occasionally as a royal justice. He was at Westminster with Glanvill in November 1188, and he met Hubert Walter, witnessing one of his charters, probably shortly before his departure for the Holy Land.[55] Ralph joined the new justiciar at Westminster in June 1194, and Hubert named him to the northern circuit of the 1194 eyre. Nothing is known of William de Sainte-Mère-Eglise before he entered Henry II's household about 1180 as a *clericus de camera,* accepting receipts for the chamber.[56] Besides his chamber work, William may have performed some duties of a chancery clerk, for he witnessed many royal charters and writs on both sides of the Channel in the years 1180–9.[57] William was abroad with Henry II almost all the time from February 1187 until the king's death; indeed, he was beside Henry's deathbed on 6 July 1189.[58]

None of this group of justices was a *familiaris* of Richard I, that is, a member of his ducal household before he inherited the throne. Only two had close ties with him. William de Sainte-

[52] *Pipe Roll 33 Hen. II*, p. 210; *Itin. Hen. II*, p. 278.
[53] Delisle, *Recueil*, introduction, p. 334; 2: 233, 240; *Itin. Hen. II*, pp. 239, 259, 253.
[54] Morey and Brooke, *Letters and Charters of Gilbert Foliot*, pp. 443–4, no. 404; meeting with papal legates, *Gesta Hen. Secundi*, 2: 4; embassy to Paris with William Marshal, *L'Histoire de Guillaume le Maréchal*, ed. Paul Meyer, Société de l'histoire de France (Paris, 1891–1901), lines 8311–34.
[55] B.L. MS.Harl. 391, f. 101. Hubert was bishop of Salisbury.
[56] Delisle, *Recueil*, 2: 230, 246, 268, 272, 281, 283, 305, 420, 421; *Pipe Roll 26 Hen. II*, p. 130; *1 Ric. I*, pp. 21, 225; *2 Ric. I*, p. 131.
[57] *Docs. preserved in France*, writs: nos. 483, 699; charters: nos. 43, 866, 1026, 1037, 1038, 1421. Delisle, *Recueil*, 2: writ, no. 669; charters, nos. 554, 580, 661, 665, 681, 687, 716, 750, 764, 765, 766, 767.
[58] Delisle, *Recueil*, Introduction, p. 499.

Mère-Eglise continued to move about with the court as a chamber clerk, and he travelled with the crusading party as it made its way across France as far as Vézelay.[59] He succeeded Hubert Walter as *protonotarius* or king's secretary in spring 1193. By that time William was closely associated with Hubert, accompanying him on a visit to the captive king in Germany and assisting in conducting the ransom money there.[60] Hubert Walter, of course, went on Richard's crusade, and it was the making of his reputation. In the Holy Land, Hubert showed outstanding qualities of leadership, and he won the respect of Richard Lionheart. When he was crossing Sicily on his return from Palestine, he learned of the king's capture and rushed to Germany to see him.[61] Richard, confident of his ability and his loyalty, named him justiciar by the end of 1193.

The other clerics among the justices started their careers in more conventional ways, only joining the *curia regis* after they had secured some experience elsewhere. Ralph Foliot enjoyed the patronage of his uncle, Bishop Gilbert Foliot, whose household he had joined at Hereford as early as 1144. Ralph remained at Hereford Cathedral as a canon after Gilbert departed for St Paul's, and he became archdeacon sometime before the spring of 1182. Probably shortly before his promotion to the archdeaconate, Ralph entered the king's service as a chancery clerk.[62]

Master Thomas of Hurstbourne can be connected with Glastonbury Abbey before he entered the royal service c. 1182–3.[63] His first patron was Abbot Robert of Glastonbury (1173–80), who named him parson of two churches.[64] He was receiving an

---

59 He witnessed expenditures for precious stones, robes, armour, etc., *Pipe Roll 1 Ric. I*, pp. 11, 225. He witnessed royal charters in England, Sept.–Nov. 1189, *Itin. Ric. I*, pp. 5, 6, 14, and in France, spring and summer 1190, *Itin. Ric. I*, pp. 26, 29, 33, 36.

60 *Roger Howden*, 3: 209, royal letter of 19 April 1193. *Pipe Roll 6 Ric. I*, pp. xiv, 242–3, for his journey to Germany.

61 Cheney, *Hubert Walter*, pp. 38, 44.

62 Brooke and Brooke, 'Hereford Cathedral dignitaries', p. 16. By spring 1182 he was at the Exchequer witnessing a grant with other royal officials, *H.M.C. Reports, Wells*, 1: 21.

63 *P.R.O., 35th Deputy Keeper's Report*, p. 16, D.L. Chtrs., Box A, no. 163. He joined Glanvill, Prince John, and royal servants in witnessing a charter.

64 To Ashbury, Berks, and Christian-Malford, Wilts, *Adam de Domerham*, 2: 487.

annual pension of ten marks by the time of Abbot Robert's death.[65] Once the abbey was vacant, it fell into the king's hand, and the royal custodian John Cumin may be the one who introduced Thomas to the royal administration. Cumin was one of Henry II's stalwarts in the Becket conflict, whose devotion to the king earned him the archbishopric of Dublin in 1182.[66] After Thomas of Hurstbourne entered Henry II's service, he worked chiefly as a custodian of ecclesiastical properties, and he continued to hold custodies after joining the judiciary in 1185. Possibly it was his zeal as an administrator of vacant ecclesiastical properties that attracted Glanvill's attention.[67]

Richard Barre's name is first found on charter witness-lists c. 1160–6, where he appears among the *familia* of Robert de Chesney, bishop of Lincoln.[68] Sometime before 1169, Richard had become a clerk of the royal household; a letter of Henry II describes him and his associates as *clericos et familiaros nostros*.[69] Barre went on two missions to the papal *curia* for the king on business connected with the Becket controversy.[70] Sometime after Richard's return from Italy in 1171, he joined the court of Henry the young king as chancellor; but he refused to follow the young king into rebellion, and he returned to Henry II with the boy's seal.[71] It must have been shortly after Richard left the court of the young king that he became archdeacon of Lisieux, most likely through the king's influence with Bishop Arnulf.[72]

From 1173 until 1190, there is little evidence of activity by the archdeacon of Lisieux, except for a diplomatic mission in 1188 made after Henry II had taken the cross. Richard Barre took royal letters to the German emperor, the king of Hungary, and the Eastern emperor at Constantinople seeking safe passage

---

[65] *Pipe Roll 27 Hen. II*, p. 15. Also he and James, a monk, received £5 *pro negotio ejusdem abbatie.*   [66] *Pipe Roll 27 Hen. II*, p. 163.

[67] The monks of Abingdon Abbey appealed to Glanvill against Thomas's exploitation, *Chron. mon. Abingdon*, 2: 297–8.

[68] *Episcopal acta*, 1, Lincoln, pp. 73–74, no. 112; p. 77, no. 119; p. 132, no. 212.

[69] He witnessed a royal charter at Bures possibly as early as 1165, Delisle, *Recueil*, 1: 536; appointment as an agent to the papal court, autumn 1169, *M.T.B.*, 7:85, no. 564.

[70] In winter 1169–70, *M.T.B.*, 7: 85; and in spring 1171, *Roger Howden*, 2: 25–8; *Gesta Hen. Secundi*, 1: 19–22; *M.T.B.*, 7: 471–5, no. 750.

[71] *Roger Howden*, 2: 46; *Gesta Hen. Secundi*, 1: 43.

[72] Delisle, *Recueil*, introduction, p. 425.

across their lands for the crusaders.[73] He was rarely in England before he surrendered his post at Lisieux to become archdeacon of Ely in 1190.[74] He crossed the channel in the train of the new bishop of Ely, William Longchamp, Count Richard's chancellor in Poitou who was to become royal chancellor now that his master had succeeded to the English crown. Through Longchamp's patronage, Barre returned to England to begin a new phase in his career.[75]

Three of the laymen among the justices seem to have had ties with Glanvill, and later with his nephew, that account for their appointment to the judiciary. Obviously, among the three is Osbert fitz Hervey, Hubert Walter's brother. No doubt, Geoffrey fitz Peter had a longstanding friendship with Glanvill going back to 1182 or earlier. He joined Glanvill and Hubert Walter in witnessing a transfer of land from the canons of Butley to the justiciar's new religious foundation, Leiston Abbey.[76] Perhaps he had already gained some experience by aiding his brother Simon in administering his several shrievalties. Certainly he had assisted Thomas fitz Bernard, *magister forestarius et justitiarius per totam Angliam*, whom he replaced when Thomas gave up his post.[77] Geoffrey followed Thomas as sheriff of Northampton-shire; he took control of Thomas's manor of Kinver, Stafford-shire; and he won custody of heirs who had been in Thomas's care.[78] The *Rotuli de Dominabus* of 1185 list Geoffrey as guardian of several heiresses, among them the two daughters of William de Say, coheirs to estates in Norfolk and cousins to the earl of Essex.[79] This wardship gave him an interest in East Anglian

---

[73] *Ralph de Diceto*, 2: 51–4.

[74] Richard's presence in England before then can be documented in only one or two instances: At Oxford with the justiciar, Sept. 1172, Charles T. Clay, 'Yorkshire final concords of the reign of Henry II', *Yorks Archaeol. Jl.*, 40 (1959): 82, no. 1; in 1184 and sometime between 1177 and 1189 he witnessed Missenden Abbey documents, *Cart. Missenden Abbey*, 1: 22, no. 247; 2: 2, no. 267.   [75] *Fasti, Mon. Cath.*, p. 30.

[76] *Monasticon*, 6, pt. 2: 881. Also Richard Mortimer, ed., *Leiston Abbey Cartulary and Butley Priory Charters*, Suffolk Charters, Suff. Rec. Soc. (1977), 1: 76–7, no. 27, date c. 1186–9.

[77] *Gesta Hen. Secundi*, 1: 323. Pipe roll entries for 1185 show Geoffrey heading forest eyres in a number of counties.

[78] *Pipe Roll 30 Hen. II*, p. 69. Thomas declared that he had delivered Kinver to 'serjeants of the forest'. *Rot. de Dominabus*, p. 29; *Pipe roll 31 Hen. II*, p. 27; *List of Sheriffs*, p. 92.

[79] *Rot. de Dominabus*, pp. 29, 39, 40.

affairs shared with Glanvill and his nephew, an interest that expanded after one of Geoffrey's wards became his wife.

Geoffrey fitz Peter was several times in Glanvill's company with the king before he first joined the justiciar in November. Also in 1188, Geoffrey had joined Glanvill in witnessing an important charter for Hubert Walter, the foundation charter for his abbey at West Dereham.[80] Another indication of Geoffrey's friendship with the justiciar is his agreement to act as a pledge for the large oblation Glanvill's son-in-law had to offer for Richard I's goodwill.[81] Geoffrey fitz Peter continued to be closely associated with the justiciarship under Glanvill's nephew, Hubert Walter.

William de Warenne's East Anglian background gave him an early acquaintance with the two justiciars. Wormegay was not far from West Dereham, Hubert's birthplace. William witnessed the foundation charter of West Dereham Abbey and also a gift made to it by the earl of Clare.[82] Hubert Walter was most likely responsible for William's career as a royal justice. William was at the Bench in Michaelmas term 1193, but his career really began in 1194 after Hubert Walter became justiciar. He was with Hubert at Reading on 14 February 1194, not long after the archbishop had become justiciar.[83] In July or August 1194, when Hubert Walter sent special justices to York to investigate the canons' complaints against their archbishop, one of those chosen was William de Warenne.[84]

Two who entered the judiciary under Richard I probably owed their appointments to the patronage of Geoffrey fitz Peter. Both Geoffrey and Simon of Pattishall were associated with the county of Northampton. In 1190 – the year Simon first served as a justice – he was custodian of escheats in Northamptonshire, and he had custody of Northampton Castle.[85] At that time the sheriff was Geoffrey fitz Peter, who held the post until the spring of 1194. Richard I on his return to England removed a number of sheriffs, and he replaced Geoffrey with Simon.

---

80 B.L. MS.Add. 46,353, f. 8; *Monasticon*, 6, pt. 2: 899.
81 *Pipe Roll 5 Ric. I*, p. 9.   82 B.L. MS.Add. 46, 353, ff. 8, 11.
83 *Mem. Roll 1 John*, p. lxxiv. He witnessed a writ.
84 *Roger Howden*, 3: 261–2; Madox, *Exchequer*, 1: 35.
85 *Pipe Roll 2 Ric. I*, pp. 6, 26. A document in *Roger Howden*, 3: 136, dated 28 July 1191, states that Simon was custodian of Northampton Castle.

Earlier, Simon had followed Geoffrey as sheriff of Essex and Hertfordshire; Geoffrey was sheriff, 1190–3, and Simon of Pattishall, 1193–4.[86] Clearly, such intertwining of careers was not solely a matter of chance, and Simon witnessed one of Geoffrey's private charters, c. 1190–1.[87] After Geoffrey became justiciar, his reliance upon Simon of Pattishall for important responsibilities at the Bench also points toward their long acquaintance.

The evidence of Geoffrey's patronage is clearer for Richard of Herriard. His first administrative post was as Geoffrey's undersheriff for Essex and Hertfordshire in 1192.[88] On the date that Richard first appeared at the Bench at Westminster – 24 May 1194 – Geoffrey was also present. Richard continued throughout his career to have close ties with Geoffrey fitz Peter; indeed, the justiciar took custody of Richard's land and heir on his death in 1208.[89] After Geoffrey became justiciar in 1198, Richard witnessed most of his legal writs, carried messages for him, went on circuit with him in summer and autumn 1202, and made gifts to one of the justiciar's religious foundations.[90] No doubt, Hubert Walter recruited him for his judiciary on Geoffrey's recommendation. Richard was a knight of two great barons, however, who may have afforded him early patronage.[91]

It is not surprising that most of the 'professional' justices serving in Richard's reign came from knightly, rural backgrounds similar to Henry II's justices. What becomes clearer in the time of Richard Lionheart is the crucial role of the justiciar in the selection of judges. Although five of them had been members of Henry II's household, Glanvill apparently was able to recruit them for his staff. Others had ties either with Glanvill or with his

---

86 *List of Sheriffs*, p. 43; *Pipe Roll 7 Ric. I*, p. 217; Harris, 'English Sheriffs in the Reign of King John', p. 200.
87 B.L. MS.Egerton, 3031, f. 45.   88 *Pipe Roll 3 & 4 Ric. I*, p. 167.
89 *Rot. Lit. Claus.*, 1: 109b. Richard witnessed one of Geoffrey's private charters, Westminster Domesday, f. 469ᵛ; and he made a gift of 5 marks to Witney Priory, *C.R.R.*, 10: 336; and building a stone church, B.L. MS.Cott. Claud. D. iii, f. 146ᵛ.
90 *Rot. de Obl. et Fin.*, p. 181; *Mem. Roll 1 John*, p. 33; *C.R.R.*, 2: 213, 231, 236; Elsa de Haas and G.D.G. Hall, eds., *Early Registers of Writs*, Selden Soc., 87 (London, 1970): lxvi.
91 Robert III earl of Leicester, *Pipe Roll 30 Hen. II*, pp. 94–5; William I earl of Salisbury, *Pipe Roll 3 & 4 Ric. I*, p. 121. Richard witnessed two charters for Earl William, *The Great Cartulary of Glastonbury*, ed. Aelred Watkins (Somerset Rec. Soc., 1947–56), 1: 200–1; *Cat. Anc. Deeds*, 4: 527, no. A10254.

nephew. None could be termed a *familiaris* of Richard I except
Hubert Walter, who became an 'inseparable companion' of the
king while with the crusading army.[92] Clearly, the justiciar had
considerable freedom in choosing his judicial bench. This marks
a contrast with Henry II's justices, at least five of whom came
from the *privata familia regis*.

4 THE REWARDS OF RICHARD I'S JUSTICES

For the ambitious, a place in the royal household or at the
Exchequer offered opportunities to move ahead. Royal office
could bring advancement, although the advance of some was
more spectacular than that of others. Obviously those justices
who moved in circles close to the throne, giving counsel on
great matters of state, were able to reap a richer reward than
were those who only did ordinary daily work of administration.
The honours, favours, and material wealth that Hubert Walter
or Geoffrey fitz Peter accumulated are in a different category
from the rewards of those who confined their work to the
Bench. The two justiciars' rise from the lower levels of the
knightly class to a place second only to the king tempted other
royal servants with the possibilities open to them, while it tor-
mented chroniclers in aristocratic monasteries who observed
such social instability with alarm. Commentators criticized
Hubert Walter for 'his extravagant outlays on living in great
state, on keeping a grand table, on a splendid throng of clerks
and knights and retainers, on rich presents, on sumptuous
buildings'.[1] In short, his lavish spending typified for them the
'self-made man'.

Three of the seven clerics among the 'professional' justices
won bishoprics at the beginning of Richard I's reign. On 15
September 1189, the new monarch named Richard fitz Neal
bishop of London, Hubert Walter bishop of Salisbury, and Godfrey de Lucy bishop of Winchester. One other entered the episcopate toward the end of the reign. In September 1198, William
de Sainte-Mère-Eglise was elected bishop of London *ex largitione*

---

[92] Cheney, *Hubert Walter*, p. 36.
[1] *Ralph of Coggeshall*, pp. 156–60; cf. *Gerald of Wales*, 1: 426–7.

regis Ricardi.[2] A difficulty in assessing the rewards that these bishop-judges accumulated is the impossibility of isolating their personal possessions from episcopal properties, a distinction they themselves sometimes found difficult to visualize. Hubert Walter and Godfrey de Lucy both worked to increase the resources of their sees, confident that in doing so they were enhancing their own wealth and power.[3]

It is useful to remember that eight justices were not in the higher councils of government, but were concentrating their energies on the work of justice. These – three churchmen and five laymen – had to be content with a lower level of expectation than the six multi-purpose officials of the old tradition. They could hardly hope to imitate Geoffrey fitz Peter in leaping from the lesser knightly level to an earldom. Yet a survey of the eight indicates that they were able to increase their landholdings, or if clerics, to secure several benefices.

A benefit of royal service was the special protection that the king extended to his servants. Barons of the Exchequer enjoyed exemption from most financial levies while in the king's service, a privilege that probably extended to the justices of the Bench as well.[4] Barons of the Exchequer also enjoyed the privilege of being excused from pleas brought against them during the Exchequer sessions, another privilege that extended to royal justices' terms.[5] When justices and other royal servants brought their own suits in the *curia regis*, they paid little or nothing for writs that were sometimes costly for ordinary litigants.

More important than these privileges was the king's provision for maintenance of his officers. He provided for them in a variety of *ad hoc* ways without any scheme for payment of salaries. A normal method of maintenance for civil servants throughout the Middle Ages was a system of fees collected for

---

[2] Hubert Walter gave 'a very broad hint' to the St Paul's chapter that William's candidacy had his and the king's support, Cheney, *Hubert Walter*, p. 80.

[3] E.g. Godfrey's attempts to regain two of the bishopric of Winchester's manors, Meon and Wargrave, *Pipe Roll 1 Ric. I*, pp. 182, 186; *Roger Howden*, 3: 18; *Cal. Chtr. Rolls*, 3: 356.

[4] *Dial. de Scac.*, pp. 46–8; pardon of payments owed by Hugh Bardolf *per libertatem sedendi ad scaccarium*, *Pipe Roll 5 Ric. I*, p. 54; *3 John*, p. 209; pardon to Richard of Herriard of payment of scutage, *Pipe Roll 10 Ric. I*, p. 69.

[5] *Dial. de Scac.*, p. 46. King John excused Richard of Herriard from suit to court in county and hundred, from transport to the treasury, and from castle ward while he was in the king's service, *Rot. Lit. Pat.*, p. 2b.

their services. Litigants paid fees for the judicial writs that the justices issued, and they and their clerks shared the money.[6] Royal officials did receive, however, grants of money or goods from time to time, although few records exist before the first liberate rolls. As early as 1183 Hugh Bardolf received 100 marks 'from the king's gift' out of the revenues of the honour of Gloucester, and about the same time the Norman Exchequer rolls record Henry II's gift of fifteen pounds to Geoffrey fitz Peter.[7] By 1195 William de Sainte-Mère-Eglise and his mother were enjoying a lifetime pension of £35 12s. provided yearly from the farm of the ducal manor of Sainte-Mère-Eglise.[8]

It was easy for the king to provide livings for his servants in clerical orders at the Church's expense. He had many churches in his gift, and he did not hesitate to request others to present his clerks to their ecclesiastical posts. Royal clerks made up a quarter, and at times a third, of the chapter at St Paul's.[9] The clerics among Richard I's royal justices were all pluralists, holding prebends, parish churches, and other ecclesiastical posts. Richard Barre, Ralph Foliot, and William de Sainte-Mère-Eglise were all archdeacons.[10] A listing of the ecclesiastical posts that William de Sainte-Mère-Eglise held illustrates well the king's piling of benefice upon benefice. The abbot of Cluny, acting at the request of Henry II, granted William the church of Saint-Côme in the Cotentin, which provided an annual income of £30 Angevin. Near the end of Henry's reign, he named William dean of Mortain in Normandy. William won other ecclesiastical appointments; whether from Henry II or Richard I cannot be determined. He was a canon of Lincoln before 1194, and after

---

[6] Margaret Hastings, *The Court of Common Pleas in the Fifteenth Century* (Ithaca, N.Y., 1947), p. 83; C.A.F. Meekings, ed., *Crown Pleas of the Wiltshire Eyre, 1249*, Wilts Archaeol. and Nat. Hist. Soc., Records Branch, 16 (1961): 13.

[7] *Pipe Roll 30 Hen. II*, p. 110; Delisle, *Recueil*, Introduction, p. 334. King John gave Bardolf 67s. for robes and armour, *Pipe Roll 1 John*, p. 36.

[8] Stapleton, *Rot. scac. norm.*, 1: clxxvi, 276.

[9] Walter R. Matthews and William M. Atkins, eds., *A History of St. Paul's Cathedral and the men associated with it* (London, 1957), chap. I, C.N.L. Brooke, 'The earliest times to 1485', pp. 29–30.

[10] Barre was first archdeacon of Lisieux, then from 1190 archdeacon of Ely, *Fasti, Mon. Cath.*, p. 50. Foliot was archdeacon of Hereford by spring 1182, Brooke and Brooke, 'Hereford Cathedral dignitaries', p. 16; William was archdeacon of Wilts by 1194, *Cartae Antiq. Rolls 11–20*, pp. 155–6, no. 550; J.S. Brewer and C.T. Martin, eds., *Registrum Malmesburiense*, Rolls Series (1879–80); 1: 440.

1193 he was also a canon of St Paul's.[11] In September 1189,
when Richard I was naming other royal clerks to bishoprics, he
made William a canon of York and dean of St Martin-le-Grand,
London, one of the richest non-episcopal posts available for a
royal clerk.[12] The other two archdeacons held plural benefices,
though they were less imposing.[13]

Not all benefices came to royal clerks by the king's gift. Some
clerks, such as Master Thomas of Hurstbourne, had received
grants of churches before they entered the royal service. His
first patron, the abbot of Glastonbury, named him parson of
two churches before 1180.[14] Other benefices came to royal
clerks from patrons sometimes in response to royal petitions,
other times in the hope of purchasing influence at court.

Monastic houses frequently presented royal clerks to churches
in their possession. Sometimes this was in response to the king's
request, as shown by Henry II's petition to the monks of
Northampton to name Ralph Foliot parson of their church at
Potton, Bedfordshire.[15] Other times the initiative may have
come from the monasteries themselves. They had an interest in
protecting themselves by cultivating powerful friends in the
curia regis, who could provide legal advice. Early in the career of
William de Saint-Mère-Eglise, the abbot of Mont Saint-Michel
gave him a pension of three marks from the revenues of one of
the abbey's churches.[16] The monks of Savigny Abbey, Normandy,

---

[11] Delisle, *Recueil*, Introduction, pp. 498–9, and 2: 245–6. William witnessed
Henry II's confirmation of Hubert Walter's foundation charter for West
Dereham Abbey as dean of Mortain, B.L. MS.Add. 46,353, f. 8ᵛ. He is ident-
ified as canon of Lincoln, *Pipe Roll 7 Ric. I*, p. xvii; also *Three Rolls of King's
Court*, p. 39. Canon of St. Paul's, *Fasti, St. Paul's*, p. 48.

[12] *Roger Howden*, 3: 16; *Gesta Hen. Secundi*, 2: 85–6; *Itin. Ric. I*, p. 22.

[13] Richard Barre had prebends at Hereford and Salisbury Cathedrals, *Salisbury
Chtrs. and Docs.*, pp. 40–1, 60; W.H.R. James, ed., *Vetus Registrum Sarisberiense*,
Rolls Series (1883–84), 1: 242–63. He was a parson of a church at Bad-
burgham, B.L. MS.Harl. 391, ff. 101ᵛ, 110ᴿ; MS. Cott. Tiber. C. ix ff. 152–
152ᵛ. Ralph Foliot was a canon of Hereford and St Paul's, Morey and Brooke,
Letters and Charters of Gilbert Foliot, p. 449, no. 410; *Fasti, St. Paul's*, p. 65. He
was parson of three churches: Cradley, Heref., W.W. Capes, ed., *Charters and
Records of Hereford Cathedral*, Cantilupe Soc. (Hereford, 1908), pp. 34–5;
Chadderley Corbet, Worcs., *P.B.K.J.*, 1: 312–13, no. 3180; Potton, Beds.,
B.L. MS.Cott. Vesp. E. xvii, f. 20.

[14] Ashbury, Berks, and Christian-Malford, Wilts, *Adam de Domerham*, 2: 487.

[15] B.L. MS.Cott. Vesp. E. xvii, f. 20.

[16] Church at Basing, Hants, *Robert de Torigni*, 2: 308. Delisle dates this grant
1175, but Round, *Docs. preserved in France*, p. 277, no. 763, dates it April
1185.

granted Ralph Foliot a portion of their tithes from Teilleul, and the abbot of Tewkesbury presented him to a church in Worcestershire.[17] Laymen with advowsons had the same motive for naming royal officials as parsons. The ecclesiastics among the royal justices, however, held few churches from laymen.[18]

Clerks in the lower levels of the royal administration were less dependent on the king than on their immediate superior for favours. For example, the chancellor might provide incomes for his chancery clerks by securing churches for them. William Longchamp, Richard I's chancellor, saw that his associate Richard Barre was presented to a church by the monks of Waltham Abbey. Thomas of Hurstbourne doubtlessly owed his prebend at Salisbury Cathedral to Hubert Walter, bishop of Salisbury before his elevation to Canterbury.

A glance at livings held by the clerics among Richard I's judges shows clearly that not all the Church's resources were available for its own purposes. Although the Church possessed enormous landholdings, the king and his officers found ways to exploit those holdings for themselves, to provide livings for clerks in their service. Employment of clerics in the royal administration was advantageous for the king apart from any question of their superior education or freedom from family interests. Medieval English monarchs relied upon clerics for their staffs not so much because of their literacy or their celibacy as because of the ecclesiastical benefices they could hold, which meant that their salaries could be secured at the Church's expense. Regular salary payments to clerics from the royal treasury were unnecessary.

It was less easy for the king to find steady sources of income for laymen in his service. The Angevin monarchs rarely rewarded their officials with permanent grants of land from the royal domain. They waited until land fell into their hand through escheat or through succession of a heiress, who could be married off to a deserving royal retainer. One of the few permanent grants – as opposed to temporary custodies – given to one of the royal justices was Henry II's grant of the barony of Bampton, Devon, to Hugh Bardolf following the flight of the

---

[17] Delisle, *Recueil*, introduction, p. 418; *P.B.K.J.*, 1: no. 3180.
[18] One of the few was William de Sainte-Mère-Eglise's church at Harewood, Yorks, a gift of William de Curci, *Rot. Cur. Reg.*, 2: 222.

heir, Fulk Pagnell. Richard I, however, took the honour into his hand following his accession, although he gave Hugh the manor of Hoo, Kent, in exchange.[19] A more modest grant was King John's charter giving Simon of Pattishall two houses in Northampton from the escheat of Benedict, a Jew of York.[20]

A common way for royal servants to rise out of obscurity and obtain new lands and higher social status was through marriage. Several justices did this, marrying widows or heiresses whose custody the king had given to them. The most spectacular example is Geoffrey fitz Peter's marriage to his ward, Beatrice de Say, daughter of William de Say and coheir with her sister to Kimbolton in Huntingdon and Saham, Norfolk. More important, however, were her connections with the powerful Mandeville family.[21] Following the death of William de Mandeville, earl of Essex, without direct descendants in 1189, Beatrice and her sister became heirs to his barony. His closest kin were descendants of his aunt who had married Geoffrey de Say. The succession was uncertain: should it pass to the younger son of the earl's aunt, Geoffrey de Say II, or to the two daughters of her deceased elder son William? The case bears some resemblance to the *casus regis*, except that the representatives of the dead elder son were female not male. At the time *Glanvill* was written, the law governing descent in such cases was not yet clear. Generally, however, the treatise follows feudal custom in showing a preference for succession of male over female heirs.[22]

Since Geoffrey fitz Peter was high in the ruling councils of England following Richard's accession, his claim was bound to win sympathetic attention. Although Geoffrey de Say offered 7000 marks for the inheritance and Geoffrey fitz Peter only 3000 marks, Geoffrey de Say never made any payments and the new king accepted the smaller fine. He acknowledged Beatrice, Geoffrey fitz Peter's wife, as 'the lawful and nearer heir' in a charter of January 1191. The claims of Beatrice's younger sister

---

[19] *Pipe Roll 34 Hen. II*, p. 166; Clay, 'Hugh Bardolf', p. 8. Later King John charged Hugh 300 marks for confirmation of the grant, *Pipe Roll 1 John*, p. 69; *Rot. de Obl. et Fin.*, p. 13.

[20] *Rot. Chart.*, p. 52. Simon was to hold for 16d. yearly.

[21] *Rot. de Dominabus*, p. 40; *Complete Peerage*, 5: 123.

[22] *Glanvill*, vii, 3–4, pp. 77–9. The uncertainty of the situation is accented by Geoffrey de Say's reopening of the case in 1212, *C.R.R.*, 6: 270.

to half the inheritance were ignored.[23] The Mandeville honour with its *caput* at Pleshy, Essex, consisted of over a hundred knight's fees in ten counties; it carried with it the title 'Earl of Essex' and the traditional payment of the third penny of the county that accompanied it. The lands of the honour and the income of the third penny were conveyed to Geoffrey fitz Peter promptly, but he had to wait for his formal investiture with the title of earl.

Four other of Richard's justices also increased their holdings through marriage to heiresses, but hardly in such dramatic manner. About 1200, King John allowed Hugh Bardolf to marry Mabel of Limesy, one of three sisters and coheirs of John de Limesy, baron of Cavendish. She brought a portion of her brother's land to her husband, including the manor of Broadwell in Gloucestershire and property in London.[24] As part of the bargain, Hugh seems to have taken on the obligation to pay a crown debt owed by John de Limesy.[25] In 1204 William de Warenne offered King John 500 marks for his marriage to Milisent, widow of Richard de Mountfichet, baron of Stanstead, Essex.[26] Even though Milisent had a son in the custody of another, she must have controlled a comfortable dower, making the match a profitable one for William. Two others married heiresses whose price and property were less. Osbert fitz Hervey paid twenty pounds at the Exchequer for his marriage to Margaret de Ria or Margaret of Brancaster, the two names hinting that she was a widow. She was a woman of some property, for a few years after the marriage she sued for a debt of 110 shillings dating from before her marriage to Osbert.[27] Richard of Herriard married sometime before 1183, Ela, daughter of Roger fitz Geoffrey, coheir of land in Somerford, Wiltshire. Richard offered the king twenty marks to have his wife's

---

[23] J.H. Round, ed., *Ancient Charters*, Pipe Roll Soc., 10 (1888): 97–9, 108–10; *Pipe Roll 2 Ric I*, pp. 104, 111; *3 Ric. I*, p. 29; *4 Ric. I*, p. 171; *5 Ric. I*, p. 5; *Roger Howden*, 4: 90.

[24] Charles D. Ross, ed., *The Cartulary of Cirencester Abbey* (Oxford, 1964), 1: 2–5, no. 6; *Cat. Anc. Deeds*, 2: 41, no. A2125.   [25] *Mem. Roll 1 John*, p. 54.

[26] *Pipe Roll 6 John*, p. 242; Sanders, *Baronies*, p. 83. William already had some interest in Milisent by Oct. 1203, for he offered a fine of 100 marks that she should have her dower 'justly and according to the custom of England', *Rot. Lit. Pat.*, p. 35.

[27] *Pipe Roll 10 Ric. I*, p. 94. In 1204 William de Bec claimed she owed him for 24 loads of barley, a loan from his bailiffs, *C.R.R.*, 3: 181, 207.

inheritance, but its division with her nephew led to litigation. In 1195 Richard offered eighty marks to have all the land 'as his right on the part of his wife'.[28]

Most royal servants had custody from time to time of lands and heirs in the king's hand. Sometimes these were temporary grants for safekeeping, or grants made for the purpose of providing payments to officials, or other times, grants for which they had bargained in the hope of increasing their income. Custodies had the advantage for the Angevin kings that they could withdraw them easily in case a royal servant aroused their anger.[29] Master Thomas of Hurstbourne, as already shown, so frequently held custody of vacant religious foundations that he can almost be considered a professional custodian. Hugh Bardolf, too, had considerable experience as a custodian of escheated lands before he took the newly-created office of escheater in 1194. Henry II had named him custodian of the honour of Gloucester, which fell vacant in 1183.[30] All Richard's judges held custodies of vacant lands at some time or other during their careers, the sizes ranging from the 327 knight's fees of the earldom of Gloucester down to a single manor.

Justices sometimes joined the race for profits that many were running by the end of the twelfth century, bidding speculatively on custodies of lands or wardships of heirs. Some speculators made bids greater than their gain, entangling them in debts to the king or to the Jews. Practically all Richard I's justices, whether clerics or laymen, played this game, although none seems to have overburdened himself with debt. One of the most avid players was Hubert Walter. He began the game early, paying 800 marks for wardship of three heirs in 1190.[31] After he had retired from the justiciarship he continued to play, offering King John 4000 marks for custody of a single heir.[32] The

---

[28] *Pipe Roll 30 Hen. II*, p. 84; *32 Hen. II*, p. 171. Richard and his wife made a final concord with Walter Mautravers, son of Ela's sister, dividing the inheritance, *C.R.R.*, 10: 17–18; *Pipe Roll 32 Hen. II*, pp. 163, 173; *33 Hen. II*, p. 198. Apparently this did not settle the matter, for in 1195 Richard offered the 80 mark fine, *Pipe Roll 7 Ric. I*, p. 139; *9 Ric. I*, p. 210; *Mem. Roll 1 John*, p. 62.   [29] Holt, *Northerners*, p. 226.

[30] *Pipe Roll 30 Hen. II*, pp. 59, 110, 149; *32 Hen. II*, pp. 118, 201–2. Hugh held the honour until 1189, when it passed to King John.

[31] *Pipe Roll 2 Ric. I*, p. 122.

[32] The son of William de Stuteville, *Rot. Lit. Pat.*, p. 30; *Rot. Chart.*, p. 108; *Pipe Roll 6 John*, pp. 191–2, 217.

archbishop bought wardships from other lords with the intention of selling them at a profit. Jocelin of Brakelond tells of the abbot of Bury St Edmunds selling the wardship of an heiress to Hubert for only £100 because he had needed the archbishop's aid in getting the girl away from her grandfather. Hubert Walter then sold the wardship for 500 marks, making an easy profit.[33]

William de Sainte-Mère-Eglise was soon following the archbishop's example. In 1194 he purchased three wardships, taking care to have specified his right to marry each ward to one of his kinswomen. The costliest of the three was the son of Robert fitz Harding II, heir to half a barony plus other lands, for whom William paid 500 marks.[34] Other justices engaged in the business of buying custodies on a less extravagant scale. Richard of Herriard promised £100 to King Richard I for wardship of the heir of a Surrey landholder, and he paid £20 as a first instalment in 1198, but nine years later he still had not completed his payments.[35] Other justices' oblations for rights of wardship and marriage ranged from forty to a hundred marks.[36]

Surveys of the possessions of the seven laymen among Richard I's justices show that all increased their landholdings beyond their inheritances. The increase was not so much due to direct royal grants as it was to marriages, grants from other lords, purchases and leases. Yet service to the king made it easier for them to acquire land. For some such as Geoffrey fitz Peter, there was a dramatic increase from a few fees of one knight or less in 1166 to over a hundred fees by 1190. Hugh Bardolf's landholdings grew less spectacularly but steadily. He inherited substantial lands in Lincolnshire, but he expanded his holdings in a number of other shires so that he had impressive estates by the time he died in 1203. Some indication of their size

---

[33] *Chron. of Jocelin of Brakelond*, pp. 123–4.
[34] Barony of Hooton Pagnell, Yorks, Sanders, *Baronies*, pp. 14, 55. William's other purchases were the heirs of Alexander de Barentin for 100 marks and the heir of Ralf fitz Amalric for 50 marks, *Pipe Roll 6 Ric. I*, pp. xxii, 95, 182, 239; *C.R.R.*, 16: 396, no. 1942.
[35] Land and heir of Robert Belet, *Pipe Roll 10 Ric. I*, p. 149; *I John*, p. 57; *2 John*, p. 217; *8 John*, p. 116; *9 John*, p. 65.
[36] William de Warenne offered 40 marks in 1194 for the heir of Hugh de Chandos, *Pipe Roll 6 Ric. I*, p. 62. Hugh Bardolf offered 100 marks in 1198 for the land and marriage of the heir of William de Bella Aqua, *Pipe Roll 10 Ric. I*, p. 43.

is the fine that Hugh's brother offered King John for recognition as his heir: £1000 plus surrender to the crown of one of his manors and transfer of another to a creditor. Added evidence for Hugh's wealth is the £1000 fine offered for his widow's marriage.[37]

More interesting is a look at justices who were not multi-purpose officials in the higher councils of governments, but who were primarily judges. Although the evidence is sketchy, it leaves an impression that they too advanced their position, though at a slower pace. William de Warenne, already a landholder of baronial rank, brought a number of lawsuits to enforce his claims to additional land.[38] Simon of Pattishall began his career as the holder of one knight's fee; by the end of his life he held at least five and three-quarters knight's fees plus other lands of varied sizes and some burgage tenures, centred around his native Northants village.[39]

Osbert fitz Hervey's gain was great enough to inspire the *exemplum* of the judge suffering in hell, depicted in 'The Vision of Thurkill', shortly after his death in 1206. It paints a picture of a corrupt judge, enriching himself by taking gifts from litigants on both sides of lawsuits.[40] Osbert evidently had earned a reputation for greed known to the East Anglian monk who was author of the 'Vision'. The surviving records do not indicate a rise so high or so rapid that it should have attracted such notice. They do reveal, however, that Osbert's lands were worth £241 10s. at the time of his death. A fine of 200 marks and two palfreys was offered for custody of his son and heir.[41] The fitz Hervey holdings were centred in Norfolk and Suffolk, with

[37] His heir was Robert Bardolf, who had to give the king the manor of Bromsgrove and Norton, Worcs., and he had to give Hugh de Neville the manor of Castle Carlton, Lincs, *Rot. de Obl. et Fin.*, p. 285. William de Braose offered the fine to have Mabel 'for the use of one of his sons', *Pipe Roll 7 John*, p. 197.

[38] He divided a marsh, taking two-thirds, with the abbot of Ramsey, *Cartularium monasterii de Rameseia*, Rolls Series (1884–93), 2: 215, 216, 380–81. He brought suit, seeking a hide of land in Sussex, *C.R.R.*, 1: 272.

[39] For a survey of Simon's holdings, see Ralph V. Turner, 'Simon of Pattishall, Northamptonshire man, early common law judge', *Northamptonshire Past and Present*, 6 (1978): 12–13.

[40] Schmidt, ed., *Visio Thurkilli*.

[41] *Pipe Roll 8 John*, pp. 33, 35; *9 John*, p. 113. William of Huntingfield won custody of the land and heir, except for the land held of the count of Perche.

some land in Essex as well.[42] Richard of Herriard was a
landholder of knightly rank, though not of the highest, when he
entered the royal service. It is impossible to measure in acres
any increase in his landholdings because of paucity of records,
and also possible confusion with his son, Richard of Herriard II.
Yet it seems certain that Richard had holdings stretching across
Hampshire and Wiltshire that he extended as far away as Middlesex by purchase and lease.[43] Michael Belet, too, increased his
landholdings beyond those he inherited from his father.[44]

The clerics among the justices were able to accumulate property as well, sometimes adding lay tenures to their spiritual properties.[45] Master Thomas of Hurstbourne bought property in
London near St Paul's. After his death, his executors disposed of
his land and house, which included a chapel, and whose windows
overlooked the brewhouse of the cathedral.[46] Richard fitz Neal,
it will be recalled, had elaborate quarters at Westminster which
he left to his successor at the Exchequer.

Several of the royal justices seem to have had supplies of ready
cash which made possible speculative ventures, such as purchases
of lands or privileges, or possibly money-lending. The justices
frequently made offerings of substantial sums for favourable
action concerning their claims to property. Figures range from
thousands of pounds offered by Hubert Walter for a rich cus-

---

[42] Manor of Dagworth, Suffolk, *Cal. Inq. Post Mort.*, 1: 147–8, no. 521; land of the
fee of William of Mountchesney, Norfolk, *Rot. Lit. Claus.*, 1: 79; land of the
count of Perche, Suffolk, *Pipe Roll 9 John*, p. 113; land at Tibenham, Suffolk,
held of St Benet Holme for £4 yearly, *Reg. St. Benet Holme*, 1: 121, 140–1, nos.
218, 260; purchase of a knight's fee at Thrandeston, Suffolk, Barbara Dodwell, ed., *Feet of Fines for Norfolk and Suffolk*, Pipe Roll Soc., new ser. 32 (1958):
152, no. 305; a knight's fee of Bury St Edmunds, Suffolk, *Feudal Docs. from
Bury St Edmunds*, pp. lxxxvi–lxxxvii, citing B.L. MS.Harl. 645, f. 25; 60 A. at
Doddinghurst, Essex, *Cal. Inq. Post Mort.*, 1: 129, no. 466.

[43] Land held of the earl of Leicester by 1184, *Pipe Roll 30 Hen. II*, pp. 94–5; land
held of the earl of Salisbury by 1191, *Pipe Roll 3 & 4 Ric. I*, p. 121. For land held
at Somerford, *Pipe Roll 30 Hen. II*, p. 84; for the church at Great Somerford,
Monasticon, 4: 399; for land at Southrope, *C.R.R.*, 1: 390. Richard of Herriard
or another of the same name gained land at Little Dartford, Kent, through his
second marriage, *Calendar of Kent Feet of Fines to the end of Henry III's Reign*, eds.
Irene J. Churchill, R. Griffin, and F.W. Hardman, Kent Archaeol. Soc., *Kent
Records*, 15 (1956): 1–2.   [44] See chap. 2, pt. 4, p. 58.

[45] E.g. William de Sainte-Mère-Eglise shortly after he became bishop received
La Haie de Morville from Richard de Vernon as a hereditary holding, returning 30s. Angevin annually, *Rot. Chart.*, p. 64.

[46] *H.M.C.*, *Ninth Report*, D & C of St. Paul's, pp. 26, 49a.

tody to half a mark offered by Richard of Herriard to have a quit-claim recorded on the pipe roll.[47] If the justices lacked cash, they seem to have had no fears about their ability to raise it. Richard of Herriard, though a relatively obscure royal officer, offered large oblations in suits to recover property: eighty marks in 1195 for land that he claimed as his wife's right, and in 1205 a hundred marks plus expenses of a knight to be sent in the king's service.[48]

Evidence shows at least one of the justices engaging in money-lending. When Hugh Bardolf died in 1203, he left a number of debtors owing him sums from fifty shillings to forty pounds. These debts indicate that Hugh was either 'a man of unusual generosity' or else did not object to 'a little usury on the side'.[49] Possibly his experience as one of the keepers of the Jews revealed to him the opportunities in this business. His assumption of a £150 debt owed by Alexander of St Vaast hints at such an explanation.[50] The meaning of the transaction seems to be that he was extending credit to a debtor who had exhausted his credit with the Jews.

A powerful factor in royal servants' struggle for lands and riches was concern for their families, a wish to push their sons a rung higher on the social ladder. They hoped to make marriages for their offspring that would advance the families' fortunes, and perhaps they sought posts in the royal administration for their sons. Evidence of concern for family is not hard to find among the justices, even those who were ecclesiastics. They were no different in this from the clerics who had served Henry II. William de Sainte-Mère-Eglise's purchase of marriages for his kinswomen reveals his concern for his family. After he became bishop of London, he may have used his position to further the careers of relatives in clerical orders. Several canons of St Paul's in the early thirteenth century took their names from Sainte-

---

[47] *Pipe Roll 1 John*, p. 130.

[48] *Pipe Roll 7 Ric. I*, p. 139; and *Rot. de Obl. et Fin.*, p. 287. William de Warenne offered fines ranging from 20 marks in 1190 for a recognition to 500 marks for his marriage, *Pipe Roll 2 Ric. I*, p. 101; *Pipe Roll 6 John*, p. 242.

[49] *Rot. Lit. Pat.*, p. 50b. The suggestion of usury is Sidney Painter's, *Reign of King John*, p. 72.

[50] *Pipe Roll 3 John*, p. 19; *Rot. de Obl. et Fin.*, p. 92.

Mère-Eglise, probably marking them as either kinsmen or *familiares* of the bishop.[51]

Hubert Walter's strong sense of family is shown by the favours that his relatives received under Richard I and John. As we have seen, one brother, Osbert fitz Hervey, had a long career in the judiciary. Another brother, Theobald Walter, won greater reward, in large measure due to his early association with Prince John, whom he must have met while a youth in Glanvill's household. He accompanied John to Ireland in 1185, was granted Irish lands, and became founder of a powerful baronial house there, the Butlers of Ormond. In 1194, through his brother's influence, he was given the wapentake of Amounderness in Lancashire.[52] Other kinsmen of Hubert Walter who won office through his influence include Theobald de Valoignes, sheriff of Norfolk and Suffolk in 1200, and possibly Hamo de Valoignes, justiciar of Ireland in the middle 1190s.[53]

Marriage was an important way of improving the family position, either increasing landholdings or creating links with other families. Geoffrey fitz Peter married his eldest son, Geoffrey de Mandeville IV, to a daughter of Robert fitz Walter, another Essex landholder. The boy's sister was married to Henry de Bohun, earl of Hereford. Their half-brother, John fitz Geoffrey, the justiciar's son by his second wife, married a daughter of Hugh Bigod, earl of Norfolk.[54] William de Warenne's only surviving child was his daughter, Beatrice, for whom he arranged a worthy marriage. She was wedded to Doun Bardolf, heir to half the barony of Shelford, Nottinghamshire, and a distant cousin of William's colleague on the bench, Hugh Bardolf.[55] Following her father's death, Beatrice de Warenne offered King John a

---

[51] *Fasti, St. Paul's*, pp. 16, 21, 52. Peter de Sainte-Mère-Eglise, cathedral treasurer, c. 1201/12–28, certainly came from William's birthplace and may well have been a relative, *Fasti*, p. 21, and Delisle, *Recueil*, Introduction, p. 500. He had been a clerk of William Longchamp, *Pipe Roll 2 Ric. I*, p. 8.

[52] Mortimer, 'Family of Glanville', pp. 9, 13; *Pipe Roll 31 Hen. II*, p. 2; *6 Ric. I*, p. 123. [53] Mortimer, p. 13.

[54] *Complete Peerage*, 5: 433–5, and genealogical table. Geoffrey found preferment for a son in clerical orders as dean of Wolverhampton and canon of Lincoln Cathedral, *Fasti, Lincoln*, pp. 126–7.

[55] *Honors and Knight's Fees*, 3: 323; Sanders, *Baronies*, p. 76; Clay, 'Hugh Bardolf and his Family', pp. 5–6.

fine of 3100 marks to have her father's barony of Wormegay, to have her dower from Doun Bardolf's lands, to be free from marrying again, and to pay her father's debts out of his chattels. Nonetheless, she did remarry, first to a certain Ralph, then in 1210–11 to Hubert de Burgh, the future justiciar of Henry III.[56] One of Simon of Pattishall's sons made a good marriage to the daughter of Richard de Argentan, which brought him two estates in Bedfordshire.[57] Nothing is known of the marriage of Richard of Herriard's son, but Richard married his daughter to Richard de Sifrewast, a member of a Berkshire landed family related to Richard Barre.[58]

Sometimes sons followed their fathers into place in the royal government, although rarely did significant offices become hereditary. Three royal justices' sons followed them into the royal administration. Master Michael Belet succeeded his father in the post of *pincerna*.[59] John fitz Geoffrey, son of Geoffrey fitz Peter, eventually followed his father in an administrative career, although he attained high rank only by the middle years of Henry III, long after his father's death. Simon of Pattishall's two sons – one a layman and one a clerk – both went into the service of Henry III and did well for themselves.[60]

If the justices succeeded in satisfying the thirst of their ambition, at least in moderate draughts, what linked their ambition with the related sins of greed and sycophancy? An important advantage of royal office was access to the king, opportunity to approach him with requests for special favours. Obviously, the six judges who were also prominent *curiales* benefited from their proximity to the king, but the others benefited as well. Their ability to approach the king for favours was a source of influence with others, winning them both patrons and clients. We can see the process in operation with Richard of Herriard's requests. The barons of the Exchequer in 1198 gave him the respite he requested from a debt 'because he says he is always prompt'. The barons were not likely to have found this a satisfactory

---

[56] *Pipe Roll 11 John*, p. 50; Sanders, *Baronies*, p. 101.

[57] *Complete Peerage*, 10: 313.

[58] *Exc. è Rot. Fin.*, 1: 72. Richard Sifrewast offered £10 to have Richard of Herriard's land in Southrope.

[59] He paid King John £100 for the privilege, *Pipe Roll 6 John*, p. 123; *Rot. de Obl. et Fin.*, p. 358.

[60] For Geoffrey's and Simon's sons, see chap. 4, pt. 4, pp. 183–4, 189.

excuse from some crown debtor from the countryside, unknown to them. For Richard, however, they agreed to defer the debt until the Michaelmas 1199 Exchequer, so that he meanwhile might pursue the matter with the king.[61] Later Richard seems to have approached King John to secure seisin of land by administrative order rather than by judicial process.[62]

Hugh Bardolf was on friendly terms with the most powerful royal counsellors from the time of Henry II into the reign of John. He was close enough to Hubert Walter to chide him about King John's appointment of him as chancellor. In a pointed reference to the martyred Thomas Becket, Hugh said to Hubert, 'We have never heard nor seen an archbishop become a chancellor, but we have seen a chancellor become an archbishop.'[63] Hugh's friendship with his fellow-justices at Westminster secured him advantages in pleas there. Hugh's clerk, representing him before the Bench, managed to get a plea against his master dismissed by simply stating *quod nescit de placito illo quicquam.*[64] Surely the judges would not have viewed such ignorance from an ordinary suitor as grounds for dismissal!

Not only could a royal servant approach the king on his own behalf but also on behalf of others. Clearly, such influence was worth something to those who needed the king's ear but had no access to court, and influence became a saleable commodity. Ralph Foliot's access to Henry II enabled him to win the king's pardon of a 100 shilling amercement for a man convicted, despite his denial, of opening up a money-lender's strongbox. The king sent his writ of pardon in 1187 at the request of the archdeacon of Hereford.[65] It is not unlikely that the man, having won his pardon, wished to express in some way his gratitude to the archdeacon.

The royal justices themselves could provide favours to those with cases coming before the *curia regis.* They could assist suitors who were their friends or clients in a number of ways without

---

[61] *Mem. Roll 1 John*, p. 19. Eight years later Richard still owed £23 10s. of the £100 debt, *Pipe Roll 9 John*, p. 65. Later King John reduced a debt of William of Warenne from 500 to 300 marks, and he postponed collection of a debt of 60 marks, *Pipe Roll 6 John*, pp. 242, 246; *Rot. Lit. Claus.*, 1: 46.

[62] *C.R.R.*, 1: 390. Ralph de Hauvill had been holding it through custody of an heiress.   [63] *Roger Howden*, 4: 90–1.

[64] *C.R.R.*, 1: 189, a plea *versus* Simon of Kyme in 1200.

[65] *Pipe Roll 33 Hen. II*, p. 33.

too openly deflecting the course of justice. Conduct that today would be condemned for compromising the impartiality of the courts was normal for justices of Richard I. They met privately with litigants to give them legal advice; they even acted as attorneys; and they consulted the barons of the Exchequer, other officials, and great men of the kingdom about politically sensitive suits. The biographer of St Hugh of Lincoln describes a suit in which, the night before judgment was to be given, the tenant's 'counsellors and supporters were in the city discussing earnestly with the justices the wording of the verdict'.[66] We can be confident that a similar discussion took place in another case; the justices alone did not decide the descent of the Mandeville inheritance in favour of Geoffrey fitz Peter. They certainly consulted the *appares* ruling England in Richard I's absence.

Among the records of Crowland Abbey is an account of a lengthy suit with Spalding Priory, 1189–1202, which illustrates vividly the need for litigants to have friends among the justices. It depicts some justices as openly partial! Robert of Wheatfield, who was still on the bench in the early years of the reign of Richard I, is described as one of the justices supporting the monks of Spalding against Crowland. The prior of Crowland came to the Exchequer sometime shortly after Henry II's death to pursue his claim to a marsh, after having earlier essoined himself of bed-sickness. Robert asked *alta voce* whether the knights who had viewed the prior on his sick-bed were present in court. Four low fellows, who were not knights at all but hired for the occasion, then presented themselves. Their testimony that the prior had not been lying abed ill when they viewed him led Robert to rule him in default. He declared that the prior should lose his seisin but not his right, *possessionem sed non proprietatem*, thus prolonging the action. Robert made his judgment in spite of the protests of the prior and all present that those claiming to be the viewers of his sickness 'were not of the knightly order nor girt with the sword, and the third of them did not know how to speak French'.[67]

---

[66] *Magna Vita Sancti Hugonis*, 2: 26, Adam de Nevill *versus* William de Hartshill in 1199, cf. *Rot. Cur. Reg.*, 1: 452. In spring 1198, Bishop Eustace of Ely appointed Richard Barre his attorney for all pleas, *C.R.R.*, 1: 33.

[67] *English Justice*, Appendix, pp. 170–1.

The case continued when the prior of Crowland came before the Bench after he had made another default. The justices disagreed about remitting the prior's default, some feeling it was made through fear and others that it was in contempt of court, and they 'wished to speak together secretly about this'. But Richard of Herriard, *fidelis vir et prudens*, stood up and argued that the prior's default should not be held against him. The other justices then accepted his view, saving the prior his seisin.[68]

The litigation between Crowland and Spalding dragged on into the reign of King John. In the autumn of 1200, the prior of Crowland went to London to seek adjournment until the new year, leaving him enough time to cross the Channel to discuss the case with John. 'A certain wise and discreet knight' arranged a meeting for the prior to win support for a long postponement. Through him, the prior 'approached certain powerful men of the court individually . . . so that they might consider his business favorably'. Among those he met were two royal justices, Simon of Pattishall and Richard of Herriard.[69]

The friendship of royal justices was clearly a valuable commodity, which magnates and monastic houses were willing to purchase. The justices did not hesitate to accept gifts from litigants in return for their legal advice or for 'expediting' causes.[70] Some of the grants, pensions, and other rewards that came to the justices were gifts from suitors in the courts, given either in anticipation of future service or in appreciation for past help. Were grants of land to Osbert fitz Hervey and Simon of Pattishall made by religious houses to ensure favourable consideration of their court cases? Osbert fitz Hervey was a tenant of two East Anglian monasteries, St Benet Holme and Bury St Edmunds. Simon of Pattishall held half a knight's fee from Bury St Edmunds plus land from three other monasteries: Bushmead Priory, Dunstable, and Cirencester Abbey.[71]

---

[68] *English Justice*, Appendix, pp. 184–5.
[69] *English Justice*, pp. 192–3. The knight was Reginald de Argentan.
[70] See below, chap. 6, pt. 3, pp. 283–8.
[71] Half a fee at Whatfield, Suffolk, of Bury St Edmunds, *Chron. of Jocelin of Brakelond*, p. 89; a croft in Pattishall plus the manor of Cold Higham and Grimscot from the prior of Dunstable, G.H. Fowler, *A Digest of the Charters preserved in the Cartulary of the Priory of Dunstable*, Beds. Hist. Rec. Soc., 10 (1926): 109, no. 312; four virgates in Eastcote from the abbot of Cirencester, *Cart. of Cirencester Abbey*, 2: 559–60, no. 665.

Once Geoffrey fitz Peter became justiciar near the end of Richard's reign, both suitors at Westminster and Exchequer debtors sought his good will. That grants of land were made to him to win his influence or to repay favours seems evident. Reward for a favour is the avowed reason for a grant recorded in an inquisition *post mortem* from the time of Edward I. According to the testimony, it was remembered that Henry de Tracy, son of one of the murderers of Thomas Becket, had returned from Normandy to seek his father's escheated barony of Bradninch, and he asked Geoffrey fitz Peter's aid. Two others were seeking the barony, and hectic bidding resulted; but the king accepted Henry's offer of 1000 marks with Geoffrey's encouragement. Grateful for recovering his inheritance Henry gave the justiciar the manor of Morton, Devon, to hold by the service of one sparrow-hawk yearly.[72]

Possibly, petitioners could curry favour with justices by making gifts to their favourite monastic foundations. The two justiciars, Hubert Walter and Geoffrey fitz Peter, were founders of religious houses, as were other royal judges.[73] The abbot and monks of Westminster Abbey sought to oblige Geoffrey by fulfilling his request for an offering to a Gilbertine house he had founded. They assigned the nuns of Shouldham Pirory tithes from one of their churches.[74]

Clearly, a place at the Bench provided means for the justices of Richard I to better themselves and their families. The increasing volume of records makes it easier to see how proximity to the centre of power gave the justices opportunities for securing favours and for increasing their wealth. Even obscure knights increased their landholdings and built up blocs of lands around their ancestral centre. Two levels continued to characterize the judicial bench just as in Henry II's last years, with six officials of high rank and political power sharing work with eight of lesser rank. Yet the backgrounds of both groups are similar. Only one justice came from an old baronial family, while the others were either of rural knightly origin or from families recently raised to

---

[72] *Cal. Inq. Post Mort.*, 2: no. 153; see Painter, *King John*, p. 38, for details of competing bids. Geoffrey also had advowson of the church at Morton, *Br. Note Book*, 3: 206–7, no. 1190.

[73] See below, chap. 6, part 1, pp. 263–5.

[74] Westminster Domesday, f. 469^V, tithes of Clarkclose.

higher rank through administrative activity. The judiciary of Richard I, like that of his father, consisted largely of 'new men'. The eight lower-ranking men were concentrating their attention on the task of justice, revealing clearly a new professional and specialized level among royal servants. With men such as Richard of Herriard or Simon of Pattishall, we see not simply professional royal officials but professionals who are concentrating on the work of the courts.

4

KING JOHN'S CORPS OF JUSTICES

1 THE COURTS OF KING JOHN AND THEIR JUSTICES

With the creation of the court *coram rege* under King John, a new branch of royal justice takes its place alongside the Bench at Westminster and the periodic eyres. The traditional view of this has been to regard it as simply part of a centuries-long process of professionalization and specialization, as distinct departments broke away from the old undifferentiated *curia regis*. The growth of professional staffs for the work of justice supports such a view. Yet the appearance of two courts which were virtually duplicates of one another in their work suggests that something else was at work: two different tendencies in medieval English government were in tension. John's creation of his own court can be seen as resistance to the tendency of offices to 'go out of court' and as a royal effort to preserve 'familiar' or 'household' government which would be more responsive to the king's will.[1]

Certainly the process of specialization and professionalization is easy enough to see if we look at the royal judges serving King John. We find seventeen men who served so regularly on the bench at Westminster, with the court *coram rege*, or on eyres to the counties that they were clearly specialists in the sphere of justice. Few of them were any longer the *familiares regis* who had formed a significant part of the judiciary in the time of Richard I: the justiciar, Geoffrey fitz Peter; two high-ranking *curiales*, William Briwerre and Hugh Bardolf; and one royal clerk Henry archdeacon of Stafford. In sum, only four out of seventeen –

---

[1] See J. E. A. Jolliffe, *Angevin Kingship* on 'familiar' government. See also Ralph V. Turner, 'The origins of Common Pleas and King's Bench', *A. J. L. H.*, 21 (1977): 238–54. See also the analysis of cases heard *coram rege*, Easter term 1204, in Turner, *King and his courts*, pp. 38–47.

counting the justiciar – were traditional multi-purpose royal servants under King John, while under his predecessor six out of fourteen justices had belonged to that category. On the other hand, King John's creation of his own court – the justices *coram rege* – conveniently near him, even if he did not himself sit in judgment with them, is evidence of his effort to preserve his personal authority in the sphere of justice. Justices of the Bench down to its demise in 1209 continued to be chiefly men of Geoffrey fitz Peter, or else men named by his predecessors whom he kept on. The members of the court following the king look as if they were chosen by John, even though he chose some of them – most notably Simon of Pattishall and James of Potterne – from among the judges experienced at Westminster. By 1205, at least, he was picking some of his justices from elsewhere.

The line separating financial and judicial staffs remained blurred, for the justices as servants of the justiciar continued occasionally to cross it, carrying out work connected with royal revenues chiefly when on circuit in the counties. Yet in most ways the line between Bench and Exchequer was becoming sharper, even though the two bodies still shared the same house at Westminster. Within the *domus de Scaccario* a division of labour was becoming apparent. William of Ely, who had succeeded Richard fitz Neal as Treasurer in 1186, did not sit regularly at the Bench as had his predecessor. Only three of the seventeen professionals among John's justices ought to be ranked as barons of the Exchequer: the justiciar Geoffrey fitz Peter and two *curiales*, William Briwerre and Hugh Bardolf. These three, along with the archbishop of Canterbury and two or three other high-ranking officials, were the king's closest associates in his work of governing the kingdom, clearly in a category apart from the other justices.

Some ninety men served King John as justices either at the Bench at Westminster, with the court following the king, or on eyres in the shires. Many, of course, were great barons, high ecclesiastics, or officers of the royal household who served only infrequently, witnessing an occasional final concord when other business brought them to the *curia regis*. No bishops sat continuously at the Bench as had Godfrey of Winchester or Richard of London under Richard I. Only seventeen men served more than five terms of court with the central tribunals. Especially were the itinerant justices likely to be temporary appointments, to supplement the corps of full-time judges from Westminster as they spread over the countryside. Twenty-nine of King John's itinerant justices never served in the central courts at all. Only three of these twenty-nine acted as justices on eyre with any frequency: Master Roger Arundel, who served on eyres from the last years of Henry II to 1206, but never sat at Westminster; Geoffrey of Buckland, who served on three general eyres, 1194–5, 1198–9, and 1201–3, and as a summer vacation judge intermittently from 1197 to 1204; and Master Henry of Northampton, who went on eyres in 1188 and 1202–3, and sat on summer vacation panels in 1203 and 1205. Arundel's career was confined to Yorkshire, where he held lands and offices;[2] all his work as an itinerant justice took place in that county. Geoffrey of Buckland, a relative of the justiciar Geoffrey fitz Peter, concentrated chiefly on financial business at the Exchequer.[3] Henry of Northampton had a long career as a royal clerk beginning as early as 1171, 'spent in obscure but useful labour', little of which involved judicial duties.[4]

Of the some sixty justices who sat on the Bench at Westminster or as justices following the king, most served no more than three or four terms. Three served five or six terms, among them Robert de Aumari, who went on the 1208–9 general eyre and then joined the judges *coram rege* until the end of 1211. Yet he left no mark on the records other than his name listed on feet of fines among the justices. Another was Reginald of Cornhill, one of King John's most trusted financial agents, who was frequently busy at other tasks. Although he was sheriff of Kent, chamberlain of London, custodian of mints and exchanges, and collector of the fifteenth, he found time to serve five terms at the Bench, to go on three eyres, and sit at a vacation court.[5] Master Jocelin of Wells, a senior chancery clerk who

---

[2] Foss, *Judges of England*, 2: 31–2. For his work on the bench, see *P.B.K.J.*, 3: Appendix III.
[3] Sidney Painter, 'Norwich's three Geoffreys', *Speculum*, 28 (1953): 803–13; reprinted in Fred A. Cazel, Jr ed., *Feudalism and Liberty* (Baltimore, 1961), pp. 185–94.   [4] *Earliest Lincs assize rolls*, pp. xxv–xxvi.
[5] Painter, *Reign of King John*, pp. 81, 88, 137, 147.

became bishop of Bath and Wells in 1206, served throughout 1204 as a justice *coram rege* and at Westminster.

King John's reign saw two general eyres: 1201–3, when groups of itinerant justices crisscrossed the country on six circuits; and 1208–9, when three groups covered the eastern counties, the Midlands, and the North.[6] Of course, other groups of itinerant justices visited some counties at more frequent intervals to take the assizes and to deliver gaols, for example, four circuits in the summer of 1206.[7] Geoffrey fitz Peter sometimes led a party of justices as far afield as the Midlands during summer vacations. Such circuits were popular with the people, as the promise in *Magna Carta* that assizes would be taken in the counties four times a year shows.

The accession of a new monarch brought no major changes in the personnel of the royal courts. John as count of Mortain had maintained a court which dispensed justice in the great chunk of territory he controlled, but no member of his comital *familia* joined the royal judiciary.[8] The justices continued to be men chosen by the justiciar, Geoffrey fitz Peter, surviving from Hubert Walter's justiciarship, or even surviving in the case of Hugh Bardolf from the days of Glanvill, until the middle years of John's reign. Five of the justices had begun their careers in the time of Richard Lionheart and one even earlier, in the time of Henry II.

The service of Hugh Bardolf antedated that of the justiciar, stretching back to 1185. Hugh was a *curialis* with multiple responsibilities, but he managed to visit almost every region of England on eyres during the reign of Richard I, and he continued to go on eyres under King John and to join the justiciar for vacation courts. Bardolf was among those who made up John's court *coram rege* on his first visit to England following his coronation, 1200–1. Hugh died in the autumn of 1203, after

---

[6] *P.B.K.J.*, 3: Appendix III, corrected by David Crook, unpublished list, P.R.O.

[7] According to Lady Stenton, there were no commissions for merely the one or the other before the reign of Henry III, *Lincs assize rolls*, p. xxviii.

[8] Charters of John as count of Mortain name his *familiares* as witnesses, e.g. B.L. MS. Cott. Vesp. E. xxv, f. 102[V]; Harl. Chtr. 45.c.9; MS. Egerton 3031, ff. 46–46[V], 90[V].

having acted as a royal justice on the summer vacation court in August.[9]

Simon of Pattishall and Henry of Whiston had begun their service on the bench in 1190, the same year that the justiciar started his service. Simon was at the Bench almost continuously until 1207, when he moved to John's court *coram rege*. King John respected Simon's ability, for he had recruited him for his own court on his early visits to England. Simon remained a member of the court following the king until its collapse in 1215. Henry of Whiston had first appeared as a justice at Westminster in 1190 and 1191, but he did not return until Easter 1198. In the intervening years he did sometimes serve as an itinerant justice. He began to sit at the Bench more regularly under King John, and he joined the justices *coram rege* in November 1200. Whiston's most active year as a judge was 1201, his last year on the bench. He served all four terms at Westminster and, in addition, went on the justiciar's summer eyre. His name does not appear among the justices after 21 November 1201, although he was still living as late as 1209, 'now old and grey-haired'.[10]

William Briwerre first sat at the Bench at Westminster in November 1191, and he found time for occasional judicial work throughout the reigns of Richard I and John. He witnessed a few final concords at Westminster every year of Richard's reign from 1195, and he went on the two general eyres of 1194 and 1198–9; but his expertise lay more in the financial sphere than in justice, and he was more often at the Exchequer than on the judicial bench. Under King John, William appeared briefly at Westminster in 1201 and 1202, but not again until the autumn of 1208. He had no part in either of the general eyres of John's reign. William sat with the justices following the king in April and May 1201 and again in May 1204, and he witnessed stray fines with the justices *coram rege* almost every year from 1204 until 1215. He returned to Westminster with Peter des Roches in the spring of 1215 during the brief revival of a court there

---

[9] Charles T. Clay, 'Hugh Bardolf the Justice', *Lincs Hist. and Archaeol.*, 1: 14–15.

[10] Papal letter dated Feb. 1207, C.R. and Mary G. Cheney, eds., *Letters of Pope Innocent III concerning England and Wales* (Oxford, 1967), p. 122, no. 737. He was party to a lawsuit as late as 1209, *Pipe Roll 11 John*, p. 16.

brought on by the king's absence in 1214. It is clear, however, that Briwerre's work on the bench was only incidental to other business which brought him to Westminster or into the king's presence. Two other of Richard I's judges remained on the bench after King John's accession. Osbert fitz Hervey was at Westminster until shortly before his death in summer 1206. Richard of Herriard's career had begun in 1194; and he remained active as a justice until 1204, although he did not die until 1208.[11]

Three men joined the bench about the time of the change in justiciars in 1198, when Geoffrey fitz Peter replaced Hubert Walter as head of the judiciary. John of Guestling first made a brief appearance at the Bench in 1197, then began regular work as a justice in January 1198. He accompanied Geoffrey fitz Peter on the great eyre of 1198–9. He served continuously on the bench either at the Westminster sessions or in the counties on the two general eyres of John's reign. Guestling rarely sat with the court *coram rege*. His judicial career underwent a long pause from 1209 until the court at Westminster re-opened following the end of the civil war in 1218. He served a total of six terms at the Bench during the minority of Henry III. James of Potterne's judicial work began with the general eyres of 1198–9, and it continued throughout the reign of John and into the reign of his successor, on eyres in 1208–9, at Westminster until 1207, and with King John's revived court *coram rege* until the king's departure for Poitou in 1214. The judicial career of Master Godfrey de Insula also began with the 1198–9 eyre, although he had participated earlier in Hubert Walter's 1194 general eyre. He served frequently at Westminster from the summer of 1200 until April 1205, when he was present at a combined session of the Bench and *coram rege* justices. Godfrey only worked as a justice once more after that, in autumn 1208, when he went on the general eyre. He did not die before 1214, however.[12]

King John's accession brought three new names to the list of judges. Master Eustace de Fauconberg joined the judiciary shortly after the death of Richard I and about the time that his master,

---

[11] For details, see chap. 3 pt. 2 above.
[12] A case before papal delegates concerning his presentation to a church, *Letters of Innocent III concerning Eng.*, p. 169, no. 1014.

the bishop of Winchester, was retiring from the bench. Eustace continued to be a justice at the Bench until shortly before its closing in 1209. He rarely missed a term of court at Westminster unless he was with the king or away on a diplomatic mission. Fauconberg went on the two general eyres of John's reign and also on less far-ranging summer circuits. Master Ralph of Stokes first appears in the role of royal justice during the king's visit to England, February to April 1200. His appearances as a justice were intermittent, chiefly among the justices *coram rege* and rarely for common pleas at Westminster. A third justice who first took his place at the Bench in 1200 was Walter of Creeping, who sat at Westminster continuously from Trinity term 1200 until its closing in 1209. He never missed a term of court at Westminster in those nine years, and witnessed the bulk of the final concords made there. Walter went on eyre to his native East Anglia during summer vacations and on the two general eyres of John's reign, an arrangement that enabled him to combine the business of hearing pleas with management of his own estates. Walter of Creeping was rarely with the court following the king. He sat with a combined Bench and court *coram rege* in the spring of 1205, and he was with the court *coram rege* again in 1209, following King John's closing of the court at Westminster. That was his last judicial work, yet he remained alive until shortly after the end of the civil war.[13]

1205 saw two new justices joining the royal courts, revealing King John's hand in appointments following his return from Normandy. Master Henry of London, archdeacon of Stafford, served as a royal justice frequently from 1205 almost until the king's excommunication in 1209. His earliest judicial experience had come at the beginning of the reign, when he joined the itinerant justices in 1199. He did not again sit in judgment until May 1205; after that he was active at the Bench and in the counties, though chiefly with the justices *coram rege*. His last appearances as a royal judge were in January and February 1209. Probably King John's excommunication later in the year made him unwilling to serve in so public a position. Richard de Mucegros' judicial career did not begin until 1205, possibly because he had

---

[13] *Rot. Lit. Claus.*, 1: 340; *C.R.R.*, 11: 141, no. 697, a 1223 suit brought by his son.

been with King John's fighting forces in Normandy earlier. In 1205, Richard sat at the Bench, with the justices *coram rege*, and on summer vacation courts. He would serve as a justice intermittently until 1211, on the 1208–9 eyre, occasionally at Westminster, but chiefly with the court following the king. In 1211, Richard served only once, and he never again sat among the royal justices, even though he lived well into the reign of Henry III.[14]

Henry II's legal innovations proved so popular that people much lower on the social scale than anticipated were soon suing each other in the royal courts for suprisingly small plots of land, sometimes only a few acres. Experiments in the construction of smoother-working machinery to cope with the growing number of suits continued under King John. The most notable change was the new importance that the court following the king took on. Although the king's own court was the feudal tribunal for his tenants-in-chief, no court *coram rege* with its own permanent staff, plea rolls, and procedures seems to have existed in the twelfth century. Henry II and Richard I did have justices accompanying them on their travels about the kingdom; yet their justices *coram rege* never became a serious alternative to the justices on eyre or the Bench at Westminster as a place for settling the common pleas of the knights and lesser freemen of the counties. It could not evolve into a permanent tribunal on account of the two kings' prolonged absences on the Continent.[15]

Whatever the role of the court following the king under Henry II and Richard I, it began to assume greater significance with King John's accession to the throne. John was no absentee monarch, for the loss of Normandy made him resident in England almost continuously after 1204; and he took an active part in day-to-day government, including justice. King John's knowledge of England, his interest in legal matters, and his almost continuous residence in the kingdom after 1204 meant that his own court, sitting nearby if not in his presence, would become a permanent part of the kingdom's judicial machinery. A dual system of central courts grew up to administer the com-

---

[14] *V.C.H., Glos.*, 8: 190.
[15] Chiefly the view of Richardson and Sayles, *Governance*, p. 172.

mon law of thirteenth-century England – Common Pleas or Bench stationary at Westminster except for periodic eyres, and *coram rege* or, later, King's Bench roaming the country – almost duplicate bodies with little to differentiate their work.[16] John's creation of his own court, staffed in part with *familiares regis*, fitted in with his plan for a government that was to be essentially household government. He may well have been aiming at the kind of 'unrealized absolutism' which J.E.A. Jolliffe asserted was the goal of the Angevin monarchs.[17]

Possibly John felt that he was merely reviving the custom of his father in hearing pleas as he moved about the land, but the accident of his continued residence in England from 1204 to 1214 meant that his court *coram rege* would become a permanent part of the English judicial system. At least, that is the version of what happened accepted by some historians. More likely, however, King John's plan from the first was to make his own court a permanent body; for almost at once the justices *coram rege* began to keep plea rolls, the first surviving one dating from the king's visit to England in the spring of 1200.[18] Although little evidence survives to identify the justices who constituted John's first court *coram rege*, two of the justices – Simon of Pattishall and Master Ralph of Stokes – can be identified. Master Ralph, a clerk borrowed from the justiciar's staff, had responsibility for keeping the roll of pleas.[19] From 1200 until 1205, the two joined the court whenever the king was in England. In the intervals, Ralph of Stokes assisted Geoffrey fitz Peter at Westminster or on summer vacation eyres from time to time. Ralph's last appearance as a justice was in September 1206, although he lived until c. 1219–24.[20]

On the king's second visit to England, October 1200 to May 1201, the justices were joined by Master Eustace de Fauconberg, and occasionally by the justiciar. Eustace joined the new court

---

[16] For the types of cases the two courts heard in 1204, Turner, *King and his courts*, pp. 33–47.   [17] Jolliffe, *Angevin Kingship*, p. 341.

[18] Feb.–Apr. 1200, printed in *P.B.K.J.*, 1: 296–310. Lady Stenton noted (p. 61) that possibly a roll of proceedings before the king was kept on John's visit to England in 1199, but if so, it has not survived.

[19] *P.B.K.J.*, 1: 57, 58; *C.R.R.*, 1: 327.

[20] Testimony in a 1224 assize of darrein presentment states that Master Ralph had died, R.R. Darlington, ed., *Cartulary of Worcester Cathedral Priory*, Pipe Roll Soc, new ser. 38 (1968): 129–31, no. 246. He was alive in 1219, *Pipe Roll 3 Hen. III*, pp. 2, 83, 84.

on John's subsequent visits about the kingdom in April and May 1204 and in May and June 1205. Following John's closing of the court of Common Pleas in the spring of 1209, Eustace again sat with the justices *coram rege* from May to October. He did not become a permanent member, however, possibly because his clerical status prevented his serving an excommunicate king. According to Lady Stenton, the work of Simon of Pattishall, Master Eustace de Fauconberg, and Master Ralph of Stokes, under Geoffrey fitz Peter's direction, 'succeeded in establishing the court *coram rege* so that it gave reasonable satisfaction to the King and his subjects'.[21]

King John grew dissatisfied with the dual system of courts, and the Bench began to decline during the years 1207–9, when more and more cases were removed from its jurisdiction until it finally ceased to exist at all. The pleas for Michaelmas term 1208 and Hilary and Easter terms of 1209 could all be recorded on a single roll. That this removal of cases resulted from a royal command is clear from the record of an assize brought before the justices at the Bench in Easter term 1209. It was adjourned for hearing *coram rege* when one of the parties declared that 'no plea ought to be held at Westminster' and vouched the king to warrant his statement.[22] Geoffrey fitz Peter had little part left to play in judgments, except for occasional appearances with the justices *coram rege* in 1212 and 1213. The absence of any permanent panel of judges at Westminster, however, meant that sometimes the Exchequer staff had to perform judicial work.[23] King John's closing of the court of Common Pleas can be seen as part of his plan for concentrating all power in his own hands. The several crises he faced – dispute with the pope, rivalry with the French king, and rebelliousness among his barons – must have fuelled John's already mistrustful nature. Lady Stenton saw that the pipe roll testimony for 1208–9 sharpens the chroniclers' portrait of 'a suspicious ruler, keeping his subjects in hand through fear'.[24]

---

[21] *P.B.K.J.*, 1: 124. [22] *C.R.R.*, 5: Preface, 327.

[23] *Justiciarship*, pp. 176–7. *Governance*, p. 385, maintain that John's distrust of his justiciar was a powerful factor in his suspension of the Bench.

[24] *English Justice*, p. 101. Yet some historians would argue that simple administrative convenience, not John's desire to control justice more closely, brought about the decline of the Bench, e.g. J.A.P. Jones, *King John and Magna Carta* (London, 1971), p. 81.

The years 1209–10 saw the greatest change in the personnel of the *curia regis* of the entire reign. King John relied on a band of only four trusted judges, occasionally bolstered by others following him about the kingdom. He could no longer rely on clerics to serve him on the bench, for many feared to endanger their souls by serving an excommunicate king.[25] Two of the clerics among the royal justices, Master Eustace de Fauconberg and Henry, archdeacon of Stafford, continued doing the king's work in other less conspicuous spheres, though not on the judicial bench. The laymen King John now relied upon included two experienced justices from Westminster, Simon of Pattishall and James of Potterne. They had been frequently with the court *coram rege* since the king's return from Normandy.

The two others were newcomers to the judiciary: Henry de Pont-Audemar and Roger Huscarl. Henry, who had been active in the administration of Normandy before coming to England, first joined the court *coram rege* in 1207. He left to take part in the general eyre of 1208, and he was absent for nearly a year from the autumn of 1212 to the autumn of 1213, but otherwise he was regularly with the *curia regis*. Roger Huscarl only joined the judiciary in October 1210, and he remained with the court following the king until John set sail for Poitou in the spring of 1214. Both men then returned to Westminster with the other justices *coram rege* to form a reconstituted court of Common Pleas. Henry and Robert last appeared as justices at Westminster in early May 1215, at the time that strife between king and baronage disrupted normal government. Henry de Pont-Audemar never served as a justice under Henry III, although he lived until at least 1223.[26] Roger Huscarl, however, served as an itinerant justice on the first general eyre of the new reign, 1218–19; and he returned to Westminster for the 1219 Easter term, much shortened because of the eyre. Eventually, his judicial experience took him to Ireland in the king's service.

One other who sat with the justices *coram rege* with some frequency, although less continuously than the other four was Robert de Aumari, autumn 1210 to autumn 1211. A second, Jocelin de Stukely, never joined the justices following the king,

---

[25] *English Justice*, pp. 97–8.
[26] He was at Westminster, taking part in a lawsuit, Hilary term 1223, *C.R.R.*, 11: 3, no. 19.

but he sat with them at Westminster during much of the spring and summer of 1214, while the king was executing his ill-fated grand design to regain Normandy. Others such as William Briwerre joined the court for shorter periods as it travelled about the kingdom, witnessing fines as justices. A particularly large number arrived and departed from the *curia regis* in 1209. With the justices in May was the justiciar, and in July the bishop of Bath, a longtime royal clerk, and the bishop of Winchester, the future justiciar, sat with them.

By early 1214 King John's attention had turned to preparations for his final campaign to recover his continental possessions, and the royal justices returned to Westminster on his departure. They joined the new justiciar, Peter des Roches, bishop of Winchester, in forming a reconstituted Bench. The revived court of Common Pleas, then, was simply the result of the justices *coram rege* settling at Westminster once the king had left England, not the justiciar's own court in the way that it had been under Hubert Walter and Geoffrey fitz Peter, both of whom were famed for their learning in the law. The bishop of Winchester was a Poitevin, chiefly a financial expert with little knowledge of the common law, and his presidency of the court was largely nominal.[27] Simon of Pattishall, the senior justice, must have played a leading part in the court's work because of the justiciar's lack of legal experience.

No plea rolls or feet of fines from a court *coram rege* survive after King John's return from the Continent in the autumn of 1214. Even at Westminster the level of Bench business fell off greatly, in evidence of the uncertainty of the times. The small number of pleas for Michaelmas 1214 and even scantier number for Hilary 1215 could all be enrolled on a single roll, later inscribed as *ultimus rotulus placitorum ante guerram*.[28] The royal courts' last recorded sessions were on 3 May 1215 when fines were made at the New Temple, London, *coram rege* and at Westminster. After that date the crisis over baronial demands for reform and the resulting civil war caused a suspension of all normal judicial activity until after King John's death. Yet judicial work did not cease entirely, for on 30 March 1216, in the

---

[27] Even though he witnessed final concords made at Westminster, his presence elsewhere on the day of the fine can be proven, *Justiciarship*, pp. 191–7.
[28] Flower, *Intro. to C.R.R.*, p. 20.

midst of the rebellion, King John found time to assign Simon of Pattishall to take an assize at Northampton.[29] Doubtless Simon had retired to his estates nearby on the disruption of normal work at Westminster.

2 ORIGINS AND TRAINING

A look at the family origins and professional background of King John's justices readily reveals that they came from knightly families similar to those of his father's and brother's judges. It also reveals their increased professionalization and specialization. Their backgrounds indicate fewer multi-purpose royal servants from the Exchequer or royal household and more men with early careers in local government. What was true for little more than half of Richard I's fourteen justices is true for at least ten of King John's seventeen. Magnates may have had some justification for their fears that government was falling into the hands of 'faceless men', unknown to them.

A comparative biographical study enables us to make some generalizations about the seventeen justices of John. First, sixteen of them were native Englishmen. Henry de Pont-Audemar, as his name indicates, came from Normandy, where he had held land and engaged in administrative activity before 1204.[1] The Pont-Audemar family, however, had held English lands long before Henry came to England. Another Henry de Pont-Audemar – doubtless his father or grandfather – held a knight's fee of the honour of Gloucester in 1187, which Henry held in King John's time.[2] In 1210 Henry claimed land in Berkshire as rightfully his through his grandfather, also named Henry de Pont-Audemar.[3] None of Henry II's inner core of justices and only one, or possibly two of Richard I's had come from across the Channel. Although John employed Normans and Poitevins widely in his government after 1204, their absence from the judiciary is not surprising. Only a native of England who had grown up with the common law and custom of the shires could

---

[29] *Rot. Lit. Claus.*, 1: 270.
[1] Henry was the man of Count Robert de Meulan, lord of Pont-Audemar, whose charter he witnessed in 1202, Prévôst, *Mémoires et notes pour l'histoire du département de l'Eure*, 1: 200; 2: 565.   [2] *Red Book Exch.*, pp. 67, 609.
[3] Half the vill of Ilsely, *C.R.R.*, 6: 73.

have mastered its complexities. It is no surprise that those native Englishmen whose origins can be traced came mainly from the South and the Midlands. Only one came from the North: Master Eustace de Fauconberg, member of a Yorkshire family.

More significant than geographical origin is the social background of the justices. Most came from the middle or lower levels of the knightly order, again offering little contrast with earlier justices. Three, however, had risen to baronial rank through service to the monarchy by the time of King John. The career of Geoffrey fitz Peter is the most spectacular example of such a rise from obscurity to the summit of power. He had held perhaps a dozen knight's fees at Henry II's death, but by 1190 had risen to the rank of an earl with his acquisition of the Mandeville honour.[4] Hugh Bardolf inherited substantial lands in Lincolnshire from his father and mother, which he steadily increased so that his holdings reached into several shires by the time of his death.[5] William Briwerre, like Geoffrey fitz Peter, was a forester's son who rose to baronial rank through service to Henry II and his sons. William accumulated so much land, scattered over several counties, that he ranked solidly among the baronage in King John's time.[6] In so far as William's holdings had a centre, it lay in Devonshire; but he never held one of the ancient titles, only a complex of tenures that he himself had built up much as Richard de Lucy had done earlier. Unlike Geoffrey fitz Peter or William Marshal, whose careers Briwerre's resembled in many ways, he never won an earldom.

Two of the justices came from families which approached baronial rank. The family of Master Eustace de Fauconberg was a distinguished Yorkshire baronial one, descended from one of

---

[4] He received the third penny of the county, valued at about £20, from Richard I, *Pipe Roll 2 Ric. I*, p. 111. King John named him earl of Essex on his coronation day, *Roger Howden*, 4: 90.

[5] His brother as his heir offered £1000 plus surrender of a manor to King John to have the inheritance, *Pipe Roll 5 John*, p. 103.

[6] 39 fees plus assorted smaller units by 1219, *Pipe Roll 3 Hen. III*, p. 24. He already had substantial lands when John confirmed his possessions early in his reign, *Rot. Chart.*, p. 28. King John in 1204 granted him the barony of Horsley, Derby, with 23 3/4 knight's fees plus two other fees of 10 knights each, *Rot. Chart.*, p. 123; the honour of Lavendon, Bucks, *Rot. Lit. Pat.*, p. 41; and an impressive group of manors, *Rot. de Obl. et Fin.*, pp. 225–6.

William the Conqueror's warriors. Eustace was the son of Peter de Fauconberg, lord of Rise and Catfoss.[7] Richard de Mucegros belonged to a branch of a family important on the southern Welsh marches almost from the time of the Conquest.[8] He inherited his father's estate of three hides plus some smaller holdings in Gloucestershire in 1200, when Richard senior retired to a monastery.[9]

Of the remaining justices under study, seven can be said with some assurance to have come from middling knightly families of the counties. At least they had relatives holding knight's fees whose names survive on lists of scutages, feet of fines, or plea rolls. Knights with the name of Guestling held fees of the archbishops of Canterbury in Kent and Sussex and some smaller holdings centred around the Cinq Ports.[10] Richard of Herriard was a knight of the earls of Leicester and Salisbury, holding lands of them in Wiltshire and Hampshire. Osbert fitz Hervey's surname was derived from a Norman tenant of the lord of Haughley, Suffolk, at the time of Domesday Book.[11] The Old English name 'Huscarl' is unexpected among the Norman-descended knights of the twelfth and thirteenth centuries, but a family of that name held three knight's fees of the honour of Wallingford. Because the name is unusual, it is likely that Roger was a member of that family, possibly a younger son sent off to

---

[7] Charles T. Clay, *Early Yorkshire Families*, Yorks Archaeol. Soc. (1973), pp. 26–7; William Farrer, ed., *Early Yorkshire Charters*, Yorks Archaeol. Soc. Rec. Ser., Extra Ser. (1914–16), 1: 419; 3: 48, no. 1322. The earliest known member of the family was Franco, related to the castellans of St Omer, lords of Faucuembergue, *Complete Peerage*, 5: 267.

[8] The family name 'Mucegros' or 'Muchgros' came from Mussegros in Normandy, seat of Roger de Mucegros, who held land in Herefs as early as 1080, Lewis Loyd, *Origins of some Anglo-Norman Families*, p. 71; *Docs. preserved in France*, p. 219.

[9] The manor of Boddington held of Westminster Abbey, *V.C.H., Glos.*, 8: 190. Richard's father and grandfather retired to Tewkesbury, *Monasticon*, 2: 75.

[10] E.g. Simon of Guestling, a tenant of the archbishop in the time of Henry II, died c. 1202, *Pipe Roll 28 Hen. II*, p. 88; *C.R.R.*, 2: 124; 11: 325, no. 1627. For John's holdings see *Red Book Exch.*, pp. 470, 725; *C.R.R.* 11: 22, no. 127; 107, no. 562; and 528, no. 2639; L.F. Salzmann, ed., *An Abstract of Feet of Fines relating to Sussex*, Sussex Rec. Soc., 2 (1903–16): 41–3, no. 167; *Cal. Kent Feet of Fines*, p. 397.

[11] For details of Richard's and Osbert's backgrounds, see chap. 3, pt. 3.

London to make his way.[12] The surname 'de Insula' or 'Delisle', on the other hand, was a common one in medieval England. In the case of Master Godfrey de Insula it doubtless denotes the Isle of Ely.[13] Possibly he was one of the Lisles of Rougemont, a family with lands in Norfolk, Suffolk, and Cambridgeshire whose rise to power began under Bishop Nigel and who continued to serve the bishops of Ely for a century.[14] Little is known of Simon of Pattishall's family, but they were apparently tenants of the honour of Wahull.[15] Henry of Whiston came from a family connected with Ramsey Abbey, which held land of the abbey in Northamptonshire and Huntingdonshire. His grandfather was the monks' tenant in 1120, and his father held three and a half or four hides of them in the 1160s. Henry's brother succeeded to the land in 1191 and eventually became steward of Ramsey Abbey. They had an aunt who married into a northern landed family, from whom Henry inherited land in Westmorland.[16]

Only one of King John's justices was of urban origin. Henry of London, archdeacon of Stafford, belonged to the Blund family, a family long prominent in the affairs of the city and with ties to the royal household. As early as the 1160s, the London Blunds were supervisors of works and suppliers of goods for the royal

---

[12] The suggestion of Doris M. Stenton, ed., *Rolls of the Justices in Eyre for Yorkshire in 3 Henry III (1218–19)*, Selden Soc., 56 (1937): xxiii. For an account of the Huscarls and their holdings, see *V.C.H., Berks*, 3: 418; and H.E. Salter and A.H. Cooke, eds., *Boarstall Cartulary*, Oxf. Hist. Soc., 88: (1930): 322. Roland Huscarl held the three fees by 1201, *Rot. de Obl. et Fin.*, p. 166.

[13] His association with Hubert Walter and with other Norfolk and Suffolk men points toward an East Anglian provenance for him: in 1198 he was a pledge in a Norfolk and Suffolk suit, *Pipe Roll 10 Ric. I*, p. 49; he was attorney in a 1203 assize concerning Norfolk land, *C.R.R.*, 2: 291.

[14] Edward Miller, *The Abbey and Bishopric of Ely* (Cambridge, 1951), pp. 180, 197. For Simon de Insula, the bishop's steward (?1202–13), see pp. 265–6.

[15] For details, see chap. 3, pt. 3, pp. 92–3.

[16] *Cart. Rameseia*, Rolls Series, 1: 146, 154; and *V.C.H., Northants*, 4: 288–9, for Henry's father, Henry senior, and grandfather, William. For Henry senior's land, *Cart. Rameseia*, 3: 49, 313. For Henry's brother William, *Cat. Anc. Deeds*, 4: 201, no. A7700; *Pat. Rolls, 1216–1225*, p. 565. In 1195 Henry offered 10 marks to have land at Crosby Ravensworth, at Lowther near Penrith, and at Whale in Lowther, Westmorland, as his inheritance from his aunt Hawise, *Pipe Roll 7 Ric. I*, p. 148; *1 John*, p. 213. These lands were part of the barony of Burgh by Sands.

family, perhaps official purchasers.[17] Henry was one of five sons born to Bartholomew Blund, an alderman of London (died c. 1201). Other sons were active in London's government: Robert, also an alderman and a sheriff in 1196–7; James, alderman, sheriff in 1199–1200, and mayor in 1216–17; and Richard, sheriff in 1198–9.[18]

The remaining justices may have had more humble origins, for they were the first of their families to leave any mark on surviving documents. All had rural origins, shown by their surnames taken from obscure villages where their fathers doubtless were freeholders. Walter of Creeping first surfaces as a charter witness in Essex sometime before 1194, but little light falls on his family or his landholdings.[19] The name 'Stoke' or 'Stokes' is so common in England that it is impossible to pinpoint the birthplace of Ralph of Stokes. A likely surmise is that he came from the manor of Severn Stoke, Worcestershire, midway between Worcester and Tewkesbury.[20] James of Potterne's name locates his birthplace in Wiltshire, two miles south of Devizes. He is described as a 'knight' in his first appearance in the public records, when he witnessed a final concord in the Wiltshire county court, 1188–9.[21]

As we have seen, a number of the justices serving King John's father and brother came from what might be termed adminis-

---

[17] Henry Blund bought falcons for the king in 1166, *Pipe Roll 12 Hen. II*, p. 130. Edward Blund oversaw repairs to royal buildings in London, Westminster, and Windsor, and purchased supplies for the royal household from 1166 to 1182, *Pipe Roll 12 Hen. II*, pp. 106, 130; *15 Hen. II*, p. 129, 170; *18 Hen. II*, pp. 144–5; *22 Hen. II*, p. 11; *27 Hen. II*, pp. 156–7. Roger Blund was one of four men accounting for the farm of London, 1169–72, *Pipe Roll 15 Hen. II*, p. 170; *18 Hen. II*, p. 143.

[18] The fifth son was John, a goldsmith, who died early. G.A.J. Hodgett, ed., *The Cartulary of Holy Trinity, Aldgate*, London Rec. Soc., 7 (1971): 90, no. 449; 129, no. 655; and Eric Saint John Brooks, 'Archbishop Henry of London and his Irish connections', *Jl. Royal Soc. Antiq. Ireland*, 20, 6th ser. (1930): 1–4.

[19] Before 1194, he witnessed a charter of Robert fitz Walter at Colne Priory, Essex, J.L. Fisher, ed., *Cartularium Prioratus de Colne*, Essex Archaeol. Soc., Occasional Pubns., no. 1 (1946): 51–2, no. 102. He witnessed charters of the abbey of St John Baptist, Colchester, before 1195, Stuart A. Moore, ed., *Cartularium monasterii Sancti Johannis Baptiste de Colecesteria*, Roxburghe Club (London, 1897), 1: 272, 2: 532, 644, 653. Other Creepings held lands of the abbey, including Walter's brother William, *Cart. St. John Bap.*, 1: 266, 272; 2: 435, 653.

[20] The manor was held by the king and the abbot of Westminster before 1167, *V.C.H., Worcs.*, 4: 192–3.

[21] *Reg. Malmesbur.*, Rolls Series, 1: 459–60, no. 136; *V.C.H., Wilts*, 7: 209–10.

trative families: eight of the thirteen under Henry II, and five of
fourteen under Richard Lionheart. The number for the justices
of King John with family ties to other royal administrators is six
of seventeen. Only one, however, came from a family in the
upper levels of government. Osbert fitz Hervey, as we have
seen, was the brother of Hubert Walter and nephew of Ranulf
de Glanvill. Those from families in lower reaches of the administration include Geoffrey fitz Peter and William Briwerre, sons
of royal foresters. Briwerre succeeded his father and grandfather
as hereditary forester of Bere, Hampshire.[22] Simon of Guestling,
a probable kinsman of John of Guestling, had been one of the
supervisors for Henry II's reconstruction of Hastings Castle in
1182.[23] A kinsman of Richard de Mucegros was also a sheriff in
Henry II's last years. Miles de Mucegros was sheriff of Hereford,
1181–3, itinerant justice, and custodian of castles on the Welsh
marches. His son Walter was in charge of King John's hounds in
1203.[24] Richard was descended from another branch of the family,
however, whose exact connection with Miles is unclear. Master
Ralph of Stokes had as kinsman Peter of Stokes, a member of
the royal household under both Richard I and John. He gained
by 1201 the post of seneschal, which he held until his death
in 1206.[25]

Ties of patronage in several instances point toward the path
which led the justices to the *curia regis*. The first step toward an
important government office for an ambitious youth was entry
into the service of some baron or bishop, possibly as a knight
but more probably by the end of the twelfth century as a clerk,
an estate steward or bailiff. By scanning charter witness-lists and
other sources, one can try to untangle the network of patronage
connecting justices to great men. The scarcity of documents,
however, means that many of the ties suggested are far from
secure. Walter of Creeping took his name from the manor of
Creeping Hall, Essex, held by Aubrey de Vere, earl of Oxford,

[22] *Rot. Chart.*, p. 39.   [23] *Pipe Roll 28 Hen. II*, p. 88.
[24] F.T.S. Houghton, 'The family of Muchgros', *Birmingham and Midland Inst.
Archaeol. Soc. Trans.*, 47 (1921): 10; *Rot. de Lib. ac de Mis.*, p. 58.
[25] *Rot. Lit. Pat.*, p. 66b. Both were associates of Geoffrey fitz Peter, Emma
Mason, *The Beauchamp Cartulary*, Pipe Roll Soc., new ser. (1980): 195–6, nos.
345, 346. Peter appointed Ralph of Stokes his attorney in a plea at
Westminster in 1200, *C.R.R.*, 1: 338; *P.B.K.J.*, 1: 314, no. 3184.

and he evidently began his career in the earl's household.[26]
Walter's brother was the *vadletus* of Aubrey de Vere II in 1216.[27]
Of course, as an Essex man with ties to the Benedictine abbey of
Colchester, Walter would have known Osbert fitz Hervey. The
manor from which James of Potterne took his name was one of
the bishop of Salisbury's holdings, and it is likely that he began
his career in the service of one of the bishops, most likely Herbert
le Poer, who succeeded Hubert Walter in 1194. Because Herbert
was often at Westminster, a member of his household could
have made contacts there for recruitment into the justiciar's
staff.

Because of Master Eustace de Fauconberg's ecclesiastical
status, his career is better documented. It began in the
household of Godfrey de Lucy, perhaps even before Godfrey
became bishop of Winchester. Eustace's name appears among
the witnesses to a quitclaim made at York in July 1187 before a
group of justices that included Godfrey. Since Godfrey de Lucy
had become archdeacon of Richmond, Yorkshire, by 1184, it
could well be that Fauconberg had already entered his service.[28]
After Godfrey moved to Winchester in 1189, Eustace witnessed
a number of his episcopal acts, in some of which he is described
as the bishop's *clericus*.[29] Eustace's master sat among the justices
at Westminster throughout Richard I's reign. This means that
Eustace was often there as well, meeting men of high rank in
royal government and observing the operations of the courts.
He picked up some experience himself, for at the end of
Richard's reign he was acting as attorney in pleas before the *curia
regis*.[30]

---

[26] *Cart. Prior. de Coln*, pp. 51–2, no. 102, where Walter joined the earl and his son
as witnesses to a charter before 1194. A later Walter of Creeping was
executor of the will of Hugh de Vere, earl of Oxford, in 1263, *Exc. è Rot. Fin.*,
2: 407. See also *Feet of Fines for Lincs*, p. xxx.

[27] *Pipe Roll 17 John*, p. 89. *Cart. St. John. Bap., Colchester*, 1: 266, indicates that
Walter and William were brothers.

[28] Charles T. Clay, ed., *Early Yorks Chtrs.*, 5: 51, no. 418; Charles T. Clay, 'Notes
on the early archdeacons in the Church of York', *Yorks Archaeol. Jl.*, 36 (1944–
7): 417.

[29] *Docs. preserved in France*, no. 768; *Cartulary of Winchester Cathedral*, ed. A.W.
Goodman (Winchester, 1927), p. 41, no. 90; Westminster Domesday, f. 580.
For other references, see Cheney, *English Bishops' Chanceries*, pp. 10, 19.

[30] For the abbot of St Vaast, *C.R.R.*, 1: 74; *Rot. Cur. Reg.*, 1: 224; and for the
bishop of Ely, *Rot. Cur. Reg.*, 1: 61.

Either Richard de Mucegros or his father had ties to William Marshal, whose marriage in 1189 made him a powerful lord along the Welsh marches where the Mucegros lands lay. Unfortunately, Richard and his father bore the same Christian name, making it impossible to sort them out before 1200 when Richard de Mucegros senior took the habit of religion. As early as 1178 a 'Richard Michegros' witnessed William Marshal's grant to the canons of Waltham. About 1190 Richard de Mucegros – senior or junior? – witnessed William Marshal's foundation charter for Cartmel Priory. At the same time, he was William's undersheriff for Gloucestershire.[31] Richard de Mucegros had some connections with Hugh Bardolf; he seems to have been Bardolf's undersheriff in Dorset and Somerset before Hugh's removal in 1194.[32]

From the time of Glanvill, when royal justices first began to hear pleas on a regular basis at Westminster, they owed their appointment chiefly to the justiciar. Osbert fitz Hervey, whose judicial career reached back to 1191, shared ties of kinship with Ranulf de Glanvill and Hubert Walter.[33] Another justice who possibly benefited from Hubert Walter's patronage is John of Guestling, a knight of the archbishopric of Canterbury. John joined the judiciary in January 1198, only a few months before the archbishop resigned the justiciarship. The change in justiciars did not affect Guestling; indeed, he accompanied Geoffrey fitz Peter on his first eyre as justiciar, 1198–9.

The evidence for Master Godfrey de Insula's connection with Hubert Walter is clearer, again because of easier documentation for clerical careers. His name is frequently found among the *clerici nostri* on witness-lists of the archbishop's charters.[34] In 1199, before Godfrey had begun to sit regularly at the Bench,

---

[31] *Cartae Antiq. Rolls 11–20*, p. 57, no. 379; *Lancs. pipe rolls*, p. 342. *List of Sheriffs*, p. 49.

[32] *Pipe Roll 7 Ric. I*, p. 228; *Chancellor's Roll 8 Ric. I*, p. 214, where Richard is responsible for a portion of the ancient farm of the county for which Hugh renders account. Earlier, c. 1184–8, Richard had joined another sheriff of Dorset and Somerset in witnessing a Wells Cathedral charter, *H.M.C. Reports, D & C Wells*, 2: 548.   [33] See chap. 3, pt. 3, p. 92.

[34] B.L. Harl. MS. 391, ff. 102^V, 106; Add. MS. 46,353, f. 12^V; Lambeth Palace MS. 1212, ff. 61^V, 107^V, 114^V. Also *Monasticon*, 6, pt. 2: 667a; *H.M.C., Ninth Report*, p. 355b, and H.E. Savage, ed., *The Great Register of Lichfield Cathedral, Magnum Registrum Album*, Col. for a Hist. of Staffs, 48 (Stafford, 1926), p. 358, no. 753.

the justices turned to him as Hubert Walter's *amicus familiaris* to verify two of the archbishop's writs.[35] The archbishop had brought several of his own clerks into the work of secular government once he became justiciar. Among the clerks was Godfrey de Insula, who went on the two general eyres of 1194 and 1198–9 as a justice. In the midst of the second eyre, Godfrey's master resigned the justiciarship, but his own career at the Bench was only beginning.

Five judges owed their appointments to a close relationship with Hubert Walter's successor as justiciar, Geoffrey fitz Peter. The ties of both Simon of Pattishall and Richard of Herriard to Geoffrey from early in the reign of Richard Lionheart have already been shown.[36] James of Potterne's first important post was as undersheriff for Geoffrey fitz Peter in Yorkshire, 1198–1200.[37] About the same time that James entered Geoffrey's service as deputy sheriff, he also began his judicial career, accompanying the justiciar on his circuit during the great 1198–9 eyre. The association on the bench between James and the justiciar continued to be close until Geoffrey fitz Peter's role in judicial affairs ended with the 1209 closing of the court at Westminster.

Master Ralph of Stokes can be found at Oxford as early as 1184, when he was among 'the knights of Oxfordshire and clerks of the archdeaconry and knights of the honor of Wallingford' taking part in an inquest before the itinerant justices. Since the archdeacon of Oxford at that time was Walter of Coutances, this inquest provides a clue to Ralph's first patron.[38] Walter, as archbishop of Rouen, was to play a major role in the government of Richard I. Ralph then fades into obscurity until early 1199, by which time he emerges as a clerk of Geoffrey fitz Peter, working on both Bench and Exchequer business. From 1199 to 1202, Master Ralph can be seen delivering messages from the justiciar to the Bench at Westminster, or to the barons

---

[35] *C.R.R.*, 7: 113.
[36] Chap. 3, pt. 3, pp. 105–6.
[37] *Mem. Roll 1 John*, p. 5. *Roger Howden* confused him with the sheriff, 4: 139–40, 158.
[38] Herbert E. Salter, ed., *Cartulary of Oseney Abbey*, Oxf. Hist. Soc. (1929–36), 4: 415–16, no. 385. For Walter of Coutances, see *Fasti, Lincoln*, p. 35.

of the Exchequer, witnessing both judicial and financial writs, or drafting and witnessing charters.[39]

Henry of Whiston seems to have been at the Exchequer, possibly in the service of Geoffrey fitz Peter, as early as 1191. He delivered money from a crown debtor to William Briwerre on Geoffrey's behalf.[40] Soon, however, Henry passed into the service of Hugh Bardolf. After Bardolf's appointment as escheator for the North of England in 1194, Henry was in charge of the accounts for Yorkshire manors in Hugh's custody.[41]

Royal patronage was the swiftest way to ascend the social ladder in the Middle Ages, enabling a few men of humble origin who attracted the king's attention to climb rapidly to the highest levels. The careers of Geoffrey fitz Peter and William Briwerre offer the most vivid picture among the judges of such an ascent. While Hugh Bardolf did not start from so low a point on the social scale and perhaps did not rise quite so spectacularly, his steady rise in political power and wealth closely approaches Geoffrey's and William's successes. William Briwerre's early career parallels Geoffrey fitz Peter's remarkably. Both men were sons of foresters who somehow won the notice of Henry II, became *familiares* of his two sons, and participated in the highest councils of government. William's path to a place in the king's company cannot be retraced, but as early as 1175 he was with Henry II at Marlborough, witnessing a charter.[42] By 1179, Briwerre had assumed office as sheriff of Devonshire, and other responsibilities in the South West soon followed.[43]

Others did not climb as high as these three *familiares regis*, yet the king may have been their patron as well. Master Henry of London, who joined the judiciary in 1205, had close connections with King John from an early date. He has been identified

---

[39] *C.R.R.*, 1: 71, 204, 391; *P.B.K.J.*, 1: 30–32; *Mem. Roll 1 John*, pp. 10, 45, 50; *Rot. Chart.*, pp. 77b, 86b, 93.

[40] *Pipe Roll 3 Ric. I*, p. 164. Henry was again passing on payments on Geoffrey fitz Peter's behalf in 1200, *Pipe Roll 2 John*, p. 52.

[41] *Pipe Roll 6 Ric. I*, p. 12; *7 Ric. I*, pp. 27–8; *9 Ric. I*, p. 116; *10 Ric. I*, p. 26; *1 John*, p. 50.   [42] *Docs. preserved in France*, p. 336.

[43] *List of Sheriffs*, p. 34. Custodian of the honour of Bampton, *Pipe Roll 32 Hen. II*, p. 203; warden of the Stannaries and tallager of the royal demesne in Cornwall, *Pipe Roll 34 Hen. II*, pp. 156, 165; itinerant justice on the southwestern circuit, *P.B.K.J.*, 3: lxxiv, lxxvi.

as the Henry of London who was a scribe of the queen mother, Eleanor of Aquitaine, c. 1193. Yet he also appears as an associate of Hugh de Nonant, bishop of Coventry, on 2 September 1192.[44] He may have owed his appointment as archdeacon of Stafford, a post he held by 1194, to Hugh. The bishop of Coventry was an associate of Prince John in his conspiracy against King Richard I, and it is likely that Henry of London was also a participant in John's plotting. The archdeacon offered a £100 fine to obtain Richard Lionheart's goodwill following his return from Germany; no doubt he had lost the king's favour as a consequence of his association with Hugh and Prince John.[45] Once John ascended the throne, Henry began to serve him in several spheres. He was one of those *curiales* functioning in a number of areas simultaneously who made Angevin government effective.[46]

Also, 1205 marks the beginning of Richard de Mucegros' judicial career. He had been absent from the records since 1200. A plausible explanation is his presence with King John's fighting forces in Normandy, perhaps accompanying the earl marshal. He first sat among the justices following the king in March 1205, and later that year served at Westminster with the Common Pleas court.

Certainly King John's voice was the decisive one in naming the justices for his own court, particularly the four who were the core of his group of justices from 1209 to 1214. While Simon of Pattishall and James of Potterne were the justiciar's men, the king recognized their experience. Henry de Pont-Audemar had no previous judicial experience in England, although he was an experienced administrator in Normandy and had been a justice

---

[44] He witnessed charters of Eleanor in favor of Bury St Edmunds, c. 1192–3 on her last visit to England, B.L. Add. MS.14,847, f. 40; C.U.L. MS. Ff.2.33, f. 29ᵛ. See H.G. Richardson, 'The Letters and Charters of Eleanor of Aquitaine', *E.H.R.*, 74 (1959); 203–5. For his tie to Hugh de Nonant, see *Cart. Worcester Cath. Priory*, pp. 163–4, no. 310.

[45] *Pipe Roll 7 Ric. I*, p. 189; *Chancellor's Roll 8 Ric. I*, p. 52.

[46] In 1200–1, he was collector of tallages, *Pipe Roll 1 John*, pp. xvii, 26, 30, 34, 77, 84, 166, 218, 227, 259, *2 John*, p. 173. He supervised transport of the king's treasure in 1200, *Pipe Roll 2 John*, p. 150. He was ambassador to the king of Navarre in 1201, *Rot. Lit. Pat.*, p. 3; *Foedera*, 1, pt. 1: 85; *Cal. Docs. relating to Ireland*, 1: nos. 199, 209, 213; *Rot. Chart.*, p. 133.

there at least once in April 1203.[47] Henry's path to the bench, then, led directly from his service to King John in Normandy before 1204.

Roger Huscarl joined the justices *coram rege* in October 1210. He came from a family holding knight's fees of the honour of Wallingford, which fell into Count John's hand in 1189 and remained with him after his coronation in 1199. Huscarl, at first glance, looks like another resident of a royal estate who entered the king's service. There is nothing to connect Roger with King John, however, until long after he had moved to London. Roger Huscarl was recruited for the court *coram rege* in October 1210, after holding only one other official position. He had served as William de Neville's undersheriff in Wiltshire from Christmas 1209 until the Easter Exchequer of 1210.[48] No clue to the reason for Roger's recruitment to John's judiciary can be found by looking for patrons. Perhaps a crisis caused by the shortage of available clerics forced King John to look about more widely for replacements.

The lay element among King John's justices is much higher than among his predecessors' judges: only five of seventeen were clerks. It is less surprising if the special circumstances of John's reign are considered. His long and bitter quarrel with the pope resulted in proclamation of an interdict upon the kingdom (24 March 1208) and the king's excommunication (7 October 1209), a situation that lasted until May 1213. During those years clerics were hesitant to serve John, at least in positions that seemed too public. Three of the clerics regularly sitting in judgment had retired before the crisis reached such a peak of hostility. Two – Master Eustace de Fauconberg and Henry archdeacon of Stafford – continued to be justices into 1209; even then they did not leave the king's service, but served him in less visible posts. The courts could function effectively without the participation of clerics. From 6 October 1209, when Eustace de Fauconberg last sat, until the courts ceased functioning in the summer of 1215 no cleric was present except Peter des

---

[47] T. Duffus Hardy, ed., *Rotuli Normanniae, 1200–1205*, Rec. Comm. (London, 1835), p. 97.
[48] *Pipe Roll 12 John*, pp. 76, 82; *14 John*, p. 147.

Roches, the new justiciar, who began witnessing final concords in January 1214.[49]

Four of the five clerics were in major orders, capable of holding benefices with care of souls. The other one, Henry of Whiston, is described in a papal letter of 1207 as 'subdeacon of the diocese of Lincoln'. Since this letter titles him only as subdeacon, and since no record survives of his ever being named rector or vicar of any church, he must have been one of those who took minor orders to secure secretarial training with no ambition for advancement in the Church.

Closely connected with the justices' clerical or lay status is the question of their education, especially study of Roman or canon law. Studies in the two written laws were flourishing in England by the beginning of John's reign, and many Englishmen had opportunities to win some knowledge of Roman legal principles. Four of John's justices – Eustace de Fauconberg, Godfrey de Insula, Henry of London, and Ralph of Stokes – had the title *magister*. The clerks who wrote out the final concords were often careless about giving judges their correct titles, yet from time to time these four are accorded the title in the records.[50] We may assume, then, that they had some advanced studies at an English cathedral school, or at Northampton or Oxford, or possibly one of the continental universities. Hardly anything definite can be known about their actual studies, but even the least sturdy straws must be grasped if we are to catch any glimpse of their schooling. Since Ralph of Stokes can be pinpointed at Oxford in 1184, it is not too rash to assume that he was studying there at the time.[51] By the latter part of the twelfth century, English bishops were sending promising young clerics from their households to study law abroad at Bologna or some other university. At home, Oxford was developing into such a centre for legal studies by the 1190s that it began to attract students

[49] Lady Stenton does record one final concord taken at the Exchequer, 10 May 1212, witnessed by the treasurer and two archdeacons, *P.B.K.J.*, 3: cclxxxiv.
[50] Walker, *Lincs Feet of Fines*, p. xxvii. For example, she shows that Eustace de Fauconberg was given the title twice in the 1200 feet of fines for Lincs, and only once on the 1202 Lincs eyre. Yet Eustace always styled himself *magister* when witnessing the justiciar's writs in 1214, *Rot. Lit. Claus.*, 207–10.
[51] *Cart. Oseney*, 4: 415–16, no. 385.

from the Continent.[52] Henry archdeacon of Stafford's selection for diplomatic missions to the Continent hints at the likelihood of his having studied Roman law.

The clerical justices had opportunities to acquire some practical knowledge of canon law while carrying out, at least in a minimal way, these duties whether or not they had any formal legal training. This is clearest in the case of Master Godfrey de Insula, a clerk in Hubert Walter's *familia*. Three members of the archbishop's household were canonists of some distinction, former teachers of canon law and authors of legal treatises.[53] It has been suggested that Godfrey's appointment to the Bench was 'as an ecclesiastic whose knowledge of canon law was useful'.[54] Eustace de Fauconberg, on the other hand, as a clerk of the bishop of Winchester, had an opportunity to observe the royal courts at work, for the bishop was active at Westminster throughout Richard I's time.

There are few straws to be grasped which will allow us to see anything of the education of the laymen on the bench. Much that was said about the education of the laymen among Henry II's and Richard I's justices remains true for John's judges as well.[55] By the late twelfth century, warfare and chivalry were clearly inadequate for the education of knights' sons, and a third discipline – letters – was becoming essential. New opportunities were opening for younger sons of knights as estate stewards for magnates who had manors dispersed over many shires. Some of John's justices may have begun their careers as estate stewards, then moved on to become undersheriffs; the work of undersheriffs differed little from the estate stewards' except in scale.

Such men were by no means illiterate in today's sense of the word. Although they may have been *illiterati* in the medieval sense of not being versed in the rules of classical rhetoric, they were not totally unlettered in Latin.[56] They had some rudiments

---

[52] Stephan Kuttner and Eleanor Rathbone, 'Anglo-Norman Canonists', pp. 323–4.
[53] Master Honorius, Master John of Tynemouth, and Master Simon of Siwell, Cheney, *Hubert Walter*, pp. 164–6.
[54] *Justiciarship*, p. 166.   [55] Chap. 2, pt. 2; chap. 3, pt. 3.
[56] Turner, 'The *Miles Literatus*', *A.H.R.*, 83: 931.

of computation as well. Their knowledge of English law did not come from books, however, but from experience gained through years of attending the courts, both private and public. As estate stewards or undersheriffs, they had to preside over various local courts.

We have already seen that religious houses had knights, noted for eloquence and learning in the law, who served as their pleaders in the secular courts.[57] Lay lords must have imitated abbots and priors in choosing one of their knights to act as pleaders. Barons and earls had the feudal obligation of supporting suits of their men in the public courts, yet they were not always able to appear personally in court with them, since their holdings spread over several shires. A specialist-pleader able to appear in their place would have been useful, and he could have substituted for them in their own suits, acting as attorney. The *Leges Henrici Primi* and *Glanvill* hint that it was not uncommon for stewards or bailiffs to act as their lords' attorneys.[58]

Most scholars date the origin of the legal profession about the first decade of the thirteenth century because they connect it with the rise of the Bench at Westminster. An assize roll for 1203, however, shows a plaintiff in a plea at Northampton speaking through his *prolocutor*, or pleader.[59] Recently Robert C. Palmer has argued that professional lawyers were needed in the county and local courts throughout the preceding century, and that it is only the lack of evidence that keeps us from seeing them earlier. In his view, the significance of the central law courts for the legal profession lies in their records, which enable us to recognize the existence of professional attorneys because of the repetition of their names on the plea rolls. He writes, 'Both for attorneys and for pleaders, it was the provincial courts probably rather more than the king's court which were more decisive for generating the legal profession.'[60]

Roger Huscarl is one of King John's justices whose name is repeated on the *curia regis* rolls enough to hint broadly that he

---

[57] Above chap. 2, pt. 2, p. 35.

[58] L.G. Downer, ed. and trans., *Leges Henrici Primi* (Oxford, 1972), pp. 100–1, cap. 7, 7a; *Glanvill*, pp. 133, 167, xi.1; xiii.33.*Dial. de Scac.*, pp. 116–17, shows barons represented before the Exchequer by their stewards.

[59] *Northants assize rolls*, xxvii and no. 719.

[60] Palmer, 'Origins of the legal profession in England', *Irish Jurist*, 11: 126–35.

was a professional lawyer. He first appears as attorney for several different people scattered over two widely separated sections of the country: some from Suffolk, Essex and Hertfordshire, and others from Somerset and Dorset. His work as an attorney extended from 1199 to 1209.[61] On the basis of this evidence, H. G. Richardson suggested, 'It is just possible that he was in fact a lawyer by profession', a suggestion enthusiastically endorsed by Lady Stenton.[62] Besides working as an attorney, acting as his absent client's *alter ego* in conducting his case at Westminster, Roger may well have worked as a *narrator* or pleader, a speaker substituting for suitors or for their attorneys, speaking in their stead. The existence of *narratores* as early as the time of King John is shadowy, for little evidence of their work survives before about 1235. Their appointment was not recorded on the plea rolls, as was appointment of an attorney. The *narratores* had no such official standing as did the attorneys, who were lawfully authorized substitutes, and their activity is only hinted at with oblique reference on rolls.[63]

Huscarl could have been active at Westminster without being a fulltime lawyer there; he may have had other employment. If the London husting, wards and sokes had left records, then we might have evidence of other legal work undertaken by him. Roger witnessed a number of charters and grants for the priory of Holy Trinity, Aldgate, after 1197.[64] This could mean that he was only their tenant, or it could imply that he was the canons' steward or other lay official holding courts for them. While it may be an exaggeration to label Roger Huscarl a 'professional attorney', he clearly was spending enough time at Westminster to attract notice and perhaps to be recommended by experienced

---

[61] He was attorney for six persons, one of them twice, and a surety for another's law, *P.B.K.J.*, 3: Appendix 2, 'Careers of minor professional men in the courts of justice', pp. cccxvi–cccxvii.

[62] Richardson, 'William of Ely, the King's Treasurer, 1195–1215', *T.R.H.S.*, 4th ser., 15 (1932): 67. Lady Stenton wrote, 'There is no doubt that the reign of John saw the emergence of the professional attorney', *P.B.K.J.*, 3: xxxvi; see her biographical sketches of professional attorneys, pp. xxxvi–xl. See also Flower, *Intro. to C.R.R.*, pp. 405–7.

[63] *P.B.K.J.*, 3: xli–xliii.

[64] *Cart. Holy Trinity, Aldgate*, p. 208, no. 1020; *Cat. Anc. Deeds*, 1: 207, no. A1760; 216, no. A1817; 2; 3, no. A1835; 10, no. A18883. Later his son was a witness, 2: 98, no. A2592.

justices to King John in 1210. How else is his selection for the court *coram rege* to be explained?

Roger Huscarl was John's only justice to come from the group of attorneys, essoiners, and pleaders growing up at Westminster. The other justices had gained practical experience in the royal administration, especially in financial duties, before their appointment to the bench. The justiciar, William Briwerre, and Hugh Bardolf all had taken on multiple responsibilities during the reign of Richard I, when they were among the *appares* sharing authority during the king's absence. Master Henry of London also had wide experience as a royal servant, though beginning later and at a lower level. Once John became king, Henry of London performed varied financial tasks, and he also went on diplomatic missions: to the king of Navarre in 1201, to Ireland in 1204 for talks with the king of Connaught, and for other assistance to the Irish justiciar.

Four justices – Richard of Herriard, Roger Huscarl, Richard de Mucegros, and James of Potterne – had found experience as undersheriffs before they came to the bench.[65] The relationship between an undersheriff and his sheriff was similar to that between an estate steward and his employer, although naturally the sheriff's assistant had more demanding duties. Undersheriffs accounted for the farm of the shire at the Exchequer in most cases, enabling the justiciar to assess their abilities and to draw them into his own service if favourably impressed.

Five other justices began their careers as local officials of other sorts before moving to posts at Westminster or with the itinerant *curia regis*. William Briwerre had served 'a typical apprenticeship in the royal service', under Henry II, holding the shrievalty of Devon and other offices in the Southwest.[66] Little evidence survives for the lives of Walter of Creeping or John of Guestling before they came to the judicial bench, and that little presents them as local figures. Walter accounted for the farm of

[65] Richard of Herriard: Essex and Herts for Geoffrey fitz Peter, 1192, *Pipe Roll 3 & 4 Ric. I*, p. 167; Roger Huscarl: Wilts, for William de Neville, 1209, Brian C. Harris, 'The English sheriffs in the reign of King John', M.A. Thesis (Nottingham, 1961), p. 212; Richard de Mucegros: Glos. for William Marshall, 1190, Harris Thesis, p. 189; and Dorset and Somerset for Hugh Bardolf, 1193–4, *Pipe Roll 7 Ric. I*, p. 228; James of Potterne: Yorks, for Geoffrey fitz Peter, 1198–1200, Harris Thesis, p. 214.   [66] See note 43 above.

Colchester in 1195 and for several years afterwards, and in 1197 and 1199 he collected tallages in his native Essex.[67] John of Guestling first surfaces in the Exchequer accounts for 1194, connected with the fortification of Hastings Castle in the face of a threatened French invasion.[68] Simon of Pattishall's earliest responsibilities had centred around his native Northampton-shire, c. 1190.

The fifth justice with a background in local government is Henry de Pont-Audemar, who had considerable administrative experience in Normandy before coming to England. As early as 1195 he was custodian of escheats in the *baillage* of the Evrecin. In 1197 he accounted for the ancient farm of the *vicomté* of Rouen, and he was also *vicomte* of Caux.[69] By 1203 Henry was busy supervising the import and export of food supplies to and from Normandy; he was licensing the export of grain and other goods from Normandy to England. Also in 1203 King John gave Henry custody of the castle of Cherbourg and appointed him a royal justice at Pont-Audemar. Again that year he presented the accounts for the forest of Roumare.[70]

The justices' work in local administration before they joined the bench had a financial aspect in most instances, which linked them to the Exchequer. A number continued to carry out occasional financial duties while in the judiciary, during va-cation visits to their own lands, while on eyres, or perhaps tem-porarily abandoning the *curia regis* to undertake some special mission. John of Guestling is typical of a significant portion of King John's royal justices in having few duties away from the bench. The tasks he did undertake illustrate the justiciar's use of members of his judiciary for financial work in the counties.

Shortly after Guestling's appointment to the Bench in 1198, he joined two Exchequer officials to amerce the men of the Cinq Ports who had been trading with Flanders in violation of the king's prohibition. John of Guestling and his companions com-

[67] *Pipe Roll 7 Ric. I*, p. 14; *Chancellor's Roll 8 Ric. I*, pp. 118, 120; *Pipe Roll 10 Ric. I*, p. 133.
[68] *Pipe Roll 6 Ric. I*, p. 229.
[69] Stapleton, ed., *Rot. scac. norm.*, 1: clxix; 2: xxii, cxxxiii.
[70] *Rot. Lit. Pat.*, pp. 25, 25b, 26; *Rot. Norm.*, pp. 82, 84–5, 86, 97; *Rot. scac. norm.*, 2: cclvii.

bined with this the hearing of an occasional plea.[71] In 1199 and
1202, John made circuits to assess amercements on counties
recently visited by the itinerant justices, a task often undertaken
by men from the Bench. The 1202 circuit took him to his native
Kent.[72] In the autumn of 1204, John of Guestling and William of
Wrotham sent word to the treasurer and chamberlains of the
Exchequer that 400 marks were owed for work done on the
king's galleys.[73] Guestling's property-holdings near the Cinq
Ports made it convenient for him to carry such messages from
the fleet to the Exchequer on his return to Westminster from
visits to his possessions.

The experience that the professionals among the judiciary
gained as justices on eyre made them useful on other sorts of
commissions to the counties. One of the conditions of the settlement of the Canterbury succession crisis in 1213 was that King
John would pay for the damage done to church property he
seized during the interdict. Three justices – Roger Huscarl,
Simon of Pattishall, and James of Potterne – were among those
assigned to investigate the injuries churches had suffered 'in
time of discord between the king and the clergy of England'.[74]

Six of King John's justices held shrievalties at the same time
that they were serving in the judiciary. This is hardly surprising
in the case of three great *curiales*, Hugh Bardolf, William
Briwerre, and Geoffrey fitz Peter, who held several shires. But
the fact that three others were sheriffs is worthy of note. Simon
of Pattishall had been a sheriff under Richard I, and he kept his
Northants post after King John's accession, holding it until
1203. John appointed James of Potterne sheriff of Wiltshire on
11 January 1204, but he held the shrievalty only until autumn.
In one of the king's experiments to improve his finances, he

---

[71] With Stephen of Thornham and Reginald of Cornhill, *Pipe Roll 10 Ric. I*, p.
209; *C.R.R.*, 1: 327, a 1200 plea between merchants of Beverly and men of
Hastings. It is noted that 'John of Guestling and Reginald of Cornhill have the
names and records'. About the same time Eustace de Fauconberg was one of
the tallagers of the lordship of Richmond, then in the king's hand, *Pipe Roll 2
John*, p. 90.

[72] Again with Reginald of Cornhill, *Pipe Roll 1 John*, pp. 29, 77, 84, 226; *4 John*, p.
216. Walter of Creeping performed this same task in Essex after he had
retired from the Bench, *Pipe Roll 13 John*, p. 121; *14 John*, p. 55.

[73] *Rot. Lit. Claus.*, 1: 13b, 3 Nov.; *Pipe Roll 7 John*, p. xiii.

[74] Huscarl to the diocese of Hereford, Pattishall to the archbishopric of Canterbury, and Potterne to the diocese of London, *Rot. Lit. Claus.*, 1: 164b.

named James sheriff *ut custos*, ensuring that he would account for
more revenues than the traditional fixed farm.[75] It is unlikely
that Simon or James personally performed the duties of the
office, for they were both almost continually at the courts during the period of their appointment. In July 1207, the king
appointed Richard de Mucegros sheriff of Gloucestershire.
Richard made a bid of 250 marks plus the promise of an annual
increment of £100 over the ancient farm. He seems to have
been the only one of the six to have gone into debt to secure a
shrievalty. Richard remained sheriff for less than a year, and by
January 1208, he was replaced with one of the king's Poitevin
mercenaries.[76] Richard's removal seems to have been more a
matter of military preparedness in anticipation of war along the
southern Welsh marches than of royal suspicions of his loyalty.[77]
    At least five of the justices who ranked below such barons of
the Exchequer as Bardolf or Briwerre nonetheless took part in
financial work at Westminster or, in the case of the archdeacon
of Stafford, with the Chamber. In 1200 Henry of London supervised the transport of the king's treasure to the sea coast, and by
1207 he can be seen acting as a Chamber officer, supplying tuns
of wine, greyhounds, and hound-handlers for the royal court.
He again served as an ambassador in the spring of 1208, setting
out for the court of the king's cousin Otto, the German
emperor.[78] Simon of Pattishall and Henry of Whiston were
named in 1198 to the Exchequer of the Jews, but in April 1200
King John replaced them and their two colleagues with new
appointees.[79] Richard of Herriard had more interesting financial
tasks; an entry on the memoranda roll for the first year of John's
reign hints that he had responsibility for paying royal pros-

---

[75] *Rot. Lit. Pat.*, p. 38; *List of Sheriffs*, p. 152. *Pipe Roll 6 John*, p. 257, lists James and
    Robert de Vipont as joint-sheriffs. See Painter, *Reign of King John*, pp. 118–21,
    on the custodian-sheriff.

[76] *Pipe Roll 9 John*, p. 215; *Rot. de Obl. et Fin.*, p. 385; *Rot. Lit. Pat.* pp. 75, 78b.
    Richard's replacement was Gerard d'Athée. Richard offered 50 marks for
    release from office and was finally acquitted in 1219, *Pipe Roll 10 John*, p. 19; *3
    Hen. III*, p. 9.

[77] On 13 Feb. 1209, John named Mucegros custodian of Chichester Castle, *Rot.
    Lit. Pat.*, p. 79.

[78] *Pipe Roll 2 John*, p. 150; *9 John*, p. 233; *10 John*, p. 86; *Rot. Lit. Claus.*, 1: 93b, 94b,
    96, 104.

[79] *Pipe Roll 10 Ric. I*, pp. xxix, 125, 165, 210, 214; Richardson, *English Jewry*,
    p. 136.

titutes. The roll records that Richard brought a woman named Hawise de Burdels before the Exchequer with a message that King John had assigned her a pension of a penny.[80]

Justices of the royal courts continued to perform varied administrative functions even as late as the time of Edward I.[81] Any idea of an independent judiciary lay centuries ahead. A biographical study of King John's judges brings clearly into focus, however, a core of royal servants concentrating on judicial activity, distinct from the Exchequer and from the *privata familia regis*. Over two-thirds of them were laymen, recruited from middle or lower-ranking knightly families. The only royal justice of urban origin was one of the five clerics. They were hardly men the barons would consider their peers! At least ten justices had begun their careers as local royal officers of one king or another, usually concerned with revenues. Perhaps they cannot yet be considered as wholly professional judges, since they still assumed some extra-judicial duties. Yet they were devoting less time to other work, and their other duties were mainly incidental to their judicial visitations to the counties, a matter of administrative convenience. From the first years of the thirteenth century, then, a professional judicial staff had definitely taken shape. The growth of judicial machinery had moved far from the men-of-all-work who made up Henry II's judiciary.

3 RELATIONS BETWEEN THE JUSTICES AND KING JOHN

The close watch that King John kept trained on his courts is widely acknowledged. Whether this attention was due to John's genuine interest in justice or due to a tyrannical aim of concentrating all power in his own hands is a matter of disagreement, however. Students of the king's character agree that he was an unlovable man, fearful and suspicious of others, and himself unable to inspire trust.[1] These problems – King John's supervision of his courts, combined with his unpleasant or unstable character – make a discussion of his relations with the royal justices relevant. John's justices were very much aware of his con-

---

[80] *Mem. Roll 1 John*, p. 12; Painter, *King John*, p. 234.
[81] *Select Cases*, 1: lxiii–lxiv.
[1] For references to John's character, see C. Warren Hollister, 'King John and the historians', *Jl. Br. Studies*, 1 (1961): 1–19; J.C. Holt, *King John*, Historical Assoc'n. pamphlet (London, 1963): W.L. Warren, *King John* (London, 1961).

stant attention to the work of justice. The king in 1207 amerced
two of his justices, Simon of Pattishall and James of Potterne, a
hundred marks each because they granted two barons leave to
agree in an appeal of felony without his permission.[2] The judges
recognized the monarch as the source of justice, and they often
marked cases *loquendum cum rege*, something that had happened
far less frequently in Richard I's time.[3] The problem hardly had
arisen in the time of John's brother because he was content to
leave supervision of judges largely to his justiciars.

The royal justices were very much the king's men, and they
had no concept of themselves as impartial arbiters standing
apart from the monarch. John's justices were faced with dual
and sometimes conflicting obligations: to render justice to all
men impartially and, at the same time, to safeguard the king's
interest. The king was a living individual, quick to anger, and his
judges sometimes witnessed the results of his *ira et malevolentia*;
for example, he closed his courts to ill-favoured suitors, or
petitioners came to them seeking to recover lands they had lost
per voluntatem regis.[4] The advantage of such a powerful master had
more concrete reality to judges than such abstract concepts as
the 'public power' of Roman law or the English concept of 'community of the realm'.

As we have seen, King John's justices still continued to combine fiscal functions with their judicial duties. They recognized
a duty to increase royal revenues. In some cases, they allowed
the king's material need to outweigh immaterial standards of
equity. Examples of this are easy to find in the plea rolls from
John's reign.[5] The justices of John's time still followed the
instructions given to Henry II's itinerant justices in 1176, 'Let

[2] *C.R.R.*, 5: 58–9; *Pipe Roll 9 John*, p. 207; *Rot. de Obl. et Fin.*, pp. 412, 417. John
    pardoned them in 1208, *Rot. Lit. Claus.*, 1: 113, 114.
[3] Turner, *King and his courts*, pp. 127–35, 157, 242. For Richard's rare interven-
    tions, see J.C. Holt, *Ricardus Rex Anglorum et Dux Normannorum* in *Atti dell
    Accademia Nazionale dei Lincei*, 378 (1981).
[4] On John's closing his courts to certain individuals, see Turner, *King and his
    courts*, pp. 60–8; on royal disseisins, see Turner, 'The royal courts treat disseisin
    by the king: John and Henry III, 1199–1240', *A.J.L.H.*, 12 (1968): 1–18.
[5] *C.R.R.*, 1: 438, pleas dismissed because the tenant was sending two knights
    overseas in the king's service; 4: 183, judgment for the defendant because he
    had offered 20s for a speedy judgment, although the plaintiff essoined himself
    de ultra mare; 7: 20, rival claimants encouraged to outbid one another in offer-
    ing oblations until those offering more – 35 marks – had their right
    recognized.

them . . . apply themselves to the utmost to act in the interest of the lord king.'[6]

Most judges in John's reign, as has been shown, were men drawn from the corps of royal servants at the Exchequer or in the counties. Few of them were members of the *privata familia regis*; yet King John must have come to know them and their work well. Certainly the justices *coram rege* travelling about the country in the king's train became well known to him, even if they did not become his intimates. They had to meet with him frequently for discussion of difficult cases.[7] What signs survive of the king's goodwill, or perhaps ill will, toward the justices? Were they able to approach him with petitions to advance their own or their friends' interests? The question becomes more meaningful near the end of the reign as discontent was growing and eventually burst into open warfare. Where did the justices stand in the crisis surrounding *Magna Carta*, baronial rebellion, and foreign invasion?

Only four of King John's seventeen justices were royal *familiares*, confidants of the king. They include three men at the centre of power – Geoffrey fitz Peter, Hugh Bardolf, and William Briwerre – and a royal clerk, Master Henry of London, whose influence grew steadily. All four had ties to John going back to his accession, or even earlier. Henry had apparently been one of John's partisans in the days of his rebellion against Richard I. He quickly became one of King John's trusted agents with multiple duties, recalling *curiales* of Henry II's time. Hugh Bardolf's position during the rebellion had been difficult. He was one of Richard Lionheart's chief agents in England, yet he was also a tenant of the honour of Tickhill and thus technically Count John's man. Because of that, he refused to join other supporters of Richard in besieging Tickhill Castle.[8]

Geoffrey fitz Peter had no such early ties with John, but he showed his loyalty at the time of Richard I's death, when he was one of the great men who persuaded the other barons to accept John as king in preference to Prince Arthur.[9] John, of course,

---

[6] Article 7, Assize of Northampton, Stubbs, *Select Charters*, p. 180; translation from *Eng. Hist. Docs.*, 2: 412.

[7] See Turner, *King and his Courts*, pp. 123–57.

[8] *Pipe Roll 5 Ric. I*, p. xix; Howden, 3: 206.

[9] *Justiciarship*, p. 102; Painter, *Reign of King John*, pp. 11–12.

kept Geoffrey on as justiciar and showered rich reward on him in years following. In the two years or so before Geoffrey's death, however, signs indicate King John's growing dissatisfaction with him. After the loss of Normandy, the king's continuous residence in England inevitably weakened the office of justiciar. After 1209, Geoffrey had no judicial duties, except on those few occasions when he joined the court *coram rege*. Even in the financial sphere, Geoffrey was having to share power with two of John's trusted officials, Richard Marsh and William Briwerre.[10] In 1212, one of the claimants to the Mandeville inheritance brought suit against Geoffrey fitz Peter, reopening the question of his right to the earldom of Essex. The king must have encouraged this suit as a means of harassing his justiciar.[11] Even if we overlook King John's supposed rejoicing at Geoffrey's death, as recounted by the unreliable Wendover and Paris, a sense of increasing ill will between the king and Geoffrey in the years before the justiciar's death remains.[12] It must be noted also that two of Geoffrey fitz Peter's sons fought for the rebels against John, although they had reasons besides the king's treatment of their father.[13]

William Briwerre had served Richard I loyally, and he so enjoyed King John's confidence that he soon won a larger share in government, perhaps second only to the justiciar and the chancellor. William was 'one of the leading financial experts of his day', and he worked closely with John on fiscal matters. He even had an agreement with the king that he would sit at the Exchequer two weeks each year.[14] King John would have admired someone like William, so skilled at extorting money from shires that they were willing to pay to be rid of him as their sheriff. In 1209 the men of Dorset and Somerset offered 1200 marks for the privilege of having as their sheriff some perma-

---

[10] *Justiciarship*, p. 171.

[11] *C.R.R.*, 6: 270; Turner, *King and his Courts*, p. 164.

[12] *Chron. Maj.*, 2: 558–9; Painter, *Reign of King John*, pp. 262, 278; J.C. Holt, *Magna Carta* (Cambridge, 1965), pp. 122–3.

[13] Geoffrey de Mandeville IV and his younger son William. Both were sons-in-law of Robert fitz Walter, *Complete Peerage*, 5: genealogical chart.

[14] *Rot. Lit. Pat.*, p. 55. J.E.A. Jolliffe, 'The Chamber and the Castle Treasures under King John', *Studies presented to Powicke*, pp. 131–2, shows that William was in charge of a provincial treasury at Exeter Castle, an important point for transfers of large sums to the Continent.

nent resident *other than* William Briwerre or one of his men.[15] John may have considered Briwerre for the justiciarship following Geoffrey fitz Peter's death in October 1213, but he chose Peter des Roches, bishop of Winchester, instead. William was associated with the new justiciar as second in authority, however, and when John made provision for government during his absence on the Poitevin campaign of 1214, William was one of two associates he left behind with Peter.[16] Writs from the king overseas commanded the bishop of Winchester to take counsel with William Briwerre on several important matters.[17]

These four *familiares regis* added to their possessions through John's favour, but other signs of their special relationship stand out. William Briwerre was reputed to be one of the king's *consiliarios iniquissimos* during the Canterbury succession quarrel. When King John seized the Church's property in April 1208 in answer to the interdict, he gave William control over all abbeys, priories, and churches lying within his lands. Certainly William stood close to John in counsel on matters concerning the Church. He was one of the royal agents sent to Dover on 13 July 1209 to meet with three bishops representing Stephen Langton.[18] When the king authorized elections in eight vacant cathedral and monastic churches following his submission to the pope in 1213, he specified that the elections should take place in the presence of William Briwerre and other royal servants.[19] William knew well the king's mind about the elections, as an account of the disputed election for abbot of Bury St Edmunds, 1213–14, shows. King John said to the abbot-elect, 'Go to William Briwerre, for he will explain fully my wishes to you.' When the abbot and monks spoke to William, he reprimanded them for 'the way you have gone about your business', warning them that they seemed to show 'contempt for his [the king's] customary liberties'.[20]

---

[15] The fine was also for quittance of the increment of the two shires' farm, *Pipe Roll 12 John*, p. 175; *Cal. Chtr. Rolls*, 1: 281–2.

[16] The other associate was Richard Marsh, *Rot. Lit. Pat.*, p. 139. Throughout autumn 1213 William had attested documents with Peter, *Justiciarship*, p. 188.   [17] E.g. *Rot. Lit. Claus.*, 1: 141, 168b.

[18] *Roger Wendover*, 3: 238; *Chron. Maj.*, 2: 351–3; *Rot. Lit. Claus.*, 1: 112b. *Gervase of Canterbury*, 2: c–ci.   [19] *Rot. Lit. Pat.*, pp. 101, 110.

[20] Rodney M. Thompson, ed., *The Chronicle of the Election of Hugh, Abbot of Bury St Edmunds and later Bishop of Ely*, Oxford Medieval Texts (Oxford, 1973), pp. 162–4.

Henry of London also stood close to King John during the period of the interdict, 1208–13. The archdeacon was a negotiator with bishops representing the pope in the crisis over the king's excommunication in 1209.[21] His possessions had special protection during the interdict, when King John ordered sheriffs not to seize the archdeacon of Stafford's lands, but to leave them in the custody of his own servants.[22] On 15 May 1213, Henry – now archbishop of Dublin – stood beside King John at the ceremony in which the king surrendered his crown to the papal legate, accepting it back as a vassal of Innocent III. Then on 1 July, the new archbishop was one of those named by King John to meet Stephen Langton on his arrival in England to assume his duties.[23] Possibly it was Henry's steady support during the Canterbury succession affair that won him the archbishopric of Dublin.

None of the other justices had ties with the king which indicate any close personal acquaintance. Only Simon of Pattishall as senior man among the justices *coram rege* approached them in contacts with King John, and his contacts were purely professional, limited to the smooth functioning of the *curia regis*. Simon and his clerk had special record-keeping responsibilities; as early as 1199, Simon was the judge who witnessed unusual original writs and an experimental judicial writ. Both Bench and *coram rege* rolls refer to writs and to notes on final concords in the keeping of Simon of Pattishall and his clerk, and pipe rolls refer to amercement lists delivered by him to the treasury.[24] Moreover, records of payments to messengers sent with letters from Simon suggest that he was the link between the justices following the king, and the Exchequer staff sitting at Westminster.[25] John clearly respected Simon's legal knowledge, for

---

[21] *Gervase of Canterbury*, 2: c–ci; *Annales Mon.*, 1: 31, 40, 59, 4: 54.

[22] *Rot. Lit. Claus.*, 1: 107b.

[23] C.R. Cheney, *Innocent III and England*, (Stuttgart, 1976), p. 333; *Rot. Lit. Claus.*, 1: 164.

[24] *P.B.K.J.*, 2: 291, no. 986; *C.R.R.*, 2: 279; 3: 48, 230, 347; 4: 46, 48, 177. *Pipe Roll 16 John*, pp. 17, 24, 155, 176. See also Elsa de Haas and G.D.G. Hall, eds., *Early Registers of Writs*, Selden Soc., 87 (1970): lxix–lxxi.

[25] *Documents illustrative of English History in the 13th and 14th centuries from the records of the Queen's Remembrancer in the Exchequer*, Rec. Comm. (London, 1844), p. 243, from *rotuli misae 14 John* (1212). For a letter addressed to Pattishall concerning a court case, see *Oseney Cart.*, 5: 67, no. 575A. The bishop of Coventry informed Simon that a church in litigation was not vacant.

in the summer of 1210 when the king was visiting Ireland, he sent for his most experienced judge. King John was trying to bring Ireland more closely under his control, and he sought Simon's help in establishing English law and custom there.[26]

A further demonstration of John's esteem for Pattishall came in 1212, when the king entrusted him with custody of Fotheringay Castle, which he had taken away from the earl of Huntingdon.[27] King John entrusted only one other justice who was not also an intimate counsellor with custody of a castle. Richard de Mucegros was given custody of Gloucester Castle while he was sheriff of Gloucestershire in 1207. When he gave up the shrievalty, he also surrendered custody of the castle; but the next year, the king named Mucegros custodian of Chichester Castle.[28]

Since the time of the barbarian invasions, kings had placed their retainers and members of their household under their special protection. The Angevin monarchs continued to grant favoured servants charters confirming them in their possessions, letters or charters of special protection, or privileges such as release from performance of traditional services. They might extend their protection to groups of officials, such as the itinerant justices, who normally received writs of protection from all pleas except assizes of novel disseisin. Or they might single out individuals for special protection. King John granted John of Guestling a special charter of protection, dated at Chinon on 2 August 1201. This charter protected all his possessions, granted the privilege of being impleaded only before the king or chief justiciar, and freed him from suits to courts of shire and hundred, and from castle-guard. This was not a simple expression of royal favour, however, for Guestling promised King John two palfreys for the charter.[29] Richard of Herriard, on the other hand, received freely a writ excusing him from the same services while he was undertaking royal tasks.[30]

---

[26] *Rot. de Lib. ac de Mis.*, p. 188, 10 marks payment to the men who arranged Simon's crossing to Ireland.

[27] Simon shared custody with another Northants man, *Rot. Lit. Claus.*, 1: 122b; *Rot. Lit. Pat.*, p. 94b.   [28] *Rot. Lit. Pat.*, pp. 71, 78b, 79.

[29] *Cartae Antiq. Rolls 1–10*, p. 88, no. 174; *Rot. de Obl. et Fin.*, p. 176. He still owed the two palfreys in 1204, *Pipe Roll 5 John*, p. 25.

[30] Richard also won release from transport to the treasury, *Rot. Lit. Pat.*, p. 2b, 8 Nov. 1201.

A favour which the justices shared with other royal officials was exemption from payment of scutages and other levies while in the king's service. Traditionally, barons of the Exchequer were freed from such obligations *per libertatem sedendi ad scaccarium*, and justices enjoyed a similar privilege.[31] A more personal gesture of favour on the king's part was the pardoning of past debts at the Exchequer. Such pardons, combined with their official privileges, made specially favoured royal officers exempt from the financial obligations that burdened other landholders. Several justices benefited from such a royal boon, most notably William Briwerre. He had promised increments – payments above the traditional fixed farm – for his shrievalties, but in two instances King John pardoned him of the payments. In June 1200 the king pardoned William of the increment of Hampshire 'for God and the salvation of his soul, and at William's request'.[32] When William surrendered Dorset and Somerset at the end of 1209, he owed increments of 225 marks; John pardoned him of 200 marks in 1210, and of the remaining 25 marks the following year.[33] More impressive is King John's pardon of 2000 marks in debts that Briwerre owed at the Exchequer in 1206–7.[34] Simon of Pattishall too benefited from royal pardon of debts, but of lesser sums.[35] John of Guestling was the only one of the lesser men in the judiciary to enjoy a pardon, although it proved to be an inconsequential sum. He was acquitted of a debt of sixteen pence by royal writ at the 1202 Exchequer, even though he still owed a fine of two palfreys.[36]

The Exchequer disciplined royal vassals and crown servants who neglected their financial obligations, and the *lex scaccarii* sometimes seemed little more than an instrument of the king's will. It dealt harshly with crown debtors who fell behind in their payments; they might find their lands and chattels distrained or

---

[31] E.g. writ releasing Henry de Pont-Audemar from payment of scutage, *Rot. Lit. Claus.*, 1: 42. See also above, chap. 3, pt. 4.

[32] *Rot. Chart.*, p. 97; *Pipe Roll 2 John*, p. 191.

[33] *Pipe Roll 12 John*, p. 98; *13 John*, p. 223.

[34] *Rot. Lit. Claus.*, 1: 2, 3, 78; *Rot. Lit. Pat.*, p. 62. Early in the reign, John acquitted William of forest exactions due from his land at Blisworth, *Cartae Antiq. 1–10*, p. 139, no. 292.

[35] E.g. the remainder of his farm of Essex and Herts in 1209, which he had owed for fifteen years, *Pipe Roll 7 Ric. I*, p. 217; *11 John*, p. 186; or the scutage of 1212, *Pipe Roll 13 John*, pp. 91, 267.

[36] *Pipe Roll 4 John*, pp. 104, 216.

themselves imprisoned. Yet royal officials who enjoyed the king's goodwill escaped the Exchequer's pressure to pay debts promptly. The debts of several justices were carried on the pipe rolls for ten years or more with no action taken to force a settlement. Richard of Herriard, for example, offered Richard I a fine of £100 to have a wardship, and he paid twenty marks as a first instalment in 1198, but ten years later he still owed £23 10s.[37] Henry de Pont-Audemar a year later also offered £100 for a wardship, and he still owed fifty marks on the fine in 1212 and was not acquitted of the debt until 1214.[38] The king's goodwill likewise proved helpful to Richard de Mucegros when he fell into debt to the Jews. The pipe roll for 1208 records that he owed £112, but he was allowed to repay at the Exchequer in annual twenty-pound instalments without any interest.[39]

From time to time, kings made gestures of gratitude towards favoured officials by making them gifts, perhaps a cask of wine, robes, or game and timber from the royal forests. By the time of Henry III such gifts came so frequently that they were practically part of their salary.[40] Earlier, however, such gifts occurred less often, and they must be considered marks of special favour. King John's gift of two tuns of good Angevin wine to Simon of Pattishall must be viewed in this way, as must the gift of thirty bucks from the park of the vacant bishopric of Chester to Henry of London just before he set sail for his archbishopric in Ireland.[41] Indications of King John's friendship with William Briwerre abound, for example, frequent gifts of timber from

---

[37] *Pipe Roll 10 Ric. I*, p. 149; *Mem. Roll 1 John*, p. 19; *Pipe Roll 9 John*, p. 65.

[38] *Pipe Roll 1 John*, p. 37. In 1212 Henry agreed to supply a knight in Poitou in place of the payment, *Pipe Roll 14 John*, pp. xxi, 21–2; *Rot. de Obl. et Fin.*, p. 484. However in 1214 he paid 40 marks and was acquitted of the debt, *Rot. de Obl. et Fin.*, p. 521. Henry of London offered 50 marks and two palfreys for a wardship in 1207, which he did not pay until 1219, *Pipe Roll 9 John*, pp. 9, 101; *14 John*, p. 62; *3 Hen. III*, p. 123. In 1219 Richard de Mucegros had owed £50 since 1208. He was acquitted of the debt with a payment of £18 3s 8d, *Pipe Roll 3 Hen. III*, p. 9.

[39] *Pipe Roll 10 John*, p. 20. Richard probably had borrowed the money to purchase the shrievalty of Glos. He had paid barely half the debt by early Henry III, *Pipe Roll 3 Hen. III*, p. 70; Exch. L.T.R. Mem. Roll, 4: m. 1; 5: m. 1d. Roger Huscarl in 1223 won a delay in paying an 8½ mark debt to the Jews, and the next year it was pardoned entirely, Exch. L.T.R. Mem. Roll, 5: m. 8; *Rot. Lit. Claus.*, 1: 587.

[40] Meekings, *Crown Pleas of the Wilts Eyre*, p. 12.

[41] Madox, *Exchequer*, 1: 70; *Rot. Lit. Claus.*, 1: 139.

royal forests.[42] A stronger indication is John's loan to William of 1000 marks in June 1204 to ransom his son, taken captive during the unsuccessful defence of Normandy. The next year the king contributed an additional 700 marks 'of heavier and stronger coins' for young Briwerre's ransom.[43]

Proximity to the king meant opportunities to approach him directly to circumvent the slow-moving legal processes. Richard of Herriard was one justice who took advantage of his opportunity, even though he was not a *curialis* in the sense of being in personal attendance on King John. He secured possession of land at Southrope, Hampshire, by administrative order and not by assize. The justices of the Bench took note of the transfer of the land away from its custodian, 'because Richard made known to the king that he [Richard] holds that land as his inheritance'.[44] Later when Herriard brought suit to secure formal title to the land, King John allowed him to have a grand assize even though in fact he was not the tenant but the claimant. The assize should have been inapplicable in his case. This was not simply an instance of King John's fondness for Richard, however; the king was acting in response to an offering of 100 marks and a knight to be sent in the king's service.[45] Master Ralph of Stokes also seems to have recovered by royal command and not by judgment seisin of land, which he had lost while overseas. At least, that was his response when his seisin was threatened by an assize of novel disseisin.[46]

Only half of King John's justices were able to take advantage of their position to win any special favours from the king. Even within that group, a wide gap lies between the four men who were royal intimates – friends is not too strong a word – and the other, lesser men who obviously did not enjoy such a close relationship with their master. A vast distance separates the rich reward William Briwerre's friendship with King John brought him from the relatively modest favours bestowed on Richard of

---

[42] *Rot. Lit. Claus.*, 1: 117b; also the gift of Henry III, p. 422b.

[43] Part of the agreement was that William would serve two weeks yearly at the Exchequer, *Rot. Lit. Pat.*, p. 55; *Rot. de Obl. et. Fin.*, p. 271.

[44] *C.R.R.*, 1: 390. Ralph de Hauvill held the land through his custody of an heiress.   [45] *Pipe Roll 7 John*, p. 129; *Rot. de Obl. et Fin.*, p. 287.

[46] *C.R.R.*, 6: 76–7, 130, John de Russes summoned before the justices *coram rege* to explain why he brought a novel disseisin against Ralph seeking land at Gislingham, Suff.

Herriard or Simon of Pattishall. Half of the judges seem not to have won any noteworthy benefits from the king by service in the *curia regis*, not even if they served with the justices *coram rege*. Of the four justices regularly following the king from 1209, only Simon of Pattishall made any particular impression on King John.

It is not too surprising, then, that the crisis at the end of John's reign found the justices divided in their loyalty. The barons' rebellion had no attraction for William Briwerre, who as one of the chief executors of the *lex scaccarii*, shared the strong views on the royal power held by Exchequer clerks. Such views are evident in Richard fitz Neal's *Dialogus*, which echoes more than faintly if not loudly Roman law notions of princely power.[47] William's own view of *Magna Carta* and the baronial cause revealed itself during discussions concerning a reissue of the Great Charter in 1223. He spoke against Stephen Langton and other advocates, arguing that 'the liberties you ask for ought not to be observed, for they were extorted by force'.[48] Briwerre stood by King John as one of the royalist military commanders once fighting broke out. John, confident to the end in William's loyalty, named him one of the executors of his will as he lay dying in October 1216.[49]

Also strongly supporting the king and his cause was Henry of London, by then in Ireland in his new post as archbishop of Dublin. During the summer of 1215, King John summoned him to England for support at this crucial time, and he was at the king's side when he set his seal to *Magna Carta* on 15 June. Later in the summer, Henry assisted the king as one of his representatives at a meeting with the rebel barons, planned for July 16.[50] Henry left England to attend the Fourth Lateran Council, probably by mid-September, and he remained at Rome for over a year. His presence there during the civil war enabled him to represent King John's position before Innocent III and to win papal support against the rebels.

Two other justices, less close to the king, also remained loyal to his cause. Master Eustace de Fauconberg had emerged from the shadows to which he retreated in 1209 to become the 'right-

[47] *Dial. de Scac.*, pp. 1–2, 28, 46, 84, 94.
[48] *Roger Wendover*, 4: 84; *Chron. Maj.*, 3: 76.
[49] Warren, *King John*, p. 255.   [50] *Rot. Lit. Pat.*, p. 149.

hand man' of Peter des Roches, the new justiciar in 1213. By the time civil war came in 1215, Eustace was a canon of St Paul's, an intellectual centre of opposition to King John, but unlike his colleagues in the chapter, his support for the royalist cause was unwavering.[51] On 3 April 1217 before the civil war had completely ended, William Marshal granted Master Eustace letters patent of protection *sine termino*.[52] Richard de Mucegros also remained loyal to the royalist cause. King John commanded the earl marshal in November and December 1215 to provide Richard with forfeited enemy lands which were in the king's hand.[53] Richard's son, Robert de Mucegros, was also a loyalist during the civil war; he had custody of one of King John's prisoners committed to him in September 1216.[54]

Five justices were less loyal, or at least, they fell under the king's suspicion and temporarily lost their lands. Of course, King John's mistrust of them is no certain proof that they were active partisans of the barons. Surprisingly, three had been John's justices *coram rege* since 1209. A royal writ of 12 May 1215 commanded the seizure of Simon of Pattishall's lands and the sale of his chattels; this came only days after Simon's last appearance on the bench.[55] Although nothing linking Simon to the rebel cause survives, something had aroused John's overly-suspicious mind. Did Simon's disappointment at inadequate reward for his many years of work incline him towards the rebel side? He had not risen to wealth and power either as rapidly or as far as had other royal officers who formed a clique of *familiares regis*. Whatever the causes for John's mistrust, they subsided quickly. On 20 May, the king issued a safe-conduct for Simon, stating, 'If it is as the abbot of Woburn said to us on your behalf, then we relax all our wrath and indignation which we had against you.'[56] By December 1215, John was seeing that Simon's property was restored to him; and the next spring, in the midst of war, the king asked him to take an assize at Northampton.[57]

James of Potterne and Henry de Pont-Audemar also fell under

[51] Richardson, 'William of Ely', p. 59; *Fasti, St. Paul's*, p. 54.
[52] *Pat. Rolls, 1216–25*, p. 53.   [53] *Rot. Lit. Claus.*, 1: 237b, 243b.
[54] *Rot. Lit. Claus.*, 1: 287. The prisoner was William de Gaugy.
[55] *Rot. Lit. Claus.*, 1: 200.
[56] *Rot. Lit. Pat.*, p. 138; *Mem. Roll 10 John*, p. 141, no. 104, letter of protection in a previously unpublished close roll.   [57] *Rot. Lit. Claus.*, 1: 244, 270.

suspicion in the troubled days of 1215–16. In October 1215, King John commanded the sheriff of Hampshire to take the manor of Over Wallop into his hand, 'if James of Potterne is not in our service'.[58] James had held the manor, part of the escheat of the Normans, at farm at least since 1204, and he recovered it by March 1217.[59] Henry de Pont-Audemar had been among the king's supporters at Runnymede in June 1215, where he took an oath to obey the baronial committee of twenty-five. Sometime afterwards, Henry fell from favour with King John and lost his possessions. A royal letter of 31 October 1217, at the end of the civil war, commanded that his property, seized during the rebellion, be restored to him.[60]

Walter of Creeping and John of Guestling, who had not served in the judiciary since the closing of the Common Pleas court in 1209, both 'withdrew from fealty and service to King John'. They received writs returning their land to them by the autumn of 1217.[61] King John showed his ill will toward Guestling in November 1215 by moving the market, outside Winchelsea, which he had granted to him earlier for his fee, inside the town to the front of the church of St Thomas.[62] The move deprived the former justice of a source of revenue, but it also won support from the inhabitants of Winchelsea, whose goodwill was worth seeking in the face of a threatened French invasion.

It is difficult to locate these two civil servants' positions, shrouded in mists of obscurity, much less speculate about their motivation. Nevertheless, we can guess that John of Guestling's friendship with members of the archiepiscopal household at Canterbury influenced him to join the opposition to King John.[63] Less substantial clues give suggestions for Walter of Creeping's discontent. Perhaps he resented an amercement of

---

[58] *Rot. Lit. Claus.*, 1: 232b.
[59] *C.R.R.*, 3: 292; *Mem. Roll 10 John*, p. 27; *Rot. Lit. Claus.*, 1: 487b.
[60] *Chron. Maj.*, 2: 605, with Roger Huscarl. Customs at Penington restored, *Rot. Lit. Claus.*, 1: 339.   [61] *Rot. Lit. Claus.*, 1: 187; 341b.
[62] *Rot. Chart.*, p. 185b; *Rot. Lit. Claus.*, 1: 237.
[63] In the years c. 1210–15, he witnessed charters for Stephen Langton, Kathleen Major, ed., *Acta Stephani Langton*, Cant.–York Soc., 5 (1950): 52–4, nos. 39, 40; and for two monastic communities at Canterbury, Aubrey M. Woodcock, ed., *Cartulary of the Priory of St. Gregory, Canterbury*, Camden Soc., 3rd ser., 88 (1956): 60–1, no. 70; G.J. Turner and H.E. Salter, eds., *Register of St. Augustine's Abbey, Canterbury*, Br. Acad. Rec. Soc. and Econ. Hist. (1915–24), 2: 456, where he is described as the abbot's *senescallus*.

twenty marks levied by the 'autumnal justices' of 1210 for unspecified *transgressiones*. This 1210 visit of justices, none of whom was from the permanent judicial staff, was a product of John's desperate financial need, and knights in nearly every shire were subjected to heavy amercements for miscellaneous offences.[64]

Either Creeping or Guestling could have felt that his loyal service had brought him inadequate reward, for neither one managed to find another post in royal government once the Bench at Westminster ceased to function. Or perhaps they had more principled reasons for joining the rebellion. Possibly genuine sentiment about the supremacy of law and revulsion at King John's arbitrary acts led them to the opposition. Chapter 40 of *Magna Carta* does constitute an indictment of much of John's earlier administration of justice, and no one could have known better the truth of the charges than two former justices.

4 THE REWARDS OF KING JOHN'S JUSTICES

With King John the different scale of reward between the few royal *familiares* in the judiciary and the majority of clerks and knights became more pronounced. In part, this is due to the obscurity of the latter group, which makes it more difficult to track down their landholdings or other sources of income. Neither are there many signs of royal generosity in the form of grants of land, marriages to rich widows, or gifts of coin or goods. Yet the process of professionalization had not proceeded far enough to provide royal justices with salary payments at fixed intervals.

Of course, these men were not dependent solely upon royal largess. Royal office was valued not only for the opportunity it presented to win favours from the king, but more so for the chance of reward from petitioners and suitors. Perhaps the king expected his officials to finance themselves through fees or 'tips' from the public they were serving. Justices and their clerks shared fees paid by litigants, such as charges for sealing judicial

---

[64] *Pipe Roll 13 John*, p. 120; for the nature of the 1210 eyre, see *Pipe Roll 12 John*, pp. xv–xxii.

writs or for drawing up chirographs.[1] But when the product sold
was not merely a document but justice itself, the possibilities for
abuse were far greater.[2]

A survey of the resources of John's seventeen justices indicates great royal reward for five men. Three of them are, not
unexpectedly, the *familiares regis* who were at the centre of
power: Geoffrey fitz Peter, Hugh Bardolf, and William Briwerre.
Another favourite of John's who succeeded in gaining great
favour was Henry, archdeacon of Stafford. Eustace de Fauconberg eventually won a bishopric, but his reward came in the
early years of Henry III, more due to his friendship with Peter
des Roches than to direct royal favour. Five of the justices seem
to have won some reward for their service to King John,
although they made no startling moves up the social scale.
Simon of Pattishall, Osbert fitz Hervey, and Richard of Herriard
had begun expanding their landholdings under Richard I, and
they continued to add to them, but none rose from knightly
rank into the baronage. Roger Huscarl's service continued
under Henry III, mainly in Ireland, where he assisted the Irish
justiciar in conducting 'the king's affairs and pleas'.[3] Master
Ralph of Stokes held five ecclesiastical benefices, enough to
mark him as a successful royal clerk. The remaining seven failed
to attract any notable royal generosity, even though two of
them were among John's small corps of justices *coram rege*.

The first act of Geoffrey fitz Peter's dramatic rise into the
upper ranks of the baronage took place in the time of Richard I.
The success story continued to unfold under King John,
especially in 1204 and 1205. By then Geoffrey had become one
of the largest landholders in the kingdom. In 1204, the king gave
Geoffrey fitz Peter the manor of Aylesbury with extensive
rights, including exemption from the murder-fine, 'a rare and
cherished privilege' granted only sparingly.[4] Greater gain came
in May 1205, when John granted him the castle and honour of

---

[1] Meekings, *Crown Pleas of Wilts eyre*, p. 13; Hastings, *Court of Common Pleas in the
Fifteenth Century*, p. 83.
[2] See below, chap. 6, pt. 3.
[3] *Rot. Lit. Claus.*, 1: 526b, 527.
[4] He held it at fee farm of £60 yearly and service of one knight. *Rot. Chart.*, pp.
127–8; Painter, *Studies in Hist. of Eng. Feudal Barony*, pp. 81–3. Earlier John had
given Geoffrey the manor of Winterslow, Wilts, *Rot. Chart.*, p. 73b.

Berkhampstead with twenty-two fees stretching across England.[5] Another large grant came from the escheat of the Normans, when John parcelled out English lands of Norman lords who had done homage to the French kings. English lands of one Norman lord worth £100 a year came to Geoffrey. King John continued to give his justiciar generous amounts of land up to 1210 or so.[6]

William Briwerre was a man after John's own heart, a sheriff skilled at extorting enormous sums for the royal coffers. As a result of his financial efficiency and expertise, rich reward came to him, particularly in 1204–5, when John gave him several honours that were in his hand. They included the barony of Horsley, Derbyshire, with nearly twenty-four knight's fees; the honour of Lavendon, Buckinghamshire, which included land to several shires; and a scattered group of manors, including the whole wapentake of Scarsdale, Derbyshire.[7] The king made the award of Lavendon although five coheirs were living at the time.[8] Briwerre, then, benefited from John's practice of ignoring rights of inheritance, which was arousing complaints from landed families.

Hugh Bardolf did not begin at such a low point as the other two, for he had a comfortable inheritance, and he had built up most of his holdings before King John's accession. In 1201, however, John made him a grant of the manor of Bromsgrove along with King's Norton in Worcestershire.[9] Fines offered to the king following Bardolf's death in 1203 attest to the value of his holdings. His brother offered £1000 for the marriage of Hugh's widow.[10]

Two of the five clerics among John's judges became bishops,

---

[5] *Rot. Chart.*, p. 151b. He held Berkhampstead at fee farm of £100 a year but at his death it was producing £400, *Pipe Roll 16 John*, pp. 12–13.

[6] *Rot. Lit. Claus.*, 154b, lands of Robert fitz Ernis. In 1205 Queen's Hithe in London, *Rot. Chart.*, p. 182; 10 3/4 fees in Essex and Herts of his honour of Gloucester sometime before 1211, *Red Book Exch.*, p. 609; part of the forest of Huntingdon as hereditary holding as late as July 1213, *Rot. Chart.*, p. 194.

[7] For Horsley, *Rot. Chart.*, p. 123; *Pipe Roll 6 John*, p. 161; for Lavendon, *Rot. Lit. Pat.*, p. 41. Also the manors of Chesterfield, Sneiton, Notts, and Axminster, Devon, with the wapentake of Scarsdale, held at fee farm of £112 and one knight's service, *Rot. de Obl. et Fin.*, pp. 225–6.

[8] *Honors and Knights' Fees*, 1: 4; Sanders, *Baronies*, p. 128.

[9] In return for a 50-mark fine, *Rot. de Obl. et Fin.*, p. 68.

[10] *Pipe Roll 6 John*, p. 212; *7 John*, p. 197.

compared with three of seven under Richard Lionheart. Henry
of London, archdeacon of Stafford, was elected archbishop of
Dublin in 1212, and Eustace de Fauconberg bishop of London
later, in 1221. Henry of London must have been one of the
greater pluralists in early thirteenth-century England. He was
parson of seven churches and canon of two cathedrals at the
king's presentation. In 1207, King John named him to prebends
at Lincoln and Exeter.[11] Since the two sees were vacant and temporarily in royal hands, John could appoint his own clerks to
prebends. Henry of London held three churches to which he
was presented by others, perhaps at the king's urging, perhaps
to win his influence.[12] He must have been rich from all his
benefices, besides other income that came to him from service
to the king.[13]

Higher ecclesiastical posts lay ahead for the archdeacon of
Stafford. In 1209 he was elected bishop of Exeter through the
king's efforts, but Stephen Langton voided the election in
1211.[14] Henry had been so confident of official confirmation
that he resigned some of his benefices in anticipation of becoming bishop of Exeter.[15] Election as archbishop of Dublin marked
the peak of Henry's success. It seems obvious that he was an
ideal candidate for Dublin from King John's point of view, a

---

[11] Churches of Cheshunt, Herts, and Faversham, Kent, in May 1202, *Rot. Lit.
Pat.*, pp. 11, 48; dean of St Mary's, Shrewsbury in 1203, *Rot. Chart.*, p. 110;
church of Harenleigh, diocese of Coventry, in 1204, but later that year the
king promised him 100 marks' return from a vacancy in his gift in the diocese
– either church or prebend – as soon as one became available, *Rot. Lit. Pat.*, p.
38b, 45; churches at Bridgnorth, Salop., and Werfield in the diocese of Chester
in 1205, *Rot. Lit. Pat.*, p. 48; dean of the collegiate church of St Mary, Stafford,
Rot. Lit. Claus., 1: 77; *Rot. Lit. Pat.*, p. 70; canon of Exeter and Lincoln, *Rot. Lit.
Pat.*, pp. 75, 78.

[12] Dean and chapter of Lichfield presented him to the church of Upper Arley,
Staffs, *Magnum Reg. Album*, p. 151, no. 308; the monks of Tutbury Priory
named him parson of Mayfield, Staffs, Avrom Saltman, ed., *Cartulary of Tut-
bury abbey*, H.M.C. Joint Pub'ns. (London, 1962), p. 31, no. 13; p. 42, no. 29.
Henry was also parson of Checkley, Staffs, presented by William Basset,
Placit. Abbrev., p. 44.

[13] In 1204, John gave him the vill of Bescot, Staffs, *Rot. Lit. Claus.*, 1: 11.

[14] Cheney, *Innocent III and England*, p. 130; Painter, *Reign of King John*, pp.
184–5.

[15] Church of Bridgnorth, *Rot. Lit. Pat.*, p. 80; church of Upper Arley, *C.R.R.*, 12:
287, no. 1412; *Magnum Reg. Album*, p. 151, no. 308.

man capable of pursuing the king's goals for Ireland. Henry had journeyed to Ireland in the summer of 1212, a visit likely related to the failing health of the archbishop, John Cumin.[16] It seems evident that Henry of London was being considered as the replacement for the elderly archbishop, even before Cumin's death in October 1212. Henry was duly elected by both the chapter of Holy Trinity and St Patrick's secular college. Although the election seems regular, the agreement of the two Dublin chapters suggests strong royal pressure.[17] Henry was consecrated in the early months of 1213, and Innocent III accepted his election without challenge.

Henry of London's election to the archbishopric of Dublin marked the beginning of a profitable and influential career in Ireland. As archbishop at Dublin, the Anglo-Norman stronghold on the island, Henry's authority went far beyond that which he had exercised in England as a royal clerk. Especially was this true in the years when his role as episcopal leader was combined with the office of justiciar. Letters patent of 23 July 1213 notified John's Irish subjects of Henry's appointment as justiciar of Ireland, a post he held until 1215 and again from 1221 to 1224.[18] Henry of London was the perfect candidate for an office that was a pivotal point in the English occupation of Ireland, a position where John required complete loyalty, amid the treacherous paths of Anglo-Irish and native Irish politics. Henry's administrative, diplomatic, and judicial experience, combined with his long association with John in troubled times, gave him the needed qualities for a difficult post.[19]

Eustace de Fauconberg, during his years of service to the crown, accumulated at least five churches plus a prebend at St Paul's. There is no evidence that King John presented him to any of the churches, although he could have been indirectly re-

---

[16] *Rot. Lit. Claus.*, 1: 118b; *Cal. Docs. relating to Ireland*, 1: 71, no. 432, £100 authorized for his expenses.

[17] Aubrey Gwynn, 'Henry of London, archbishop of Dublin', *Studies (Irish History)*, 38 (1949): 296.

[18] *Cal. Docs. relating to Ireland*, 1: 75–6, no. 466.

[19] For Henry's career in Ireland, see Diana Primelles, Ph.D. Dissertation, 'The archbishops of Dublin and the Normanization of Ireland: 1182–1228.' The Florida State University, 1980.

sponsible.[20] Neither is there evidence that Eustace's secular landholdings came to him by royal grant. In 1203, he paid scutage on half a knight's fee of the honour of Tickhill, and he had other holdings.[21] Fauconberg's most impressive reward came after John's death, when he became royal treasurer and bishop of London.

In John's last years, Master Eustace was more closely associated with Peter des Roches, the justiciar, than with the king personally. Fauconberg disappeared from royal government from October 1209 until 1214. Possibly scruples about serving an excommunicate king sent him back to Winchester, where he had begun his career as Godfrey de Lucy's clerk. By 1214, however, he was emerging from the obscurity that had engulfed him; and he appears as the 'right-hand man' of Peter des Roches, who had succeeded Godfrey as bishop of Winchester and had become justiciar following the death of Geoffrey fitz Peter in 1213. Fauconberg's work for the justiciar was no longer judicial but largely financial. In Peter des Roches' service, Eustace seems to have concerned himself with making many of the routine payments that kept royal government functioning, leaving the justiciar free to concentrate on greater problems.[22] His financial work earned him the office of treasurer by autumn 1217, when the civil war ended and the Exchequer reopened. The crowning of Eustace's career came with his elevation as bishop of London in February 1221, following the retirement of William de Sainte-Mère-Eglise.[23] He continued to take part in secular government after his consecration as bishop, holding the office of treasurer until his death in 1228.[24]

---

[20] The monks of Pontefract presented Eustace to Catwick Church, Farrer, *Early Yorks Chtrs.*, 3: 48, no. 1322; *Pontefract Chart.*, 2: 550–1, no. 445. Archbishop Geoffrey Plantagenet presented him to Rampton, in Notts, *C.R.R.*, 10: 219; and the mother of Thomas de Camvill presented him to a church at Goddington, Oxon., *C.R.R.*, 10: 250–1. He also held churches at Kirkleatham, Yorks, *C.R.R.*, 8: ix, 67; and at Thurlton, Norfolk, *C.R.R.*, 8: 321. For his prebend, see *Fasti, St. Paul's*, p. 54.

[21] The Tickhill fee was held of Adam of Bedingfield, *Pipe Roll 5 John*, p. 173; *9 John*, p. 118; land at Cheam, Surrey, *C.R.R.*, 4: 248, 289, and possibly land in Dorset and Somerset, a grant by Henry fitz Reiner of land from Robert de Harcourt's fee, *Cat. Anc. Deeds*, 1: 194, no. A1665.

[22] *Rot. Lit. Claus.*, 1: 207–13; see also *Justiciarship*, pp. 197, 201–2, 210.

[23] *Fasti, St. Paul's*, p. 2.

[24] First mention of Eustace as treasurer is 4 Nov. 1217, *Rot. Lit. Claus.*, 1: 340. He went on embassies to the French court in 1223 and 1225, *Rot. Lit. Claus.*, 1: 556; 2: 41.

Ranking near Master Eustace de Fauconberg are five other justices who won some modest reward at the hands of King John. The only clerk among the five is Master Ralph of Stokes. He too held five churches, but evidently no cathedral prebends. In 1203 King John presented him to the church at Alrewas, Staffordshire.[25] The others do not seem to have been at the king's presentation, although he could have had a hand in them.[26] There are few signs, then, that Master Ralph benefited from direct royal favour, although he may have benefited indirectly.

Simon of Pattishall had success in increasing his landholdings from only one knight's fee to five and three-quarters plus several smaller holdings. He sought to make his land at Pattishall the heart of his holdings, for they were concentrated around his native village near Northampton, and in neighbouring counties, although he had some holdings farther away. King John made no hereditary grants to Pattishall, but he sometimes gave him temporary possession of escheats, which provided an income. As early as 1199, Simon held land at Willaveston, Rutland, at a farm of twenty shillings, and such grants continued until 1212.[27] John's grants could include urban as well as rural property. In 1200 the king granted Simon two houses in Northampton for sixteen pence yearly, part of the escheat of Benedict the Jew of York.[28] John rarely granted his servants hereditary holdings, preferring to let lands at fee farm or some other temporary arrangement that could be withdrawn in case the farmer aroused his displeasure.[29]

With Roger Huscarl, we seem to be approaching the salaried civil servant. While little evidence of grants of land or goods survives, several instances of money grants to him for expenses while on the king's service do survive. In October 1212, the king

[25] *Rot. Lit. Pat.*, p. 40b.
[26] Church at Woodford, Northants, patron unknown, *Placit. Abbrev.*, p. 41; church at Bainton, Yorks, presented by the abbot of York, *Br. Note Book*, 3: 323–4, no. 1339; church at King's Somborne, Hants, presented by William Briwerre, *Reg. St. Osmund*, 1: 262; church at Overbury, Worcs., presented by the prior of Worcester, W.H. Hale, ed., *Register of the Priory of St Mary Worcester*, Camden Soc., old ser. (London, 1865), pp. 76b–77b.
[27] Land of John de Mallium, *Pipe Roll 1 John*, p. 20. Simon held the escheated land of Josce of Wallingford by service of eighteen geese in 1201, *Pipe Roll 3 John*, p. 178. By 1212 he held at the king's will the escheated manor of Waddesdon, Bucks, *Red Book Exch.*, 2: 600. In May 1215 the manor was given to another, *Rot. Lit. Claus.*, 1: 200.
[28] *Rot. Chart.*, p. 52. [29] Holt, *Northerners*, p. 226.

notified the treasurer and chamberlains of 100 shillings of prests to be paid to Roger, and in 1214 he was to be paid 20 shillings.[30] Prests were advances to a royal servant, either advances against sums which he had to repay at the Chamber or Exchequer out of funds he later collected in the course of his work or else advances to be deducted from future salary payments. In December 1222, Huscarl received five marks for the expenses of his crossing to Ireland as a *nuntius* to Archbishop Henry of Dublin.[31] No doubt, he was sent on his Irish mission because of his experience as a judge, and he continued his judicial work there, taking part in a 1224 general eyre.[32] Roger received £20 in 1225 to be paid either in coin at the Irish Exchequer or in land, and the next year his salary was increased to £25, a substantial salary in the early thirteenth century.[33] Little mention of other cash payments to royal justices occurs in the Exchequer accounts.[34]

No evidence points toward any particular favours flowing from the king personally to the remaining seven justices. No heiresses or widows in the king's gift provided brides with rich landed estates. Indeed, except for the survival of legitimate heirs, there is little evidence for the existence of wives. John of Guestling did leave a widow, Barbota, whose suit for her dower gives an indication of her husband's landed wealth. She sought only an unimpressive collection of small plots of a few acres and

---

[30] *Rot. Lit. Claus.*, 1: 125b; *Pipe Roll 16 John*, p. 124.

[31] *Rot. Lit. Claus.*, 1: 52b.

[32] K.W. Nicholls, 'Inquisitions of 1224 from the Miscellanea of the Exchequer', *Analecta Hibernica*, 27 (1972): 105, an inquest into what seems to be articles of the eyre at a court held at Limerick on 22 Oct. 1224 before William Marshal, Roger Huscarl, and others. *Chart. St. Mary's Dublin*, 1: 64–5, a charter made *coram Rogero Huscarl et ceteris fidelibus domini regis in assisi apud Pontem Drogheda*. *Cal. Close Rolls 1279–88*., pp. 55–6, enrolment of the verdict of a 1280 inquest, referring to the seizure of the liberty of Meath into the king's hand when Henry of London was justiciar of Ireland. The seizure was said to have been made by the justiciar with the advice of Roger Huscarl, then justice 'of the Bench at Dublin'.

[33] *Rot. Lit. Claus.*, 2: 32b, 40, 125; *Cal. Docs. relating to Ireland*, 1: 192, no. 1271; 196, no. 1295; 212, no. 1400. He was given the manor of Baliscadden in Aug. 1225, *Cal. Docs. relating to Ireland*, 1: 199, no. 1320.

[34] One of the few is a payment of 10 marks to Walter of Creeping by justiciar's writ in 1206, *Pipe Roll 8 John*, p. 65. In 1214, King John gave Henry de Pont-Audemar 60s in annual customs from a salt pit belonging to the borough of Southampton, *Rot. Lit. Claus.*, 1: 206b, 372.

a few shillings' return.[35] Neither is there much evidence of appointment to royal offices which would enable the justices to improve their position. We have seen that few of them were sheriffs. A problem is the difficulty of making a reasonable guess at judges' property-holdings which will allow a glimpse of any acquisitions. Richard de Mucegros, for example, was already a substantial landholder through his father, but he does not seem to have increased his holdings significantly, either with temporary custodies or with permanent grants. His one speculative venture for profit was his purchase of the shrievalty of Gloucestershire in 1207, and that proved to be an unprofitable one.[36] Certainly none of the seven who were not *curiales* managed to leap from their knightly level into higher social circles.

Documentation for clerics is sometimes easier to find than for laymen because of better care given to the Church's records. Yet that rule does not hold true for the two clerics among the seven: Master Godfrey de Insula and Henry of Whiston. Since Henry was only in minor orders, he could not hold benefices with care of souls. He held secular holdings in the North which were in part, if not wholly, inherited from his aunt.[37] Henry seems to have had plenty of cash available. In 1195 he offered a sixty-mark fine for an heiress, and a little later he lent four silver marks to a Northamptonshire man in return for a gage of his land.[38]

After his retirement from the royal administration, Henry seems to have remained wealthy. In 1207, he sought release from a crusading vow which he had taken at the time of the Third Crusade, 'on account of the love and favor of the king's father Henry II, whose clerk he was, rather than out of piety'.

---

[35] In 1223 she claimed 28s return from Winchelsea, two-thirds of a mill, the marsh of Sneps, six acres of Stanmareis, a third of two perches of land in Guestling wood, and 24 acres at Guestling, *C.R.R.*, 11: 22, no. 129; 107, no. 562; 528, no. 2639.

[36] See above, part 2, p. 157.

[37] Land of the barony of Burgh by Sands, *Pipe Roll 7 Ric. I*, p. 148; *1 John*, p. 213; a third of an advowson at Lodore, Cumberland, *P.B.K.J.*, 3: cxix; a claim to advowson of the church at Crosby Garrett, Westmorland, *C.R.R.*, 6: 163, 267; *Pipe Roll 11 John*, p. 16. He also had land at Syston, Leics, *C.R.R.*, 2: 26.

[38] Fine for the daughter of Philip de Neubald, *Pipe Roll 7 Ric. I*, p. 191; *Chancellor's Roll 8 Ric. I*, pp. 54–5. Gage on four virgates at Duddington, *C.R.R.*, 1: 141.

Whiston had never fulfilled his vow, and he was 'now old and grey-haired', incapable of carrying out his intention. The pope released him from his vow on condition that he pay twenty-five marks initially and afterwards twenty-five pounds annually to the Knights Templars at London for relief of the Holy Land.[39] At a time when a knight's income was often only ten to twenty pounds, such a payment was quite large. Henry of Whiston must have had a much larger annual income, supplemented from sources that must remain hidden from us.

Hardly any evidence survives of rewards Master Godfrey de Insula earned by his long service to the king and to Hubert Walter. King John gave him a moiety of the chapel at Launceston Castle at some unknown date; the other moiety belonged to the canons regular of Launceston. They challenged the king's right to present to the chapel, and the case was assigned to papal judges-delegate, sometime between 5 October 1214 and 22 August 1215.[40] The ecclesiastical court's decision is not extant; perhaps the civil war prevented its convening. Master Godfrey had the right of presentation to the church at Reymerston, Norfolk, which he later gave to the nuns of St Radegund at Cambridge.[41]

Royal servants had many means of adding to their wealth, and they did not necessarily depend directly on the king for reward. Their work provided other possibilities for supplementing their income. Justices, along with others at the centre of government, had opportunities to bargain for profitable custodies. Of course, the king sometimes awarded custodies freely as a way of providing for servants. At least eleven of the seventeen justices held wardships of widows or heirs, for which several had offered fines. William Briwerre bought a half-dozen or more wardships, for which he offered sums ranging from ten to a thousand marks.[42] Lesser men purchased wardships as well, and their usual fine was around £100.[43]

---

[39] *Letters of Innocent III concerning England*, p. 122, no. 737.

[40] *Rot. Lit. Pat.*, p. 153b; *Letters of Innocent III concerning England*, p. 169, no. 1014.

[41] *C.R.R.*, 9: 26–7. A certain William Gebram had given the advowson to Godfrey de Insula.

[42] E.g. 10 marks for custody of Matilda, daughter of Hamo de Andelos, *Rot. de Obl. et Fin.*, p. 399; 210 marks for heirs of Ralph Murdac and Walter de Glanvill, ibid., p. 10; 1000 marks for heir and widow of Hugh de Aubervill, p. 473.

Perhaps the opportunity to collect gifts from petitioners at court was a more powerful attraction for royal office than the uncertain chance of royal generosity. Great *curiales* such as Geoffrey fitz Peter or William Briwerre obviously had influence for which those seeking royal favour would pay, willingly or unwillingly. Since their goodwill was useful for suitors in the *curia regis* or for Exchequer debtors, they were not so much guilty of sycophancy themselves as they were objects of sycophancy from suitors. Such is the explanation for Henry de Tracy's grant of the manor of Morton, Devon, to the justiciar. Geoffrey fitz Peter's aid was recalled in an inquisition *post mortem* from the time of Edward I. According to the testimony, Henry de Tracy gave Geoffrey the manor in gratitude for his help in recovering his father's barony.[44]

Among the magnates who bestowed manors on William Briwerre are Fulk Paynell and Rose of Dover. Their large grants of land to him look suspiciously like rewards for his aid in recovering lands in the king's hand and in Briwerre's custody. Paynell gave William two manors and other land once he regained his barony of Bampton, Devon, from King John.[45] Rose of Dover won half the Lucy inheritance, and she – by pre-arrangement or in gratitude – promptly gave William seven manors and the service of eleven knights, the major part of her inheritance.[46] A more brazen example of purchase of favour is an offering of sixty marks and a palfrey to King John, and another palfrey to William Briwerre, by a Somerset man seeking his inheritance in 1200.[47]

Henry of London seems to have won lands in similar circumstances in 1214. Hugh Hose, who had been in the king's wardship until then, gave the new archbishop of Dublin the manor of Penkridge, Staffordshire, with some dependent vills and a fair. He doubtless made the gift in return for favours while

---

[43] E.g. Henry of Whiston 60 marks in 1195; Hugh Bardolf 100 marks in 1198; Richard of Herriard £100 the same year; Henry de Pont-Audemar £100 in 1199; and Henry of London 50 marks and two palfreys in 1207.

[44] For details see above, chap. 3, pt. 4, p. 124.

[45] *Rot. Chart.*, p. 28. For other gifts of Fulk Paynell, see *Cal. Inq. Post Mort., Hen. III*, p. 34, no. 139; *P.R.O. 35th Report*, D.L. Charters, pp. 9, 26. For William as custodian of Bampton, see *Pipe Roll 6 Ric. I*, pp. 30, 167, 172.

[46] *Rot. Lit. Claus.*, 1: 127; *Rot. Chart.*, p. 189. For a fuller sorting-out of the complications of the Lucy inheritance, see Painter, *Reign of King John*, pp. 75–6.   [47] *Rot. de Obl. et Fin.*, p. 95.

he had been in the king's custody. King John then added his own gift: advowson of the deanery of Penkridge, to be held by the archbishop and his successors at Dublin 'provided that they were not Irishmen'.[48]

Even lesser men in the judiciary could be worth cultivating by large landholders who were often involved in litigation. As we have seen, justices sometimes met privately with litigants to give legal advice.[49] No doubt, they received a consideration for their time and expertise. Royal justices thought nothing of accepting pensions, grants of land, or presentation to churches from magnates or monastic houses in return for their legal advice. John of Guestling, Richard of Herriard, Osbert fitz Hervey, and Simon of Pattishall all held land of religious houses. During the years 1209–18, when John of Guestling was absent from the courts, he returned to his native South East and found employment as the *senescallus* of Abbot Roger of St Augustine's, Canterbury.[50] Neither did the justices find it unfitting to accept the hospitality of prominent county families or great monastic houses when they made their eyres, even though their hosts might have suits pending before them.[51]

Of course, the justices' familiarity with the work of the courts and friendship with colleagues in the *curia regis* gave them advantages in their own lawsuits. A 1212 action brought against Master Ralph of Stokes illustrates this. Ralph's response was to claim that his opponent was a bastard, incapable of inheriting the land in question; and he offered a mark for an inquest into his legitimacy. The case received careful attention from the justices *coram rege*, revealing Ralph's friendship and influence with them after his retirement from the bench. They ordered a jury of twenty-four, twelve men from Warwickshire and twelve from Derbyshire. Later they found the jurors to be *inutiles*, and new ones – both knights and lawful men – were ordered selected. When the new jurors defaulted, causing another adjournment,

---

[48] *Rot. Chart.*, p. 218; *V.C.H., Staffs*, 3: 299; 5: 108–9.
[49] See chap. 3, pt. 4, pp. 122–3.
[50] G.H. Turner and H.E. Salter, eds., *Register of St. Augustine's Abbey, Canterbury*, Br. Acad. Records of Soc. and Econ. Hist. (1915–24), 2: 456. Guestling held land of the abbot of Fecamp for 12d yearly, *Sussex Feet of Fines*, p. 4, no. 13; *Docs. preserved in France*, 1: 53, no. 151; and 90 acres of the abbot of Battle for 3d, *Sussex Feet of Fines*, p. 24, no. 102.
[51] See below, chap. 6, pt. 3, for details.

the justices commanded the sheriff to 'inquire diligently' whether anyone could be found who had been present at the marriage of the mother of Master Ralph's opponent.[52] Clearly, Ralph was to have every possible opportunity to prove his opponent's illegitimacy.

A concern for family interest moved King John's justices to seek advantage for their kinsmen, just as it had those of Henry II and Richard I. Again, those closest to the king had greater success in securing favours for their kinsmen. Geoffrey fitz Peter was in an easy position to provide for his children: three sons and a daughter from his first marriage, and a son and possibly two daughters from his second.[53] His eldest son, Geoffrey de Mandeville IV, was heir to the Mandeville inheritance, centred on the honour of Pleshy with other holdings of his father.[54] Young Geoffrey married first a daughter of Robert fitz Walter, another Essex lord who later became one of the baronial leaders opposing King John. Geoffrey married a second time in 1214 to Isabel, heir to the honour of Gloucester and the king's divorced wife. He apparently was pressured into this marriage by King John, who extorted a 20,000 mark fine for it. There was no way young Mandeville could pay such an enormous debt, and it was enough to drive him to join his former father-in-law in the rebel forces.[55] But the earldom of Gloucester soon reverted to the crown, for Geoffrey was killed in a tournament in 1216, leaving no children behind.

Geoffrey de Mandeville's heir was his younger brother, William, who married another daughter of Robert fitz Walter. He had acquired some of the lands his father had gained during his lifetime with the restorations made after Runnymede, but lost them in a year's time when he too joined the rebellion.[56] He

---

[52] *C.R.R.*, 6: 237, 300, 354. Roger fitz Alan brought an action *quare intrusit* against Ralph and Isabel, widow of Roger de Wichenor. They shared custody of the son and heir of Roger de Dumervill, heir to Alrewas, Staffs, *Book of Fees*, 1: 142. [53] *Complete Peerage*, 5: genealogical table.

[54] *Rot. de Obl. et Fin.*, pp. 502–3.

[55] *Rot. Lit. Pat.*, p. 109b; *Rot. de Obl. et Fin.*, p. 520. See also Painter, *Reign of King John*, pp. 283–4.

[56] He gained the manor of Aylesbury and the honour of Berkhampstead, *Rot. Lit. Claus.*, 1: 217. John had taken Berkhampstead into his hand on Geoffrey's death, *Rot. Lit. Pat.*, p. 105b. The royal grant of Berkhampstead, however, had specified that it was to go to Geoffrey's heirs by his second wife, *Rot. Chart.*, p. 151b.

died in 1227 also without heirs of his body. Since the third brother, Henry was in clerical orders, he was ineligible for the succession. His father had found him a place as a royal clerk, and he became dean of the collegiate church at Wolverhampton, a royal chapel, in 1205 and a canon of Lincoln Cathedral in 1207.[57] The inheritance then went to his sister, Matilda, who had married Henry de Bohun, earl of Hereford; and the bulk of the estates Geoffrey had built up passed to the Bohuns, an old baronial family.[58]

Geoffrey fitz Peter had a son by his second wife, Avelina, widow of William de Mountchesney and daughter of Roger de Clare, earl of Hereford. This son, John fitz Geoffrey, was under age at the time of his father's death. He received a portion of his father's lands following his half-brother's death in 1227, in return for a 300 mark fine.[59] He married into a baronial family, taking as wife a daughter of Hugh Bigod, earl of Norfolk. John followed his father into an administrative career, and he shared his father's interest in legal matters. John held a number of offices in the middle years of Henry III, including justice of King's Bench and justiciar of Ireland.[60]

William Briwerre exploited his position shamelessly to provide for his family. He had two sons and five daughters to look after, and he sought lands and good marriages for them. When Walter Brito III died in 1199 having only two sisters as heirs, Briwerre sought his honour of Odcombe, Somerset, for his eldest son Richard. The sisters' descendants inevitably viewed William's efforts as an unjust violation of their rights, but the hereditary principle was not yet fully binding on the king. One sister's son had his right recognized by an assize in 1200 for which he had paid 200 marks, but somehow he was persuaded to surrender promptly his half of the honour to William Briwerre for his son.[61] Two years later, after William had given King John a 500 mark fine, the other half of the honour was given to

[57] *Rot. Lit. Pat.*, p. 75. King John named him to a prebend at Lincoln in 1207. See also *Fasti, Lincoln*, pp. 126–7.

[58] Sanders, *Baronies*, pp. 72, 92.   [59] *Complete Peerage*, 5: 124, 433.

[60] John was sheriff of Yorks, justice of King's Bench, steward of Gascony, and justiciar of Ireland, Turner, ed., *Brevia Placitata*, pp. xxvi–xxviii, xxxi. Also Westminster Domesday, ff. 348b, 381b, where he witnesses charters in 1241 as *capitali forestiario Angl.*

[61] Walter Croc, *Pipe Roll 1 John*, p. 238; *2 John*, pp. 99–100; *C.R.R.*, 1: 239.

Richard Briwerre, William's eldest son. Many years afterwards, jurors in an inquisition *post mortem* declared that these lands had been 'alienated from their just heirs through the power of Lord William Briwerre the elder'.[62]

Richard Briwerre died by 1215, and William's heir then became his second son, William Briwerre, junior. He married Joan, daughter of William de Reviers, earl of Devon, a union that signalled the Briwerre family's rise to the highest level of feudal society.[63] When William II died without any offspring in 1232, his heirs were his five sisters, and the Briwerre estates were partitioned among them.[64] All five had found husbands from rich and powerful families, in two instances because their father had married them off to his wards. Isabel's first marriage seems to have been to the son of Fulbert de Dover, who was in her father's custody. Joan married William de Percy, heir to Topcliff, another ward of her father.[65] Lesser-ranking men could imitate Briwerre's practice of marrying off daughters to heirs in their wardship, for Henry de Pont-Audemar seems to have done the same thing.[66]

William Briwerre's sense of family extended beyond his own children to his nephew. He married Richard Gernun, a nephew, to Joan de Morvill, coheir to a Cumberland barony.[67] Another nephew entered the clergy, and his uncle's influence aided his advancement. William Briwerre, bishop of Exeter 1222–4, was precentor of Exeter before his election. Probably it is no coincidence that at the time of his election his uncle, William Briwerre, had custody of the vacant see's property.[68] Briwerre, like any magnate, had a host of *familiares*, household clerks,

---

[62] *Pipe Roll 4 John*, p. 256; *Rot. Chart.*, p. 195n; *Cal. Inq. Post Mort.*, 1: 191, no. 597; 2: no. 150.

[63] Dugdale, *Baronage*, 1: 702.   [64] *Book of Fees*, 1: 396–401.

[65] Isabel married secondly Baldwin Wak, heir to the honour of Bourne, Lincs, *Pipe Roll 3 Hen. III*, p. 130; Sanders, *Baronies*, pp. 107, 111, 123, 148.

[66] He purchased custody of the heir of Miles Neirnuit, *Pipe Roll 1 John*, p. 37. Later records name his daughter as widow of Richard Neirnuit, S.F. Hockey, ed., *The Beaulieu Cartulary*, Southampton Records Ser., 17 (1974): 116–17, no. 146.

[67] Burgh by Sands, Sanders, *Baronies*, p. 24. The marriage was purchased for 50 marks for his son, or if her relatives agreed, for Richard Gernun, *Rot. de Obl. et Fin.*, p. 184.

[68] *Pat. Rolls 1216–25*, p. 415. For the identification of the bishop as the royal official's nephew, see George Oliver, *Lives of the Bishops of Exeter* (Exeter, 1861), pp. 34–6.

knights, and other servants, for whom he had to provide. If skil-
ful, he could secure benefices for his clerks from the king. He
did this in 1224, securing royal presentation of one of his clerks
to a church belonging to the abbey of Tavistock, which was temporarily without an abbot and in the king's hand.[69] Thus the presentation cost neither William Briwerre nor Henry III anything,
and the abbey was saddled with the salary of William's clerk.

William Briwerre's and Geoffrey fitz Peter's rise from
obscurity to high rank is dramatic enough to set beside the
biography of William Marshal, only lacking a poet to sing their
praises. They illustrate well the rise of 'new men' that conservative churchmen and old landed families alike resented. Despite efforts of the two to build up great blocks of lands, their
ambition of founding dynasties to stand alongside the old
baronial houses was unfulfilled. The chances of birth – too many
daughters and not enough surviving sons – thwarted their
ambitions.

The two clerics among John's judges who were elevated to
bishoprics found it possible to offer patronage to kinsmen and
familiares. Three men bearing the surname 'Fauconberg' appear
among the canons of St Paul's during Eustace's episcopate, two
of whom became cathedral treasurers. Not only *consanguines* but
associates in the royal administration owed their prebends at St
Paul's to the favour of their master Bishop Eustace, who was
also treasurer. Luke the Chaplain, controller of the king's wardrobe, 1224–7, was a canon of St Paul's about the same
time.[70]

Among the clerks who came from England to take up posts in
the Irish Church were Blunds of London, nephews and other
relatives of Henry, archbishop of Dublin. His nephews held two
of the chief offices in the secular college of St Patrick's church,
Dublin, which Henry was transforming into a full cathedral
chapter. Simon Blund, son of Robert Blund, served his uncle as

---

[69] *Pat. Rolls 1216–25*, p. 435, Master Adam presented to the church of
Hatherleigh, Devon. In 1202 King John named Hugh Bardolf's chaplain,
Master Henry of Derby, vicar of the church of Melbourne, diocese of Carlisle,
Rot. Lit. Pat., p. 7.

[70] Philip de Fauconberg, canon by 1223, and archdeacon of Huntingdon about
the time of Eustace's death; Thomas, archdeacon of Essex shortly before
Eustace's death; and William treasurer by 1228, *Fasti, St. Paul's*, pp. 13, 21, 33,
37, 62–3. For Luke, *Fasti*, p. 70.

a clerk in Dublin. Henry secured for him the church of
Kirkham, Lancashire, the advowson of which belonged to a
prominent Anglo-Irish family, the Butlers. He became precentor
of St Patrick's Cathedral under Archbishop Henry.[71] Another
nephew, William of London or William fitz Wydo, son of Henry's
sister, became the archbishop's first dean of St Patrick's. In 1216
King John granted him a house at Oxford which had been in the
hands of Jews. By 1218 he was a canon of his uncle's cathedral in
Dublin, he became dean about 1220, and he came to hold the
manor of Esker, County Dublin. He witnessed many deeds for
his uncle, the archbishop.[72] Several other Englishmen who held
prebends at Dublin may have been kinsmen of Henry.[73]

Henry of London's nephews who remained laymen also came
to Ireland in search of opportunity. He was not above alienating
the archbishopric's lands to find gifts for them. Andrew Blund,
brother of Simon, held considerable property in England,
including two-thirds of the manor of Penkridge, which his uncle
gave him. He visited Ireland in 1226 and 1228, and the
archbishop granted him the manor of Kinsaley, County Dublin,
but he later sold all his Irish lands.[74] John of London, another
son of Henry's sister, received the town of Portmachyueran
from his uncle about 1224.[75] Besides his four nephews, Henry
had a niece, or just possibly a natural daughter, Matilda
Scorchvillein. She married William, son of Geoffrey Marsh, justiciar of Ireland in the interval between the archbishop's two
appointments. Her uncle endowed her at the time of her
marriage, sometime before 1226, with three Irish manors, one
of which King John had previously given to the Church. The
couple met a bad end, for William Marsh eventually turned to
piracy, was captured and executed in 1242, and his wife was
imprisoned for a time. After her release, she struggled to
recover her lands, which the archbishop's successor at Dublin
claimed on the ground that Henry had wrongly alienated them

---

[71] St John Brooks, 'Archbishop Henry's Irish connections', pp. 4–5; see also
genealogical chart, p. 22.   [72] St John Brooks, pp. 7–11.
[73] *Fasti Ecclesiae St. Patrick*, ed. H.J. Lawlor (Dundalk, 1930), pp. 5, 53, 60, 83,
124, 155, 189, 190; J.T. Gilbert, ed., *Register of the Abbey of St. Thomas, Dublin*,
Rolls Series (1889), pp. 286–7, 382; *Chart. St. Mary's, Dublin*, 84, 466.
[74] *V.C.H., Staffs*, 5: 109; St. John Brooks, pp. 5–7.
[75] St John Brooks, pp. 11–14.

from the Church, and which the king also claimed as escheat on account of her husband's outlawry.[76]

Those justices who did not stand so close to the king seem to have had less luck in securing advantage for their kin. In most cases, it is next to impossible to learn much more than the names of heirs. This in itself is significant, indicating that their sons fell back into the shadows out of which they had appeared. There is little evidence for administrative dynasties among the families of John's judges. Only two of the twelve lesser-ranking men had sons who followed them into administrative careers.

One of the two was Richard de Mucegros, who had two sons.[77] Robert, the elder son, followed his father into the royal administration and surpassed him in prominence with a career lasting until 1254. He had joined the king's service as a knight as early as 1212, and he was with the forces in Poitou in the summer of 1214. Also that year Robert was keeper of six of the treasury's chests.[78] As we have seen, Robert remained with his father on the royalist side during the baronial rebellion. In 1216 he had custody of Glastonbury Abbey, and he was told later that year to commit the custody of the convent of Shafesbury to another, if he could not take it himself.[79] By early 1227 Robert had become the steward of Stephen Langton, archbishop of Canterbury,[80] but he returned to Henry III's service before 1230. That year his service on the campaign to Poitou won him a remission of interest on his debt to the Jews.[81] The next year he became custodian of Isabel, the king's younger sister, and she remained in his care until her marriage to the German emperor in 1235. Later that year, Robert was one of the ambassadors sent to

---

[76] St John Brooks, pp. 15–21. Cf. *Cal. Docs. relating to Ireland*, 1: nos. 2262, 2280, 2328.

[77] *Exc. è Rot. Fin.*, 1: 74, list of pledges for a debt of Robert includes Richard de Mucegros, 'father of Robert', and Richard de Mucegros 'junior'. Richard junior is described as Robert's brother when appointed his attorney in 1213, *C.R.R.*, 7: 14.

[78] *Pipe Roll 14 John*, p. 169, lists his expenses for a squire, four grooms, and four horses. *Rot. Lit. Claus.*, 1: 169b, shows him in Poitou with the king in July 1214; *Rot. Lit. Pat.*, p. 112, order to deliver chests.

[79] *Rot. Lit. Pat.*, p. 175; *Rot. Lit. Claus.*, 1:259b. For Shafesbury to the abbot of Sherbourne, *Rot. Lit. Claus.*, 1: 286b.

[80] *Cart. St. Gregory, Canterbury*, pp. 15–16, no. 19; *Acta Stephani Langton*, p. 50, no. 121. For ms. references, see Kathleen Major, 'The "Familia" of Archbishop Stephen Langton', *E.H.R.*, 48 (1933): 547–8.

[81] *Close Rolls 1227–31*, p. 414.

Provence to arrange the marriage of Henry III to Eleanor of Provence. He entered the service of Queen Eleanor, and at his death, he was described as her seneschal and *de familia reginae speciali*. He found time, however, to be custodian of Marlborough and its castle, responsible for construction there.[82]

Simon of Pattishall also had two sons, both of whom followed him in the king's service. Walter served Henry III as itinerant justice in 1218-19 and as sheriff of Bedford and Buckingham, 1224-8; he made a good marriage which brought him property in Bedfordshire.[83] Another son, Hugh of Pattishall, had a more impressive career centred at Westminster. He began as a clerk of the Exchequer, rose to treasurer in 1234, eventually earning as reward the bishopric of Coventry and Lichfield. On his election as bishop in 1236, he had to resign some six benefices.[84] More significant than heirs of Pattishall's body, however, is his spiritual heir. Martin of Pattishall, his clerk at the *curia regis*, followed him into the judiciary and became better known than his master through citations in *Bracton*.[85]

No precise figures for the wealth of these less well-known justices can be calculated, but a look at the evidence leaves an impression of some additions to their landholdings. One who managed to increase his holdings is Simon of Pattishall. The additions that some others made to their possessions must be measured in acres rather than in manors or knight's fees. It is difficult, for example, to reconstruct the holdings of Roger Huscarl, for plea rolls and feet of fines reveal only small plots: a messuage here, five acres there, and so on.[86] The records do show that his lands were scattered around Stepney in southeast

---

[82] Houghton, 'Family of Muchgros', pp. 21-2; *Chron. Maj.*, 5: 535. For his custody of Marlborough, *C.R.R.*, 16: 51, no. 149E.

[83] *Complete Peerage*, 10: 313; *Honors and Knights' Fees*, 1: 93, *D.N.B.*, s.v. 'Pateshull, Walter of'. *Pipe Roll 14 Hen. III*, p. 119, indicates that Walter was sheriff until 12 Hen. III.

[84] *D.N.B.*, s.v. 'Pateshull, Hugh of'. For his work as Exchequer clerk, see *Pipe Roll 14 Hen. III*, pp. 129, 317. For his benefices, see A. Hamilton Thompson, 'Pluralism in the medieval Church', *Lincs Architect. and Archaeol. Soc., Reports and Papers*, 33 (1915): 52-3.   [85] See below, chap. 5, pt. 2, p. 211.

[86] Pleas contesting half a virgate and a messuage at Stepney in 1200, *Rot. Cur. Reg.*, 2: 262; *C.R.R.*, 1: 345; and warranty of five acres in 1204-5, *C.R.R.*, 3: 204, 328. Other justices' pleas also involved small plots: Walter of Creeping gained 12 acres at Little Ellingham, Suffolk, by a final concord in 1208, *C.R.R.*, 5: 119, 294-5; James of Potterne won 30 acres of pasture in a 1219 lawsuit, *C.R.R.*, 6: 207-8, 232.

Middlesex, although he held some land as far away as Bruton, Somerset.[87] Huscarl later held land lying in the forest of Ros, Ireland, of William Marshal the Younger, who gave him permission to enclose it 'saving to us the wild beasts'.[88] Roger also had temporary grants of land 'for sustaining himself in the king's service'.[89] If Roger Huscarl had arrived in London a landless younger son, then he had done well for himself.

Several justices seem to have had substantial sums of cash available. Perhaps this wealth was ill-gotten, as the moralist Ralph of Coggeshall labelled Osbert fitz Hervey's riches in the 'Vision of Thurkill'. Henry of Whiston, as we have seen, could afford to give twenty-five pounds a year to the Church during his retirement. John of Guestling possessed an income-producing weekly market and an annual fair near Winchelsea.[90] None of the justices left large debts to the crown on their deaths, even though they had sometimes joined on a small scale the speculation in wardships that was catching others in the Exchequer's clutches.

The record of success by the seventeen justices of King John indicates that the spectacularly successful ones were still multi-purpose officials, *curiales* who likely had a close personal acquaintance with the king. Those who were concentrating chiefly on the work of justice found more modest reward. This is true even of those who worked closely with the king in his court *coram rege*. Not even Simon of Pattishall, the most important of the justices, won outstanding reward from John. Perhaps this simply reflects the professionalization of the judiciary, but it hints at some lack of generosity on the king's part. He may have felt, however, that office was its own reward, providing opportunities for the justices to satisfy their greed at litigants' expense.

[87] Final concord of 1200, W.J. Hardy and W. Page, eds., *A Calendar of the Feet of Fines from London and Middlesex, Ric. I–12 Eliz.* (London, 1892–3), p. 5; assize of novel disseisin in 1219, *C.R.R.*, 8: xi. He claimed seven acres at Walesmere, Middlesex, in 1212, *C.R.R.*, 6: 282, 392. He gave a sparrowhawk in 1217–18 for a quitclaim to land in Somerset, Emanuel Green, ed., *Pedes Finium for the County of Somerset*, Somerset Rec. Soc., 6 (1892): 29. His younger son, Alexander, claimed a tenement at Babcary, Somerset, ten miles away from Bruton, in 1229, *Pat. Rolls, 1225–32*, p. 291. [88] *Chart. St. Mary's, Dublin*, 2: 157.
[89] The land of Roger of Tanton (Stainton?), probably at Cowstead (in Stockbury), Kent, assigned to Huscarl in 1212, *Rot. Lit. Claus.*, 1: 204b; and 20 Sept. 1215, p. 229. Also land at Baliscadden, Ireland; see above.
[90] *Rot. Chart.*, p. 185b.

5

PATTISHALL, RALEIGH AND THEIR COLLEAGUES

1 THE JUDICIAL BENCH IN EARLY HENRY III, 1217–39

The machinery of normal government came to a standstill during the baronial rebellion that broke out at the end of John's reign, and royal justices only resumed their work in the fall of 1217 or in early 1218. The justiciar Hubert de Burgh took a number of assizes in Norfolk and Suffolk in the summer of 1218.[1] The promise made in *Magna Carta* that common pleas 'shall be heard in some fixed place' (cap. 17) demanded that the minority council turn its attention to reopening a court at Westminster as soon as possible. Apparently William Marshal and others in the ruling council heard pleas at Westminster in Michaelmas term 1217, and a regular court of Common Pleas was functioning throughout 1218, although no plea rolls survive before Trinity 1219.[2] The accession of Henry III, a boy of nine, marked a return to conditions that had prevailed before the loss of Normandy. Just as the king's absence then precluded a court *coram rege*, so now the king's minority meant that again the Bench at Westminster would be the only central common law court. James of Potterne, one of the small band of *coram rege* justices in King John's last years, received a command in 1218 to turn over to a royal clerk estreats and writs in his possession from the previous reign.[3] Obviously, the order is connected with the re-establishment of the Bench.

The first surviving final concords from Henry III's reign begin only with Hilary term 1218. Fines for that term include as witnesses William Marshal *rector regis et regni* and Hubert de Burgh,

---

[1] *Pipe Roll 2 Hen. III*, pp. 26–8.
[2] *P.R.O. Lists and Indexes*, Suppl. Ser., 1, *List of various common-law records* (reprint, 1970), p. 10. *Br. Note Book* does record some 1218 cases, and *Pipe Roll 2 Hen. III* (1218) lists fines offered for assizes to be taken at Westminster.
[3] *Rot. Lit. Claus.*, 1: 382.

the justiciar, along with four lesser-ranking professionals. Arrangements for government during the minority of Henry III are comparable to those made during Richard I's absence on crusade. A council composed of barons, bishops, and high-ranking officials was in charge in each instance. The council governing England in the young king's name had no court associated with it comparable to King John's court *coram rege*; its occasional judicial interventions were noted on the rolls of the Bench at Westminster.[4] The council was too busy with other matters to spend much time hearing pleas, and the volume of cases coming into the royal courts required the attention of fulltime professionals.

The burden of handling judicial work at Westminster was falling on a small and stable band of professionals. During the years from the revival of the Bench until William of Raleigh's retirement from the judiciary in 1239, a total of forty-five different names appear as witnesses to final concords at Westminster. This is in contrast to higher figures for the previous reigns, which were shorter in number of years. Of these forty-five, thirteen served at the Bench and on eyres long enough to group together as the core of the judiciary between 1217 and 1240. The remaining thirty-two were present for only a few sessions at Westminster, not enough to be considered professional justices.

Only four justices were survivors from King John's judiciary. The civil war marks a greater break in judicial personnel between the reigns of John and Henry III than that which had punctuated earlier changes in rulers. Simon of Pattishall, the mainstay of John's *curia regis*, probably died around 1217. William Briwerre ranked high among the young king's counsellors, but he was too busy as a baron of the Exchequer to hear cases at the Bench. John of Guestling, who had been a justice before King John closed the court at Westminster, served five terms between 1218 and 1220. The only others with judicial experience from the previous reign to return to the Bench were Eustace de Fauconberg, now treasurer, Geoffrey of Buckland, and Roger Huscarl. Eustace was present for three terms of

---

[4] *Select Cases*, 1: xxxiii–xxxiv; F.M. Powicke, *King Henry III and the Lord Edward* (Oxford, 1947), pp. 38–40.

court, the other two for only one term each plus participation on the 1218–19 eyre. James of Potterne, one of King John's little band of *coram rege* justices, also went on the 1218–19 eyre, but never joined Henry III's justices at Westminster. It is significant that John of Guestling, the one who served longest, had been among the rebels in 1216 and 1217. At the other end of the period – the late 1230s – we find some justices beginning to serve whose careers lie mainly outside the limits of our study. Henry of Bath, for example, joined the Bench in the summer of 1238, and he would become chief justice at Westminster in 1245 and chief justice *coram rege* in 1249.[5]

Further evidence that the judiciary was almost fully in the hands of professionals is the absence of magnates or high-ranking royal officers among the judges. Earlier justiciars had maintained the fiction of their presence at Westminster by witnessing all final concords whether or not they were there in person. Hubert de Burgh, Henry III's justiciar, abandoned any such fiction, no longer witnessing final concords. Hubert owed his appointment as justiciar chiefly to his military success, and he lacked the judicial experience of his predecessors.[6] West's study of the justiciarship concludes that Hubert played a smaller part in judicial matters than had earlier justiciars, and that he 'no longer devoted the greater part of his time to judicial work as had Geoffrey fitz Peter'. He left routine administration of justice to professional judges.[7] The same situation prevailed after his sudden fall in the summer of 1232. Although Stephen of Segrave, Hubert de Burgh's successor, was an experienced judge, senior common law justice in the realm after Martin of Pattishall's retirement, he never witnessed final concords in his capacity as justiciar.

We no longer need to divide the judges into two categories of high-ranking multi-purpose royal servants and judicial specialists. The former category is almost totally lacking after the revival of

---

[5] For a biographical sketch, see Meekings, *Crown Pleas of the Wilts Eyre 1249*, pp. 128–9. Another justice whose career began in the later 1230's and continued well after 1239 is William of Culworth.

[6] Michael Weiss, 'The Castellan, the early career of Hubert de Burgh', *Viator*, 5 (1974): 235–52.

[7] *Justiciarship*, pp. 253–4. G.O. Sayles earlier noticed that Hubert 'never left his mark upon the plea rolls as his predecessors ... had done', *Select Cases*, 1: xxxii.

the courts in 1217. Only eight men of baronial or episcopal rank were present at Westminster with the justices for any length of time, and those eight put in appearances only during the early minority, before 1222. Besides William Marshal and the justiciar, they included three bishops: William Cornhill, bishop of Coventry; Richard Marsh, bishop of Durham and chancellor; and Peter des Roches, bishop of Winchester and the boy-king's *tutor*. Another high-ranking ecclesiastic who sat at the Bench for a term in 1219 was the abbot of Ramsey, Hugh Foliot. Two earls were also at the Bench occasionally: William d'Aubigny, earl of Arundel in Michaelmas 1218; and Robert de Ver, earl of Oxford, present for over a year, from Trinity 1220 through Michaelmas 1221. Eustace de Fauconberg, the treasurer, might also be included in this group of high-ranking officials. He was the only one of them with any significant legal experience.

In the first years of Henry III's minority, the professional justices included Martin of Pattishall, the senior justice, Stephen of Segrave, Ralph Hareng, and Simon de Insula. None of these four had belonged to King John's judiciary. The first two would have long careers at the Bench, with Pattishall serving as senior justice until his retirement in February 1229, a few months before his death on 14 November 1229. Segrave succeeded him as senior justice, served briefly as justiciar, then fell into disgrace, but returned to the judiciary as justice *coram rege* in 1239. Ralph Hareng remained at Westminster until Michaelmas term 1223, when he withdrew to his estates. Simon de Insula failed to become a permanent member of the judicial bench; he disappeared in 1220 after only two years in the judiciary. Occasionally joining the justices in 1218, 1219, and 1220 was Thomas of Heydon, who became a regular member of the Bench by 1221 and remained there until the summer of 1227, although he lived until 1235.[8] Thomas's last work as a royal justice was in the summer and autumn of 1228 on eyre in Norfolk and Suffolk with Martin of Pattishall. One of the longest judicial careers was that of Robert of Lexington who first joined the justices on eyre in 1218, then was at Westminster in the autumn of 1220, returned for Easter term 1221, and remained a justice of the Bench and leader of eyres until his retirement in 1244.

---

[8] For his dates, *Exc. è Rot. Fin.*, 1: 276; *Book of Fees*, p. 1362.

Three new justices, all knights, made appearances in the middle 1220s. Geoffrey le Sauvage III first sat as a justice at Westminster in autumn 1222, and he was present for every term of court for a period of four years, through Easter 1226; he also took part in a circuit for assizes and gaol deliveries in the summer of 1225. He did not die until the autumn of 1230, when he fell ill at Nantes during the last days of the king's continental campaign.[9] Thomas of Moulton had participated in the general eyre of 1218–19 visiting the North West, but he did not appear at Westminster until the spring of 1224. He was active as a justice for twelve years, until the autumn of 1236. From the summer of 1234 until his retirement, he was the senior justice at Westminster. The third knight, William de Insula, had a commission for assizes and gaol deliveries with Martin of Pattishall in September 1225, then participated in the general eyre of 1226–7, and first appeared at Westminster in Easter term 1227. Two of the regular Bench justices, Moulton and Segrave, were busy at that time leading circuits of the general eyre. William was a justice for about ten years, last serving on the general eyre that ended in November 1236, two or three years before his death.[10]

The end of the decade marked some changes in the composition of the courts, following Martin of Pattishall's retirement in 1229. William of Raleigh, his longtime clerk, was promoted to the Bench on 5 or 6 May 1229, and he would serve at Westminster until named to the newly revived court *coram rege* at the end of May 1234. He was chief justice *coram rege* until he resigned in 1239 to accept a bishopric. Stephen of Segrave was senior justice of common pleas after Pattishall's departure; but he left the court in 1230 to assume other responsibilities, first as one of the regents while Henry III was campaigning on the Continent, then as justiciar from autumn 1232 to May 1234.[11]

In the autumn of 1229 another justice joined Segrave and Raleigh at Westminster. Master Robert of Shardlow was appointed a junior justice of the Bench, and he served as Bench

---

[9] He fell ill before 4 Oct. and died by 4 Nov., *Close Rolls 1227–31*, p. 451; *Exc. è Rot. Fin.*, 1: 205.

[10] Meekings, *1235 Surrey Eyre*, p. 212.

[11] He was at Westminster for Michaelmas 1230 and again for Hilary 1232, his last appearance there.

and eyre justice until his disgrace and dismissal in July 1232 for complicity in the agitation against foreign clerics holding benefices in England.[12] Although this crisis in the summer of 1232 contributed to Hubert de Burgh's fall from the justiciarship, the change had little impact on the judiciary, aside from Shardlow's removal. Master Ralph of Norwich joined the justices for Easter term 1230, and he served at Westminster and on eyre until February 1237, when he left England for Ireland where he had served earlier. At the beginning of Easter term 1231, William of York first took his place at the Bench as justice. He had long been a clerk at the Bench and had served as itinerant justice to Cumberland in 1227. After Raleigh left Westminster in 1234, William of York became the second ranking justice, a position he would occupy until his own departure for the court *coram rege* in early November 1241. Adam fitz William won appointment to the Bench at the beginning of Hilary 1232 because several of the regular justices were away from Westminster on an eyre in Kent. He heard pleas at Westminster and in the counties through Easter term 1238. He seems to have died in mid-May 1238, just as he was about to set out on an *iter* to Cornwall.[13]

The crisis in the summer of 1234 which broke the power of the Poitevins over the government resulted in William of Raleigh's transfer to the newly-created court *coram rege*. It brought other changes in personnel at Westminster, both at the Exchequer and the Bench. Three new justices were appointed to the common law court at Westminster, apparently through the power of the bishops and barons who had toppled the Poitevins. The aim must have been to win some measure of control over proceedings in the courts, but their appointees did not remain on the bench long enough to master its procedures and rules, much less influence its judgments.[14]

The general eyre – *iter ad omnia placita* – had been a prominent feature of English justice since Henry II's time, and it would flourish through the thirteenth century. During the reign of

---

[12] *1235 Surrey Eyre*, p. 241.
[13] Meekings, *Studies*, article 8: 14.
[14] The three were Robert of Rookley, Reynold de Mohun, and Robert de Beauchamp, *C.R.R.*, xvi. Only Rookley witnessed any fines, and he did so only during Trinity term 1234.

Henry III, the justices were sent on nine general eyres. The first eyre got underway in the autumn of 1218, not long after the civil war had ended, part of a programme for reasserting the central government's authority, assuring those dwelling in the country-side that strife and instability were at an end. Fifty justices organized into eight circuits itinerated in 1218 and 1219 with their work completed by three circuits in 1220–1. To lend greater prestige to the parties, all except two had at their head a bishop or an abbot. Such sweeping judicial investigations often took several years to complete, and five to eight years separated the beginning of one from the beginning of another.[15] Almost yearly, however, some justices made visitations of a more limited scope. General eyres continued past the time of Edward I; 1294 effectively marks their end as a significant part of judicial machinery, however.

By the time the treatise attributed to Bracton was written, the king could give several types of commissions. The itinerant jus-tices of Henry III fall into three main groups: the general eyre, commissions to take the assizes, and commissions of gaol delivery. As we have seen earlier, the groups of justices appointed for a general eyre received lists of questions, *capitula itineris*, to ask of local juries. The justices heard all pleas of writs plus pleas of the crown acting on presentments of juries and on private appeals. The articles of the eyre reveal that the justices still had administrative tasks in addition to their judicial work; the articles commanded them to make inquiries about all sorts of matters of interest to the king. The itinerant justices of 1218–19 were com-manded to inquire about serjeanties, escheats, widows in the king's gift, minors who were royal wards, advowsons belonging to the king, and encroachments on the king's land.[16]

The justices on a general eyre formed as much a *curia regis* as did the justices at Westminster or those following the king. Leaders of the parties of justices making circuits were always senior men from the Bench. On the five general eyres before 1240, Martin of Pattishall, Stephen of Segrave, Thomas of

---

[15] The eyres of early Henry III are: 1218–22; 1226–9; 1231–2, cut short by the *coup d'état* of 1232; 1234–6, following the Poitevins' overthrow; and 1239–41. C.A.F. Meekings, 'General eyres 1218–1272'.

[16] Powicke, *Hen. III and Lord Edward*, p. 29; Meekings, *1235 Surrey Eyre*, pp. 90–4.

Moulton, Robert of Lexington, and William of York all headed
parties. Until 1249, a general eyre meant suspension of sessions
at Westminster for a term or longer while the professional justices left the Bench to lead parties of part-time justices about
the country. Cases pending at Westminster were adjourned for
hearing before itinerant justices. If the business of an eyre was
not completed in the allotted time, the itinerant justices sometimes gathered at Westminster to conclude their work.

Despite this evidence for the equality of the courts, when it
came to a test, the itinerant justices' jurisdiction was inferior to
the other two branches of the *curia regis*. Justices at Westminster
sometimes adjourned pleas involving very small plots of land for
hearing in the counties.[17] Itinerant justices received instructions
to reserve novel points of law or procedure for later consideration, and 'Let the parties appear at Westminster' was the conclusion to many cases beyond their competence. The justices
kept a memoranda roll on which they recorded cases that they
were unwilling to judge, either because the law was uncertain or
because the litigants were persons of high position. By the late
1230s the court *coram rege* under William of Raleigh was exercising firm control over the eyre justices.[18]

The second form of commission authorized justices to 'take
the assizes', that is, to deal only with possessory assizes. Sometimes itinerant justices went to the counties with an even more
specific commission, to deal solely with assizes of novel disseisin. Such commissions were popular with the king's subjects,
for they made it possible for suitors to avoid the trouble and
expense of a trip to Westminster or the long delay between
general eyres. In *Magna Carta*, King John promised that the
possessory assizes would be taken four times a year in the counties
in which they arose. Later editions of the Charter retained this
provision, although the number of visitations promised fell to
one a year.[19]

During Henry III's reign, it became common for justices to be
specially commissioned to take individual assizes in the counties.
The earliest example of this occurs in the midst of the civil war,
March 1216, when King John called on Simon of Pattishall to

---

[17] E.g. *C.R.R.*, 8: 94, 97, plots of an acre or less.
[18] *1235 Surrey Eyre*, p. 9.
[19] *Magna Carta* (1215), cap. 18; (1225), cap. 12.

take an assize at Northampton.[20] Those who wanted unusually speedy justice were willing to pay for a special assize on the spot. The patent rolls record innumerable examples of appointments of such commissioners to take a single assize. Sometimes four local knights took the assize; other times one justice from Westminster was named and instructed to associate one or two local knights with him. Judges who had retired from active service at Westminster frequently received commissions to take an assize in regions near their place of residence. An example is Geoffrey le Sauvage, who left the Bench after Easter term 1226, but who continued to be commissioned for judicial work in the counties. His last appearance as a justice was in August 1227, when he and three other men received an appointment to try several accused criminals at Wallingford.[21]

Thirteenth-century justices were sometimes commissioned for gaol deliveries, or occasionally for both gaol deliveries and assizes. Those appointed for this task were usually two professional justices asked to associate four knights of the county with them, in accordance with *Magna Carta*'s provisions. By the last years of Henry III, most accused criminals were tried before commissioners of gaol delivery rather than before justices of the general eyres.[22] Justices usually had commissions to take assizes or to deliver gaols during vacation time, when they could combine this work with visits to their country estates or rectories to attend to private business. On the journey to and from Westminster, they might stop along the way to take an occasional assize or to take care of other court business. For example, William of Raleigh saved his neighbours the inconvenience of making payments of a composition ending a lawsuit at Westminster in 1225. Instead, they could pay at his house at Blatherwycke, Northants, while he was spending his summer vacation there.[23]

[20] *Rot. Lit. Claus.*, 1: 270.
[21] *Pat. Rolls 1216–25*, pp. 393, 576; *C.R.R.*, 12: 129, no. 644. For his other commissions, see *Pat. Rolls 1216–25*, p. 562; *Rot. Lit. Claus.*, 2: 76–7. Ralph Hareng was also commissioned to take assizes after he left the Bench, *Pat. Rolls 1225–32*, pp. 218, 301, 306.
[22] Pollock and Maitland, 1: 200; 2: 645; Alan Harding, *The Law Courts of Medieval England* (London, 1973), pp. 74–5.
[23] Meekings, *Studies*, article 11: 165, citing *C.R.R.*, 553 (P.R.O., K.B. 26/90, m. 5d).

The king was almost constantly on the move about his kingdom, but a permanent court following him did not reappear after John's death. It did not even immediately reappear after Henry III declared himself of age in 1227. Occasionally pleas coming before the justices at Westminster were postponed for hearing in the king's presence, beginning as early as 1221; and Henry was present for the pleas of Easter and Trinity term 1227, perhaps to impress upon his people that he had reached his majority. After Henry III's return from the Continent in 1230, there are 'slight indications' that Stephen of Segrave joined the royal household from time to time to hear pleas before his appointment as justiciar at the end of summer 1232.[24] But no plea rolls from a separate court *coram rege* exist for the years before 1234.[25]

A permanent court *coram rege* was re-established as part of administrative changes that followed the crisis of 1232–4. There was a long delay between the time Henry III officially came of age and the time he actually took command of his government. Hubert de Burgh, his justiciar, was more the governor of England than the king was for the years from the earl marshal's death in 1219 until summer 1232. But then the powerful justiciar fell from favour and a new group of royal intimates took control of the country. The faction that assumed power is called the 'Poitevins' after its two most prominent members, Peter des Roches and his nephew Peter des Rivaux, but native Englishmen such as Stephen of Segrave also participated. The Poitevins soon pushed Henry III into arbitrary acts that alienated many of his former friends, and they lost the king's favour by 1234.

Henry then sought to bring all his officers and all branches of government more closely under his own control.[26] Maitland wrote that after the dismissal of Stephen of Segrave and the Poitevins, 'It looks as if the king had determined to get all the

---

[24] Meekings, *Studies*, article 11: 171; and article 4: 176. In March 1231 and May 1232, Segrave went to the Welsh marches to meet with the prince of Wales, and for several months, June–Aug. 1231 and June–Aug. 1232, he was away from court on eyre.

[25] E.g. 15 Oct. 1226, a plea touching the king is adjourned for hearing before Henry III and Martin of Pattishall, *Rot. Lit. Claus.*, 2: 142. The first *coram rege* roll, *curia regis* roll 115B, dates from 19 June 1234.

[26] Chrimes, *Intro. to Admin. Hist. of Medieval England*, pp. 86–7; Powicke, chap. 3, 'Reform at the Exchequer', 84–122 and 329.

highest justice of the realm done under his own eye by professional judges who would not be too powerful, whom he could trust, whom at all events, he could watch.'[27] Henry III need not have had any fear about being unable to watch over the Bench at Westminster. The two senior justices at Westminster after William of Raleigh left to head the court *coram rege* were Robert of Lexington and William of York, both career royal judges. Once Henry took personal charge of his government, the practical need for a court accompanying him became greater, for the justices of the Bench had to consult him about more and more questions, making for delays in judgments. The solution was a return to two central law courts, as there had been under King John, 1204–9: one group of justices following the king and another seated at Westminster.

Two scholars who studied closely the revival of a court *coram rege* under Henry III are G.O. Sayles and C.A.F. Meekings.[28] They both linked its revival to the reforms in government in the spring of 1234, following the fall of the Poitevins. Among the changes were a number of new appointments in late May and June at the Exchequer and other offices, but no one was appointed to the post of justiciar. Also among the reforms was the creation by Henry III of a court of his own, later to be called King's Bench. In Sayles' view, this was not an unusual step in spite of the seeming illogic of two central courts with parallel jurisdictions, because the royal household needed a court to settle domestic disputes, and the king's household stewards had sometimes taken on judicial tasks.[29] Yet Meekings points out that the immediate political situation had significance, for Henry III needed an experienced judge following his dismissal of Stephen of Segrave as justiciar to preside over important political cases that were coming before the king and his council. For one reason or another, the office of justiciar remained vacant, giving William of Raleigh, the senior justice *coram rege*, greater stature in judicial work and in the council.[30]

---

[27] *Br. Note Book*, 1: 58–9.
[28] Sayles, *Select Cases*, 1: i–xl; 4, Selden Soc., 74 (1955): xxvi–xxxviii; and *The Court of King's Bench in Law and History*, Selden Soc. Lecture (London, 1959). Meekings, *List of Common-law Records*, pp. 36–9; and introduction to *C.R.R.*, 15: xxi–xxxix.
[29] *Select Cases*, 4: xxx–xxxi; 7, Selden Soc., 88 (London, 1971): xli–xliii.
[30] *C.R.R.*, 15: xxvii–xxviii.

Neither Meekings nor Sayles weighed in full measure the part the political situation played in the revival of the court *coram rege*. The fall of Segrave was followed by a concentration of power in the hands of household officials, and a household court to rival Common Pleas in much the same way that the Wardrobe rivalled the Exchequer was not to be unexpected. Henry III had managed to rid himself of two troublesome and ambitious justiciars within only a few years, and he may have felt that another court, in effect a household court dependent on the king, would be a useful counter-weight. He could not have known that he would be successful in leaving the office of justiciar unfilled until 1258. He may have feared that he might have to fill the office once again with someone who might hedge his power or give him bad counsel. He may even have felt that the barons and bishops who had sympathized with Hubert de Burgh and opposed the Poitevins might force him to appoint someone from the baronial ranks.

Henry III's court *coram rege* was not at first the equal of common pleas. Much of the business of the newly created court was 'small and miscellaneous' in the summer of 1234, but it often involved persons associated with the court or the chancery.[31] Some of the court's business had, indeed, a wider importance; a number of actions were brought against Peter des Rivaux, Stephen of Segrave, and their followers, men whom Henry III resented for having pushed him into a crisis through their misuse of power, 1232–4.[32] A sign of the *coram rege* court's inequality was that in its early days it was something of a vacation tribunal active between terms of Common Pleas, or when the justices dispersed from Westminster to lead eyres. Its rolls did not begin to approach the Bench rolls in bulk; it took *coram rege* rolls for several terms bound together to equal the roll of only one term of Common Pleas in number of membranes.[33] For another

---

[31] *C.R.R.*, 15: xxxi.

[32] *C.R.R.*, 15: xxxii, lists actions against Peter des Rivaux and Stephen of Segrave. See also Hubert de Burgh's actions to regain his lands, *C.R.R.*, 15: 234–5, no. 1058; 298, no. 1207; 478, no. 1895; also *Br. Note Book*, 3: 126–8, no. 1108; *C.R.R.*, 15: 244–5, no. 1076; also *Br. Note Book*, 3: 129–30, no. 1111; also pp. 156–7, no. 1136; and p. 161, no. 1140.

[33] *Curia Regis Roll* 115B consists of 35 membranes for Trinity and Michaelmas terms 1234 and Hilary and Easter 1235. Bench rolls in the years before the revival of King's Bench, c. 1230–4, range from a high of 33 membranes to a low of 7 a term.

thing, King's Bench did not yet possess the professional character of the group of judges who had followed King John. From 27 May 1234 until early 1239, the court consisted of only one career justice sitting with one or more of the household stewards. William of Raleigh was the only professional present until shortly before his election as bishop of Norwich in the spring of 1239. Then the rehabilitated Stephen of Segrave replaced him. The earliest evidence for Segrave as chief justice *coram rege* dates from 29 June 1239, but he probably began sitting with Raleigh about Candlemas (2 February).[34] Raleigh's successor then had a career judge to join him in his last year on the *coram rege* bench, only months before his death in October 1241: Jeremy Caxton, who joined Stephen just after 20 January 1241.[35]

Not until 1236 did the court *coram rege* regain the equality with Common Pleas that it had enjoyed in the years 1204–9. It moved towards superiority in Easter term 1236, when it took steps to correct a procedural mistake made by an understaffed Bench the previous term. The judges were summoned before Henry III where they acknowledged that they had proceeded wrongly, 'But that they did not know how better to proceed'.[36] As a result, Adam fitz William, a justice enjoying Raleigh's confidence was recalled to the Bench to strengthen it at a time when many regulars were away on eyre. Also a writ was sent to the justices at Westminster ordering them in cases where they were in doubt not to give judgment without the king's consent.[37] Meekings writes, 'In short, in the spring of 1236 the court *coram rege* seems to be taking steps to control, where necessary, cases pending before the Bench or assize commissioners in ways which had not been explicit before under Henry III.'[38]

This raises an important question: what distinguished the work of the Bench at Westminster or justices of Common Pleas from the court *coram rege* or King's Bench? A cause for confusion is the uncertain meaning of the term *communia placita*. In the early twelfth century, the author of *Leges Henrici Primi* had

---

[34] *C.R.R.*, 16: xxi.
[35] For the household stewards, see *C.R.R.*, 15: xxxvii–xxxix; 16: xxv–xxvi. For a biographical sketch of Caxton, see *C.R.R.*, 16: xxii–xxiii.
[36] *C.R.R.*, 15: xix–xx; *Br. Note Book*, 3: 179–80, no. 1166.
[37] *Close Rolls 1234–37*, p. 348.
[38] *C.R.R.*, 15: xxxv.

applied the phrase broadly as meaning any failure of justice.[39] As
Sayles said, 'The "commonness" does not relate to the case at
all, but to the litigants', meaning that common pleas were those
brought by private persons, where the king was not one of the
parties to the action.[40] Criminal cases could be common pleas if
they were brought by an individual's accusation and not by a
jury of presentment; indeed, a writ of appointment for justices
in 1253 adds to 'common pleas' the phrase 'pertaining to lands
as well as to the crown'.[41] It was not until the early fourteenth
century that the task of trying suspects named in indictments
began to set King's Bench apart from Common Pleas.[42]

No noticeable differences in procedure distinguish the two
courts, for both followed the pattern that had developed from
the writs, plaints, and juries of the twelfth century. Yet scholars
such as G.O. Sayles have professed to see some distinction in
their work. He pointed out that cases heard by the Bench at
Westminster were chiefly proprietary and possessory actions,
those with 'a system of procedures that precluded haste and
were conveniently heard in a sedentary court', while the court
coram rege had a higher jurisdiction, reviewing miscarriages of
justice and unlawful proceedings. Sayles admits that the appor-
tionment of tasks was not so logical, and that often the only factor determining where a plea should be heard was the
importance it had in the king's eyes.[43] Many pleas touched him
in some way, since he was not only monarch but the greatest land-
lord in the kingdom. His court was still the feudal court for royal
tenants-in-chief. Lawsuits between private persons – common
pleas – could often raise questions about royal grants or charters, bringing them to the court *coram rege*. Also many persons,
particularly heads of religious houses, had the privilege of having their suits settled *coram rege*. Naturally, 'state trials', proceedings against the once-great who had fallen from royal favour,
were heard *coram rege*.

---

[39] L.J. Downer, ed. and trans., *Leges Henrici Primi* (Oxford, 1972), cap. 59, 19, pp.
188–89.

[40] *King's Bench in Law and History*, p. 5; cf. *Select Cases*, 4: xxxii, xxxvi.

[41] *Cal. Pat. Rolls 1247–58*, p. 227.

[42] *King's Bench in Law and History*, pp. 12–14; *Select Cases*, 2: xxxiv–li.

[43] *Select Cases*, 1: xxxviii; 4: xxxi–xxxii. On the distinction between the two
courts, see also Ralph V. Turner, 'The Origins of Common Pleas and King's
Bench', *A.J.L.H.*, 21 (1977): 250–4.

King's Bench did have in some measure, then, a high jurisdiction. It heard cases removed from Bench or eyre because of some difficult question, or because of some miscarriage of justice, even though it was not technically an appeals court. *Bracton* described the justices *coram rege* as those 'whose duty it is to correct the wrongs and errors of all others [i.e. other justices]'. By the time that was written, it seems that the court *coram rege* was coming to be seen as superior to the Bench and the itinerant justices, even though all these courts were *curiae regis*.[44]

The two central tribunals of thirteenth-century England were not the result of defining different jurisdictions; neither were they products of different procedures. Inquisitorial methods borrowed from Roman law belong to the Tudors' prerogative courts, not the thirteenth-century *coram rege* court. Twin law-courts doing much the same work and using nearly identical procedures were the result of two divergent tendencies in Angevin government. For Common Pleas, it was a slow process of specialization and professionalization as a government office concerned with justice took shape under the great justiciars Glanvill and Hubert Walter. But the desire of the monarchs – John and Henry III – for personal supervision of justice cannot be neglected. Certainly the creation of the court *coram rege* by King John and its revival by his son represent efforts to keep justice close to the king, to strengthen 'household' government.

2 JUSTICES' ORIGINS AND PATHS TO THE BENCH

The origins of the thirteen justices active in Henry III's early years reflect little change from the pattern in earlier reigns. They came largely from the middle or lower levels of knightly society with several from administrative families. Although more documentation came into existence in the second and third decades of the thirteenth century, the origins of five remain hidden. The pattern remains constant, however, for the clerics continue to provide few clues about their families as in other reigns. All the five with uncertain origins happen to have been ecclesiastics; we can be definite about the background of

---

[44] *Bracton*, 2: 307, f. 108; Michael T. Clanchy, *Writ File of the Berkshire Eyre*, Selden Soc., 90 (1972–3): xix.

only two clerks. Seven of the justices had taken clerical orders, a number not very different from the number under Henry II and Richard I. Special circumstances of John's reign – the long interdict – explain the paucity of clerics among his judges.

Not surprisingly, all thirteen justices were native-born Englishmen. Even after Henry III began appointing foreigners to office, the judiciary remained entirely English. The geographical origins of the thirteen show a shift from East Anglia, which had produced so many judges due to the influence of Ranulf de Glanvill and Hubert Walter. Only two of Henry's justices had East Anglian origins: Thomas of Heydon in Essex and Master Ralph of Norwich. A majority of the justices – eight – came from the Midlands with one each from Buckingham, Derby, Leicester, Lincolnshire, Nottingham, and Warwicks, with two from Northants. One each came from the South East and South West with Adam fitz William from Hertfordshire and William of Raleigh from Devon. As usual, the North was thinly represented, with William of York the only northerner on the bench.

The ancestry of the justices continued to be knightly in the main, since seven of them came from families which were definitely knightly in rank. Six of the knights on the bench came from families holding several fees. Adam fitz William belonged to a family which may have descended from a Domesday tenant of several Hertfordshire manors.[1] The family seat was the manor of Hatfield, later called Symondshyde, held of the bishops of Ely. But Adam held other fees of Robert fitz Walter, a baronial leader in the 1215–17 rebellion. He held of Robert Almshoe, Radwell, and Gravely also in Herts. The last was one of the three castleguard fees of Dover Castle which Adam held of fitz Walter, while the other two that he held lay in Kent. Adam eventually came to have other interests in Herts and Kent, and possibly property in Essex as well.[2]

At least three men bearing the name Ralph Hareng – father, son, and grandson – appear in twelfth and thirteenth-century records as knights of the honour of St Valery in Oxford and Buckinghamshire. A Ralph Hareng, father or grandfather of the

---

[1] Adam son of Hubert of Ryes, Meekings, *Studies*, article 8: 2.
[2] Ibid., pp. 2–4.

royal justice, held land in Sussex in the time of King Stephen.[3]
The Harengs became tenants of the St Valery barony holding
substantial lands, including the manors of Radclive and
Thornton with the adjoining smaller manor of Hasley, Bucks,
and land at Holton, Norton, and Thrupp, Oxfordshire.[4]
William de Insula also had a name that can cause confusion. The
royal justice was a Northants knight, not to be confused with
another William de Insula, a knight of Kent and Surrey, active
about the same time (c. 1200–35). The Northamptonshire
William had his chief estates at Brampton Ash and Harringworth,
and he held others at Flore, Maidwell, Sibthorpe, and Stoke
Doyle.[5]

Thomas of Moulton took his name from the village in the
Lincolnshire fen country, east of Spalding Priory, where his
father and grandfather had been knightly landholders. His
grandfather, Lambert, held land at Moulton of Spalding Priory,
half a knight's fee at Bourne of the earl of Lincoln, and other
South Lincolnshire land of Conan, earl of Richmond. His father,
also named Thomas, succeeded to Lambert's lands c. 1166–7.[6]
Thomas senior joined his neighbours in an attack on the
marshland property of Crowland Abbey in 1189 in an effort to
enforce rights to pasturage against the Crowland monks' enclos-
ing policies. The attack led to lawsuits in the *curia regis* that lasted
until 1202.[7]

Stephen of Segrave's name comes from a village in Leicestershire, north of the county town, where his grandfather had

---

[3] *Docs. preserved in France*, p. 510, no. 1391, a grant of tithes of Shopwick to Lewes
     Priory.
[4] Radclive, *Luffield Priory Charters*, ed. G.R. Elvey, jt. publns. of Northants Rec.
     Soc. and Bucks Rec. Soc., 18 (1975), 2: 1; Holton, *C.R.R.*, 12: 212, no. 1039;
     Thrupp, *Cart. Oseney*, 4: 131, no. 91A; *C.R.R.*, 14: 399–400, no. 1869; Norton
     (Brize Norton or Chipping Norton?), *Feet of Fines for Oxon.*, pp. 62–3, no. 53.
     Ralph had advowson of the church at Thornton by 1219, W.P.W. Phillimore,
     ed., *Rotuli Hugonis de Welles, episcopi Lincolnensis*, Cant. and York. Soc., 1
     (1909): 36.
[5] Meekings, *1235 Surrey Eyre*, p. 212, citing P.R.O. CP 25(1)/172/24, no. 259; 26,
     no. 316; 27, no. 332; 173/28, no. 369.
[6] *Complete Peerage*, 9: 397–8. Foss, *Judges of England*, 2: 415–16, gives Lambert as
     Thomas's father, apparently confusing the father and grandfather. Other
     sources make clear that his father was Thomas, *English Justice*, App. V, *Historia
     Croylandensis continuato*, p. 154; *C.R.R.*, 13: 37, no. 168.
[7] *English Justice*, p. 154; for an account of the Crowland-Spalding conflict, see
     V.C.H., Lincs, 2: 107–8.

held land in the early twelfth century, granted to him by either one of the earls of Leicester or an abbot of St Mary de Pré, Leicester.[8] Gilbert of Segrave, Stephen's father, held a quarter fee at Brailes, Warwickshire, of the earl of Warwick in 1166, apparently before he fell heir to his father's lands. Later under Henry II and Richard I, Gilbert secured other holdings in Leicestershire and in the town of Leicester.[9] He clearly prospered, for in 1199 he was assessed 400 marks for an aid, although he was not a tenant-in-chief of the king.[10]

The name Geoffrey le Sauvage presents difficulties in sorting out family and holdings. First, two families bore that name, and in both the christian name Geoffrey was common. A Staffordshire Geoffrey le Sauvage was active c. 1175–1210.[11] The royal justice belonged to the Warwickshire Sauvages, a family of knightly rank. They produced four men named Geoffrey from early in Henry II's reign to 1248; Henry III's justice was Geoffrey le Sauvage III, who died in 1230. His father whose name he shared was alive at least as late as 1222.[12] He left lands centred in Warwickshire, but stretching into neighbouring shires. On the death of Geoffrey I in 1195, Geoffrey II had paid 100 marks for possession of his Warwickshire lands.[13] Geoffrey I had held half a fee at Newton Regis in chief of the king, a grant from Henry II in 1159, and half a fee in Derbyshire, enfeoffed by Earl Robert II de Ferrers.[14] A knight's fee at Leak Wootton had come to Geoffrey

---

[8] *Complete Peerage*, 11: 596–97, n. 'c'. In 1218, the abbot and the bishop of Lincoln reached agreement about the manor and mill of Segrave. The bishop surrendered his claim to the abbot, C.W. Foster, ed., *Registrum Antiquissimium*, Linc. Rec. Soc., 3 (1935): 218–21, no. 875.

[9] *Red Book Exch.*, p. 326; *Honors and knights' fees*, 2: 71. Isaac H. Jeayes, ed., *Descriptive Cat. of MSS. in the possession of Lord Harding at Berkeley Castle* (Bristol, 1892), pp. 14, 16–17, nos. 24, 29–32; *Pedes Finium de Regno Regis Ricardi I*, Pipe Roll Soc., 20 (1896): 133, no. 169.   [10] *Pipe Roll 10 Ric. I*, pp. xxiv, 160.

[11] He held a fee at Trentham, *Pipe Roll 22 Hen. II*, p. 165; *23 Hen. II*, p. 140; *24 Hen. II*, p. 97; *31 Hen. II*, p. 164; *9 Ric. I*, p. 142. The existence of two Geoffreys is shown in a 1210 fine that Hugh de Neville offered; he wanted Geoffrey le Sauvage of Staffs summoned to cross to Poitou instead of Geoffrey le Sauvage his undersheriff for Hants, *Pipe Roll 12 John*, p. 35.

[12] *Rot. Lit. Claus.*, 1: 491; 2: 94; *Exc. è Rot. Fin.*, 1: 83, 84.

[13] *Pipe Roll 7 Ric. I*, p. 190.

[14] For Newton Regis, *Pipe Roll 6 Hen. II*, p. 35; *13 Hen. II*, p. 160; *Red Book Exch.*, pp. 18, 689, 690. For Tissington, Derby, *Red Book Exch.*, p. 339; *Cal. Inq. Post Mort.*, 1: 125, no. 453.

II, probably through his marriage to the sister of Henry de Arden.[15] Another manor, Baginton, along with two carucates in Worcestershire also came to Geoffrey II through marriage.[16]

Robert of Lexington's father Richard was a new man, who first appears in the records in 1204 as one of King John's servants.[17] Nothing is known of his forebears, but some tenuous evidence makes it tempting to suggest that Richard's father was an illegitimate son of Robert de Cauz, baron of Shelford.[18] The family took its name from the manor of Laxton, Nottinghamshire, fifteen miles west of Lincoln. The manor was part of the Cauz barony, and Richard of Laxton served as King John's custodian of it and acquired some land there. He had temporary grants of land to maintain himself in the royal service, but he acquired some permanent possessions, for he made small grants of land to Rufford Abbey.[19] His lack of sufficient lands must have been a factor in the decision of Robert and his brothers to seek out the schools and ecclesiastical careers. All the five sons of Richard of Lexington proved to be remarkable men, rising high in the service of Church and monarch. Their rise from low levels of knightly society is witness to the force of ambition coupled with education in the thirteenth century.[20]

Thomas of Heydon, another cleric on the bench, had an unusual family background for someone living in the thirteenth century. He was the son of a priest, Godfrey, parson of the church at Heydon, Essex. Henry II had presented Godfrey to the church, probably c. 1164–6 when the abbey of Walden which held the advowson was in the king's hand. Eventually Thomas replaced his father as parson, and he held the church

---

[15] A 1203–4 lawsuit forced him to give up a third of the fee, *C.R.R.*, 2: 259; *Warwicks Feet of Fines*, eds. Ethel Stokes, Lucy Drucker, *et al.*, Dugdale Soc., 11 (1932): 29, no. 149, final concord with Henry de Armentiers. See also *V.C.H., Warwicks*, 6: 168.

[16] Baginton was held for half a knight's service and Eastwood, Worcs, for a quarter knight's service, *V.C.H., Warwicks*, 6: 23; *Cal. Inq. Post Mort.*, 1: 25, no. 453.

[17] *Rot. Lit. Claus.*, 1: 7.

[18] C.J. Holdsworth, ed., *Rufford Charters*, 1, Thoroton Soc. Rec. Ser., 29 (1972): xcii–xciii.

[19] *Rufford Chtrs.*, p. xciii.

[20] For the Lexington brothers' careers, see Gavin I. Langmuir, 'The knight's tale of young Hugh of Lincoln', *Speculum*, 47 (1972): 470–2, 474–7.

throughout the rest of his life.[21] We have with Godfrey and Thomas of Heydon, then, a late example of an hereditary parsonage.

The family backgrounds of the remaining five clerics among the justices are less easy to see. The fathers of two clerics, William of Raleigh and William of York, most likely were knights. Nothing is known of William of York's family or early life. Doubtless the manor of Eske in the East Riding, which William conveyed to his brother, was the family seat.[22] William of Raleigh's toponymic derives from the Devonshire village, but it is uncertain to which of several branches of the Raleigh family he belonged. Historians have differed in his identification with the William of Raleigh who was sheriff of Devon 1225–8. H.G. Richardson maintained that William of Raleigh, clerk and royal justice, was the same William of Raleigh, knight, who had been coroner and who became sheriff in October 1225. Lady Stenton, however, found Richardson's identification 'doubtful'.[23] C.A.F. Meekings felt the problem to be without a definite solution, but that 'the probability seems on the whole very much against the identification'. He demonstrated that Raleigh the future justice was on eyre in the North as Martin of Pattishall's clerk at the same time the new sheriff of Devonshire was taking up his duties. Meekings accepted that the two Raleighs were relatives, and that William of Raleigh *miles* belonged to the senior branch of the family.[24]

The origin of three clerical justices lies completely hidden: Martin of Pattishall, Ralph of Norwich, and Robert of Shardlow. We know little more about them before they entered the king's service than what their toponymics tell. Martin of Pattishall evidently came from the same Northamptonshire village as his

---

[21] *C.R.R.*, 16: 58, no. 180. Stephen Marsh, claiming presentation in 1238, stated that Henry II had presented Thomas; his opponent, the abbot of Walden, said that the abbot and monks of Walden had presented him; the jurors said they did not know whether anyone had presented him. For Walden's right to Heydon, see *Letters and charters of Gilbert Foliot*, p. 474, no. 439.

[22] To his brother Nicholas c. 1240/6, *Early Yorks Chtrs.*, 7: 250. William also had an aunt named Sibyl, *C.R.R.*, 13: 309, no. 1435.

[23] *Pat. Rolls 1216–25*, p. 554; Richardson, 'Azo, Drogheda and Bracton', *E.H.R.*, 59 (1944): 28–9. Stenton, *Rolls of the Justices in Eyre for Lincs and Worcs*, Selden Soc., 53 (1934): xviii.

[24] Meekings, *Studies*, article 11: 159–60, 172–5; and article 5: 496.

longtime master, Simon of Pattishall. A Martin the clerk whom we may identify as Simon's clerk first appears on the plea rolls in early 1203. The name recurs, often as attorney for absent suitors.[25] No contemporary records ever refer to Martin as Simon's kinsman, but Simon must have known the young Martin and his family well, and he must have chosen him as his clerk because he saw the promise of talent. The editor of many *curia regis* rolls described Martin's handwriting as 'characteristic of a man who thought and wrote rapidly'.[26] No doubt, the barons, bishops, and other officials restoring central authority in 1217–18 knew well Simon of Pattishall's reputation as a judge, and they needed his longtime clerk's experience in re-establishing the courts. Choosing a professional without any clear partisan identity was also a promise of impartiality for the revived Bench, a gesture of reconciliation.

Another clerk about whom nothing is known before he began his career in King John's service is Master Ralph of Norwich. His toponymic suggests that he may have come from the *bourgeoisie*, although that remains no more than a suggestion. His title of *magister* indicates study at a university or cathedral school sometime in the first years of the thirteenth century, but nothing more can be said concerning his early life. Little more can be said about Master Robert of Shardlow. His family came from the village of Shardlow, Derbyshire, about midway from both Derby and Nottingham, and they apparently had knightly status. At least, by 1238, Robert and his brother held land in Derbyshire, Nottingham, Leicestershire, and Suffolk.[27] He too took a master's degree, and we can deduce from his employment as a royal agent at Rome that it was in canon law.

Only four of the thirteen justices came from administrative families, or at least had fathers active in the royal administration. It is difficult to distinguish between Ralph Hareng II, the royal justice, and his father, Ralph Hareng I. Throughout the decade 1190–1200 both were active; they sometimes wit-

[25] *C.R.R.*, 2: 162, 279; 3: 20, 347; 4: 46, 177; *Rot. Chart.*, p. 180; *Earliest Northants assize rolls*, nos. 666, 817.
[26] Flower, *Intro. to C.R.R.*, p. 9; cf. Stenton, *Northants assize rolls*, p. xviii.
[27] *Close Rolls 1237–42*, p. 48. Robert's brother was named Hugh, and he had a sister also, *Close Rolls 1227–31*, p. 303.

nessed charters together as 'Ralph Hareng and Ralph his son.'[28]
We can assume that it was Ralph senior who took on minor
administrative tasks in Richard I's time. He was one of the
deputies for William de Sainte-Mère-Eglise, escheator for the
South, in 1195 and 1196. Also in 1196, he was a member of a
special commission to remedy a complaint by the prior of
Leighton Buzzard about his tenant's services. The following
year he was one of the assessors of tallages in Bucks and
Bedfordshire.[29]

Robert of Lexington's father, Richard, was one of King John's
minor officials. The king named him forester and custodian of
the manor of Laxton from 1204 to 1207, and in 1212 he made
Richard grants of land to maintain himself while in the royal service. His career was not completely successful, however. Twice
in the course of carrying out his duties he fell foul of King John
and had to offer fines *pro benevolentia regis*.[30]

Geoffrey le Sauvage's grandfather Geoffrey I (died c. 1196)
had some minor administrative assignments from Henry II. He
was present at the *curia regis* in 1175, when he witnessed a royal
charter. From 1176 to 1179 he was custodian of an estate of the
honour of Chester, which had fallen into the king's hand.[31]
Geoffrey le Sauvage II (died c. 1222), the judge's father, had an
administrative career in the service of Hugh de Neville, King
John's chief forester. He was Hugh's undersheriff for Oxfordshire, 1197–9, and for Hampshire, 1210–12.[32] In the interval
between these two appointments, Geoffrey continued to be
active on royal business in Oxfordshire. He had custody of the
escheated manor of Kirklington and of the royal manor of

---

[28] Ralph I was of age by 1160 or earlier and died c. 1200/5. Ralph Hareng II's gift
to Luffield Priory then hints at his father's recent death, *Luffield Priory Chtrs.*,
2: 90–1, no. 396.

[29] Assistant escheator, *Pipe Roll 7 Ric. I*, p. 61; *Chancellor's Roll 8 Ric. I*, pp. 190–2;
commissioner for complaint, *curia regis* roll for Hilary 7 Ric. I, printed in *Mem.
Roll 10 John*, p. 73; tallager, *Pipe Roll 9 Ric. I*, p. 205.

[30] *Rot. Lit. Claus.*, 1: 7, 21, 65, 83, 90b; *Pipe Roll 6 John*, pp. 161, 172; *7 John*, pp.
221, 226; *8 John*, pp. 79, 81; *9 John*, pp. 118, 124–7; *11 John*, pp. 112, 116–17; *12
John*, p. 127. For his fines, see *Rot. de Obl. et Fin.*, pp. 392, 437, 570.

[31] Charter of 20 July 1175, *P.B.K.J.*, 3: lvii. Custodian of Alstonfield, *Pipe Roll 25
Hen. II*, p. 98.

[32] *Pipe Roll 9 Ric. I*, p. 33; *10 Ric. I*, p. 189; *1 John*, p. 219; *12 John*, p. 182; *13 John*,
p. 197; *14 John*, p. 91. Geoffrey witnessed an agreement that Hugh made for
his sister's *maritagium*, *P.R.O. 35th Report*, p. 23, from D.L. Chtrs., box A,
no. 238.

Woodstock, and he had responsibility for forest payments from nearby Cornbury.[33]

Stephen of Segrave's father Gilbert engaged in administrative activity similar to that of Geoffrey le Sauvage II. He was one of the custodians of the vacant abbey of St Mary de Pré, Leicester, for Henry II in 1187.[34] During the reign of Richard I, he was undersheriff of Warwicks and Leicestershire for the sheriff Hugh de Nonant, bishop of Coventry, and later for William d'Aubigny.[35]

In nearly every instance, we have evidence for the early careers of Henry III's justices which indicates the kinds of experience thought suitable for future judges. A practical apprenticeship still provided a useful introduction to a judge's work.[36] Six of the thirteen justices began their careers in other branches of royal government as chancery clerks or as members of the Exchequer staff. One of them had been the personal clerk of Brian de Insula, but moved into King John's service just as the civil war was breaking out. Three clerks at the Bench advanced into the judiciary. Several laymen had earned experience in local, county affairs, including two who had been estate stewards. Three had been sheriffs for brief spells, although Thomas of Moulton's experience as sheriff was unsuccessful and doubtless extremely unpleasant for him.

Three royal justices began their careers in the chancery, although their paths did not proceed directly from chancery clerk to judge. Master Robert of Shardlow's earliest known work in royal government was as a diplomat at Rome. That may be evidence enough to classify him with the chancery staff. Thomas of Heydon paused for a number of years before proceeding to the Bench. He apparently began his career in the service of Eustace, vice-chancellor for Richard I by 1194, later chancellor, and finally bishop of Ely by 1198. Thomas was a chancery clerk with Richard Lionheart from late summer 1198 to February 1199, when charters identify him as 'then acting as

---

[33] *Rot. Lit. Claus.*, 1: 141; *Pipe Roll 6 John*, pp. 106, 112–13; *9 John*, pp. 43–4. He incurred a 200 mark amercement as custodian of Woodstock and offered fines for the king's goodwill, *Rot. Lit. Claus.*, 1: 14b, 25, 26b.

[34] *Pipe Roll 34 Hen. II*, p. 215.

[35] *List of Sheriffs*, p. 144; *Pipe Roll 9 Ric. I*, p. 169; *2 John*, p. 183.

[36] See Frank Pegues, 'The *clericus* in the legal administration of thirteenth-century England', *E.H.R.*, 71 (1956): 529–9.

vice-chancellor'.[37] He remained a chancery clerk under King John and returned to Normandy in his service.[38] Thomas seems to have retired to Ely and joined the household of his patron, Bishop Eustace, following the king's return to England at the end of 1203. He retained some ties at court, however, for he received permission to approach the king on Eustace's behalf at the time of the proclamation of the interdict in 1208.[39]

Thomas returned to royal government as a justice in 1218–19, when he joined Henry III's first eyre. No doubt, Thomas was chosen because of his knowledge of conditions in Cambridgeshire and surrounding counties. Thomas continued his work in 1220–1, joining Martin of Pattishall and his fellows for pleas in December 1220 and December 1221. Perhaps his performance on the first eyre of the new reign impressed Martin of Pattishall and Stephen of Segrave, and they sponsored him for the Bench.

William of York, another justice who began his career as a chancery clerk, first comes into view in the years just following the civil war. Henry III himself reminded William after he had become a powerful bishop, 'I raised you from the depths; you were the scribbler of my writs.'[40] Although the servant of Ralph de Neville, the chancellor, William was usually found at the Bench. From the time the court reopened following the civil war until summer 1231, he served as a clerk at Westminster. He also went on eyres with the justices from Westminster; he accompanied Martin of Pattishall as clerk on his circuit of the North in autumn and winter 1226–7.[41] He was not the personal clerk of one of the justices, but was a chancery clerk assigned to the Bench, following the chancellor's orders.[42] The *curia regis* rolls reveal William of York drawing up chirographs, drafting

---

[37] *Itin. Ric. I*, pp. 133–8, 140, 143; *Cartae Antiq. Rolls 1–10*, pp. 65–6, no. 118; pp. 90–1, no. 181.

[38] *Rot. Cur. Reg.*, 2: 217, plea postponed because Thomas was on the king's service and absent from the kingdom. Also *Rot. de Obl. et Fin.*, p. 142; *Rot. Lit. Pat.*, p. 27b; *Pipe Roll 1 John*, p. 125, 40s. for Thomas's passage.

[39] *Rot. Lit. Claus.*, 1: 108. Thomas witnessed a grant by Richard Barre, archdeacon of Ely, sometime before Sept. 1204, and he witnessed several episcopal charters, W. Rich-Jones, ed., *Sarum Charters and Documents*, Rolls Series (1891), p. 60; C.U.L., MS. Liber M (Ely Cart.), ff. 159b–167; B.L. MS. Harl. 391, f. 110.

[40] *Chron. Maj.*, 5: 374.   [41] Meekings, *Studies*, article 5: 496.

[42] Meekings, *1235 Surrey Eyre*, pp. 259–60; also his unpublished paper, 'Coram rege justices, 1239–1258.'

charters, taking custody of writs and suspected false charters. Possibly an otherwise unidentified 'William' or 'William of the Bench' also appearing on the plea rolls as a clerk at the *curia regis* should be identified as William of York.[43]

William clearly regarded Ralph de Neville as his patron. Six letters 'written in a frank and lively manner' from York to his patron survive from 1226–8. In them William reveals himself clearly. He once wrote to the chancellor, seeking to escape duty on an eyre to remote Cumberland, that he would not go, 'even if I have a royal mandate, unless I get a special order from you'.[44] Years later, William of York was an executor of Ralph's will.[45]

It is likely that William of York in his role as the chancellor's representative at the Bench was a forerunner of the keeper of rolls and writs of the Bench. The formal existence of this office is not usually acknowledged until May 1246. The first royally appointed keeper was William's former clerk, Roger of Whitchester; but his 1246 appointment may have come because Alan of Wassand, another of William's former clerks then acting as keeper, had moved into the judiciary.[46]

William of York's early experience shows that the *curia regis* was becoming capable of supplying its own justices, as clerks were sometimes apprentice-judges before taking seats on the bench. The two most famous justices – Martin of Pattishall and William of Raleigh – were not seconded from the chancery, but were judges' personal clerks. Each justice had his own clerk, who kept a roll of pleas for him.[47] Martin was the longtime clerk of Simon of Pattishall, as we have seen, and William of Raleigh was in turn Martin's clerk. There seems no reason to doubt this, although H.G. Richardson in his accustomed search for con-

[43] Meekings, *Studies*, article 11: 166.
[44] Ibid., pp. 495–503. Shirley, *Royal Letters*, gives the text of three: Meekings' letter no. 1 equals Shirley, 1: 342–3, no. 281; Meekings' no. 2 equals Shirley, 2: 222–3, no. 583; Meekings' no. 4 equals Shirley, 1: 421–2, no. 350.
[45] *Close Rolls 1247–51*, p. 522; cf. p. 335.
[46] Meekings, *Studies*, article 13: 468. Pegues, '*Clericus* in legal administration', p. 546, writes, 'Presumably there had been a clerk of the rolls and writs ever since there was a chancellor'.
[47] References to rolls of individual justices occur frequently on the plea rolls, e.g. *C.R.R.*, 8: 99, references to the rolls of Simon of Pattishall and Eustace de Fauconberg; 14: 105, no. 534, the roll of Lord S. of Segrave. See Stenton, *Lincs assize roll*, p. xxxii; *Intro. to C.R.R.*, pp. 8–10.

troversy called the accepted view into question. He stated that Raleigh's work, especially after 1225, was quite incompatible with the discharge of the duties of a clerk to a judge of the bench.[48] Numerous references in the *curia regis* rolls, however, depict Raleigh clearly as holding notes for chirographs, collecting payments, and carrying out other tasks perfectly consistent with the work of Pattishall's own clerk. He may even have written a large part of the first of Pattishall's five extant plea rolls.[49] He accompanied his master Martin on the 1221 and the 1226–7 eyres.[50] C.A.F. Meekings' exhaustive survey of the evidence led him to conclude that it points toward Raleigh's 'personal service and loyalty to Martin Pattishall' from 1219 definitely, and perhaps from 1214. Meekings, to clinch his conclusion, cited a deed Raleigh made in 1235 or 1236 in which he described Martin of Pattishall as 'of good memory my sometime lord'.[51]

Richardson denied that apprenticeship through serving as a judge's clerk was the normal path to the Bench in the thirteenth century. Certainly it was not the only route to a judgeship, but it was becoming more and more common as the century progressed. The best known case is Henry of Bracton's service as clerk to William of Raleigh, a fellow Devon man. Of course, Richardson rejected stubbornly the notion of a Pattishall-Raleigh-Bracton dynasty, and he denied that Bracton was Raleigh's clerk.[52] Samuel E. Thorne, who has lived with Bracton's ghost for years, maintains that Bracton probably began his career as Raleigh's personal clerk in 1234 and that he had become senior clerk of the court *coram rege* by 1239, when his patron

---

[48] Richardson 'Azo, Drogheda and Bracton', p. 28; *Bracton: the problem of his text* (London, 1965), p. 4.

[49] E.g. *C.R.R.*, 7: 267; 8: 23, 40, 77, 145, 186, 206, 390; 9: 208; 10: 10, 78, 94, 181–2; 12: 112, no. 553; 178, no. 1258; 13: 96, no. 413; 123, no. 532; 345, no. 1831. For Raleigh as scribe for Pattishall's plea rolls, see *Intro. to C.R.R.*, pp. 8–10, 32, 271. Meekings, 'Pateshull and Raleigh', p. 164, says that Flower's claim is not fully established.

[50] *C.R.R.*, 7: 267; Doris M. Stenton, ed., *Rolls of the justices in eyre for Gloucestershire, Warwickshire, and Shropshire (1221–2)*, Selden Soc., 59 (1941): xvi; Meekings, *Studies*, article 11: 158–9, 177–8.

[51] P.R.O., D.L. 42/2, Hants no. 43, cited in Meekings, *Studies*, article 12: 229.

[52] *Bracton*, pp. 4, 7–8.

retired.[53] He eventually succeeded to the court *coram rege* himself by 1247.

Other mid and late thirteenth-century justices came to the judiciary by way of a court clerkship. Roger of Thurkelby, justice c. 1240–59, spent nearly a decade as a clerk at the Bench. He became one of William of Raleigh's clerks as early as 1231. Roger of Whitchester, justice 1254–8, was William of York's clerk by 1230, then keeper of Bench writs and rolls in 1246.[54] Roger's predecessor as keeper was Alan of Wassand, who became a royal justice in 1246; he had been a clerk at Westminster and keeper of rolls and writs, also associated with William of York.[55] Robert of Nottingham, justice 1244–6, had been Robert of Lexington's clerk from 1241 to 1243; and Nicholas de Turri, who became justice *coram rege* in 1251, had served as a chancery clerk and *coram rege* clerk.[56] Later several of Edward I's justices served apprenticeships as clerks before joining the judiciary.[57]

Some judges won their early experience in other branches of the royal administration. The connection between the Exchequer and courts of justice was no longer so close. Only three or possibly four of the professionals moved from financial activity to the judiciary. William de Insula began his career about 1205 on the staff of Reginald of Cornhill, head of the London merchant family and King John's financial agent. Several times between 1205 and 1215 William was charged with transferring treasure for the king. By 1218 he had the title 'marshal of the Exchequer'.[58] William de Insula performed a number of tasks between 1215 and his appointment to the

---

[53] Lecture at Exeter University, *Henry de Bracton 1268–1968* (Exeter, 1970), pp. 5–8. Lady Stenton held a similar view, although she believed that Raleigh had introduced Bracton to Martin of Pattishall sometime before 1229, *Rolls for Lincs and Worcs*, pp. xix–xx.   [54] Meekings, *Studies*, article 14: 104–5.

[55] Meekings, *Studies*, article 13: 468.

[56] Meekings, *Studies*, article 10: 133; article 14: 119.

[57] W.H. Dunham, ed., *Casus Placitorum, and reports of cases in the king's courts (1272–8)*, Selden Soc., 69 (1950): xxxv. E.g. Ralph of Hengham had been clerk to Giles of Erdington.

[58] *Rot. Lit. Claus.*, 1: 39 and 104, where he is described as a *serviens* of Reginald; 214b; and 350, 353, where he is described as *marescallus*; *Rot. Lit. Pat.*, p. 143.

Bench in 1225, not all of which were purely financial in nature. He was a keeper of Boston fair and a collector of the fifteenth, and he was also constable of castles, keeper of forests, and sheriff of Rutland, 1216–18. He joined Simon of Pattishall in March 1216 in the midst of the civil war to take a Northants assize.[59] William's professional career as a judge began under Martin of Pattishall at the Northampton assizes and gaol deliveries of September 1225. Doubtless, he was already acquainted with Martin through other county activities.

Master Ralph of Norwich was a *clericus regis* by February 1215, although he had entered King John's service earlier.[60] In 1217 the council commanded in Henry III's name that the justiciar of Ireland suitably reward Ralph, since he had served 'the lord king our father and us well and faithfully for a long time'.[61] Ralph was clearly connected with Exchequer business in both England and Ireland, even though he never bore the title *clericus de Scaccario*. He spent much of his time on the king's business in Ireland, first travelling there as a royal messenger in 1216. Between February 1217 and October 1222, he made five journeys to Ireland.[62] He returned to Ireland in August 1227 on a mission connected with collection of the clerical sixteenth, and he remained there until 1230, when he brought funds to the treasury at Winchester Castle.[63] In the intervals between visits to Ireland, Ralph of Norwich engaged in administrative duties in England, mostly financial.[64] He may have acted as one of the justices of the Jews sometime between October 1222 and August 1227, although the evidence is scanty, resting on 'a single ambiguous passage' on the close roll.[65]

Robert of Lexington began by 1214 to undertake tasks for King John that might be classed as financial. He had begun his

[59] For a biographical sketch, see Meekings, *1235 Surrey Eyre*, pp. 212–13.
[60] *Rot. Lit. Claus.*, 1: 187b; *Rot. Lit. Pat.*, p. 185.
[61] *Cal. Docs. relating to Ireland*, 1: 115, no. 762.
[62] 31 May 1216, *Cal. Docs. relating to Ireland*, 1: 107, no. 696; 110–11, no. 723, when he was a confidential messenger from the council to the Irish justiciar; *Rot. Lit. Claus.*, 1: 431, when he was sent to collect an aid.
[63] *Pat. Rolls 1225–32*, pp. 133, 254, 329; *Cal. Liberate Rolls 1226–40*, p. 167; *Close Rolls 1227–31*, pp. 302, 351.
[64] Collector of customs at Bristol and keeper of Northampton fair, *Pat. Rolls 1216–25*, pp. 136, 153, 178; *Rot. Lit. Claus.*, 1: 353b, 383; messenger to the archbishop of York, Shirley, *Royal Letters*, 1: 39.
[65] *Rot. Lit. Claus.*, 2: 47; Meekings, *Studies*, article 4: 179, 186–7.

career earlier as the clerk of Brian de Insula, one of King John's trusted administrators and military captains. He assisted Brian as custodian of the vacant bishopric of Lincoln in 1212 and of the honour of Peverel in 1214. Also in 1214 Robert took custody of the archbishopric of York for the king.[66] As the civil war approached, he took charge of maintaining the king's house at Clipstone, Nottinghamshire, and supplying forty serjeants who were to hold Nottingham and Derbyshire for John.[67]

Geoffrey le Sauvage was carrying out some financial duties in the counties about the time that he began his judicial career. He was first a member of a judicial commission to take single assizes in 1220 and 1221. Also in 1220 he was an assessor of the carucage in Hants, and in 1222 he was one of those appointed to tallage the borough of Southampton. Then in 1226, about the time Geoffrey was leaving the Bench, he headed a party collecting the fifteenth in Wiltshire.[68]

Several of the laymen among the justices acquired early experience in legal work in the counties as local officials of one sort or another. Adam fitz William was prominent in Hertfordshire affairs after the civil war in tasks that normally fell to knights of the counties. Such tasks gave him the practical legal experience that many knights who came to the judiciary had earned. Beginning in 1220 he occasionally had commissions to take individual assizes, and he was one of the knights bearing the record of a case from the Hertford county court to Westminster that autumn. He was a justice for assizes and gaol deliveries in 1225; he served as juror during the 1227 eyre to Essex and Hertfordshire; and at the end of the eyre he was sworn in as coroner.[69] Martin of Pattishall and William of Raleigh had an opportunity to observe his work on the 1227 eyre.

Stephen of Segrave's early career also centred on activities as a knight of the county. As early as 1206, he served as coroner in Leicestershire.[70] Unlike Adam fitz William, who supported the

---

[66] *Pipe Roll 14 John*, p. 2; *16 John*, p. 67; *17 John*, p. 11; *Rot. Lit. Claus.*, 1: 208.
[67] *Rot. Lit. Claus.*, 1: 209b, 210b.
[68] Assize commissions, *Pat. Rolls 1216–25*, pp. 306, 310; tallages, *Rot. Lit. Claus.*, 1: 182b, 208b; carucage, *Book of Fees*, p. 1444; the fifteenth, *Rot. Lit. Claus.*, 2: 146b.   [69] Meekings, 'Adam fitz William', pp. 5–6.
[70] *C.R.R.*, 5: 18. *D.N.B.*, repeating a slip of the pen by Dugdale, *Baronage*, p. 671, mistakenly states that Stephen was constable of the Tower of London in 1203.

baronial side in the 1215–17 rebellion, Stephen served King
John loyally and moved closer to the centre of government. In
February 1215, the king sent groups of royal agents throughout
the kingdom to explain to the men in the counties 'our business', probably the royalist version of the quarrel brewing between king and barons. Segrave belonged to the group sent to
Worcestershire.[71] Once fighting broke out, he received from
King John custody of land in Lincolnshire and Leicestershire
that had belonged to one of the rebels.[72]

During John's last years, Stephen of Segrave came to know
well the king's lieutenants who would take command after his
death. Stephen and his father were tenants of Ranulf, earl of
Chester, holding some land at Segrave of the honour of
Chester.[73] Even before the end of the twelfth century, the earl
gave Stephen a manor in Warwicks; and a short while later, he
gave him land and advowson of a church in Leicestershire.
Several other grants to Stephen from Earl Ranulf followed.[74] In
July Segrave received custody of half the honour of Leicester,
until then in Ranulf's hands, clearly because he was to be the
earl's substitute as custodian while he was away on crusade.[75] On
the earl's death, Stephen served as one of the executors of
his will.[76]

We have seen that in previous reigns, knights sometimes started
their administrative work as estate stewards to barons or
bishops. That holds true for two of Henry III's professional justices, Geoffrey le Sauvage and Ralph Hareng. The Sauvage
family had ties with the Nevilles, an important administrative
family. Geoffrey served an apprenticeship as estate steward for
Ralph de Neville, who had been keeper of the king's seal since
1213 and would win the title of chancellor by 1226.[77] Geoffrey

---

[71] *Rot. Lit. Pat.*, p. 128b.

[72] Stephen de Gant, *Rot. Lit. Claus.*, 1: 246.

[73] *Honors and Knights' fees*, 2: 71, citing B.L. MS.Harl. 4748, f. 10.

[74] Manor of Caludon, *V.C.H., Warwicks*, 8: 121, citing P.R.O. E. 164/21, f. 57; 8
virgates and advowson at Kegworth, Leics, Jeayes, *Cat. of Berkeley Castle MSS.*,
nos. 152, 153, Harl. MS. 4748, f. 8; vill of Bretby, *Honors and Knights' fees*, 2: 43;
a quarter fee at Mountsorel, 2: 62; and land at Smisby, Derby, 2: 34, 39.

[75] Ranulf held the honour of Leicester for Simon de Montfort sr., 1215–18, then
again, 1220–31, when Simon jr. came to England.

[76] *Cal. Pat. Rolls 1232–47*, p. 185.

[77] Jacques Boussard, 'Ralph Neville évêque de Chichester et chancelier
d'Angleterre (+1244) d'après sa correspondance', *Revue Historique*, 176
(1935): 217–33.

served Ralph de Neville as steward of an estate at Thorpe (Leicestershire?) sometime during the years 1214–22, before Ralph was elected bishop of Chichester. Several of Ralph's letters to him survive; they concern such matters as Ralph's need for cash, purchases of a horse and pigs, and everyday details of estate management.[78] Geoffrey's service with Ralph de Neville inevitably involved him in the work of government, and during the baronial rebellion he became a royal messenger.[79]

Geoffrey le Sauvage first sat as a justice at Westminster in the autumn of 1222. Undoubtedly, his sponsor was his employer, the bishop-elect of Chichester, who worked closely with the justices of the Bench in his capacity as vice-chancellor. Ralph was a friend of Martin of Pattishall, the senior justice, and the two exchanged letters. Martin wrote to him in 1226 and 1227 about eyre business, but also to thank him for sending *rumoribus curie* and to ask for more news from court.[80]

Ralph Hareng was Thomas de St Valery's estate steward as early as 1199, and in summer 1200 he was Thomas's attorney in a plea at Westminster.[81] Ralph seems to have remained responsible for the St Valery lands throughout John's reign, either as Thomas's steward or as royal custodian when they were in the king's hand. King John first seized the St Valery honour in the spring of 1207, and in autumn 1211 those lands were still in Hareng's charge. Ralph had orders once more to take custody of the St Valery lands in July 1213, in August 1216, and again in 1225 and 1226. He remained custodian until August 1227, when the king granted the barony to Richard earl of Cornwall.[82] Cus-

---

[78] P.R.O., SC.1/6, nos. 2–6. Nos. 2–4 are translated in W.H. Blaauw, 'Letters to Ralph de Neville', *Sussex Archaeol. Collections*, 3 (1850): 39–41.

[79] *Rot. Lit. Claus.*, 1: 180; 236b, 275, 416, a *liberate* of 1220 for 12d. to Geoffrey going to East Anglia 'with our writ'. In 1218–19, Geoffrey – II or III? – was doing the king's business in Wilts, taking custody of lands of the late earl of Huntingdon and serving on a forest eyre, *Pat. Rolls 1216–25*, pp. 163, 211.

[80] P.R.O., SC.1/6, no. 76, Latin text printed in Boussard, 'Ralph Neville', p. 223, n. 1. Also 1/6, nos. 75, 127, 128; no. 75 is translated by Blaauw, pp. 42–3.

[81] *Mem. Roll 1 John*, p. 55. The Christian name is missing. Madox, *Exchequer*, 1: 673, gives an undated charter of Thomas de St Valery witnessed by *Radulf Harengo tunc temporis Senescallo meo.* Ralph again appears as steward in April 1207, *Rot. Lit. Claus.*, 1: 82; and c. 1210, *Cart. Oseney*, 2: no. 1045. Ralph as attorney, *C.R.R.*, 1: 174.

[82] *Rot. Lit. Pat.*, p. 71; *C.R.R.*, 6: 137; *Pipe Roll 13 John*, pp. 203–4. P.R.O., Exch. L.T.R. Mem. Roll 1, n. 2d; *Rot. Lit. Claus.*, 1: 138, 281; 2: 22, 26, 198; *Pat. Rolls 1225–32*, p. 129.

tody of the St Valery barony was a heavy responsibility, for it consisted of some fifty knight's fees.[83] It gave Hareng considerable experience in conducting courts.

Ralph Hareng's work as royal custodian attracted the attention of King John. On 2 July 1215, the king named him sheriff of Buckingham and Bedfordshire, one of several changes made to strengthen the royalist position.[84] Sometime during the civil war, however, John removed Ralph and replaced him with Fawkes de Breauté. His removal was a military matter, not a reflection on his loyalty to the royalist cause: King John entrusted to Fawkes eight counties forming a line across the Midlands.[85] Throughout the civil war, Ralph received royal safe-conducts for travel, indicating that he remained an active royalist supporter.[86]

Ralph Hareng was often present at Westminster on legal business during King John's reign, and this led Lady Stenton to suggest that he was a professional lawyer.[87] Her suggestion seems unwarranted, however. Hareng was in court several times as a juror, other times as Thomas de St Valery's steward, or on his own business, but only once as attorney for anyone other than Thomas. In 1218, about the time he was beginning his work as a royal justice, he was Earl William de Ferrers' attorney.[88] His only judicial activity before he joined Henry III's Bench came in the autumn of 1208, when he accompanied Simon of Pattishall on his eyre to the northern counties.[89] Certainly, Ralph Hareng had opportunities to become well acquainted with Martin of Pattishall and the Common Pleas staff before he joined them as a judge in early 1218.

Although Thomas of Moulton had a noteworthy judicial career under Henry III, his activity under King John held little promise for an administrative career. Thomas had no place in royal government before his appointment as sheriff of Lin-

---

[83] Under John scutage was owed on only 10, but under Henry II the total number of fees had been 50, Sanders, *Baronies*, p. 10.

[84] *List of Sheriffs*, p. 1; *Rot. Lit. Pat.*, p. 145h.

[85] Carl H. Caldwell, 'The role of Faulkes de Breauté in English medieval history', M.A. Thesis (Ohio University, Athens, 1968), pp. 30–1.

[86] 13 Aug. 1215, *Rot. Lit. Pat.*, pp. 192b–3; 13 Jan. 1217, *Pat. Rolls 1216–25*, p. 24; 10 May 1217, *Pat. Rolls 1216–25*, p. 63.

[87] *P.B.K.J.*, 3: xl, cccxiii–cccxiv.

[88] P.R.O., Exch. L.T.R. Mem. Roll 1, m. 1d.

[89] *P.B.K.J.*, 3: cclx–cclxi.

colnshire in 1205. He was first at Westminster in May 1200, when he witnessed a charter there.[90] He was involved in lengthy litigation throughout John's early years, seeking to expand his holdings in the south Lincolnshire marshes, and lawsuits doubtless brought him to Westminster from time to time.[91] It seems likely that during part of the period 1201–3 Moulton was fighting in Normandy with King John. Matthew Paris's obituary describes him as *miles in armis* during his youth.[92]

Thomas of Moulton was one of three justices in Henry III's early years to have been a sheriff. Thomas was not a typical curialist sheriff, who held some other post at Westminster or with the royal household and depended upon a deputy to perform his duties. Thomas purchased the shrievalty of Lincolnshire from King John in December 1205 to hold for seven years in return for a proffer of 500 marks and five palfreys, plus a yearly increment of 300 marks in addition to the ancient farm of the county.[93] This purchase was part of an attempt by local notables to win control of the office. As the local candidate, Thomas had to consider their interests; and his ties prevented his being an unscrupulous sheriff, capable of raising large sums for himself and for the Exchequer. Thomas was soon falling behind on his promised payments, and he was subject to the harsh *Lex Scaccarii*. At the Easter Exchequer of 1208, he was removed from office, imprisoned in Rochester Castle, and amerced 1000 marks. King John commanded that he remain in prison until he paid all that he owed 'to the last penny'.[94] Apparently Thomas had also angered the king for being an ineffective administrator, and in 1207 he was amerced

---

[90] *Cartae Antiq. Rolls 1–10*, pp. 71–2, no. 134. Perhaps he was present for a lawsuit, for he had made a final concord on 14 Apr., *Lincoln Records: abstracts of final concords*, ed. W.O. Massingberd (London, 1896), p. 12.

[91] Holt, *Northerners*, pp. 58–9.

[92] Thomas offered 40 marks in 1201 not to cross the sea in the king's service, but commands sent to Westminster appear to place him with John's forces in Normandy, *Pipe Roll 3 John*, pp. 22–3; *Rot. de Obl. et Fin.*, p. 173; *C.R.R.*, 2: 40, 133. An added clue is John's pardon in 1204 of tallage on his lands, *Rot. de Lib. ac de Mis.*, p. 91.

[93] *Rot. de Obl. et Fin.*, p. 338; *Rot. Lit. Pat.*, p. 57–7b. He paid a quarter of his fine in 1206, *Pipe Roll 8 John*, p. 103.

[94] *Pipe Roll 10 John*, pp. xviii, 76–7; *Rot. Lit. Pat.*, p. 85b. See also Holt, *Northerners*, pp. 156, 182–3.

200 marks for incorrect statements he had made *in curia regis*.[95]

By 1210 Moulton had come to terms with John concerning his debts, and he took part in the campaign against the Welsh in 1211. The king assigned him some minor administrative tasks in the following years.[96] Thomas was among the knights who served on the Poitevin campaign in the summer of 1214, although many had opposed any obligation to serve overseas.[97] It is no surprise to find Thomas of Moulton among the 'Northerners' who rebelled following the king's return from the Continent. He fits readily into the profile of those rebels outlined by J.C. Holt. Thomas had close ties with other Lincolnshire gentry who had suffered similar disappointments in their search for office and riches and were similarly in debt to the crown.[98] Because of his role in the rebellion, Rochester Castle again became Thomas's prison.[99]

Soon after peace was restored, Thomas found himself in trouble with the barons and royal officials ruling in young Henry III's name. He married without their leave a prominent widow, Ada de Morvill, coheir to the Morvill barony in Cumberland. The council reacted by seizing Thomas's land and chattels, but he had come to terms by September 1218.[100] About the time that he was reconciled with the rulers during the royal minority, they chose him to be a justice on the first general eyre of the reign, visiting the North West where his new wife's lands lay.

We can only speculate about how Thomas, a prominent rebel, won such quick acceptance by King John's companions

---

[95] Thomas said that he had attached Thomas de Scotigny by gage and pledges and later denied it, *Pipe Roll 9 John*, p. 28. Also in 1207 an investigation was made concerning tolls Thomas had taken at Boston fair, *C.R.R.*, 5: 45.

[96] Farrer, *Lancs Pipe Rolls*, p. 242, pardon of the scutage of Wales. *Rot. Lit. Claus.*, 1: 124b, to deliver money from the Temple to the king: *Rot. Lit. Claus.*, 1: 164b; *Rot. Lit. Pat.*, p. 97, to investigate complaints against the sheriffs of Yorks and Lincs; *Rot. Lit. Claus.*, 1: 164b, to investigate damages to ecclesiastical property during the interdict.

[97] *Pipe Roll 16 John*, p. 152; also *Rot. Chart.*, p. 200, where he witnessed a charter at Niort.

[98] When Thomas purchased his shrievalty, 10 of his 11 pledges were future rebels, Holt, *Northerners*, pp. 74, 77.

[99] He was taken prisoner 30 Nov. 1215, *Rot. Lit. Claus.*, 1: 241b; *Gervase of Canterbury*, 2: 110. He raised 300 marks ransom and regained lands and freedom by 3 Sept. 1217, *Rot. Lit. Pat.*, pp. 161b, 162; *Pat. Rolls 1216–25*, pp. 69, 83, 85.

[100] He fined for £368 and assumed his wife's debt of 164/8/1, *Rot. Lit. Claus.*, 1: 354b; *Pat. Rolls 1225–32*, p. 208.

now in command. It is necessary to look beyond Hubert de Burgh for the appointment of justices during the minority. Thomas had connections with two magnates prominent in the council. Through his marriage to Ada de Morvill, he had family connections with William Briwerre.[101] Thomas had links to another royalist stalwart, Ranulf earl of Chester. He and his father had been the earl's tenants during the ten years that he held the honour of Richmond. Thomas continued to hold some land of the honour of Chester, and he sometimes witnessed the earl's charters.[102] Perhaps the council consciously tried to select one or two representatives from former rebels for the first general eyre as a conciliatory move. By 1224 when Thomas joined the justices at Westminster, he had proven himself through local administrative activity in Cumberland and Lincolnshire.[103]

The justices chosen during Henry III's early years undoubtedly reflect the choices of the regency council. Ties of some to leading counsellors are clear; for example, Thomas of Moulton and Stephen of Segrave both had feudal links with Ranulf earl of Chester. The vice-chancellor Ralph de Neville had some role in appointments, for two of his clients became justices: his clerk at the Bench, William of York, and his steward, Geoffrey le Sauvage. For others, the council may have relied upon the recommendation of Martin of Pattishall, who was doing much of the judicial work that justiciars traditionally had done. William de Insula can be described as one of Martin's protégés. Absence of ties of patronage between the justiciar and the justices points up the separation of the justiciar from the courts that had been widening since Geoffrey fitz Peter's death. Only one of the justices, Master Robert of Shardlow, seems to have been Hubert de Burgh's protégé.[104] After Martin's retirement,

---

[101] Ada's sister Joan was the wife of Briwerre's nephew, Richard Gernon, Sanders, *Baronies*, p. 24.

[102] Land at Bourne held mediately of Osbert fitz Nigel, *Honors and Knights' fees*, 2: 163; *C.R.R.*, 13: 37, no. 168. Charters, P.R.O., D.L. 42/2, ff. 249d, 261d, 262.

[103] E.g. as a forest justice in 1219, *Rot. Lit. Claus.*, 1: 434b, *Pat. Rolls 1216–25*, p. 218; a commissioner into customs owed by the burgesses of Carlisle, *Pat. Rolls 1216–25*, p. 312; commissioner to investigate a shipwreck on the Lincs coast, *Rolls of justices for Lincs and Worcs*, pp. 332–3, no. 687.

[104] Meekings, *1235 Surrey Eyre*, p. 241.

the other senior justices at the Bench must have been powerful voices in naming replacements for vacancies. Henry III chose his own justices *coram rege* once that court was re-established, selecting them, however, from the Bench.

3 BOOK-LEARNING IN THIRTEENTH-CENTURY ENGLISH LAW

of Chosen

It is possible to speak more positively about the education of royal justices as a group by the early thirteenth century, although pinning down the schooling of any single judge is no easier. While practical experience in the royal administration was still the most usual path to the judiciary, some of these experienced administrators – both clerics and laymen – may have picked up some formal study of the law earlier. We can say little about the education of the clerics among Henry III's justices except that two of the seven – Ralph of Norwich and Robert of Shardlow – had the title *magister*. It is impossible to tell where they took their degrees or whether they were masters of laws. Roman and canon law studies had become well established in England by the last quarter of the twelfth century, and centres for teaching the two laws continued to exist in the thirteenth century. Of course, Oxford remained a centre for legal studies, but a school seems to have existed at London as well until Henry III ordered it closed in 1234[1]

Alongside Roman and canon law was English law, which was becoming a subject for academic study from the first years of the thirteenth century. Although this is a murky area, an increasing number of manuscripts surviving from the years between *Magna Carta* and the Statute of Merton enable us to penetrate the gloom. Surviving texts show that knowledge of English law no longer had to depend upon an oral tradition. Our brightly shining beacon is the treatise on the laws and customs of England long attributed to Henry of Bracton.[2] But a growing

---

[1] *Close Rolls 1234–37*, p. 26, Dec. 1234. Little more is known of this school than what Maitland says, Pollock and Maitland, 1: 122–3. Perhaps its closing was part of the reaction to events earlier in 1234, which had led to the dismissal of the Poitevins. There was hostility toward Henry III's legists, e.g. Master Roger de Cantelu (or Cantilupe?), Powicke, *Hen. III and Lord Edward*, p. 135, n. 2.

[2] Samuel E. Thorne, trans. and G.E. Woodbine, ed., *Bracton on the laws and customs of England (Bracton De Legibus et consuetudinibus Angliae)*, 4 vols. (Cambridge, Mass., 1968–70).

number of less compendious legal manuscripts from the 1220s and 1230s also serve as landmarks.

Evidence for lay literacy in Latin becomes easier to spot by the beginning of the thirteenth century.[3] Canonists and theologians were aware of literate laymen, capable of replacing ecclesiastics as secretaries to secular princes; and they urged rulers to assign such laymen to tasks involving the shedding of blood. Peter the Chanter and Robert of Courson, two early thirteenth-century theologians at Paris, advised that secular rulers assign to literate laymen the drafting of documents imposing sentences of death.[4]

The early lives of laymen are still so ill-documented in the thirteenth century that little can be learned about an individual's schooling. Of the six laymen among Henry III's professional justices, no statements survive to shed any light on their education, except in Stephen of Segrave's case. That one statement issues from the pen of Matthew Paris, part of his attempt to smear Segrave. The *Chronica Majora* states that Segrave surrendered his clerical status in favour of the knightly life, only to submit to the tonsure again in order to plead benefit of clergy when he was in disgrace and danger.[5] No other evidence supports this tale of a tonsure rejected and reclaimed, and it may be a product of Matthew Paris's overworked imagination. A more charitable explanation, however, is that his awareness of Segrave's schooling led him to assume that the fallen justiciar had taken ecclesiastical orders in his youth. Stephen's appointment in 1219 as a *procurator* to the papal legate, along with two *magistri* and *clerici*, in a dispute between the English and Scottish kings perhaps confirms Matthew Paris's view that he had been a clerk in his youth.[6]

Matthew's tale, coupled with confusion over the meaning of the terms *clericus* and *literatus* in medieval writings, has led modern scholars to assume that any *miles literatus* was always *nuper clericus*.[7] Too many students still suppose that any knight of proven

---

[3] Turner, 'The *Miles Literatus*', *A.H.R*, 83: 928–45; Clanchy, *From Memory to Written Record*.

[4] Ralph V. Turner, 'Clerical judges in English secular courts, the ideal versus the reality', *Medievalia et Humanistica*, new ser., 3 (1972): 87–8.

[5] *Chron. Maj.*, 3: 293; 4: 169.   [6] *Pat. Rolls 1216–25*, p. 197, 21 July 1219.

[7] E.g. Pegues, 'The *Clericus* in legal administration', p. 557.

literacy must once have been in clerical orders; their view is that otherwise he would have been illiterate.[8] They find reinforcement for their mistaken view in their assumption that all students in all schools north of the Alps were always members of the clergy, wearing tonsures.[9] Students' clerical status had more to do with the jurisdiction of the Church courts than it did with religious professions. Furthermore, tonsuring was not an irreversible process, and nothing prevented those who had taken minor orders for educational advantage from later choosing to lead secular lives. Clerics did occasionally change careers and exchange their ecclesiastical vows for knightly oaths.[10]

In the thirteenth century, practical treatises were being written for laymen in four professions: common lawyers, estate stewards, conveyancing clerks, and accountants. These were closely related fields, and an individual might concern himself with more than one of them. Indeed, many knights of the counties had such varied responsibilities that they needed some expertise in all four spheres. Some knights were also stewards of great estates, who had to keep accounts and to conduct correspondence in Latin. There is little reason to doubt the literacy of two laymen among Henry's justices who were former estate stewards: Ralph Hareng and Geoffrey le Sauvage. As we have seen, several letters from Ralph de Neville to his steward Geoffrey treating everyday matters of estate management survive. Neither is there reason to doubt William de Insula's literacy, for his early career in the royal financial service would have demanded it.

Treatises on accounting were being written for such men by about 1225, and by mid-century or a little later, treatises on estate-management were being written for them as well.[11] Knights also needed legal handbooks to guide them in holding

---

[8] Turner, 'The *Miles Literatus*', pp. 930–1; Clanchy, *From Memory to Written Record*, chap. 7, 'Literate and illiterate.' [9] Murray, *Reason and Society*, p. 264.

[10] E.g. 'Lord Richard of Healing *nunc miles* had been presented to the church of Healing', Charles W. Foster, 'Institutions to benefices in the diocese of Lincoln, *sede vacante*, 1200–3; 1234–5', *Associated Architect. Soc. Reports and Papers*, 39 (1929–30): 186. John Mansel's father was a deacon, who married, but secured an annulment and re-entered the Church, *Cal. Papal Reg.*, 1: 269, 362–3; *Chron. Maj.*, 5: 129.

[11] Dorothea Oschinsky, *Walter of Henley and other treatises on estate management and accounting* (Oxford, 1971).

their own courts, in doing the work of shire and hundred, and in arguing their causes in the *curia regis*. Works that would fill such a need were being written by the first half of the thirteenth century.

An illustration of the legal literature being collected by thirteenth-century knights is the compilation of Robert Carpenter, a freeholder on the Isle of Wight (d. 1280).[12] Although Carpenter was not a professional scribe, he copied some material for his collection by his own hand while on a visit to Westminster. He collected an updated *Glanvill*, copies of such legal texts as *Magna Carta*, the Statute of Merton and the Provisions of Westminster, articles of the Hants eyre for 1265, tracts on drafting deeds and keeping manorial accounts, and tracts on legal procedure. Some of these materials were old enough for Robert to have inherited copies from his father (d. 1249). The revision of *Glanvill* probably dates from the 1220s or 1230s, composed at Oxford. The legal treatise is *Consuetudines diversarum curiarum*, written no later than 1244 and perhaps at the same time as the revised *Glanvill*.[13] It concludes with a *tractatus*, *De criminalibus placitis coram justiciariis itinerantibus*, which Carpenter himself composed.[14] The collection is, in Meekings' words, 'a typical collection of a mid-thirteenth-century hundred juror'. He adds that though it seems unique today, many similar compilations must have existed in the thirteenth century.[15] A knight such as Adam fitz William, who had busied himself with county affairs before coming to the Bench in 1232, may well have possessed one of them.

Sons of knights who became estate stewards could obtain some education beyond the elementary level in the business schools that were springing up by the end of the twelfth century. In the reign of King John, Oxford became a centre for business studies: *ars dictaminis* or letter-writing, accounting, and some elementary law. It was a curriculum that prepared youths for

---

[12] Caius College, Cambridge, MS. 205, discussed by Noël Denholm-Young, 'Robert Carpenter and the provisions of Westminster', *E.H.R.*, 50 (1935): 22–35; and Meekings, *Studies*, article 3: 260–9.

[13] *Glanvill*, appendix, 'Glanvill revised', pp. 195–8. H.G. Richardson and G.O. Sayles, *Select Cases of procedure without writ under Henry III*, Selden Soc., 60 (1941): cxci–cxciv; text of *Consuetudines*, cxcv–cciii.

[14] Richardson and Sayles, *Procedure without writ*, pp. cci–cciii.

[15] Meekings, *Studies*, article 3: 269.

careers in the service of bishops, barons, or other great
landholders as accountants, estate-stewards, scribes, and attorneys.[16] They might, of course, graduate into the service of some
great officer of state, or even of the king himself.

In the early thirteenth century several Englishmen composed
treatises on the *ars dictaminis*, which are extant.[17] Growing out of
the *ars dictaminis* was the *ars notaria*, which taught the drafting of
legal documents. In Italy where this discipline first developed
the *ars notaria* course trained notaries public. This did not happen in England because the common law failed to recognize the
notarial instrument, and seals served as the means for auth-
enticating English documents, even in the Church courts.[18]
H.G. Richardson, however, found a curious compilation made
at Oxford, c. 1202–9, which apparently represents an Oxford
master's attempt to compile a similar formulary for English
students' use. It contains sample documents and letters, a
collection of legal precedents, and portions of an *ordo judiciarius*.
Richardson was certain that similar collections were circulating
in England by the early part of Henry III's reign.[19]

The *ordines judiciarii* were primarily manuals of procedure,
practical guides for litigants in both civil and ecclesiastical
courts. Several of these handbooks written in either England or
Normandy survive from the late twelfth century.[20] The best
known of them is *Practica legum et decretorum*, written c. 1181–9 by
William Longchamp, Richard I's chancellor.[21] William of

---

[16] H.G. Richardson, 'The Oxford law school under John', *Law Qtrly. Rev.*, 57
(1949): 319–38; 'Business training in medieval Oxford', *A.H.R.*, 46 (1941):
259–80. Richardson held that an earlier business school had existed at
Northampton, 'The School of Northampton in the twelfth century', *E.H.R.*,
56 (1941): 595–605. See also Clanchy, '*Moderni* in education and government', *Speculum*, 50: 686.

[17] E.g. Geoffrey de Vinsauf, John of Garland, Gervase of Melkley, and some-
what earlier Peter of Blois, a longtime resident in England. See Noël
Denholm-Young, 'The *cursus* in England', in F.M. Powicke, ed., *Oxford Essays
in Medieval History presented to Herbert Edward Salter* (Oxford, 1934), pp. 75–80;
and C.H. Haskins, 'The early *Ars Dictaminis* in Italy', in his *Studies in medieval
culture* (Oxford, 1929), p. 191.

[18] C.R. Cheney, *Notaries Public in England in the Thirteenth and Fourteenth Centuries*
(Oxford, 1972), pp. 12, 52.

[19] Walters Art Gallery, Baltimore, MS. W.15, ff. 79b–81b; discussed by
Richardson, 'Oxford law school', pp. 319–29. See also his 'An Oxford teacher
of the fifteenth century', *Bull. John Rylands Lib.*, 23 (1939): 445–52.

[20] Kuttner and Rathbone, 'Anglo-Norman canonists', pp. 290–1.

[21] E. Caillemar, 'Le droit civil dans les provinces anglo-normands', *Mémoires de
l'Académie de Caen* (Paris, 1883).

Drogheda's *Summa Aurea*, written at Oxford about 1239, had a similar practical purpose. William was an advocate in the Church courts as well as an Oxford master, and his treatise was a textbook on ecclesiastical procedures.[22] Such manuals of procedure and formularies made it possible for men who did not take university degrees, even laymen such as Stephen of Segrave, to pick up a smattering of Roman legal principles.[23]

At Oxford and possibly at Westminster, elementary legal instruction co-existed with more advanced legal studies of the *Digest*, *Institutes*, and the *Decretum*. The division between academic and practical subjects was not as precise as it would become later in medieval universities, and the business schools did not stand completely isolated from the liberal arts faculties.[24] Students preparing for careers in the civil service in the late twelfth and early thirteenth centuries could easily obtain some grounding in Roman legal principles without taking a degree in civil law.

Advanced Roman and canon law studies continued to flourish in thirteenth-century England. Several English canonists made their way to Bologna to join the faculty there at the beginning of the century.[25] Others, however, remained active in England. Prominent among them were three clerks in the household of Hubert Walter who had earlier lectured at Oxford: Master Simon of Siwell, John of Tynemouth, and Master Honorius.[26] The career of Thomas of Marlborough (d. 1236) makes clear the vitality of civil and canon law studies in early thirteenth-century England. He was a teacher of law at Exeter and Oxford who became a monk at Evesham about 1200, bringing to the monastery his large personal library which included *libros utriusque juris, canonici scilicet et civilis*.[27] He frequently represented his house as an advocate in ecclesiastical causes at Rome and in England. In 1205, returning from one of his journeys to Rome, he paused at Bologna for six months' study to refresh his knowledge of the

[22] *Bio. Reg. Univ. Oxf.*, 1: 594–5.
[23] Richardson and Sayles, *Procedure without writ*, p. cxiv.
[24] Clanchy, '*Moderni* in education and government', p. 683.
[25] E.g. Richard de Morin or *Ricardus Anglicus* and *Alanus Anglicus*, Kuttner and Rathbone, 'Anglo-Norman canonists', pp. 328–9, 339; John Wallensis, J.C. Russell, *Dict. of Writers of Thirteenth Century England*, p. 78.
[26] Kuttner and Rathbone, pp. 304–9, 325–7.
[27] W.D. Macray, ed., *Chronicon Abbatiae de Evesham*, Rolls Series (1863), p. 267.

written law.[28] Evesham was not the only English religious house
to have a learned lawyer among its monks.[29]

The language of Roman law was making its way onto the plea
rolls by the time of Richard I. As early as 1194, some crimes were
labelled *laesio majestatis*. An individual bringing an action of trespass in 1198 borrowed from the libellary procedure of canonists
and civilians.[30] By King John's time, the vocabulary of Roman
law was seeping into statements issuing from the chancery. A
1205 summons to a great council spoke of the *communis regni
utilitas*. Towards the end of John's reign, the mandates drawn up
for his *procuratores* or ambassadors began to use formulae which
showed the written laws' influence on the royal chancery.[31]
Doubtless some of John's advisers were learned in the law of
Rome. As we have seen, four of his justices had the title *magister*.
Although this is no indication in itself of a law degree, other
evidence leads to the conclusion that two of the four – Master
Godfrey de Insula and Master Henry of London – had some
acquaintance with canon and Roman law.[32]

After the middle of the thirteenth century, English students
no longer took the road to Bologna in great numbers. Roman
and canon law continued to be widely known in the first half of
the century, however, and they had an impact on the common
law in that period. Some scholars see a connection between the
action of trespass and the canonist *actio injuriarum*.[33] The author
of *Bracton* – whoever he is – clearly was an able Romanist, capable
of discussing the common law with 'the unmistakable technical
vocabulary of the schools'.[34]

---

[28] *Chron. Evesham*, p. 147. For a biography of Thomas, see Russell, *Dict. of writers*,
pp. 166–8.

[29] Richard de Morin taught at Bologna c. 1194–7, then retired to Merton c.
1198, and was elected prior of Dunstable in 1202, Kuttner and Rathbone,
'Anglo-Norman canonists', pp. 329–38. Master Nicholas of Dunstable, a
monk at Bury St Edmunds, had a legal education, Rodney M. Thomson, ed.,
Chron. of election of Hugh Abbot of Bury St. Edmunds, p. xx. A John Wallensis,
abbot of Malmesbury (1222–6), had been a professor at Bologna and authored
canonistic glosses, Russell, *Dict. of writers*, p. 78.

[30] *Rot. Cur. Reg.*, 9: 31, a disseisin made *in laesionem coronae domini Regis*; Roger Howden,
3: 242, Gerard de Camvill appealed *de laesione regiae majestatis*. *Rot. Cur. Reg.*, 1:
203; *C.R.R.*, 5: 132; 6: 156.

[31] Stubbs, *Select Charters*, p. 277; Gaines Post, *Studies in medieval legal thought: public
law and the state, 1100–1322* (Princeton, 1964), pp. 106–7.

[32] Chap. 4, pt. 2, p. 151.

[33] E.g. Richardson and Sayles, *Procedure without writ*, pp. cviii–cxxxiv.

[34] Thorne trans., *Bracton*, 1: xxxvi.

Henry III found servants with degrees in the written law useful as his representatives in lawsuits at the papal *curia*. A law degree enhanced a royal proctor's skills in dealing with curial documents and in negotiating. One of the royal justices, Master Robert of Shardlow, evidently was a brilliant canonist, for he began his career in Henry III's service as a royal agent at the papal court in 1227 and 1228.[35] We can discover the names of other servants of Henry III who had legal training, for Matthew Paris railed against the king's *legistae*.[36] The royal justice Robert of Lexington had a brother, John, who entered the king's service in 1235 after spending several years at a university outside England, possibly Bologna. Henry III gave him assignments that 'suggest unusual familiarity with church matters and canon law', and also postings as ambassador to the Scots. Although a layman, John became keeper of the king's seal in 1247. A chronicler described him as *vir utroque jure, canonico scilicet et civile, peritus*.[37] John of Lexington's successor as keeper of the king's seal was Master William of Kilkenny, a clerk who had served Henry III in 1234 and 1237 as his proctor at the papal *curia*. Matthew considered him learned in the two laws as well, *in iure canonico et civile peritus et circumspectis*.[38] These two keepers of the seal, both experts in written law, may have contributed to Henry III's political notions which were approaching Roman imperial ideas of authority.

Two continental visitors who came to England in the 1230s and 1240s were learned in the law, and they contributed to Henry's increasingly absolutist views. Henry of Susa, a Savoyard canonist known later by the name of Hostiensis, was on Henry's staff for several years, serving in England and at Rome.[39] Some

---

[35] First, to deal with the Fawkes de Breauté affair and a year later in connection with a disputed Canterbury election, *Pat. Rolls 1225–32*, pp. 141, 204; *Close Rolls 1227–31*, pp. 80, 118.

[36] Simon of Estelant, *Chron. Maj.*, 3: 268, 491; Master Roger de Cantelu (Cantilupe?) 3: 483; Master Odo of Kilkenny, 3: 491; Alexander Saecularis, 3: 491; 4: 266. Roger de Cantilupe was a lawyer for the monks of Christ Church, Canterbury, c. 1240–5, Norma Adams and Charles Donahue, jr., eds., *Select cases from the ecclesiastical courts of the province of Canterbury c. 1200–1301*, Selden Soc., 95 (1978–9): 13. Master Odo was a royal advocate before King's Bench in 1244, *Close Rolls 1242–47*, p. 245.

[37] *Annales Mon.*, 1: 345. For John's career, see Langmuir, 'Knight's tale of Hugh of Lincoln', pp. 469, 474–7.

[38] *Chron. Maj.*, 5: 130; *Bio. Reg. Univ. Oxf.*, 2: 1048–49.

[39] *Chron. Maj.*, 4: 133, 286, 351–53; *Cal. Pat. Rolls 1232–47*, pp. 252, 365, 409, 412, 413, 414, 416.

of Henry III's opinions on the royal power came from canon law through parallels with papal practice.[40] Another foreigner was the imperial protonotary Peter de Vinea, who visited England in the fall and winter of 1234–5. He too had an influence on the king's thinking. Peter had helped Frederick II draft the *Liber Augustalis*, a law code for the Sicilian kingdom much influenced by the law of the Roman Empire. A writ of Henry III issued in 1244 much resembles a chapter of the *Liber Augustalis* on the royal duty to resume rights wrongly alienated from the crown. Henry's statement on the need to limit liberties being exercised without specific royal warrant echoes a passage from Peter de Vinea's work.[41]

Most powerful evidence for the continued strength of Romano-canonical studies in early thirteenth-century England is the great treatise on the laws of England, long known by the name of *Bracton*. Its latest editor Samuel E. Thorne, however, has brought all previously accepted opinion about the author and date into question. He shows conclusively that the book was written much too early for Henry of Bracton to have been its author, for parts of it date from the 1220s and 1230s. In Thorne's view, much of it already had been written by the time of the Statute of Merton in 1236.[42] It may have had its start even earlier. Paul Brand suggests that 'the initial impulse for the writing of *Bracton* may have come from the work done in preparing a statement of English law for promulgation in Ireland by King John in his charter of 1210.[43] The book underwent numerous revisions, growing from a series of small *tractates* on particular topics, arranged 'in a practical rather than a systematic way',

---

[40] E.g. his insistence that he could abrogate his own and his predecessors' charters, Michael T. Clanchy, 'Did Henry III have a policy?' *History*, 53 (1968): 210.

[41] Henry's writ, *Close Rolls 1242–47*, p. 242, quoted by Powicke, *Hen. III and Lord Edward*, p. 111; see also Clanchy, 'Did Henry III have a policy?' pp. 210–11. For Peter de Vinea's continued influence in England, see Ernst H. Kantorowicz, 'The prologue to *Fleta* and the school of Petrus de Vinea', *Selected Studies* (Locust Valley, N.Y.), pp. 167–83. A Wardrobe clerk in Edward II's time possessed a *liber dictaminis* by Vinea and Thomas of Capua, T.F. Tout, *Chaps. in admin. history*, 2: 226, n. 3.

[42] *Bracton*, 3: preface and xiv–xv, 1. The manuscripts closest to the archetype did not mention Bracton as author. The earliest 'unambiguous reference' to Bracton as author dates from 1277.

[43] Paul Brand, 'Ireland and the literature of the early common law', *Irish Jurist*, 16 (new ser. 1981): 97, 112.

until it reached something like its present shape in the late
1250s.[44] This new dating clears up the mystery of why nearly all
the references to suits in *Bracton* belong to the years when
Pattishall and Raleigh were on the bench.

The additions made in the 1230s were all connected with cases
that William of Raleigh heard, and they are likely due to one of
his clerks, possibly Henry of Bracton. The forerunner of the
treatise was very likely in his hands by 1234. It becomes evident,
thanks to Thorne's lifelong labours, that 'the prime mover
behind the *De Legibus*' was Raleigh.[45] He may have begun writing
some *tractates* before 1229, while he was Martin of Pattishall's
senior clerk. If Raleigh himself did not compose the titles and
paragraphs that constituted the original version, he at least
inspired the work, and the author was surely someone in his circle,
one of the clerks at the Bench.

Thorne's working out of the stages through which *De Legibus*
passed from c. 1230 to c. 1258 settles once and for all the question 'How far can Bracton be described as learned in Roman
law?' Maitland's explanation for *Bracton's* seeming ineptness was
that the author was 'a beginner groping his way among uncouth
terms and alien ideas'.[46] We must now turn back to Hermann
Kantorowicz's *Bractonian Problems*, in which he defended the
author of *Bracton* as an accomplished Roman lawyer, capable of
correctly using Roman legal terminology. He first proposed the
theory of a redactor to explain the book's apparent errors in use
of Roman law.[47]

The author of *De Legibus* was no novice civil lawyer, for
scholars have now identified quotations from about 500 parts of
the *Digest* and *Code*, and the author also used and understood a

---

[44] *Bracton*, 1: xl, xliv; 3: xv–xx.
[45] *Bracton*, 3: xxx, xxxv.
[46] *Select passages from the works of Bracton and Azo*, Selden Soc., 8 (1894): xix.
Scholars long continued to accept Maitland's finding. H.G. Richardson described 'Bracton' as an 'imperfectly trained' Romanist, who had studied at
Oxford but left before completing his degree, *Bracton, the problem of his text*.
Lady Stenton described 'Bracton's' Romanism as 'the hardly won learning of
an able man who from the books available to anyone who . . . could afford
them, had eagerly absorbed the current knowledge of the great Roman system', review of Richardson, *Bracton, E.H.R.*, 82 (1967): 113. Her view accords
with that of Plucknett, *Early Eng. legal lit.*, p. 48. For a brief survey of differing
opinions, see Thorne's lecture, *Henry de Bracton 1268–1968*.
[47] Hermann Kantorowicz's *Bractonian Problems* (Glasgow, 1941).

number of manuals of Roman and canon law.[48] Thorne shows
through his textual criticism that Kantorowicz's theory of an
incompetent redactor is basically correct, for he points out what
even Maitland had overlooked: that the redactor handled
English law just as badly as he did Roman law. Thorne concludes
that all extant manuscripts of the treatise must be traced to 'a
slip-shod copy of Bracton's original'.[49] He sees the author of the
lost original *De Legibus* as 'a trained jurist with the principles and
distinctions of Roman jurisprudence firmly in mind, using them
. . . to rationalize and reduce to order the results realized in the
English courts'. Roman law supplied *Bracton*'s author with tools
for shaping English materials into 'an articulated system of principles'. One of the most useful of these tools was 'a precise
technical vocabulary, infinitely more subtle than the language
of the plea rolls'.[50]

The circle of justices and their clerks assembled at Westminster
in the years following the civil war was an exceedingly capable
group. There can be no doubt that some of them had studied
with the greatest masters at Oxford, if not at Bologna itself. The
plea roll description of a difficult case heard in 1237 places the
judges in the mainstream of legal currents. They declared that
they did not wish to judge by examples from overseas regions,
and that they had never seen such a case *in jure scripto*.[51] Nonetheless, it is practically impossible to speak with any certainty about
any single judge's schooling. As we have seen, only two were
addressed as *magistri*, and we can only deduce from indirect
evidence that one of those, Master Robert of Shardlow, was a
canonist. Matthew Paris commented in his usual caustic manner
on the education of Master Ralph of Norwich, noting that he
was 'more learned in the *curia regis* than in the school of
liberal arts'.[52]

Thomas of Heydon, one of the oldest men on Henry III's
bench, had spent a good part of John's reign at Ely in the
household of his patron, Bishop Eustace. During his retreat in

---

[48] *Bracton*, 1: xxxv–xxxvi. See Fritz Schultz's articles, 'Critical studies on Bracton's
      treatise', *Law Qtrly. Rev.*, 59 (1943): 172–80; 'Bracton on Kingship', *E.H.R.*,
      60 (1945): 136–76. Also J.L. Barton, 'Bracton as a civilian', *Tulane Law Rev.*, 42
      (1968): 555–83.
[49] *Bracton*, 1: xxxiv.   [50] *Bracton*, 1: xxxiii.
[51] *C.R.R.*, 16: 39–40, no. 136C. The question was division of the earldom of
      Chester among heiresses.   [52] *Chron. Maj.*, 5: 560.

the fen country between 1203 and 1218, he had an opportunity to absorb some legal learning. Eustace of Ely was an active ecclesiastical judge, learned in both civil and canon law.[53] Also at Ely was Richard Barre, the archdeacon and longtime royal justice, who had studied at Bologna many years earlier.[54] Throughout John's reign, Martin of Pattishall had been at the Bench serving as Simon of Pattishall's clerk. Perhaps he had received some advanced schooling before Simon recruited him for his staff, probably at nearby Northampton; but his main preparation for a judicial post must have been practical, earned through years of observing his master, King John's ablest judge.

Nothing is known of William of Raleigh's life before 1214, by which time he had become Martin of Pattishall's clerk. It is not too far-fetched to suppose that he was at Oxford or some other legal centre before seeking a career at the *curia regis*. The friendship that two scholar-bishops, Robert Grosseteste of Lincoln and Edmund Rich of Canterbury, felt for him is testimony to the great judge's learning. Although the bishop of Lincoln stoutly opposed Raleigh on several issues – most notably on the differing definitions of bastardy in common law and canon law after the provisions of Merton – they conducted an amicable correspondence, trying to convince each other. The exchanges reveal that they regarded one another as intellectual equals.[55] No more is known of William of York's or Robert of Lexington's careers before they became clerks. They may well have studied at one of the emerging business schools in the first years of the thirteenth century, if not at a university. Since Robert's four brothers all secured superior educations, we must suspect that he too gained some advanced training.

Besides *Bracton*, less learned books were becoming available for the study of English law, perhaps more useful for those involved in the day-to-day work of the courts. Purely oral transmission of legal learning was no longer adequate even for

---

[53] See *Letters of Innocent III concerning England*, pp. 95–6, no. 562, for replies to a number of points of canon law about which Eustace had consulted the pope.   [54] See chap. 3, pt. 3, pp. 95–6.

[55] *Letters of Robert Grosseteste*, p. 95, no. 24. Cf. other letters, pp. 63–5, no. 17; pp. 76–94, no. 23; pp. 271–2, no. 86; p. 333, no. 113. The dying archbishop of Canterbury addressed his last letter in 1240 to Raleigh, Powicke, *Hen. III and Lord Edward*, p. 333.

laymen on the *curia regis* staff or standing on its fringes as attorneys and *narratores*. The knights among Henry III's justices may have gleaned some of their legal knowledge from books they had studied at the business schools, or from compilations of legal texts similar to Robert Carpenter's.

Knights and clerks had access to registers of writs, seven of which survive from the years before 1236.[56] They may derive from an early master register in existence before 1200, although scholars disagree about this, and the editors of *Early Registers of Writs* discreetly declare that the question of such a master register 'remains open'.[57] The earliest surviving one, the 'Irish' register previously dated at 1227, may actually date from November 1210, a product of King John's transplantation of English common law to his Irish lordship.[58] Chancery clerks and clerks at the Bench obviously needed registers of writs in order to copy off writs for suitors, although they may have had no official compilation, only their personal copies. In the late 1230s a copy was made for a clerk in the recently revived court *coram rege*.[59] Lawyers needed copies in order to choose the writs which best fitted their clients' needs. Religious houses, often drawn into suits in defense of their property and privileges, found it useful to have a register in their libraries. Of course, collections of writs soon proved useful as textbooks for students hoping for places as clerks, lawyers, or judges in the royal courts.

---

[56] Early registers include the 'Irish' Register of 1227, B.L. MS. Cott. Julius D II; also B.L. MSS. Harl. 746, Add. 8167, and Add. 25005; Nat. Lib. of Wales, Peniarth 390C. C.U.L. Ii.vi.3, also probably from the 1220's; and Corpus Christi College, Cambridge, MS. 297, a late thirteenth-century ms., but the register itself is pre-1236. See De Haas and Hall, *Early Register of writs*, pp. xxxiii–xliv, lxxx–lxxxiv, xcviii, cxix–cxxi. A possible eighth is P.R.O. E. 163/1/27, based on a register in use at the Bench in the 1220's. Meekings, *Studies*, article 1: 209–21.

[57] De Haas and Hall, pp. cxvii, cxxiii–cxxv. Maitland argued that there was no authoritative master register, 'The history of the register of original writs', *Harvard Law Rev.*, 3 (1889): 97–115, 167–79, 212–25; reprinted in *Collected Papers*, ed. H.A.L. Fisher (Cambridge, 1911), 2: 110–73. Plucknett, *Early Eng. legal lit.*, pp. 31–3, follows Maitland. Richardson and Sayles, *Law and legislation*, pp. 79, n. 3, and 110, maintain that a primitive register existed early enough to provide a guide for the treatise *Glanvill*.

[58] Brand, *Irish Jurist*, 16: 100–6.   [59] Meekings, *Studies*, article i: 210.

In addition to collections of writs, the plea rolls were becoming objects of interest. Martin of Pattishall was probably responsible for the survival of Simon of Pattishall's assize rolls. Martin apparently had Simon's rolls in his possession, studied the cases, and made notes on them.[60] Compilations of cases excerpted from the plea rolls were being made in the 1220s and 1230s. *Bracton's Note Book* is only one of several such collections of excerpts, unique to us today simply because it survived and all the others perished. It may have been neither the work of Bracton nor a preparatory study for the treatise; indeed, the pleas collected come not directly from the rolls but from other transcripts of cases.[61] This work of excerpting the plea rolls, probably by 'the *minores* of the judicial establishment', shows that the common law was being studied in a sustained manner by the fifty or so clerks at Westminster. Possibly junior clerks copied entries marked on a plea roll by a senior clerk to master the art of enrolling pleas. Collections of cases were also helpful to novice attorneys and pleaders, who needed examples to supplement the textbooks' general rules. *Bracton's Note Book* and its lost companions may be 'the rudimentary predecessors of the *Novae Narrationes* and the Year Books'.[62]

The expression 'school of Pattishall and Raleigh' that Maitland first used, then, means more than a circle of judges and their clerks. It rightly carries the meaning of a school in the literal sense, a centre for study of the common law. It was a school that operated on two levels: practical instruction for novices in the procedures of the *curia regis*, based on writs and plea rolls; and for judges and clerks with canonist or Romanist learning, exercises in shaping English law into a rational system. Thanks to the presence of both knights and churchmen on the bench, this 'school' combined the best of two traditions of legal training – the practical education of lawmen in the secular courts and the academic discipline of the Roman and canon lawyers – two traditions that had first come together in the age of *Glanvill*.

---

[60] Of the 12 assize rolls that survive from John's reign, 11 are from Simon's eyres, Stenton, *Earliest Northants Assize Rolls*, p. xix. De Haas and Hall, pp. cxvi–cxvii.

[61] *Bracton*, 3: xxxv–xxxviii.   [62] *Bracton*, 3: xxxviii.

4 REWARDS REAPED BY FULLTIME JUSTICES

The professional status of Henry III's justices becomes clearer when the rewards they won are examined. For one thing, we no longer need to divide the justices into two categories of multi-purpose royal servants and judicial specialists. The thirteen men regularly on the bench were all fulltime judges, even though two of them exercised other significant responsibilities. Second, a system of salary payments was beginning to take shape, although salaries were not the only means by which the king provided for judges' maintenance. Salaries were often insufficient and were rarely paid on schedule. Finally, we see the judiciary conferring greater status than ever. Several judges became intimate counsellors of Henry III and won wealth for themselves and their families primarily through judicial activity. This is perhaps clearest in the case of Stephen of Segrave, but is also seen in a quartet of clerics who devoted their lives to the judiciary: Pattishall and Raleigh, Robert of Lexington, and William of York.

Justices continued to be called upon occasionally to labour at non-judicial tasks. Some of these, of course, were administrative chores that had been assigned to justices since the beginning of the eyre system.[1] Other duties were those the justices could perform during vacations, combining visits to their own lands with the king's business. For example, Thomas of Heydon in 1223 was named clerk to a group in Northamptonshire collecting money due to the king for tree-fallen wood. Travel with the commissioners enabled Thomas to visit two Northants churches that he held.[2] Adam fitz William added the office of escheator to his duties as royal justice for about two years. He became one of the two joint-escheators south of the Trent in June 1234, and he remained active in the post until about April 1236.[3]

It is surprising to find five justices serving on occasion as

[1] E.g. Ralph Hareng's commission to assess tallages in 1223, *Pat. Rolls 1216–25*, pp. 403–4; *Rot. Lit. Claus.*, 1: 538, 540b. Or Thomas of Moulton's appointment to head a party of Lincs assessors of the fifteenth, *Pat. Rolls 1216–25*, pp. 561–2; *Rot. Lit. Claus.*, 2: 146b.

[2] Cold Higham and Raunds, *C.R.R.*, 16: 60, no. 195. For his appointment as clerk, *Pat. Rolls 1216–25*, p. 400.

[3] *Cal. Pat. Rolls 1232–47*, p. 54; *C.R.R.*, 15: xx.

sheriffs and constables. To see Thomas of Moulton and Stephen of Segrave occupying such offices is less astonishing than it is to see three clerics. These clerics' appointments, however, are connected to the process of professionalization in thirteenth-century royal government and are in fact indications of the passing of the old multi-purpose royal servants. Robert of Lexington took charge of the castles of Peak and Bolsover in 1223, and he continued to be their keeper until 1227.[4] The transfer of the two castles to him was part of a programme for resumption of royal castles from magnates' custody and their placement in the hands of professional royal servants. Master Robert of Shardlow was named sheriff of Surrey and custodian of Guildford Park in early 1231; through these positions he also became constable of Guildford Castle.[5] His appointment was in the tradition of the curial sheriff, and a deputy performed the duties of the office while he remained at Westminster. Shardlow was removed from his shrievalty after a year and a half because of his implication in anti-foreign agitation.[6] His removal may have represented a stage in the Poitevins' struggle to bring down Hubert de Burgh, his patron. Once the justiciar's power was broken, the Rivaux regime began naming professional royal servants to additional offices. Doubtless, William of Raleigh's appointment as keeper of Rockingham Castle 'for his whole life' on 16 July 1232 was part of their programme.[7]

Only two justices approached in activity the old multi-purpose servants of the crown who had sat at the Bench in earlier times. Thomas of Moulton and Stephen of Segrave, unlike their colleagues, still combined work at the Bench with significant responsibilities elsewhere. Moulton had a prominent place in the North of England as a royal agent, largely because of the baronial holdings he accumulated in Cumberland and

---

[4] *Pat. Rolls 1216–25*, p. 418; *1225–32*, p. 28; *Cal. Lib. Rolls 1226–40*, pp. 1, 107; *Rot. Lit. Claus.*, 2: 102b. For a time Lexington handed Bolsover to William Briwerre, *Rot. Lit. Claus.*, 2: 6b. Lexington was named sheriff of Oxon. in autumn 1229, but was almost immediately replaced, *List of Sheriffs*, p. 107.

[5] *Pat. Rolls 1225–32*, p. 419; *Close Rolls 1231–34*, p. 36.

[6] *Pat. Rolls 1225–32*, p. 486.

[7] *Pat. Rolls 1225–32*, p. 490; *Close Rolls 1231–34*, p. 88; Meekings, *Studies*, article 11: 177.

Westmorland through his marriage to Ada de Morvill. Also because of this second marriage, he became hereditary forester of Cumberland. This was an important post, not an empty title, for the royal forest covered a large part of the county.[8] Thomas became sheriff of Cumberland and constable of Carlisle Castle in 1233, responsibilities which he held for three years.[9] His appointment was one of numerous changes in sheriffs that occurred in 1233 following Hubert de Burgh's fall. Thomas remained active in the affairs of his native Lincolnshire as well. In 1226 he was joint-custodian of the Boston fair, and in 1230 he was one of the keepers of Lincolnshire ports.[10] Much of his work in the North had to be left to deputies or handled during vacation visits, since Thomas was regularly at Westminster for judicial sessions until his retirement in 1236.

Stephen of Segrave won appointment to a number of important posts between 1220 and his disgrace in 1234. Perhaps most significant were the multiple shrievalties that he held. He became sheriff of Essex and Hertfordshire in the autumn of 1220, and he continued to be sheriff of those counties until 1223. At Christmas 1221, he also received the shrievalty of Lincolnshire, which he held until 1234; and in February 1222, he became sheriff of Lancashire. He added Northamptonshire, Buckingham and Bedfordshire in autumn 1228, and in November 1229 he received in addition Warwick and Leicestershire.[11] Stephen's plural posts as sheriff were in the tradition of sheriffs under Henry III's father and grandfather, who appointed *curiales* to multiple shrievalties with undersheriffs carrying out the actual duties of office.

Not long after Stephen of Segrave became senior justice of common pleas, Henry III selected him – along with Ralph de Neville – to be one of the two regents during the king's absence from the realm, May to October 1230.[12] Stephen's judicial

---

[8] Thomas received letters close concerning the taking of deer or wood, *Close Rolls 1227–31*, p. 197; *1231–34*, pp. 67, 90, 487; and he served as forest justice in Cumberland and other northern counties, *Rot. Lit. Claus.*, 1: 434b; *Pat. Rolls 1216–25*, p. 218; *Close Rolls 1231–34*, pp. 137–8.

[9] *Close Rolls 1231–34*, p. 298; *Cal. Pat. Rolls 1232–47*, p. 8.

[10] *Pat. Rolls 1225–32*, p. 40; *Close Rolls 1227–31*, pp. 356, 357–8, 367. His son Alan had charge of the port of Grimsby.

[11] *List of Sheriffs*, pp. 1, 43, 72, 78, 92, 144; *Close Rolls 1227–31*, p. 259; *Cal. Chtr. Rolls*, 1: 166.   [12] *Pat. Rolls 1225–32*, p. 339.

experience, his long acquaintance with the king, and his 'pliability', made it natural that Henry III should appoint him to replace Hubert de Burgh as justiciar at the end of summer 1232.[13] Stephen had been one of Henry III's intimates as early as January–February 1227. A writ from that time to a party of justices in Hertfordshire explains that Segrave could not join them 'because the lord king retained [Stephen] next to him for certain business'.[14] By the time Stephen became senior justice of the Bench, he was, according to Matthew Paris, *regis tunc consiliarius, vir quidem sui solius amicus*.[15] It was about this time that Segrave became sheriff of five counties, holding them on very favourable terms.

Henry dismissed his justiciar in the summer of 1234, he appointed special justices to collect evidence of Stephen's misdeeds, and he summoned him to answer charges concerning his misconduct as justiciar. The king ordered Stephen outlawed and exiled from England, but his anger eventually cooled, and he rescinded his order on 2 January 1235.[16] Stephen of Segrave was reconciled with Henry III in early 1235, after paying a fine of 1000 marks, and he eventually returned to royal service.[17] By early 1239, Stephen had been restored fully to the king's favour, and he succeeded William of Raleigh as chief justice *coram rege*. Although he never again held the multiple posts he had before 1234, he was one of Henry III's chief counsellors by the time of his death. Indeed, Matthew Paris had the impression that he was involved in nearly all the business of the kingdom.[18]

Other royal justices became close associates of Henry III largely because of their position in the judiciary, unlike royal *familiares* in earlier reigns whose judicial work had been only one

---

[13] On 7 Aug. Hubert was commanded to surrender eight castles to Stephen, *Pat. Rolls 1225–32*, p. 496.

[14] *Rot. Lit. Claus.*, 2: 171. In the years 1227–32, Stephen witnessed on 11 different dates 15 royal charters out of a total of 38, Meekings, 'Charter roll witnesses 1227–43' (typescript at P.R.O.)

[15] *Chron. Maj.*, 3: 187. Cf. *C.R.R.*, 13: 406, no. 1934, Easter 1229, where the king issued a command *per dominum S. de Segrave*.

[16] Shirley, *Royal Letters*, 1: 445, no. 373; *Close Rolls 1231–34*, pp. 574–5; *1234–37*, p. 332; Powicke, *Hen. III and Lord Edward*, pp. 137–8.

[17] He had commissions for assizes by autumn 1236, Meekings 'Coram rege justices 1240–1258', citing *Pat. Roll 20 Hen. III*, m. 2d, 3d. In June 1237 he became justiciar for the vacant earldom of Chester, *Close Rolls 1234–37*, pp. 538–9; *Cal. Pat. Rolls 1232–47*, p. 188.   [18] *Chron. Maj.*, 4: 169.

of many responsibilities. The king knew his judges well, and several ranked high among his counsellors. Henry III became well acquainted with William of Raleigh in the years 1234–9, when he was senior justice *coram rege* and accompanying the royal household on its travels. Raleigh became the king's chief adviser on legal matters.[19] William of York frequently witnessed royal charters, as justice *coram rege* 1241–5 and as bishop of Salisbury. He was *domini regis clericum familiarissimum* at the time of his election. When Henry III sailed to Gascony in 1242, he named William one of three custodians of the realm.[20] Robert of Lexington stood close enough to the king to witness royal charters with some regularity.

Some of the less prominent judges received marks of favour from the king that reveal his personal acquaintance with them. Geoffrey le Sauvage accompanied Henry III on his continental expedition of 1230, several years after he had left the judiciary. When Geoffrey fell ill at Nantes sometime before 4 October, the king showed his concern, commanding that money be lent to him and a doctor found for him. Despite the doctor's care – or perhaps because of it – Geoffrey was dead by 4 November 1230.[21] The favours bestowed on Master Ralph of Norwich in 1235 and 1236, while he was busy with a general eyre, are more typical of the benefits that the king might offer. Henry III pardoned Ralph of a debt of twenty marks owed to the Jews; he excused his justice from suit to county and hundred court and from sheriff's aids and tallages from his land in Buckinghamshire; and he presented him with deer and oaks from the royal forest of Brill.[22]

Provision for regular payments to royal servants was more adequate by the beginning of Henry III's reign, or at least better documentation for salaries survives. In either case, this is evidence for growing professionalization. Not all royal servants

---

[19] E.g. Raleigh's role in the Statute of Merton, Powicke, *Hen. III and Lord Edward*, pp. 151–2.

[20] *Chron. Maj.*, 4: 587; 5: 534; *Cal. Pat. Rolls 1232–47*, p. 283; *Annales Mon.*, 3: 159 (Dunstable). [21] *Close Rolls 1227–31*, p. 451.

[22] *Cal. Pat. Rolls 1232–47*, p. 133, exemption for Chetwode; *Close Rolls 1234–37*, p. 125, pardon of debt; p. 299, gift of two deer; p. 399, gift of eight oaks. William de Insula also received a charter freeing him from jury duty and suit to court of county and hundred, *Close Rolls 1231–34*, p. 60.

received salaries, however; some had other sources of income. Laymen might be given escheats or wardships, while ecclesiastical benefices could support clerics. Proof of this policy are the temporary allowances frequently granted to royal clerks until suitable benefices could be found for them.[23] Earliest evidence for salaries dates from 1218, when justices at Westminster received payments in January and July of 100 shillings each.[24] By 1221 Stephen of Segrave's semi-annual payment had quintupled to twenty-five pounds, and the next year Ralph Hareng's salary jumped from 100 shillings to 100 marks.[25]

Such salaries seem large when compared with the payments made to royal servants about the middle of the century. From 1237 to 1239 William of Culworth, a junior justice at Westminster, was receiving an annual salary of twenty pounds.[26] Bracton's salary when he first appeared on the royal payroll in 1240 was forty marks, later raised to fifty pounds. While Bracton's salary was 'well up towards the top of the scale' for senior men in the civil service, Stephen of Segrave's figure surpassed it once he returned to the king's service. In 1240 he was receiving the opulent sum of 100 marks.[27] Rules regularizing royal justices' salaries were finally laid down in 1278. At that time, the chief justice's salary was set at sixty marks and other justices' salaries at forty or fifty marks each.[28]

In addition to salaries, justices received grants of money for their expenses on eyre. These grants ranged from six pounds to fifteen marks, with ten marks the most common figure. They apparently were not automatic, for William of York expressed anxiety about receiving his allowance in letters to his patron. He sought Ralph de Neville's intercession on his behalf, asking his

---

[23] In 1220 Ralph of Norwich assigned a salary of 20 marks a year until a benefice could be found for him, *Pat. Rolls 1216–25*, pp. 252, 298. John of Lexington, a layman, later received £20 yearly until he could be provided with the equivalent in escheats or wardships, *Cal. Lib. Rolls 1226–40*, p. 252.

[24] *Rot. Lit. Claus.*, 1: 350, 365.

[25] *Rot. Lit. Claus.*, 1: 459b, 472, 489. In 1226, Roger Huscarl's salary as a justice in Ireland was £25 yearly.   [26] *Cal. Lib. Rolls 1226–40*, pp. 295, 376.

[27] *Cal. Lib. Rolls 1226–40*, pp. 180, 445. For Bracton's salary, see Plucknett, *Early Eng. legal lit.*, pp. 44–5.

[28] Francis Palgrave, ed., *Parliamentary Writs and Writs of Military Summons*, Rec. Com. (1827–34), 1: 382; *Close Rolls 1272–79*, pp. 503–4.

help in getting 'a fat blessing' on his next eyre.[29] Allowances did
not reach the justices until the eyre had ended, for they frequently
came from amercements which the sheriff collected after the
justices' visits.[30] Expenses on eyre could he heavy with costs of
horses and servants, fodder, food and shelter, and the judges
wished to cut costs whenever possible. They readily accepted
hospitality from local dignitaries or occasionally from one
another. William of York wrote to Stephen of Segrave in 1240,
expressing thanks for kindnesses Lady Segrave had shown him
during his stop at their manor house at Alconbury, while he was
in Huntingdon on legal business.[31]

All royal servants, including judges, received frequent payments in the form of goods, particularly products from royal
forests. Grants of timber, firewood, and deer can almost be considered supplements to their salaries. Sometimes royal presents
had a special one-time purpose, such as Henry III's 1222 grant to
Ralph Hareng of twenty-four beams from the royal forest for
rebuilding his chapel.[32] Often encountered in the records are
gifts of fish from the royal fishponds and wine from the king's
cellars. In 1228, the king allowed Master Ralph of Norwich to
take twenty live bream from the fishpond at Kenilworth Castle
for a pond that he was starting.[33] By mid-century gifts of robes at
Christmastime were becoming common perquisites of Henry
III's servants; William of York received a 'complete and fitting'
robe for Christmas 1243.[34]

The real test of a royal servant's success lay in his achievement
in adding to his family possessions. The seven laymen among
Henry III's justices were no less ambitious than their predecessors. They too had widely varying degrees of success in this

---

[29] Meekings, *Studies*, article 5: 498–9. Ralph Hareng had an allowance of £6 in
1219 for expenses on eyre, *Pipe Roll 3 Hen. III*, p. 158. On 1226–8 eyres,
William of York received allowances of £10 to be paid out of amercements,
Rot. Lit. Claus., 2: 119b, 151; *Cal. Lib. Rolls 1226–40*, pp. 48, 76.

[30] E.g. 10 marks assigned to Ralph Hareng out of Worcs and Glos amercements
in 1221, *Rot. Lit. Claus.*, 1: 459b–460.   [31] *C.R.R.*, 16: 490, no. 2474.

[32] *Rot. Lit. Claus.*, 1: 519, 520. Also a gift to one of Stephen of Segrave's knights
of four oaks from the royal forest to rebuild his house, which had recently
been burned, 2: 200.

[33] *Close Rolls 1227–31*, p. 18. Also p. 224, 10 large bream and 40 small ones to
Stephen of Segrave; a tun of wine to Stephen, *1231–34*, p. 1; another tun, *Pipe
Roll 26 Hen. III*, ed. H.L. Cannon (New Haven, 1918), p. 139.

[34] *Close Rolls 1242–47*, p. 143.

sphere, and their success was not always directly related to their judicial appointments. Stephen of Segrave accomplished the most notable expansion of landholdings, raising himself from the knightly level to baronial holdings. Indeed, his descendants became barons by writ from 1295 until the male line failed in 1353. Stephen expanded his family holdings to some eighteen manors, mostly held as fees of one knight which spread from Leicestershire over five other Midland counties, but stretched as far south as Buckinghamshire and as far north as Lancashire.[35] Grants of nine manors came to Stephen from the two kings he served. They began when King John gave Stephen the royal manor of Kineton, Warwickshire, in July 1216 to hold at fee-farm.[36]

Thomas of Moulton had an almost equally spectacular rise. In early manhood he was a knight of the Lincolnshire fenland, but he died in 1240 a baron of Cumberland. Thomas's second marriage enabled him to climb from the Lincolnshire gentry into the baronage. He married in 1218 Ada de Morvill, coheir to the barony of Burgh-by-Sands and widow of Richard de Lucy. He married this prominent heiress and widow without royal consent, arousing the anger of young Henry III's counsellors, but he was reconciled with them by autumn.[37] At the other extreme from Segrave and Moulton is William de Insula, who began and ended his career as a Northamptonshire knight. He was a substantial knight of the county when he joined the judiciary in 1225, and his eleven years of service to the crown brought no spectacular change in status.[38]

---

[35] B.L. MS. Harl. 4748, Segrave Cart. or 'Red Book', gives the holdings. For a calendar of Leics portions, see John Nichols, *The History and Antiquities of the County of Leicestershire* (London, 1795–1815), 2, pt. 1: 108–20.

[36] *Rot. Chart.*, p. 223; *Rot. Lit. Claus.*, 1: 278, 471. Other royal grants include the manor of Alconbury, Hunts, *Rot. Lit. Claus.*, 1: 415; *C.R.R.*, 16: 478, no. 2409; Cotes, Derby, *Cal. Chtr. Rolls*, 1: 81–82, 84; *Cal. Inq. Post Mort.*, 1: 89, no. 334; wapentake of Goscote, Leics, *Cal Chtr. Rolls*, 1: 95; *Close Rolls 1227–31*, p. 170; manor of Finedon, Northants, *Cal. Chtr. Rolls*, 1: 116; *Close Rolls 1227–31*, p. 317; manor and soke of Kirton, Lincs, *Close Rolls 1231–34*, pp. 163, 395; Melbourne, Derby, *Cal. Chtr. Rolls*, 1: 175; *Close Rolls 1231–34*, p. 198; Leyland, Lancs, and Fen Stanton, Hunts, *Cal Chtr. Rolls*, 1: 187, 250; *Close Rolls 1231–34*, pp. 281, 368.

[37] *Rot. Lit. Claus.*, 1: 354b; *Exc. è Rot. Fin.*, 1: 17; P.R.O., Exch. K.B. Mem. Roll I, m. 1.   [38] Meekings, *1235 Surrey Eyre*, pp. 212–13.

The fortunes of the other knights – Adam fitz William, Ralph Hareng, and Geoffrey le Sauvage – lie somewhere between the two extremes. They succeeded in increasing their landholdings, but not to any dramatic degree and without direct royal grants. Adam fitz William was a prominent Hertfordshire landholder with some holdings in Kent and Essex, and he made modest additions to his lands in 1235 and 1236, while he was on the bench.[39]

Ralph Hareng's family held manors in Buckinghamshire with additional land in Oxfordshire. He added to these holdings until he had become tenant of most of the St Valery honour by the end of King John's reign. During his years as a royal justice, his main concern was consolidation of his holdings, not large scale acquisitions.[40] An impression of Ralph's holdings can be formed from the listing of his son's lands in the inquests of 1242–3. Ralph III held two and a third fees in Bucks of the earl of Cornwall, part of the old St Valery honour. He also held of the earl a socage tenure for two shillings annually. In Oxfordshire, he held three and a third fees of the St Valery honour and one other fee through his wife's inheritance.[41]

Geoffrey le Sauvage was also solidly within the knightly class, heir to lands centred in Warwickshire but stretching into the neighbouring counties of Worcestershire and Derbyshire. Although Geoffrey acquired no land by direct royal grant, he did gain land at Hampton Gay, Oxfordshire, through his marriage into the Despenser family.[42] On Geoffrey's death in 1230, his father-in-law offered a fine of fifty marks for custody of young Geoffrey IV and the boy's mother.[43]

Like their predecessors, Henry III's judges accepted gifts from suitors in the courts. Indeed, some of the judges seem to have accepted such substantial presents that they must have

---

[39] Meekings, *Studies*, article 8: 2–4.
[40] He acquired Westbury manor, Bucks, from his brother-in-law in 1200, *C.R.R.*, 1: 183; *Feet of Fines Oxon.*, p. 230, no. 30. See a 1221 exchange of Oxon. and Bucks land, *Feet of Fines Oxon.*, pp. 62–3, no. 53, and a suit for the manor of Chilworth Valery, Oxon., pp. 71–2, no. 82.
[41] *Book of Fees*, pp. 822, 823, 826, 871.
[42] To Petronilla, daughter of Hugh Despenser, *Complete Peerage*, 4: 260; *Cart. Oseney*, 6: 52, no. 967A; 63 no. 975B.
[43] *Exc. è Rot. Fin.*, 1: 205; *Pat. Rolls 1225–32*, p. 413.

been longtime legal consultants to have merited such reward. William of York held a Yorkshire living in the patronage of William de Forz, titular count of Aumale.[44] The pattern of patron and client was expected to be mutually beneficial and William of York sought to look out for the count's interests at court. He was successful in protecting his patron in 1235, when the king pardoned William de Forz 'at the instance and petition of William of York' of an amercement incurred on William's eyre in Yorkshire.[45] Another likely case of purchase of influence at court is a gift of land and houses which the prior and canons of Holy Trinity, Aldgate, made to Ralph Hareng sometime around 1217–21. They described Ralph as 'our chosen friend'.[46] More striking examples of attempts to purchase influence are the many grants of land made to Stephen of Segrave as he rose higher and higher in royal favour. A royal charter of 1233, made when Stephen's power was at its height, confirmed grants to him from two earls of Chester, the earl of Derby, Earl William de Mandeville and the countess of Essex, his wife, and from the countess of Eu.[47] Persons of less than baronial rank also made grants to Segrave.[48]

The measure of success for clerics among the judges is their ecclesiastical preferment. As we have seen, some justices always succeeded in piling benefice upon benefice despite the Church's opposition to pluralism. A moderately successful royal clerk would accumulate three or four livings from the king's gift or from others, while those who won special favour could expect more. Thomas of Heydon became parson of three or four churches long before he joined Henry III's judiciary; Richard I presented him to two sometime after 1190, and as we have seen, he was hereditary parson of Heydon.[49] Master Ralph of Norwich

---

[44] Easington in Holderness, *C.R.R.*, 12: 457, no. 2283.

[45] *Close Rolls 1234–37*, p. 62.

[46] *Cart. of Holy Trinity, Aldgate*, p. 122, no. 620.

[47] *Cat. of Berkeley Castle MSS.*, pp. 78–9, no. 231.

[48] E.g. half a fee at Roslinton, Derby, from Roger de Mohaut, the earl of Chester's seneschal, Jeayes, *Cat. of Derby Chtrs.*, p. 255, nos. 2025–6; ten virgates at Thurlaston, Warwicks, from William de Cantilupe, former steward of the royal household, *Book of Fees*, pp. 376, 1279; *V.C.H., Warwicks*, 6: 82; manor of Bericote, Warwicks, from Boscher son of Henry, *V.C.H., Warwicks*, 5: 105.

[49] Cold Higham and Raunds, Northants, *C.R.R.*, 16: 60, no. 195. He was possibly also parson of Pulham, Norfolk, *C.R.R.*, 12: 144, no. 709.

also began receiving benefices while still a royal clerk. In 1217 the regent, William Marshal, named him dean of the royal chapel at Wallingford Castle.[50] Then in 1221 Henry III presented him to the church at Oakley, Buckinghamshire, and Master Ralph also held the church on the royal manor of Brill, which was a chapel of Oakley.[51] His service in Ireland brough him a prebend at St Patrick's, Dublin, by 1227.[52] Master Robert of Shardlow's reward took the form of a shrievalty, and no evidence survives for his presentation to churches in the king's gift. He held only one living, and he was presented to it by William of St Johns before July 1228, shortly after he joined the royal service.[53]

The remaining four clerics on the bench had outstanding success in securing benefices. None of them, however, could equal the record of John Mansel, one of Henry III's most trusted counsellors and probably the thirteenth century's most notorious pluralist. He began to collect benefices about 1241, and by his death in 1265 he was said to have held over 300 livings which brought him an annual income of 4000 marks.[54] Martin of Pattishall had his preferment estimated at a value of over £1000 at the time of the clerical sixteenth in 1226. Later Pattishall won appointment to other substantial offices that increased his income; he became archdeacon of Norfolk by September 1227 and dean of St Paul's, London, a year later.[55] The benefices that William of York held in 1242 brought him some £800 a year gross income, and he must have realized half that or more as net income. Among his holdings was the provostship of Beverley, 'that perquisite of great royal servants' which was worth over fifty pounds yearly.[56] The value of Robert of Lexington's and William of Raleigh's livings remains uncalculated, but they most likely approached those of Pattishall and York. A preliminary listing of their properties shows five or six churches plus two or three prebends for each. In addition, Raleigh won

[50] *Pat. Rolls 1216–25*, p. 27.
[51] *C.R.R.*, 11: 337, no. 1791; *Rot. Lit. Claus.*, 1: 631; *Cal. Pat. Rolls 1247–58*, p. 471.   [52] *Chart. St Mary's, Dublin*, 1: 41.
[53] Church of Harty, Kent, Meekings, *1235 Surrey Eyre*, pp. 240–1.
[54] Thompson, 'Pluralism in the mediaeval Church', pp. 50–2.
[55] Based on his payment of 100 marks, *Pat. Rolls 1225–32*, p. 249. One prebend alone was valued at 80 marks, *Reg. St Osmund*, 2: 74. *Fasti, Mon. Cath.*, p. 65; *Fasti, St Paul's*, p. 6.   [56] Meekings, *Studies*, article 10: 136; article 5: 503–4.

the office of treasurer of Exeter Cathedral sometime after 1229.[57] All four began collecting benefices before joining the judiciary either as early as King John's reign or during his son's minority.[58]

Clerics in the king's service also accumulated lay properties. Royal clerks sometimes acquired houses in London. For example, William of York purchased a house in the parish of St Benet's Woodwharf, and he added to its grounds in 1244 and 1245.[59] Sometimes they built up land in the country as well. Master Ralph of Norwich acquired parcels of land at Chetwode, Buckinghamshire, totalling fourteen virgates. He held other plots at Barton Hartshorn, Buckinghamshire, and at Goddington nearby but lying in Oxfordshire. In 1245 he conveyed ten virgates of his land to an Augustinian priory he founded at Chetwode.[60]

Perhaps most successful among the clerical justices in building up lay holdings was Robert of Lexington. He began by 1228 to acquire manors centred around Laxton in Nottinghamshire, but he expanded his holdings into Derbyshire and farther away into Oxfordshire.[61] Robert's land acquisitions were due less to royal favour than to his own shrewd, even sharp business practices. As a cleric with ample preferment, he did not need these landholdings. By 1237 he had passed a large portion on to his brother John, the only one of his four brothers not in clerical orders.

The supreme mark of success for clerics in the king's service had always been elevation to a bishopric. Two justices – William of Raleigh and William of York – won election as bishops, while a third – Master Ralph of Norwich – narrowly missed becoming

[57] *Fasti, St Paul's*, p. 37.

[58] Pattishall was a canon of Lincoln in 1220, *Fasti, Lincoln*, p. 132. York was presented to the church of King's Ripton, Hunts, by 1220, Meekings, *Studies*, article 5: 496. King John presented Robert of Lexington to a prebend at Southwell, Notts. and to the vicarage of South Stanley, Yorks, *Rot. Lit. Pat.*, p. 115; *York Minster Fasti*, 2: 139, no.89. He presented William of Raleigh to the living of Bratton Fleming, Devon, *Rot. Lit. Pat.*, p. 93b.

[59] On his election as bishop, he gave the property to the Chapter of St Paul's, D & C St Paul's, Deeds A–4, nos. 685, 687–8, cited by Meekings, '*Coram rege justices.*'

[60] *Cal. Feet of Fines, Bucks*, pp. 54, 61, 86; *H.M.C. Reports*, 78, R.R. Hastings MSS., 1: 268–9.

[61] *Rufford Chtrs.*, 1: xciv; Langmuir, 'Knight's tale of Hugh of Lincoln', p. 471.

an archbishop. Henry III followed episcopal elections closely, and he frequently nominated a candidate of his own. Since many elections were a result of royal pressure, we may suspect the spontaneity of the electors' choices. In some elections, however, the canons, eager to please the king, selected someone they thought to be high in his favour. According to Matthew Paris, the canons of Salisbury elected William of York their bishop in 1246 because they feared the king would accept no one except an *aulicium et curialem*[62]

William of Raleigh won election in 1239 to two bishoprics: first to the see of Coventry and Lichfield, then in April to Norwich. Raleigh accepted Norwich, the king gave his approval in June, and he was consecrated on 25 September 1239.[63] The next year the monks of Winchester elected Raleigh to succeed Peter des Roches as bishop, and this time royal approval was not forthcoming. Henry III had his own candidate for the wealthy see of Winchester, first one of the queen's Provençal uncles and then another. The king appealed to Rome, refused to accept the pope's finding for Raleigh, and then sought to prevent Raleigh from exercising his episcopal authority. A long and bitter struggle ensued, and Henry III came to regard his former friend as his worst enemy. The king only managed to calm his anger and to accept Raleigh as bishop of Winchester by July 1244.[64]

Master Ralph of Norwich had a long career in Ireland after leaving the English judiciary in 1237. He was chancellor of Ireland from 1249 until 1256, when he was elected archbishop of Dublin. He won Henry III's approval, but Pope Alexander IV refused to accept him. The electors were criticized for choosing 'a man wholly secular, and at that moment occupied with custody of the Irish treasury under the king's patronage'.[65] According to one account, Robert of Lexington also was elected to a bishopric. The Dunstable annals state that he was elected to the see of Coventry and Lichfield in 1239, but that he declined the

---

[62] *Chron. Maj.*, 4: 587; Powicke, *Hen. III and Lord Edward*, pp. 264–6.
[63] *Fasti, Mon. Cath.*, p. 57.
[64] Thorne, ed., *Bracton*, 3: xl–xliv; Powicke, *Hen. III and Lord Edward*, pp. 270–3.
[65] *Cal. Pat. Rolls 1247–58*, pp. 471–5; *Cal. Papal Reg.*, 1: 333; *Chron. Maj.*, 5: 560.

election because of uncertainties surrounding the rivalry between the monks of Coventry and the chapter of Lichfield over right of election.[66]

While royal justices benefited from the favour of the king and others, they themselves wished to be in a position to dispense favours to family and friends. Fulfilment of the desire to provide for their progeny can be seen on a modest level in Ralph Hareng's provision for his children and on a grander scale with Thomas of Moulton's or Stephen of Segrave's plans for their sons. On Ralph Hareng's death early in 1230, his heir was his eldest son, Ralph Hareng III.[67] Young Ralph had married Alice Murdak, coheir with her three sisters to lands through both her parents. Through her father, Ralph Mardak III, she was coheir to two hides at Doddington in north Oxfordshire; and through her mother, Eva de Grey, she was coheir to a fee of four knights in Oxfordshire held of the earl of Devon.[68] Ralph Hareng left at least two other children: Jordan, parson of two Oxfordshire churches at the time of the interdict in 1208, and a daughter Joan, married off to Simon de St Liz.[69]

Thomas of Moulton arranged profitable marriages for his sons, which raised them into the baronage. These marriages did not come to him through royal favour or because of his influence in the judiciary, but through his willingness to take financial risks. Thomas played a dangerous game in 'the no man's land between business and politics', making a 1000 mark proffer to King John for the custody and marriage of Richard de Lucy's two daughters.[70] The girls' father had been one of several claimants to the vast northern lands of Alice de Rumilly (d. 1187), lying in Cumberland, Westmorland, and Yorkshire. Thomas of Moulton married Richard de Lucy's widow, as we have seen, and he promptly married off the two heiresses in his

---

[66] *Annales Mon.*, 3: 140. Matthew Paris makes no mention of Robert in his account of Hugh of Pattishall's election, *Chron. Maj.*, 3: 542.

[67] *Close Rolls 1227–31*, p. 296; *Exc. è Rot. Fin.*, 1: 194; *Mem. Roll 14 Hen. III*, p. 94.

[68] *C.R.R.*, 13: 362, no. 1718; 16: 65–6, no. 228; 415, no. 2041; *Exc. è Rot. Fin.*, 1: 455; *Cal Inq. Post Mort.*, 1: 290, no. 842.

[69] Jordan held Chesterton and Mixbury, *Rot. Lit. Claus.*, 1: 114. For Joan and her husband, see *Cart. Oseney*, 5: 231–2, nos. 723–4.

[70] *Rot. de Obl. et Fin.*, pp. 482–3. The phrase is Holt's, *Northerners*, p. 57.

custody to his sons by his first wife. Lambert, the elder son, married Mabel, and Alan married Alice de Lucy.

These marriages involved the Moultons in the complex problem of partitioning Alice de Rumilly's inheritance, which had occasioned litigation for years. The case was revived in 1223–5, probably as part of a plan to reduce the power of William de Forz, count of Aumale, and the chief rival to the Lucy girls' claims. This northern magnate had recently refused to surrender castles in his custody and staged a short-lived rebellion, which had earned him little goodwill from the ruling council.[71] He was summoned to Westminster in the autumn of 1223 to explain why he withheld half the Rumilly inheritance, which should have passed to the daughters of Richard de Lucy. Though an interested party, Thomas of Moulton acted as the king's attorney.[72] He made certain that he kept in touch with Westminster while he was away on judicial business in Lincolnshire in the summer of 1225, sending letters detailing his itinerary to the king and to the chancellor.[73] The eventual partition of the Rumilly lands gave the count of Aumale the Yorkshire estates and the castle of Cockermouth in Cumberland with its manor, while the remaining Cumberland territories went to the Lucy daughters. Mabel, wife of Lambert of Moulton, took the barony of Egremont, while her younger sister Alice, wife of Alan of Moulton, took half of Papcastle.[74]

This financial gamble which Thomas took in purchasing the Lucy heiresses ultimately paid off; his sons were now among the leading men of Cumberland. He had other children for whom he had to provide: another son and a daughter by his first wife and three sons by his second wife. The third son from his first marriage, also named Thomas, became a clerk.[75] The daughter, Juliana, married in 1209 Robert Vavassor, a Yorkshire knight who had been undersheriff of Lancashire in 1197.[76] Thomas had offered a fine of 300 marks and three horses for her marriage,

[71] Ralph V. Turner, 'William de Forz, count of Aumale', *Proc. American Philos. Soc.*, 115 (1971): 238–41, 244–5.
[72] *C.R.R.*, 11: 247, no. 1223.   [73] P.R.O., SC 1/4, no. 96; SC 1/6, no. 70.
[74] The count also had to pay damages of 600 marks, *C.R.R.*, 11: 544, no. 2710; 12: 66–7, no. 360; 177–9, no. 866; 324–5, no. 1576; *Early Yorks Chtrs.*, 7: 14.
[75] *Pat. Rolls 1216–25*, pp. 15, 69, 83.   [76] Holt, *Northerners*, p. 59.

but the debt was transferred to her husband's account because he had married her 'by the king's will'.[77]

Of Moulton's three sons by Ada de Morvill, the eldest was also christened Thomas. Sometime before his father's death in 1240, he married the heiress to the barony of Irthington (or Gilsland), Cumberland. Thomas junior was heir to the Morvill barony through his mother and through his aunt, who died without direct heirs. In addition, Thomas conferred on the boy in 1231 two of his Lincolnshire estates, although they were to be in the custody of Thomas's colleague on the bench, William of Raleigh, *sicut senescallo*.[78] Thomas of Moulton, then, brought three sons into the baronial class through marriage, perhaps something of a record.

Stephen of Segrave raised one son to baronial rank, although he had three. His eldest son, John, preceded him in death; but two or three years before the boy died in 1230, Stephen married him to an heiress in his custody, the daughter of Roger de Cauz III. Her father was a Buckinghamshire and Berkshire landholder who also held a serjeanty tenure at Water Eaton, Bedfordshire.[79] Following John of Segrave's death, Stephen offered the king £100 to have his daughter-in-law's marriage.[80]

Gilbert of Segrave, Stephen's second son, became his heir after 1230. Gilbert shared in his father's rise, fall, and restoration to royal favour. Gilbert married before September 1231 Mabel, daughter and coheir of Robert of Chaucombe. Her father gave the couple his manor of Dalby, Leicestershire.[81] Young Segrave became active in the royal service by 1232, and he shared in the rich reward his father was winning as one of the Poitevins, 1232–4. He had custody of two royal castles, and he received land for maintaining himself in the king's service: the manor and soke of Horncastle, Lincolnshire, and the earl marshal's land at Burton, Northants. When Henry III called for the return of the manor of Burton, the king maintained that he

[77] *Pipe Roll 11 John*, pp. 75, 139.

[78] Young Thomas's bride was Matilda, daughter of Herbert II de Vaux, *Complete Peerage*, 9: 405–6; Sanders, *Baronies*, p. 124. Manors of Whaplode and Holbeach, *C.R.R.*, 14: 419, no. 1941.

[79] *Rot. Lit. Claus.*, 2: 174, 183; G.H. Fowler, ed., *A Digest of the charters preserved in the cartulary of the priory of Dunstable*, Beds Hist. Rec. Soc., 1 (1913): 295, no. 211.   [80] *Exc. è Rot. Fin.*, 1: 204; *Pat. Rolls 1225–32*, p. 412.

[81] *Complete Peerage*, 11: 603; *Cat. of Berkeley Castle MSS.*, p. 76, no. 223.

had given it to Gilbert 'by the counsel of Stephen of Segrave his father'.[82] Gilbert's career in the royal administration eventually resumed, and he followed his father onto the judicial bench. Gilbert's heir was his son Nicholas, whom Edward I formally recognized as a baron; and his daughter married William Mauduit V, heir to the earldom of Warwick.[83]

Little is known about Stephen of Segrave's third son, also christened Stephen, other than that he was a cleric. Due to his father's influence, the king presented him to two ecclesiastical livings. In 1222 he received a moiety of the church at Burnham, Lincolnshire, which was temporarily in the king's gift. Henry III named him to the church at Dilwyn, Herefordshire, in 1229 following Martin of Pattishall's resignation of the living.[84] Stephen's sense of kinship embraced those beyond his immediate family, and in 1221 he found a benefice for a nephew which would enable him to attend the schools.[85]

Although clerics in major orders supposedly loosened their ties to the world, concern for family interest was still a powerful motivating force. Almost all seven clerics among Henry III's justices sought favours for relatives; five of them had kinsmen in clerical orders whom they helped to obtain benefices.[86] Sometimes they arranged for a relative to succeed them when they resigned a living. While William of York was still a court clerk in 1228, he wrote to his patron Ralph de Neville that he was supporting in the schools 'a certain poor scholar and relative of mine'. He sought to secure for this kinsman presentation to his church of King's Ripton, which he was resigning, and the chancellor obliged. William persuaded the Cluniacs of Lewes Priory to present another kinsman to their church at Gratton.[67]

---

[82] *Br. Note Book*, 3: 130–1; *Close Rolls 1231–34*, pp. 249, 263, 344, 427. For details of Gilbert's activity, see *Complete Peerage*, 11: 602–3.

[83] *Beauchamp Cart.*, p. xxxi.

[84] *Pat. Rolls 1216–25*, pp. 359, 379; *1225–32*, p. 268.

[85] Robert received the church at Syston, *Rot. Hug. Welles*, 2: 278.

[86] William of Raleigh's kinsman, Philip of Sideham, was rector of Lilleford in 1238, *Cal. Papal Reg.*, 1: 169; his brother Robert was parson of Marsh Gibbon, Bucks, by 1230, *Rot. Hug. Welles*, 2: 78. The nuns of Woodchurch presented the nephew of Martin of Pattishall to the church of Dallington, c. 1220, *Rot. Hug. Welles*, 2: 102.

[87] Master John Paulin, *Pat. Rolls 1225–32*, p. 177; Meekings, *Studies*, article 5: 501, no. v; William, Meekings, *1235 Surrey Eyre*, p. 260. William had a brother, Nicholas, to whom he gave his manor of Eske, *Early Yorks Chtrs.*, 7: 250.

Robert of Lexington had four brothers, three of them in clerical orders, for whom he felt responsible. This Nottinghamshire family proved to be a talented group who took important parts in both ecclesiastical affairs and royal government. Robert, 'the real founder of the family fortunes', must have accumulated his properties in order to aid his younger brothers. His least known brother, Peter, earned a master's degree by 1237, but spent most of his life as a country parson. Henry became treasurer of Salisbury Cathedral by 1241, doubtless with aid from his brother Robert, who was a canon there. Later he moved to Lincoln, where he was dean in 1245 and bishop a few years later, following Robert Grosseteste's death. The third brother in orders was Stephen, who studied at Paris and Oxford. He was studying theology at Oxford in 1221, when he suddenly left the schools to become a Cistercian monk. Stephen had a brilliant career as a monastic administrator, becoming abbot of Stanley about 1223, then crossing the Channel where he served successively as abbot of Savigny and of Clairvaux.[88]

The only layman among the five brothers was John of Lexington, who rose rapidly in Henry III's government, surpassing Robert in influence after 1235. He was one of those well-lettered knights who were among the king's most influential counsellors. John became steward of the king's household, keeper of the seal on several occasions – the first layman to have that responsibility – and justice *coram rege*. He won infamy when Henry III charged him with looking into allegations of the ritual murder of little Hugh of Lincoln by Jews in 1255, and his inquiry led to the execution of nineteen Jews on extremely dubious evidence.[89] John became a substantial landholder through the generosity of his brother, who enfeoffed him with two Nottinghamshire manors between 1235 and 1237. On Robert's death in 1250, he inherited his brother's estates, except for some lands bequeathed to religious houses.[90]

Royal justices had to dispense patronage to others besides their relatives. Naturally, they sought benefices for clerks they employed. An example is Martin of Pattishall's effort to find a

---

[88] On the Lexington brothers' careers, see *Rufford Chtrs.*, 1: xcv–xcix; Langmuir, 'Knight's tale of Hugh of Lincoln', pp. 471–2.

[89] Langmuir reconstructs both John's career and the whole episode of the persecution of Lincoln Jews, 'Knight's tale.'

[90] For John's holdings, *Rufford Chtrs.*, 1: xciv–v, xcvii.

living for William of Raleigh at the time of his retirement in
1229. When Martin left the Bench he also resigned his rectory of
King's Somborne. He persuaded the prior of Mottesfont, who
had the right of presentation, to appoint Raleigh the new rector.[91] William of York in 1242 presented his chaplain to a church
that he had earlier secured for a poor kinsman.[92] As has been
shown, Roger of Whitchester was William of York's clerk, and
he succeeded him as keeper of writs and rolls at the Bench.
Roger was a cleric in minor orders in 1244 when he fell heir to
his father's estates, but he did not wish to renounce his clergy
and take up knighthood. William of York's influence enabled
him to retain his ecclesiastical status. The king issued orders
releasing Roger of Whitchester from undergoing the ceremony
of knighting 'because we desire that clerks in our service should
be in better condition than others and . . . Roger . . . has borne
himself laudably in William of York's service'.[93]

Clearly, the web of patronage binding servants of the crown
together continued to be woven tightly. It was enabling the
ambitious to climb to higher social rank, just as it had in Henry
II's time and would continue to do for centuries. The rise of professional royal servants to positions of wealth and power continued to spread alarm among conservative social critics in
Henry III's day, as Matthew Paris's malicious obituaries
show.

[91] Meekings, *Studies*, article 12: 227–8.
[92] *Rotuli Roberti Grosseteste, episcopi Lincolniensis*, ed. F.N. Davis, Cant.–York Soc.,
     10 (1913), and Lincoln Rec. Soc., 11 (1914): 284.
[93] *Close Rolls 1242–47*, p. 247; Meekings, *Studies*, article 14: 105.

6

THE WORK OF THE JUSTICES

1 THE JUSTICES' MENTALITY

The judges of the Angevin kings – except for Richard fitz Neal and the authors of *Glanvill* and *Bracton* – wrote little that might cast light on their feelings about their work. The earliest surviving letters of royal justices date from Henry III's early years. They were hardworking royal servants with little time and probably little inclination for reflection or writing. We have seen that at least half the justices were laymen, whose training in the law was primarily practical. Ten of the clerks among the judiciary had some higher education, seen by their title of *magister*, but evidence for law degrees is extremely thin. It is only certain that one, Richard Barre, studied at Bologna, although *Bracton* is evidence that justices in William of Raleigh's circle were accomplished Romanists.

Medieval judges were not required to give reasoned judgments, and the plea rolls rarely record principles of jurisprudence, for most cases concluded with a jury's verdict, a statement of fact, or with 'wager of law' or compurgation, not with a judge's authoritative statement. Royal justices did pronounce the law, however, on procedural matters or in spheres where the law was uncertain. *Glanvill* notes instances in which judgment could be made *de consilio curie ex equitate*, and *Bracton* discusses questions where there was *contentio inter maiores*.[1] Decisions on procedure were often decided 'by counsel of the court', and the judges' decisions generally aimed at rational resolution of the problem with concern for the convenience of the parties.[2]

The plea rolls alone present an incomplete and misleading picture of the justices' work. They leave an impression of the judges as merely chairmen whose judgments are little more than

---

[1] *Glanvill*, ii, 12, p. 32; iii, 3, p. 39; iii, 7, p. 42; vi, 10, p. 63; vii, 1, p. 74. *Bracton*, 3: 321, f. 282; 4: 154, f. 367. For a discussion of judges' differing interpretations, see Lady Stenton, *Rolls of Justices for Lincs and Worcs*, pp. xxii–xxiii.

[2] See below, pp. 266–7.

ratifications of jurors' verdicts. In fact, justices were active in the courtroom in a way that the Latin passive voice beloved by the scribes often disguises. The scribes' innocuous *queritur si . . .* lessens the impact of the questions that the justices actually asked. *Bracton* describes in detail the questions that justices should ask when hearing an assize of novel disseisin, questioning first both plaintiff and tenant to make sure that an action lies, then ascertaining whether an exception is available to the tenant, and ensuring the accuracy of the information contained in the writ. Once they were satisfied on those points, the judges could allow the case to go to a jury.[3] In criminal proceedings begun by presentment the justices acted as prosecutors, questioning the accused. In *Glanvill*'s words, they were to discover the truth by 'many and varied inquests and interrogations' and by 'considering the probable facts and possible conjectures both for and against the accused'.[4]

It is possible to penetrate the judges' silence and to sense something of their thoughts about their work. There is no reason to assume that they were cut off from the main currents of legal thought, and we can safely attribute to them ideas that were 'in the air' during their lives. Many legal ideas and practices grew not so much out of the learned speculations of clerics and schoolmen as they did out of the collective traditions of lay communities.[5] Like all medieval men, royal judges felt the weight of custom, and phrases such as *lex terrae* or *consuetudo regni* crossed their lips from time to time. Yet it is difficult to determine whether such phrases were matters of common form or whether they had some deeper meaning for the justices.[6] The justices of the Bench in 1228 warned a tenant that his grand assize would proceed on the appointed day whether he was present or not, *secundum antiquam consuetudinem*. In this case, their use of the phrase was not a matter of form; it was a wish that the

---

[3] *Bracton*, 3: 68–70, ff. 183b–184b; cf. ff. 288b, 289, 290b. See also Donald W. Sutherland, *The Assize of Novel Disseisin* (Oxford, 1973), p. 73.

[4] *Glanvill*, p. 171.

[5] Susan Reynolds, 'Law and communities in Western Christendom, c. 900–1140', *A.J.L.H.*, 25 (1981): 205–24.

[6] Lady Stenton argued that they were not merely common form, *English Justice*, pp. 89–90. Yet it appears that by 1220 or so, such phrases were standard in ordering outlawry of accused criminals, *C.R.R.*, 8: 198, 237; 9: 220, no. 1079.

tenant know the law as set forth in *Glanvill*.[7] Other times, the judges seem to be contrasting *lex terrae* or *consuetudo Angliae* with the legal innovations of the Angevins. For example, the justices used these terms most commonly in their orders to sheriffs to proceed with the ancient process of outlawry.[8] They also used such phrases when contrasting the law of the *curia regis* with canon law, or with special commands of the king.[9]

Custom was not such a heavy weight that royal justices could not look about and apply practical lessons they had learned in administrative posts or in management of their own estates. They formed part of the movement for rationalizing procedures that was influencing many areas of life in the twelfth and thirteenth centuries, ranging from better accounting methods for estate stewards to rejection of the ordeal as a mode of proof. They were in the vanguard of the movement for rationalization, as seen in their eagerness to curtail the ordeal and encourage the inquest even before the Fourth Lateran Council's ban in 1215. Paul Hyams has shown that canonists' and theologians' learned arguments are not the full explanation for rejection of the ordeal by the secular courts.[10]

Although surviving evidence does not permit us to piece together any consistent social theory held by the justices, nothing points toward startlingly new tendencies. Works such as Richard fitz Neal's *Dialogus de Scaccario*, which reflect views of the circle of *curiales* from which many justices came, show acceptance of conventional views of society. Fitz Neal exhibited prejudices against those engaged in trade, *burgenses* or *cives*. Merchants seemed to him to be greedy; they 'strive with all their strength and by every means to multiply their possessions'.[11] At

---

[7] *C.R.R.*, 13: 96, no. 414; *Glanvill*, ii, 16, pp. 33–4.

[8] Earliest example, *C.R.R.*, 5: 49, Michaelmas term 1207.

[9] *C.R.R.*, 8: 198, order to a sheriff to outlaw those who resist with force the implementation of the verdict of an assize of novel disseisin. *C.R.R.*, 10: 52, on the question of a legacy; p. 148, plea to proceed in county court in spite of its being placed at Westminster by the king's command; 12: 62, no. 344, inquest goes against a tenant, but he may implead the complainants *secundum legem terre*, if he wishes.

[10] Paul R. Hyams, 'Trial by ordeal: the key to proof in the early common law', in *On the Laws and Customs of England, Essays in Honor of Samuel E. Thorne*, eds. Morris S. Arnold, Thomas A. Green, Sally A. Scully, and Stephen D. White (Chapel Hill, N. Car., 1981), pp. 90–126.

[11] *Dial. de Scac.*, p. 109; translation *Eng. Hist. Docs.*, 2: 555–6.

the same time they seek to hide their wealth, not displaying it openly and proudly as would the landed classes. Richard felt this justified their harsher treatment under the law of the Exchequer. A knight whose chattels were to be sold for debt, however, could retain his horse, 'lest having attained the rank of knight, he should be compelled to go on foot'. If he actually practised the profession of warrior, he could also keep his armour. [12]

Royal officials could urge compassion for the poor on occasion. By the twelfth century, the monarch's obligation to protect the poor from oppression by the powerful had become almost a cliché among writers on kingship. [13] Martin of Pattishall combined compassion with practicality, as seen in his letter to the chancellor concerning the 1226 eyre. He notes that he had heard many complaints because two of his colleagues held sessions at harvest time, when the poor were busy gathering their crops. Because of *gravamina pauperum*, he would adjust his schedule to free them from the burden of attending the courts during the harvest season. [14] Some of the justices who must be placed among the greediest and most ambitious of royal servants made special provision for the poor by their ecclesiastical benefactions, six of them by founding hospitals. In addition, several gave gifts for maintenance of paupers in already existing almshouses. [15] This concern for the poor carried over into their judicial work. Especially during the minority of Henry III, justices' pardons of amercements 'on account of poverty' appear on the plea rolls. [16] Yet such sympathy for the poor did not lead to any radical rulings in their favour. In fact, the effect of judgments defining villein status was to reduce the rights of the nonfree, not enhance them. [17]

Although knights often appear in medieval and modern

---

[12] *Dial. de Scac.*, p. 111; *Eng. Hist. Docs.*, 2: 557.

[13] Paul R. Hyams, *King, Lords and Peasants in Medieval England: the common law of villeinage in the twelfth and thirteenth centuries* (Oxford, 1980), p. 261.

[14] P.R.O., SC 1/6, no. 76; printed by Sayles, *Select Cases*, 1: cxlii.

[15] E.g. Richard of Ilchester's provision for doubling the number of poor fed by a Winchester hospital from 100 to 200, David Knowles and R. Neville Hadcock, *Medieval religious houses, England and Wales* (London, 1971), p. 404; or Hubert Walter's gifts to hospitals at Canterbury and Reading, Young, *Hubert Walter*, p. 163. William Briwerre set aside a manor for his foundation at Mottisfont to provide food and clothing for an additional four paupers, *Monasticon*, 6: 480–3.

[16] Turner, *King and his courts*, pp. 155–6.   [17] Hyams, *King, lords and peasants*.

literature as either ruthless plunderers of Church property or superstitious purchasers of salvation with bribes, they were not incapable of genuine religious feeling.[18] It is next to impossible to probe their minds, but their ties of family, friendship, and patronage to saintly men tell something of their religious sentiments. Richard of Herriard, a hardworking justice under Richard I and John, stood surety for a debt owed by John of Ford, abbot of the Cistercian house and author of devotional works.[19] Signs of some depth of devotion among the clerics on the bench are easier to find, for example, Richard Barre's compilation of a book of biblical quotations.

We can deduce from the justices' religious benefactions that they were conventionally pious. Evidence survives of gifts by about half the justices to monasteries and churches. They range from William Briwerre's foundation of four religious houses to Adam fitz William's gift of a silk cloth to St Albans.[20] Historians have long noted that administrators of the Angevin kings favoured the Austin canons and Premonstratensians for their foundations.[21] Nine of the royal justices founded a total of sixteen new religious houses, and of these, five were Augustinian houses and three Premonstratensian.[22] Four founders were men

[18] E.g., Fred Cazel, jr., 'Religious motivation in the biography of Hubert de Burgh', in Derek Baker, ed., *Religious motivation: biographical and sociological problems for the Church historian, Studies in Church History*, 15 (Oxford 1978).

[19] A debt of 10 marks owed to William of Wrotham in 1200, *C.R.R.*, 1: 240. On John of Ford's career, see Russell, *Dict. of Thirteenth Century Writers*, pp. 62–3.

[20] For Briwerre's foundations, see below note 22. For Adam's gift, *Chron. Maj.*, 6: 390.

[21] Richard Mortimer, 'Religious and secular motives for some English monastic foundations', *Studies in Church History*, 15: 80–4.

[22] William Briwerre founded Torre Abbey, Premonstratensian; Mottisfont, Austin canons; Dunkeswell Abbey, Cistercian; and the hospital of St John, Bridgewater. Geoffrey fitz Peter founded Shouldham Priory, Gilbertine canonesses; and a hospital at East Tilbury, Essex. Glanvill founded Butley Priory, Austin canons; Leiston, Premonstratensian, and a hospital at West Somerton, Norfolk. Hubert Walter founded the abbey of West Dereham, Premonstratensian, and was planning at the time of his death a Cistercian house at Wolverhampton. Ralph of Norwich founded the Austin priory of Chetwode; and William de Warenne founded Wormegay Priory, another Augustinian house. Richard of Ilchester founded Hartland Abbey, Austin canons, and a hospital at Winchester. Henry of London founded a hospital in Dublin, and Thomas of Moulton founded one outside Boston at Skirbeck. See Aubrey Gwyn and R. Neville Hadcock, *Medieval religious houses: Ireland* (London, 1970); and Knowles and Hadcock, *Medieval religious houses, England and Wales*.

of the highest rank, including three justiciars. The fourth, William Briwerre, was the most lavish in his generosity. He used much of the land and wealth he accumulated to found four new religious houses, among them Torre Abbey, the richest Premonstratensian abbey in England.[23] A fifth founder, William de Warenne, had baronial standing though not in the inner corps of King John's officials. He founded Wormegay Priory in Norfolk, a house of Austin canons.[24] The least prominent founder was Master Ralph of Norwich, whose foundation at Chetwode, Buckinghamshire, never had more than three or four canons.[25] A new means of providing perpetual prayer was appearing in the thirteenth century: the chantry chapel. Three of Henry III's justices – Ralph Hareng, Robert of Lexington, and Stephen of Segrave – maintained chantries.[26]

Stephen of Segrave prepared for his death with pious gifts before he returned to his old refuge at St Mary de Pré, Leicester, to die in the habit of an Austin canon.[27] Although Stephen was rich in lands, he never parted with any to endow a new monastic foundation. Nonetheless, Matthew Paris, impressed with the good death that Stephen made, gave him an obituary more kindly in tone than those he penned for other royal justices.[28]

Evidence survives for gifts to existing houses by at least sixteen other justices. They made grants mainly to houses of monks or nuns which stood near their estates. Sometimes they were family foundations, where tombs of their kinsmen lay, and where they would be laid to rest.[29] Several made gifts to the

---

[23] Foundation charter, P.R.O., E 164/19, ff. 4–5ᵛ; his wife's charter, f. 9; cf. *Monasticon*, 6, pt. 2: 923–5.

[24] *Monasticon*, 6: 591; *Early Yorks Chtrs.*, 8: 32; *V.C.H., Norf.*, 2: 407.

[25] *H.M.C. Reports*, 78, 1: 268–9; *V.C.H., Bucks*, 1: 380; 4: 165–6.

[26] The Harengs maintained a chantry chapel at Thrupp, Oxon., which Ralph gave to Oseney Abbey, c. 1221/9, *Oseney Cart.*, 4: 131, no. 91A. Robert of Lexington endowed a chantry at Southwell, Notts, *Rufford Chtrs.*, 1: xcv. The abbot of Leicester issued charters for a canon to say mass perpetually for Stephen of Segrave and his relatives, supported by Stephen's gifts., Nichols, *Hist. and Antiq. Leics*, 2, pt. 1: 115, cal. of B.L. MS. Harl. 4748.

[27] He gave the Cistercians of Stoneleigh, Warwicks, the manor of Bericote, *V.C.H., Warwicks*, 5: 105. He gave Leicester Abbey a wood in Warwicks, Dugdale, *Baronage*, p. 672.   [28] *Chron. Maj.*, 4: 169.

[29] E.g. Michael Belet's gifts to the Austin canons of East Rudham, Norfolk, a house founded by his wife's family, Coxford Cart., ed. H.W. Saunders, *Original Papers of Norf. and Norwich Archaeol. Soc.*, 17 (1909–10): 286, 297, 356. Or Roger fitz Reinfrid's gifts to St Mary Clerkenwell, where his mother and his wife were to be buried, *Cart. of St Mary Clerkenwell*, pp. 67–8, no. 101; 70–1, no. 105.

religious houses which they selected as the sites for their tombs.[30] The judges' grants reflect family feeling as much as religious devotion. Sometimes the signs of love and respect for kin are still touching. For example, Michael Belet provided funds for the Austin canons to keep a lamp perpetually burning over his mother's tomb, a light which was extinguished in the sixteenth century if not earlier.

Religious benefactions sometimes showed devotion to the monarch as well as to the founder's family. Foundation charters of William Briwerre's religious houses always solicit the residents' prayers for the souls of Henry II and his sons as well as for the founder and his family. At a chapel Briwerre maintained at Northampton a special mass was to be said for the souls of the four kings he had served.[31] He gave a gold chalice to Worcester Cathedral on its restoration in 1217 following a fire.[32] Perhaps Worcester held a special place in his thoughts because it sheltered King John's tomb. A lesser-ranking royal servant, Ralph Hareng, took care to state that his 1222 grant to the nuns of Godstow was for the souls of Henry III and King John as well as for his own and his family's souls.[33]

Many clerics in the king's service were men of little or no spirituality. They, like other ecclesiastics throughout the Middle Ages, ignored the conflict between the Church's ideal of withdrawal from the world and their own active lives in service to a secular prince. Obviously their worldly offices distracted them from ministering to the souls entrusted to their care, yet few felt any strain from the conflicting demands upon their time. William of Raleigh's request to Robert Grosseteste, bishop of Lincoln, that he institute to a church 'a mere boy, still learning his letters' shows how seriously he estimated a parson's spiritual duties.[34] Raleigh had asked the wrong person, for Grosseteste was preoccupied with the clergy's responsibility for

---

[30] Simon of Pattishall's gifts to Pipewell Abbey, the site for his burial, *Cal. Chtr. Rolls*, 1: 205; William de Warenne's gifts to the priory of St Mary Overy, Southwark, which he chose for his burial, *Monasticon*, 6: 169, 171; *Early Yorks Chtrs.*, 8: 33; and Robert of Lexington's selection first of Newstead Priory and then of the Cistercian house of Rufford for his burial, with gifts to each, *Rufford Chtrs.*, 1: xcv.

[31] *The Percy Chartulary*, ed. M.T. Martin, Surtees Soc., 117 (1911): 384.

[32] *Annales Wigorn.*, in *Annales Mon.*, 4: 409, 418.

[33] Andrew Clark, ed., *The English register of Godstow Nunnery*, Early Eng. Text Soc., 142 (1911): 84–5, no. 86.   [34] *Letters of Robert Grosseteste*, p. 63, no. 17.

cure of souls. He opposed use of ecclesiastical benefices to maintain clerks in the king's service. Grosseteste and other reformers saw that it led to the twin abuses of pluralism and absenteeism, but their complaints had little effect on the pluralists' consciences. While some royal clerks were scrupulous enough to seek papal dispensations for holding benefices in plurality, others did not. Henry III himself did request from the pope dispensations for Pattishall, Raleigh, Lexington, and William of York.[35]

Canons from the earliest councils had urged the clergy to shun the courts of princes. Theologians and canon lawyers constantly sought to limit the secular activities of ecclesiastics, particularly their involvement in judgments of blood.[36] Even William of Raleigh once he became a bishop presided over councils forbidding such worldly involvements, although as a royal justice he had handed down the death sentence many times. Henry III, opposing Raleigh's candidacy for the bishopric of Winchester, pointed out that William had killed more men with his tongue than a rival candidate had with his sword.[37] Robert of Lexington shocked the saintly Robert Grosseteste not merely by trying capital cases but by doing so on Sunday, the Lord's day.[38] Nothing indicates that pronouncing the death penalty troubled Raleigh's or Lexington's consciences. Neither they nor other clerics hesitated to accept appointments as justices of gaol delivery, when they knew that hanging would be the fate of most men they tried.[39]

It is not necessary to think that the royal justices were without conscience, however. They could sometimes show compassion for the poor, as we have seen. Scattered throughout the plea rolls are innumerable instances of the justices settling suits *per consilium curiae*, disregarding the strict letter of the law in favour of a more merciful solution. For example, they might allow a plea to go forward even though they had some grounds for dismissing it, such as a flaw in the writ.[40] An increase in such judg-

---

[35] *Cal. Papal Reg.*, 1: 102, 168. See also Thompson, 'Pluralism in the mediaeval Church', pp. 35–73.

[36] Turner, 'Clerical judges in English secular courts', pp. 95–8.

[37] *Chron. Maj.*, 3: 494.   [38] *Letters of Grosseteste*, pp. 266–8, no. 84.

[39] Turner, 'Clerical judges', pp. 91–2.

[40] *C.R.R.*, 6: 80–1, 171. The abbot of St Albans sought the court's consideration whether he ought to respond to a writ issued in the justiciar's name although the king was in England. The justices allowed the plea to go forward.

ments seems noticeable on the rolls from the minority of Henry III.[41] Although justices of the Bench heard fewer criminal cases than the itinerant justices, they did hear enough to leave evidence of their efforts to protect the rights of the accused. In 1219, they adjudged the appeal of several men by an informer to be invalid because the sheriff and others testified that they were *legales homines*. The next year they dismissed an appeal against a man who was so old that he could hardly walk.[42]

It seems that itinerant justices, who were often prominent local men, not professional civil servants, were more likely to express independent views. Occasionally individual judges sought to dissociate themselves from their colleagues' decisions. The king's council in 1219 found that a group of itinerant justices had wrongly and unjustly hanged two suspects. The head of the party of itinerant justices, Jocelin of Wells, had absented himself when sentence was given. Evidently, he had not wanted to share responsibility for a judgment that he regarded as a miscarriage of justice.[43]

Not all the itinerant justices were so scrupulous, and a glance at the *curia regis* rolls reveals a dozen or so instances of carelessness or incompetence by them which the justices of the Bench took care to correct. Hugh Bardolf once allowed his chaplain and constable to hear a case in his absence. Because they had wrongly allowed the assize to proceed, even though the tenants had vouched a warrantor and presented charters, the justices at Westminster had the task of correcting their careless act and restoring the victims to their property.[44] One of the justices of gaol delivery in the summer of 1234 came to the justices at Westminster to tell of his disagreement with his colleagues' judgment concerning nine prisoners held for homicide.[45] About

---

[41] E.g. *Rolls for Lincs and Worcs*, p. 490, no. 991, a poor widow technically guilty of a novel disseisin is assisted in securing rent and arrears due from the land she took. See also pp. 92–3, no. 218; p. 381, no. 789; p. 526, no. 1052; and pp. 530–1, no. 1061, for other illustrations of the justices' use of their discretion.

[42] *C.R.R.*, 8: 142, where the informer was ordered hanged, and p. 270. Also the abbot of Waltham was found in mercy for forcing men to undergo the ordeal of water *contra consuetudinem regni*, 8: 41–2.

[43] *C.R.R.*, 8: 80–1. As an ecclesiastic, Jocelin had a legitimate excuse for absenting himself from a 'judgment of blood'. In 1227, the council saved a Scotswoman from a less dire fate; they acquitted her of petty larceny *quia justiciarii itinerantes erraverunt*, *C.R.R.*, 12: 248, no. 1217.

[44] *C.R.R.*, 3: 87, 97. [45] *C.R.R.*, 15: 248, no. 1089, John de Braitoft.

the same time itinerant justices were amerced for hearing an assize of darrein presentment after a lapse of six months and in spite of an essoin made by the tenant. They pleaded ignorance, and their amercement was remitted, 'because they had acted through ignorance rather than malice'.[46] Especially were commissions of amateur justices appointed to take a single assize likely to make mistakes which justices of the Bench had to correct.[47] Examples of errors by the justices at Westminster themselves are far less frequent. The first correction by the justices *coram rege* of an error made by the justices of the Bench came in 1236. The judges were summoned before King Henry III, where they acknowledged that they had proceeded wrongly, 'But that they did not know how better to proceed in the matter.'[48]

Despite occasional cases of incompetence, and as we shall see, some venality, the justices generally displayed a strong sense of responsibility. The plea rolls are rarely eloquent, but the account of a case in 1226 does express well their sense of the monarch's – and his judges' – responsibility for justice. Two men were called to answer why they were impeding the sheriff of Lincolnshire and his deputies in their work of holding shire and wapentake courts. The justices asked of them, 'Why do they not permit right to be done to those who complain of injuries, as the king is bound and wishes that full right should be done by him and his bailiffs, according to the custom of the realm to all in the kingdom concerning injuries and wrongs done to them?'[49]

2 THE JUSTICES' VIEWS ON KINGSHIP

We can hardly perceive the justices' political philosophy from the plea rolls. Yet a wide field of sources does allow us to winnow out their thoughts on kingship. Feudal societies based on personal relationships between individuals and on private rights had lost sight of the Roman *respublica*, the abstraction of the state. The early Angevins' royal justices had little sense of serving the 'public power' of the Roman tradition or the native concept of 'community of the realm'. In the Becket conflict, Henry

---

[46] *C.R.R.*, 15: 368, no. 1429.
[47] E.g., *C.R.R.*, 16: 237, no. 1263. See also Sutherland, *Novel Disseisin*, p. 62, for other references.
[48] *Br. Note Book*, 3: 179–80, no. 1166.   [49] *C.R.R.*, 12: 461, no. 2312.

II's defenders had used the phrase 'public power' less than his enemies, although the phrase does occur in the *Dialogus de Scaccario*.[1] The king and his advantage had more meaning for the royal justices than such abstract concepts. In their work of doing justice, they had no sense of being set apart from other branches of royal government; they were men 'who approached their task from the point of view of the organizer, the higher civil servant'.[2] The views expressed in *Glanvill*, the *Dialogus*, and *Bracton* reflect the feelings of other professional royal servants serving as judges.

These writers reflect medieval confusion about the character of kingship. They easily lost their way in the thicket of medieval political thought with its underbrush growing up from tangled Christian, Roman, Germanic, and feudal roots. They were convinced that the royal power came from God alone, and that the king was responsible to God, not to man, but they felt uneasy about the lack of limitations. *Glanvill*, for example, in the Prologue repeats the Roman law maxim *quod principi placet legis habere vigorem*. The author later stated his concept of kingship in another way: 'For the king can have no equal, much less a superior', a statement echoed in *Bracton*. Yet throughout the two treatises, the laws are described as made by the king with the advice of his great men.[3] Richard fitz Neal, however, indicated his acceptance of the Roman law doctrine that the king could issue legislation on his own initiative 'under the compulsion of necessity and for the peace of the realm'. Fitz Neal also had an exalted view of kingship coming from Christian tradition; he defended the doctrine that kings were accountable only to God.[4] In the *Dialogus*, he took pains to assure his pupil that the laws of the Exchequer were not arbitrary, but he admitted that the king sometimes acted arbitrarily. He acknowledged that Henry II denied justice: 'For to some he shows the fullness of justice freely out of regard for a service rendered solely out of

[1] Beryl Smalley, *Becket Conflict and the Schools*, p. 229. *Dial. de Scac.*, p. 100; the translation in *Eng. Hist. Docs.*, 2: 552, is clearer.
[2] T.F.T. Plucknett, 'The Relations between Roman Law and English Common Law down to the Sixteenth Century', *Univ. of Toronto Law Jl.*, 3 (1939–40): 32. Cf. C.A.F. Meekings' view that they approached their work in the same way as did estate stewards, who held their lords' courts, *Crown pleas of Wilts eyre, 1249*, p. 7.   [3] *Glanvill*, pp. 2, 28, 84, 167; *Bracton*, f. 1, 2: 19; f. 107, 2: 305.
[4] *Dial. de Scac.*, pp. 1–3, 101–2.

charity; but to others, by the law of human circumstance, he will not yield for love or money.'[5]

Medieval English judges were special representatives of the king, who was the source of all secular justice in the kingdom. King John recognized their position, when he sent a writ ordering a plea to proceed in spite of letters of protection which one of the parties had presented seeking to have the suit postponed for hearing before the king or justiciar. John stated, 'All pleas that are held before the justices of the Bench are understood to be held before the lord king or the chief justiciar.'[6] *Bracton* stressed the king's need to choose capable men to be judges, since they were acting in his place. Henry III may have been echoing the treatise when he said in 1249·of the duties of royal justices, 'To root out [evil] I have appointed wise men that, together with me, they may rule and guard my realm. I am but a single man; I neither want, nor am able, to bear the burdens of the whole realm without assistance.'[7] Judges, according to *Bracton*, should be 'wise and God-fearing men in whom there is the truth of eloquence, who shun avarice which breeds covetousness'. He urged wisdom as a necessary quality for justices, and he warned of divine punishment for those guilty of evil judging.[8]

As agents of a Christian prince, judges had to render justice impartially to all; yet they were servants of a living, breathing man whose property and privileges they had to protect. Obviously, judges were faced with dual and sometimes conflicting duties: to render justice impartially and, at the same time, to

---

[5] *Dial. de Scac.*, p. 120. This translation is from *Eng. Hist. Docs.*, 2: 564. Fitz Neal also admitted the arbitrary nature of the forest law, pp. 59–60.

[6] *C.R.R.*, 2: 462. In 1214, however, when royal letters of protection were again presented, the justices were uncertain about proceeding and postponed the plea until they could consult the king and the justiciar, *C.R.R.*, 7: 83. During the minority of Henry III, the justices proceeded with an assize despite letters of protection presented by Pandulf, newly elected bishop of Norwich, *C.R.R.*, 9: 382. Such letters of protection conflicted with the provision in *Magna Carta* (article 13 of the 1217 ed.) that assizes should be held in the county to which they related, *C.R.R.*, 10: 7, 140.

[7] *Chron. Maj.*, 5: 57. For an account by Henry III of the duties of itinerant justices, see his letter to the pope in which he described 'discreet and noble judges dispatched to certain parts of our land to hear and correct the quarrels which many brought to our ears concerning the rapine and spoliation of their lands and goods, according to the custom prevailing in our kingdom and approved since olden times', *Royal Letters*, 1: 225.

[8] *Bracton*, f. 2, 2: 21–2; f. 108, 2: 306–7.

protect the king's interests. They had not learned to separate the king and the crown, the living individual who is their ruler and the impersonal institution of monarchy. A concept of the 'crown' with interests which they ought to protect apart from the personal, private interests of the king would prevent conflicts in treating suits to which the monarch was a party. *Bracton* made this conflict clear, without recognizing it himself, in his account of the justices' oath. His is the first detailed description of their oath, although it was in use long before his treatise was written. The *justicias errantes* named in 1176 had taken an oath 'to preserve the king's interest in the regions to which they were sent.[9] According to *Bracton*, the justices swore to do right to rich and poor alike, to carry out the articles of the eyre, and to do what is right and just in hearing pleas of the crown. But the treatise states that after the oath, 'Let each of them be instructed to promote, to the best of his ability, the advantage of the lord king.'[10] The problem of impartiality in suits to which the king was a party was one which few writers could face openly. They could only fall back on pious hopes for the king's fear of eternal punishment.

Richard fitz Neal probably represents the feeling of most royal justices that their chief responsibility was to safeguard the king's interests. In the *Dialogus*, he echoes the instructions given to the eighteen justices Henry II sent on circuit in 1176. They were authorized to hear suits involving small tenures without reference to the king, but were admonished, 'Let them, nevertheless, apply themselves to the utmost to act in the interest of the lord king.'[11] Fitz Neal's pupil made the point, 'I observe that with all your moderation you never lose sight of the king's interests.' The Treasurer felt that service to the king was a high calling, suitable for clerics, since the royal power comes from God.[12] Biographical information about royal justices indicates that several would have held similar views. For example, those justices in clerical orders who remained faithful to Henry

---

[9] Ralph de Diceto, *Ymagines*, 1: 404.   [10] *Bracton*, f. 109, 2: 309.

[11] Article 7, Assize of Northampton, Stubbs, *Select Charters*, p. 180; translation from *Eng. Hist. Docs.*, 2: 412.

[12] *Dial. de Scac.*, pp. 1, 109. Cf. p. 13, '. . . yet the purpose of all the offices [at the Exchequer] is the same, namely to watch over the King's interests, due regard being paid, however, to equity, according to the established rules of the Exchequer'.

II and John during their troubles with the Church must have shared Richard fitz Neal's sentiments.[13] Others had acquaintance with Roman law, which gave them grounds for seeking the king's interest. Certain phrases in the *Dialogus*, *Glanvill*, and chancery documents show that officials of Henry II and his sons were beginning to recognize the concept of *necessitas* or *utilitas* in Roman law, which provided justification for princes to override the letter of the law in pursuit of the common good. Roman theories of political authority proved useful to King John in his several struggles, for example, providing a theoretical justification for the thirteenth of 1207. A little later, the author of *Bracton* also recognized the ruler's overriding responsibility for the public interest or *res publica*.[14]

The royal judges often gained experience in financial posts before their appointment to the bench, and they continued to have financial functions when on eyre. Chroniclers depicted the judicial eyres as more concerned with increasing royal revenues than with rendering justice. Roger Howden's complaint of the cost of the 1198 eyre, 'By these and other vexations, whether just or unjust, the whole of England from sea to sea was reduced to poverty', was echoed by later chroniclers.[15] Payments recorded on the pipe rolls reveal that inhabitants of the shires shared this view. For example, the men of Leicester paid eighty marks in 1180 to be free from a visitation by itinerant justices,

---

[13] E.g. John of Oxford, Geoffrey Ridel, Richard of Ilchester, and Richard Barre during the Becket controversy, or Henry of London, archdeacon of Stafford during the Canterbury succession crisis.

[14] G.L. Harriss, *King, Parliament, and public finances in medieval England to 1369* (Oxford, 1975), pp. 20–1. Such terminology is rare in the plea rolls, though we do find in Nov. 1194 a disseisin described as *in lesionem coronae domini Regis Ricardi*, *Rot. Cur. Reg.*, 1: 31; cf. *Three rolls of the King's Court*, p. 50. On the phrases *utilitas* and *necessitas* in twelfth and thirteenth-century England, see the works of Gaines Post, *Studies in Medieval legal thought*, and 'Status Regis', *Studies in Med. and Ren. Hist.* (Univ. of Nebraska, 1964), 1: 1–103. See *Bracton*, f. 6, 2: 34.

[15] *Roger Howden*, 4: 62. The Dunstable annalist recorded cryptically that when the itinerant justices came to Cornwall in 1233 everyone fled to the woods in fear, *Annales Mon.*, 3: 135. This story has become a 'stock example of the eyre's unpopularity', but the situation was unusual because no eyre had been held in Cornwall for over thirty years. C.A.F. Meekings, 'The Eyre *ad omnia placita*', unpublished paper read at the Anglo-American Conference of Historians, July 1954. Matt. Paris wrote of the justices on the 1240–1 eyre, 'Under the pretence of justice, they collected a huge sum for the use of a king who squandered everything', *Chron. Maj.*, 4: 51.

and in 1194 men of several shires offered fines 'for kindly treatment' by the justices.[16] The justices recognized a duty to increase royal revenues, and complaints against their extortions were oftentimes due not so much to their own greed as to their excessive zeal in promoting the king's interest. Examples are not hard to find in the records of King John's reign in which judges allowed the king's material need to outweigh immaterial standards of equity.[17] This enthusiasm for raising royal revenues can be seen in a letter by one of Henry III's justices. William of York's letters to his patron, the royal chancellor, 1226–8, are rare evidence for the thoughts of a royal justice at the beginning of his career. They indicate pride in his part in raising royal revenues; he noted that his eyre was producing forty marks a day for the king.[18]

The plea rolls offer evidence of the justices' concern for protecting the king's interests. Although they knew that most cases should proceed *secundum legem et consuetudinem Angliae*, at the same time they recognized the reality of the royal *voluntas*. Old notions of the 'tutorial' character of the ruler meant that justice could be seen not as a right but as a royal boon to be given or denied as the king saw fit. *Glanvill* describes the grand assize as a *regale beneficium*, 'granted to the people by the goodness of the king'.[19] Justices must have been uncertain where law and custom left off and the king's will began.[20] For example, the law of inheritance for feudal tenures was still uncertain where the eldest son did not survive, and the king as overlord granted fees to whatever relative he chose, sometimes ignoring the claims of closer kin. Because the monarch was the source of justice, he had a necessary role in the work of the courts. The justices

---

[16] *Pipe Roll 26 Hen. II*, p. 101.
[17] *C.R.R.*, 1: 438, pleas dismissed because the tenant was sending two knights overseas in the king's service; 4: 183, judgment for the defendant because he had offered 20s for a speedy judgment, although the plaintiff essoined himself *de ultra mare*; 7: 20, rival claimants encouraged to outbid one another in offering oblations until those offering more – 35 marks – had their right recognized.
[18] Meekings, *Studies*, article 5: 497, no. ii; 499, no. iv; 503, no. vi.
[19] *Glanvill*, ii, 7; p. 28.
[20] J.C. Holt, *Magna Carta*, p. 90; Walter Ullmann, *Principles of Government and Politics in the Middle Ages* (London, 1961), p. 156; and *Law and Politics in the Middle Ages* (Ithaca, N.Y., 1975), p. 58.

recognized his role, and they sometime marked cases *loquendum cum rege*.[21]

Many suits touched the king in his capacity as feudal lord, and the justices sought to safeguard his interests. When John de Braose was making a final concord in 1221, regaining his grandfather's honour of Bramber which King John had confiscated, the justices warned him that, 'as he loves his residence on the king's land, to seek no means whereby harm may come to the king there'.[22] The justices were careful to consult the king on questions about royal grants or charters. Henry III insisted that he alone was the interpreter of royal charters, and his judges declared, 'The testimony of the lord king by charter or by word of mouth exceeds all other proof.'[23] After Henry III came of age, the justices were anxious to protect him from injury by deeds done in his name when he had been under-age. The citizens of London in 1244 maintained that whatever was done in the young Henry's name ought to stand, since 'the king had always been king from the day of his coronation'. But the justices of the London eyre replied that because the king was under-age, nothing done in his name then that prejudiced his interest should be allowed to stand.[24]

Ideally, the king had no special privileges when he was plaintiff in a suit, but in practice he had advantages. He was not bound by the ordinary forms of action, but could order inquests without writ. As the justices of Henry III stated, 'The lord king has this privilege . . . that he impleads in his court whenever he wishes by any writ, as well for plaints as for trespasses and for every kind of plea of land and debt.'[25] The justices could specify

---

[21] Turner, *King and his courts*, pp. 127–35, 157, 242.

[22] *C.R.R.*, 10: 134–5, a postponement; the actual agreement with his uncle, Reginald de Braose, is found in *C.R.R.*, 12: 533, no. 2672, Easter term 1226.

[23] *Br. Note Book*, 2: 182–3, no. 239; also *C.R.R.*, 16: 412, no. 2121. For Henry's opinion, see *Chron. Maj.*, 5: 339, where he said in 1252, 'Does he [the pope] not abrogate previously granted charters by inserting the clause *non obstante*? So also will I annul this and other charters . . .'

[24] Helena M. Chew and Martin Weinbaum, eds., *The London Eyre of 1244*, London Rec. Soc. Pubns., 6 (1970). 122, no. 300. See also *C.R.R.*, 16: 340, no. 1704; 226–7, no. 1199, for other attempts to undo acts that had injured the king during the Minority.

[25] Richardson and Sayles, *Procedure without Writ*, p. 36, no. 34. Cf. *C.R.R.*, 1: 375–6, where the court answered a litigant who demanded view of a writ that no writ was needed because the plea had begun with an inquest commanded by the king.

special juries in cases questioning royal rights, and they often directed that knights be selected. In one case, they could not contain their anger at a sheriff who was dilatory in collecting knights for a jury. The plea roll reads, 'Be it known that the sheriff acts warmly in the business of others since becoming so negligent in the king's business . . .'[26]

Twelfth and thirteenth-century justices knew that the king was a man who could do wrong. From time to time, they witnessed the king's anger; for example, he closed his courts to certain suitors because of ill will toward them. Sometimes too they heard allegations of disseisin *per voluntatem regis*. Since distraint of land was commonly used by feudal lords as a means of disciplining their tenants, it was difficult to label such royal acts unlawful. Obviously, the assize of novel disseisin did not lie against the king, and the courts offered little help to victims of royal disseisin before 1234. Then Henry III was forced to admit in a court chaired by William of Raleigh that he had wrongfully disseised one of his subjects.[27]

Yet the impact of the royal will upon the courts can be exaggerated. The justices heard hundreds of 'common pleas' each term of court, and the overwhelming majority came to a conclusion without the king's intervention. For example, some 240 pleas of dower were concluded before King John's justices without any evidence of royal interference.[28] Sometimes even in pleas concerning the king, the justices would go their own way. Early in John's reign the justices at Westminster ordered new jurors selected in a suit brought by the king, for the first picked 'were not such men as would give anything to the king or take anything away from him'.[29] Occasionally the judges can be observed disregarding the king's writ and hearing a plea he had commanded postponed.[30] The justices of Henry III adjourned an action touching the king because one of the parties was under-age, although in other pleas touching the king minority

---

[26] *C.R.R.*, 9: 232. See also Turner, *King and his courts*, pp. 117–18, 214, 216, 233.

[27] Ralph V. Turner, 'The royal courts treat disseisin by the King: John and Henry III, 1199–1240', *A.J.L.H.*, 12 (1968): 1–18.

[28] Sharon T. Ady, M.A. Thesis, (The Florida State University, 1974).

[29] *C.R.R.*, 1: 287.

[30] *C.R.R.*, 1: 194; 4: 41. Or the reverse: *C.R.R.*, 10: 148, where they sent a plea to the shire court despite its being placed at Westminster by the king's command.

was not considered an adequate excuse for postponement.[31] Actions for advowsons brought by John and Henry III can be counted. Of thirteen such actions brought by King John which can be traced through the *curia regis* rolls to their conclusion, the king won seven and lost six. Eighteen suits brought by Henry III before 1240 can be traced, and he won eleven, lost five, and divided two advowsons with their possessors.[32]

Sometimes judges' biographies supply clues to their attitudes. A look at justices' stands during the baronial rebellion against King John can indicate their sentiments about the law and the king's arbitrary acts. One longtime royal justice, one of John's 'evil counselors', was William Briwerre, as we have seen. He revealed his feelings about *Magna Carta* when he opposed its reissue in 1223 on grounds that it had been originally exacted by force. Other justices, however, may have felt differently. King John confiscated the lands of five of his professional justices and two future justices of his son because he doubted their loyalty. Of course, John's distrust is no certain evidence that they were supporters of the baronial cause; no more is their support of the rebels evidence for high principles of law and equity. Yet at least one of them, John of Guestling, was associated with the *familia* of Stephen Langton, a centre of ideological opposition to the king.

While we can only speculate on the true feelings of John's professional justices, a group of itinerant justices in the minority of Henry III pronounced their views clearly in a letter. They protested the action of the royal council in reversing one of their judgments for political expediency's sake. They stated their concept of their duty in dignified language:

Since you chose us – we did not choose ourselves – and since you appointed us in this eyre for the peace of the lord king and his kingdom, bound to do justice to one and all, rich and poor alike without respect of persons, it would seem becoming and honourable . . . that you should not so readily . . . believe evil of us. . . . We call Him as witness who is witness of our consciences and the searcher of hearts and the knower of secrets that, sitting as a tribunal, we have done nothing of our certain knowledge according to our understanding and intelligence which ought to displease God or men of good will. . . . And therefore it is not expedient for the king's honour and ours . . . [that]

---

[31] *C.R.R.*, 14: 128, no. 647, discussed in *King and his courts*, p. 222.
[32] Turner, *King and his Courts*, pp. 229–31.

we who should be judges are made contemptible in the sight of those to whom we are sent.[33]

They went on to ask that the judgment they had given 'in accordance with the due custom of the kingdom' be allowed to stand. These justices were not professional royal servants, but were important in their own right. They included Hugh of Wells, bishop of Lincoln; John Marshal, the regent's nephew; and William d'Aubigny, a leader in the late rebellion. In this period just after *Magna Carta*, the judges were taking seriously their responsibility for rendering justice impartially to all men regardless of the king's wishes. Although devoted to protecting the royal interest, they felt a duty as the king's deputies to maintain a high standard of justice.

3 THE QUALITY OF JUSTICE

The professional judiciary was in a position to direct the course of proceedings to favour the cause of some to the injury of others, if it chose. The incomplete state of English law in the twelfth and thirteenth centuries made it necessary for the justices to decide many matters on the basis of equity. As we have seen, they had discretionary power at several stages of proceedings, sharply questioning the parties before a question could be framed for a jury to answer. The justices could halt an action at an early stage by deciding that the original writ was inaccurate or inappropriate for the remedy sought.[1] Or they might rule that one of the litigants' status – for example, an excommunicate – made him ineligible to plead.

Royal justices could make summary judgments concerning defaults and essoins. *Glanvill*'s discussion of essoins indicates several points where the justices exercised discretionary powers, such as the length of time to allow for a delay.[2] The law concerning certain aspects of defaults and essoins was not

---

[33] A suit between the count of Aumale and Gilbert de Gant, *Royal Letters*, 1: 21; translation by Lady Stenton, *Rolls for Lincs and Worcs*, p. 61, no. 151.

[1] E.g. *Rolls for Lincs and Worcs*, p. 381, no. 789, a woman brought a writ of novel disseisin when she should have brought a writ of entry *cui in vita*. The court considered that she could sue in another way if she wished.

[2] *Glanvill*, 1, 27–9, 33, pp. 15–17, 21.

always clear, and the judges themselves were sometimes uncertain and had to take counsel among themselves. Both *Glanvill* and *Bracton* noted that the law concerning defaulters in pleas of land was unclear, and *Glanvill* gave the different opinions of three judges on punishments due defaulting demandants, while *Bracton* commented on the *contentio inter veteres* and *dissensus antiquorum* on the rights of tenants who lost their suits by default.[3] The Battle Abbey chronicler pictures Henry II's justices several years before *Glanvill* 'displeased at the useless vexation of the abbot and at the subterfuge of the opposing party' in delaying his appearance in court. Finally, in exasperation, they assigned him a day without allowing the possibility of any further essoin.[4]

Such uncertainties gave royal justices the right to pronounce general principles of law from time to time. For example, in 1204 the justices *coram rege* had to deal with a plea of land delayed by essoins first by a husband and then by his wife. The justices declared, 'It is not the custom that a man and his wife both should have essoins concerning the same plea when the essoins were made on different days.'[5] They were in effect declaring a general rule of law. Such statements are not common, and of the few expressions of general principles that are found, a good number come from Simon of Pattishall's rolls.[6] They are not unknown on other justices' rolls, however. William of York's party on the 1241 Surrey eyre stated clearly the law limiting women's right to bring appeals, when they rejected a woman's appeal because it was not for one of the two allowable grounds: 'the violation of her body or for the death of her husband killed within her arms'. This statement is almost identical to the one in *Bracton*.[7]

As we saw in cases touching the king's interest, justices had wide discretionary powers concerning the composition of

---

[3] *Glanvill*, i, 32, p. 20.
[4] *Chron. of Battle Abbey*, pp. 232–4. Suit between Abbot Walter and Hamo Peche concerning an advowson, c. 1164–70. This was before the assize of darrein presentment had been devised.   [5] *C.R.R.*, 3: 105.
[6] *Earliest Lincs assize rolls*, p. xxiii, nos. 404, 426, 513, 690, 764, 811. Simon was on the bench when the above statement was made as well.
[7] P.R.O. JUST.1/869, m. 3, cited by Meekings, *1235 Surrey Eyre*, p. 123. *Bracton*, f. 148; 2: 419.

juries. *Glanvill* states this clearly when discussing selection of the twelve knights for a grand assize. He wrote concerning the naming of jurors, 'It is better to rely on the discretion of the court than to insist on the settled law and custom of the court; in this way it is left to the foresight and judgment of the lord king or to his justices so to adjust this assize as to make it more practical and equitable.'[8] Any number of times, the *curia regis* rolls record measures by the justices to ensure capable and impartial jurors. They sometimes removed jurors they found to be *inutiles et indiscreti*, they varied the number of jurors, and they took care on at least one occasion to find jurors 'who are not related to either party and who know best the truth of the matter'.[9]

It is difficult to draw a line between substantive law and procedural rules in the age of *Glanvill* and *Bracton*. The English courts were so preoccupied with pleading and procedure that justices could make many decisions on such matters which might work to the advantage of one party. Yet they could also pronounce the law on substantive issues in instances where custom was not yet fixed and certain. The clearest illustration of such law-making by the justices concerns inheritance of military tenures, for their heritability was only coming to be recognized in law by the late twelfth century. An illustration is *Glanvill*'s discussion of the justices' disagreement over the succession to land when a landholder is survived, not by his eldest son, but by a younger son and a grandson born of his deceased eldest son, the so-called *casus regis*. The treatise states that some justices support the younger son's claim, while others favour the grandson.[10] *Glanvill* discussed a similar problem: who has the right to land granted by a brother to his younger brother, who then dies before his elder brother? Dispute might arise between the elder brother and his own sons concerning the inheritance, although it would seem that the land ought not revert to the grantor, for then he would be both tenant and lord. The author noted that such a problem provoked discussion among those learned in the

---

[8] *Glanvill*, ii, 12, p. 32.
[9] *C.R.R.*, 5: 69; 6: 300, 354; 8: 320. Also *C.R.R.*, 1: 376, they allowed the plaintiff to remove those jurors he reasonably could ask to be removed; and *Lincs assize rolls*, p. 57, no. 327, an assize is adjourned until 'better jurors can come'.
[10] *Glanvill*, vii, 3, pp. 77–8.

law, and that a decision was sometimes reached *de consilio curiae ita ex equitate*.[11]

Justices of the *curia regis*, then, could make decisions in the course of hearing a plea which might injure the cause of one of the parties. They might even make rules of law that would injure whole categories of the king's subjects. The judges belonged to the landholding class, and they shared its outlook. There is no reason to think that they had more advanced views than their kinsmen among the knights, unless a presumption in favour of the royal power. As Paul Hyams has recently shown, the myth that thirteenth-century royal justices adopted the Roman law principle of *favor libertatis* in cases questioning villein status has no basis. He can find no evidence that they ever bent common law rules to find in favour of freedom for alleged villeins.[12]

Did the judges make their judgments impartially, or did they divert the course of justice for personal gain and the advantage of family and friends? To answer this question, we must fill in the bare-bones outline provided by the plea rolls with detail drawn from other sources. Any accounts of a proceeding apart from the plea rolls are scarce, but monastic writers sometimes left descriptions of their houses' lawsuits which flesh out the skeletal framework of the official records. In addition, a few surviving letters give further shape to the outline. By looking at these materials, we should be able to see the judges in the round and to estimate the standard of justice they handed down.

The monks of Crowland Abbey kept a detailed record of their dispute with Spalding Priory, which dragged through the royal courts for over a decade, 1189–1202. It reveals much about the justices' conduct that the spare plea roll accounts fail to record. The judges consulted magnates present at Westminster and barons of the Exchequer about the case, and they evidently sought to give advantage to the prior of Spalding's suit. Probably the prior's powerful friends, among them the earl of Chester, can explain the justices' favouritism.[13] The Crowland chronicler accused one justice, Robert of Wheatfield, of supporting their opponents and wrongly ruling that the abbot had falsely essoined himself. Later, however, the abbot of Crowland did

---

[11] *Glanvill*, vii, 1, pp. 72–4. For cases settled *ex equitate*, see *Rolls for Lincs and Worcs*, pp. 92–3, no. 218; p. 461, no. 942; pp. 530–1, no. 1061.
[12] Hyams, *King, Lords and Peasants*, pp. 201–19.   [13] *English Justice*, p. 149.

succeed in arranging a private meeting with Simon of Pattishall and Richard of Herriard, 'so that they might consider his business favorably'.[14]

Other monastic chroniclers record instances of improprieties by the justices. Another private discussion with litigants is recorded in the *Magna Vita* of St Hugh of Lincoln; it describes a meeting between justices and one of the parties to a plea the night before judgment was to be given.[15] The susceptibility of judges to influence from the king and magnates is noted also. St Hugh's biographer describes another of his pleas, one the earl of Leicester brought against him, which the bishop expected to win. His confidence astonished his associates, for they had heard that the earl had the king's support and that of almost all the justices.[16] The monks of Kirkstall Abbey, seeking a grange from King John, had the aid of the constable of Chester *et omnes magnates curiae qui amici ejus erant*.[17] Also in King John's time, the abbot of Bury St Edmunds defended his abbey's right to two manors, presenting a charter as proof, but the charter carried no weight *quia tota curia erat contra nos*. The plea roll record confirms the monks' charge that the jurors gave no importance to the abbot's chirograph (not a charter), but based their verdict on the long possession of the claimant's father and grandfather.[18]

Monastic accounts of proceedings at the *curia regis* are obviously prejudiced and cannot be considered entirely trustworthy. An example is another episode from the biography of St Hugh of Lincoln. It supposedly shows the bishop's steadfastness in preventing a cleric from bringing an accusation of treason, which he felt to be false and which was, furthermore, a judgment of blood before a secular tribunal. Hugh repeatedly excommunicated the clerk only to have his ban lifted by Archbishop Hubert Walter, who felt that giving up the prosecution once it was set in motion would be *contra honorem regium*.[19] The *curia regis* roll account of this 1194 case shows that the cleric's appeal was

---

[14] See above, chap. 3, pt. 4, pp. 122–3.   [15] See above, chap. 3, pt. 4, p. 122.
[16] *Magna Vita Sancti Hugonis*, 2: 83–4, concerning the manor of Knighton in the suburbs of Leicester.   [17] *Monasticon*, 5: 531–2.
[18] *Chronicle of Jocelin of Brakelond*, pp. 123–4; *C.R.R.*, 1: 430, Easter 1201, pleas *coram rege*: Margaret of Cockfield, ward of Thomas de Burgh, sought the manors of Semer and Groton. She had been the ward of Bury St Edmunds, sold first to Hubert Walter, and then to Thomas de Burgh.
[19] *Magna Vita*, 2: 28–30.

not for treason, but for felony and breach of the king's peace. The accused band of murderers and robbers raised the exception of their accuser's excommunicate status in an attempt to get the appeal dismissed. Hubert Walter removed the excommunication not because the clerk enjoyed royal protection, as Hugh's biographer alleged, but in order to prevent the accused from escaping trial for serious crimes.[20] The saintly bishop of Lincoln had more interest in maintaining his discipline over members of the clergy than in seeing men accused of serious crimes stand trial.

In addition to chroniclers' complaints of bias by the justices, condemnations of them for greed were frequent in the twelfth and thirteenth centuries, reaching a climax in the time of Edward I. Did profits come to the justices beyond the opportunities their presence at the Exchequer or with the royal household offered? We must divorce ourselves from modern conceptions of judicial propriety which have no meaning in discussions of medieval judges' conduct. Royal justices' pleas sometimes came before the *curia regis* without them withdrawing from the bench. Simon of Pattishall remained sitting among the justices when one of his suits came to Westminster in 1214, although he did leave the bench in another case when his own final concord was being made.[21] As the Crowland Abbey case shows, justices were willing to meet privately with litigants to give legal advice.

Ties of dependence, family, or friendship with suitors did not embarrass medieval judges. Everyone assumed that such ties involved mutual exchange of favours, and they expected justices, like everyone else, to discharge their duty toward friends or patrons. Royal justices and their clerks even acted as attorneys for their patrons and for the king. Bishop Eustace of Ely appointed as his attorney for all pleas at Westminster in 1198 his archdeacon, the royal justice Richard Barre. Another justice, Master Eustace de Fauconberg, also acted as an attorney for the bishop of Ely near the end of Richard I's reign.[22] Thomas of Moulton acted as the king's attorney in the Rumilly inheritance case, brought against the count of Aumale, 1223–5, when Thomas was beginning his career as a royal justice. Henry III was ostensibly seeking land from the count which belonged to the inheritance of two royal wards. In fact, the two girls were in Thomas of Moulton's custody, and he had married them to his sons.[23]

As early as the time of Henry II, if not earlier, great men had written letters to *curiales* on the bench seeking their influence in suits, and the practice continued in the time of Henry II's sons and grandson. Hubert Walter, after he had retired from the justiciarship, did not hesitate to send letters to the justices on behalf of friends. He wrote them in support of Lanthony Priory's suit, 'Please expedite the prior's business so as to earn our thanks, for you know what affection we bear to the prior and his house.'[24] Later Stephen of Lexington, abbot of Savigny, Normandy, wrote more than once to his brother, asking him to look kindly toward Cistercian houses which had suits coming before him.[25]

More serious are the continuous assertions that justices accepted gifts from parties to lawsuits that they were hearing. *Bracton* warned royal justices against taking gifts, quoting with approval *Ecclesiasticus* (20: 31), 'Presents and gifts blind the eyes of judges.' And the writer reminded them that flattery and

---

[22] *C.R.R.*, 1: 33; *Rot. Cur. Reg.*, 2: 61. Fauconberg was an attorney for the abbot of St Vaast as well, *C.R.R.*, 1: 74. A Master Eustace, possibly Fauconberg, was attorney for the bishop of London in 1199, *Rot. Cur. Reg.*, 2: 35, 66. Osbert fitz Hervey's clerk was attorney for Butley Priory in 1194, *Rot. Cur. Reg.*, 1: 44. John of Guestling's clerk Anselm *Lascivus* acted as his attorney, *C.R.R.*, 4: 131. And in 1219, 'a certain clerk of the justices' was attorney for the prior of Newstead, *Rolls for Lincs. and Worcs.*, p. 437, no. 910. For justices acting as attorneys for the king, see *Select Cases*, 1, cx–cxii.

[23] Turner, 'William de Forz, count of Aumale', pp. 244–5.

[24] P.R.O., SC 1/1 (19), cited by Cheney, *Hubert Walter*, p. 110. For another letter, see p. 109. See also *C.R.R.*, 1: 279, where he insisted that a plea brought by a youth in his custody proceed, arguing that according to custom it could go forward even though the boy was under-age.

[25] Bruno Griesser, ed., *Reg. Epist. Stephani de Lexinton*, in *Analecta Sacri Ordinis Cisterc.*, 2 (1946): no. xliv; 8 (1952): no. lvii, letters on behalf of the house at Stanley, Wilts. Also 8: no. clxi, letter on behalf of the canons of St Barbe-en-Auge, Normandy.

immaterial favors were as much gifts as material goods.[26] As we
have seen, justices had numerous ways in which they could
influence the result of a plea without pronouncing openly a false
judgment. Yet it is quite possible that competing gifts from
both sides to suits tended to neutralize their effect, and that
they failed to influence the justices significantly.[27]

Royal justices did not consider it improper to accept the hospitality of great monastic houses or prominent county families
when they made their eyres, even though their hosts might have
suits coming before them.[28] Among the records of St Augustine's Abbey, Canterbury, are plans – *informationes* – to win the
goodwill of the justices on the 1313–14 Kent eyre.[29] The monks
presented them with weekly rations of bread, wine and ale, and
less frequent gifts of wood and straw. The manual also instructed
the monks to invite the justices and their clerks to dinner once
or twice during the eyre. St Augustine's was at some disadvan-
tage because the head of the party was not residing with them,
but at St Gregory's Priory. In addition, the instructions called
for gifts to be offered to the leader of the justices on his arrival
and, if he refused them, they should be offered again at the end
of the eyre. Although this evidence is late, similar plans to enter-
tain judges must have appeared almost as soon as eyres became
regular events in county life, about a century and a half earlier.
No one would have questioned the judges' propriety in accepting such hospitality.

Larger gifts raise more serious questions of propriety. High-
ranking *curiales* could offer influence with the king, and they
obtained rich reward from petitioners. Grants of land from
those with shaky hereditary claims to lordships made to such
figures as William Briwerre illustrate the practice of 'pay-offs'.[30]

---

[26] *Bracton*, f. 2, 2: 21; f. 106b, 2: 302–3.
[27] Frank Pegues, 'A monastic society at law', *E.H.R.*, 87 (1972): 560.
[28] Meekings, *Crown Pleas of Wilts eyre*, pp. 13–14, for the hospitality of the bishop
of Winchester. The Dunstable chronicle in *Annales Mon.*, 3: 174, notes two
itinerant justices at Dunstable for two days *ad custum prioris*. Then in 1286, the
prior of Dunstable spent £33 on the Bedford eyre, although the chronicle
does not itemize the expenses, *Annales Mon.*, 3: 335. An English priory of Bec
paid 55s 2d for the expenses of an itinerant justice and 3s for his men in 1288–
9, Marjorie Chibnall, ed., *Select Documents of the English Lands of the Abbey of Bec*,
Royal Hist. Soc., Camden 3rd ser., 73 (1951): 129, 133.
[29] Pegues, 'Monastic Society', pp. 553–60.   [30] See chap. 4, pt. 4, p. 181.

One of the opposing parties claiming patronage of a church might promise presentation to one of the justices in exchange for his assistance.[31] The specialist justices, such as Simon of Pattishall, accepted grants of land or, in the case of clerics, presentations to churches from barons, bishops, and religious houses, presumably in return for legal advice.[32] Surviving financial accounts of magnates or monastic houses date from no earlier than the mid thirteenth century. By that time, the new evidence makes clear that they were paying regular pensions to royal justices, causing the problem of judicial corruption to merge with the larger one of retainers. Public criticism of their acceptance of retaining fees first appeared among the barons' complaints against Henry III which they submitted to Louis IX in 1264, and it mounted during the fourteenth century, prompting Parliament to make periodic attempts at reform.[33]

Yet there was a line – however shadowy – between acceptable gifts from litigants and unacceptable favours or bribes. John of Salisbury conceded that judges might receive gifts so long as they did not 'shamelessly extort' them.[34] Apparently gifts of food and drink or firewood for use at once were always acceptable, even to judges in the ecclesiastical courts.[35] Judges regularly received gifts for 'expediting' pleas as late as the seventeenth century, as Sir Francis Bacon's impeachment proves.[36]

[31] E.g. Richard of Ilchester and the churches of Luton and Houghton, *Gesta Abb. S. Albani*, 1: 124; Martin of Pattishall and the church of Rampton, Notts; and Robert of Nottingham and the church of Stoke Goldington, Bucks, Meekings, *Studies*, article 10: 135.

[32] *Select cases*, 1: lxxvi–lxxviii; 7 (Selden Soc., 74 for 1971): xxv. See Edmund King, *Peterborough Abbey 1086–1310* (Cambridge, 1973), pp. 133–4, for a late-thirteenth-century example, Elias of Beckingham.

[33] R.E. Treharne and I.J. Sanders, eds., *Documents of the Baronial Movement of Reform and Rebellion 1258–1267*, Oxford Medieval Texts (Oxford, 1973), pp. 270–3. Documents associated with the arbitration of St Louis, Jan. 1264, no. 37C. See also J.R. Maddicott, 'Law and lordship: royal justices as retainers in thirteenth and fourteenth-century England', *Past and Present*, Suppl. 4 (Oxford, 1978). [34] *Policraticus*, Dickinson translation, p. 117.

[35] E.g. the Provisions of Oxford or Edward I's reforms, for which see below. For ecclesiastical judges, see Richard Helmholz, 'Canonists and standards of impartiality for papal judges delegate', *Traditio*, 25 (1969): 386–404.

[36] S.F. Hockey, ed., *Account Book of Beaulieu Abbey*, Royal Hist. Soc., Camden 4th ser., 16 (1975): 257, expenses of the keeper of pleas, ca. 1269–70: *pro diversis ne [gociis exp]ediendis coram justiciariis et aliis* 67 s 6 d. For discussion of later periods, see E.W. Ives, 'The reputation of the common lawyers in English society, 1450–1550', *Univ. of Birmingham Hist. Jl.*, 7 (1960): 148–50; J.H. Baker, ed., *The Reports of Sir John Spelman*, vol. 2, Selden Soc., 94 (1978): 141–2.

By the late thirteenth century, justices sometimes crossed the line separating acceptable and unacceptable gifts, and the king had to take action. The first recorded move against a justice specifically for corruption is Henry III's removal of Henry of Bath in 1251. It seems likely that Henry of Bath's dealings in lands had conflicted with the interests of some old Midland families, and they complained that some of his transactions had been illegal. The complaints triggered charges of misconduct in office by disgruntled litigants. Although Henry may have been guilty of illegal or at least unethical conduct in his private business dealings, none of the accusations of official corruption was ever proven.[37] He had to offer a fine of 2000 marks to regain royal favour,[38] but Henry III's wrath quickly cooled, and the former justice soon found himself restored to the judiciary. By 1253 Henry of Bath had become chief justice of the court *coram rege*, and from 1256 to 1258 he was chief justice of common pleas as well.

The Henry of Bath case, then, may not signify increasing judicial corruption. One of the Provisions of Oxford in 1258, however, hints at abuses in the justices' acceptance of gifts from suitors. It declares, 'And justices shall accept no gifts except presents of bread, wine, and the like – that is, such food and drink as is customarily brought daily to the tables of important men.'[39] The strong monarchs and the active justiciars of the Angevin period doubtless kept a close watch over justices, not allowing their gift-taking to get out of bounds. The first wide scandal involving a number of justices occurred in the time of Edward I following a period of royal absence on the Continent and, of course, the lack of any chief justiciar. Edward I, following his return from Gascony in 1289, removed from office on account of corruption a number of his servants, among them ten judges, including the chief justices of King's Bench and Common Pleas. After this, Edward required his justices to swear that 'they will take nothing from anyone without permission from the King',

---

[37] Conclusion of C. A. F. Meekings, '*Coram rege* justices, 1240–1258', (unpublished paper at P.R.O.), pp. 95–104, a thorough examination of the whole Henry of Bath case. Cf. *Chron. Maj.*, 5: 213–15, 223–4; *Annales Mon.*, 4: 101.

[38] *Cal. Pat. Rolls, 1247–58*, p. 101; Fine Roll 35 Hen. III, m. 16.

[39] *Docs. of the baronial movement*, pp. 106–9, chap. 16 of the Provisions.

although he agreed that they could accept daily gifts of food and drink.[40]

All this talk of gifts must be put into context. Not until the early years of Henry III do the royal records show payments to royal justices at regular intervals, and not even then can we be sure that the king paid all his justices regular salaries.[41] One of the reforms proposed in the Provisions of Oxford was payment of adequate salaries to justices, 'so that they shall have no need to accept anything from anyone else'. Yet the justices' expenses, especially when on eyre, were heavy, not always covered fully by royal generosity. Because they received inadequate salaries, royal officials had to exploit their opportunities in order to gain a living for themselves. No one expected them to do otherwise. Public office in the Middle Ages was viewed as a licence to levy fees on the public.[42] Tales of the many advocates, clerks, ushers, and other minor functionaries crowding the papal *curia* and fleecing naive northerners make that plain.

In spite of complaints about the sale of justice, the end of the twelfth and beginning of the thirteenth centuries saw a surge of suits before the *curia regis*. By Henry III's time, the average roll of civil pleas totalled four or five hundred cases.[43] Many of these were proceedings between smallholders involving lands of little consequence, often only a few acres. Henry II's assizes, first created with landholders of knightly rank in mind, had quickly proved popular with lower-ranking freeholders.

Apparently most Englishmen found the royal justices' standard of conduct acceptable. Certainly the standard they found in the courts of the Angevin kings was no lower than that in the Church's courts, including the papal *curia* at Rome. The cost of justice in the ecclesiastical courts was notoriously high, and complaints against its price gave rise to stinging satires.[44]

[40] Powicke, *Hen. III and Lord Edward*, p. 335; also Powicke, *The Thirteenth Century*, pp. 361–6.

[41] *Select Cases*, 1: lxxi; Meekings, *Crown Pleas of Wilts Eyre*, pp. 12–13.

[42] Much of what Trevor-Roper wrote about payments of public officers in the Renaissance must have held true centuries earlier. See. H.R. Trevor-Roper, 'The General Crisis of the Seventeenth Century', in Trevor Aston, ed., *Crisis in Europe 1560–1660* (New York, 1967), p. 79.

[43] M.T. Clanchy, ed., *Civil Pleas of the Wilts Eyre, 1249*, Wilts Rec. Soc., 25 (1971): 9.

[44] For this literature, see J.A. Yunck, *The Lineage of Lady Meed* (Notre Dame, Ind., 1963).

Bishops and abbots engaged in suits at Rome could easily spend thousands of marks on salaries for proctors, fees for curial staff, and gifts for cardinals and the pope himself.[45] Frequent legislation by ecclesiastical councils forbidding judges to accept presents indicates that bribery was not uncommon. Hubert Walter, as papal legate, presided over a council at York in 1195 which prohibited ecclesiastical judges from taking money for giving judgments or for withholding, hastening, or delaying justice. Continued enactment of such canons in the thirteenth century shows that the problem lingered.[46]

The question of payments for judges perplexed canonists and theologians. Their writings make clear that within the Church the assumption was that the parties to suits should provide for ecclesiastical judges' expenses, paying something like a salary. Papal judges-delegate commonly assessed fees or procurations for their time, travel, and other costs. Theologians, such as the early thirteenth-century circle of Peter the Chanter at Paris, wrestled with the problem of payments for judges. They sought without much success to distinguish between just remuneration for expenses and the sale of justice, which they labelled simony.[47]

Not only costs but other difficulties in ecclesiastical proceedings hint that the standard of justice may actually have been higher in the English *curia regis* than at the papal *curia*. Canonical suits tended to suffer interminable delays because of abuse of the right of appeal to far off Rome. Suits in the English courts – at least the possessory assizes taken in the counties – had the advantage of speedy settlement. Donald Sutherland's study of the assize of novel disseisin notes that Bracton in the early 1250s was nearly always able to give a final judgment on the first day that an assize came before him. Sutherland concludes that justices taking assizes 'kept in general to a remarkably high standard of efficiency'.[48]

---

[45] See the examples cited by Cheney, *Innocent III and England*, pp. 109–10; and Sayers, *Papal Judges-Delegate in Canterbury*, p. 267.

[46] Sayers, p. 135; Cheney, *Hubert Walter*, p. 121. Cf. Stephen Langton's legislation, F.M. Powicke and C.R. Cheney, *Councils and Synods* (Oxford, 1964), 2: 34.

[47] John W. Baldwin, *Masters, Princes, and Merchants: the social views of Peter the Chanter and his circle* (Princeton, 1970), 1: 191–2.

[48] Sutherland, *Novel disseisin*, p. 128.

Not only was the distance between Rome and northern Europe a difficulty, but that coupled with reliance upon written documents in ecclesiastical proceedings afforded opportunities for fraudulent claims and forgeries impossible in the English courts.[49] The pope and his judges, ignorant of geography north of the Alps and unfamiliar with the circumstances surrounding cases from far away, could easily be deceived by unscrupulous petitioners. Other unscrupulous suitors could easily secure forged documents, present them to local judges-delegate as legitimate products of the papal chancery, and win wrongful judgments. Awareness of these possibilities made the popes and their lawyers hesitant to limit the right of appeal in ecclesiastical cases. Royal justices familiar with local conditions and taking oral testimony from jurors prevented such abuses in England. The justices' experience in other aspects of government and their ties to county society could be an advantage.

[49] See Stanley Chodorow, 'Dishonest litigation in the Church courts, 1140–98', in Kenneth Pennington and Robert Somerville, eds., *Law, Church and Society: Essays in honor of Stephan Kuttner* (Philadelphia, 1977), pp. 187–206.

CONCLUSION: THE JUDGES AND THEIR CRITICS

A survey of forty-nine justices from late Henry II to Henry III's personal rule shows change from a group of largely unspecialized royal servants to a professional corps. Mainly responsible for Henry II's *curia regis* were the justiciar, the treasurer, and three bishops, aided by an inner core of eight knights and clerks; this group of justices also consituted a large bloc of the barons of the Exchequer. Only two men among Henry II's justices – Godfrey de Lucy and Robert of Wheatfield – seem to have concentrated on the work of the courts. After Hubert Walter became justiciar by 1194, we still see a number of high-ranking *curiales* playing an active role in justice at Westminster, but we can also identify a group of eight lesser-ranking justices who were giving most of their attention to the courts. Most noteworthy were two, Richard of Herriard and Simon of Pattishall, both of whom remained prominent justices after Geoffrey fitz Peter succeeded to the justiciarship. Hubert Walter, who was responsible for so many administrative reforms, also deserves credit for setting up a judicial bench separate from the Exchequer board.

By the time of King John, the process of professionalization and specialization is easier to see. Only four of seventeen justices were *familiares regis*, men-of-all-work close to the king. The rest were rather obscure men, clearly concentrating on the work of justice. This is most evident with John's *coram rege* court, the only central court in England, 1209–14. The best known figure among its members was Simon of Pattishall. Although we know little of the division of labour among the justices, it seems likely that lesser-ranking men were taking charge of day-to-day administrative work connected with the courts. Herriard and Pattishall, for example, seem to have had special responsibilities, leaving the justiciar free for great matters of state.

Once the courts reopened in 1217 following the civil war, a professional judiciary takes even clearer shape. None of the thirteen justices regularly at Westminster was a great man comparable to William Briwerre or a multi-purpose *curialis* comparable to the archdeacon of Stafford. Not even the justiciar sat regularly with the Bench any longer. It becomes clear that the senior justice on the bench, a professional such as Martin of Pattishall, was actually in charge at Westminster; and that would be true of the court *coram rege* as well, once it was revived in 1234 with William of Raleigh presiding.

Scholars have long assumed that clerics predominated among the royal justices until laymen began to be recruited from the ranks of professional lawyers by the time of Edward I.[1] As we have seen, however, about half the judges were laymen (25/49), even as early as the time of Henry II. There is no reason to think that these laymen were mere window-dressing, sitting idly while clerics did the actual work. Knights brought to the bench knowledge badly needed, not only about the facts of landholding in the shires but also about the law. Many twelfth and thirteenth-century knights had a wide knowledge of English law, and they were as capable of contributing to its growth as were their clerical colleagues with learning in the written law. This is true even though only one of the laymen – Roger Huscarl – came from the ranks of professional lawyers.

Reconstruction of the lives of these early royal justices should enable us to put into perspective the criticisms their contemporaries made of them. As we have seen, contemporary preachers and scholars often lumped them with *aulici, curiales, familiares regis* as objects of scorn. Does a picture of any clarity emerge from the sources surveyed? Were the chroniclers, moralists, and satirists justified in their condemnations of the judges for ambition, sycophancy, and greed?

We must remember that for medieval thinkers who valued a stable social order ambition was not a virtue, but a vice. Many conservative thinkers considered it a sin linked closely to the sin of avarice.[2] Their complaints about the low origins of royal justices may signify uneasiness at opportunities the civil service offered to clever newcomers, which traditionally had come only

---

[1] E.g. John P. Dawson, *A History of Lay Judges* (Cambridge, Mass., 1960), p. 130; Plucknett, *Early Eng. Legal Lit.*, p. 82; Pollock and Maitland, 1: 133–5, 205.
[2] Murray, *Reason and Society in M.A.*, pp. 102–4.

to warriors of unusual courage. Ambitious the justices were! Their ambition operated on two levels, however. About 27 per cent (13 or 14/49) can be considered great *curiales* or *familiares regis* who stood at the centre of government, in constant contact with the monarch, who could attain their almost limitless ambitions. Men such as Geoffrey fitz Peter, William Briwerre, or possibly Stephen of Segrave were as much politicians as civil servants. They succeeded in advancing from middling knights to powerful magnates. Perhaps the prime example of the opportunities open to them is Hubert Walter, son of an obscure East Anglian knight, who wielded power over both the English Church and secular government in a way not to be seen again until Cardinal Wolsey in the sixteenth century.

Those justices who were not among the king's men-of-all-work, but who were giving their main attention to judicial matters, had to set more modest goals for themselves. This latter group contained some men from the fringes of knightly society, although most were securely within that level of county society that would later be labelled 'the rising gentry'. A number of justices 47 per cent (23/49) came from families with a tradition of service to the royal government: eight of thirteen under Henry II, five of fourteen under Richard I, and six of seventeen under John, while under Henry III the numbers are four of thirteen. Others were the first of their family to join the king's service, and they used their posts as pathways to higher social position. While they rarely benefited from direct royal grants, most were able to increase their holdings, slowly building up blocs of land surrounding their native villages, leaving a worthy inheritance. Plotting the holdings of a Richard of Herriard, a Simon of Pattishall, or a Ralph Hareng on the map illustrates graphically this goal. They clearly sought to push themselves and their families from the fringes into the centre of their county's society.

Justices, like all medieval men, felt a strong sense of family, and we have seen numerous examples of their efforts on behalf of *consanguines*. Obviously, they wished their sons to do well, and in a few cases sons surpassed their fathers in prominence. Three ready examples are Gilbert, son of Roger fitz Reinfrid, who rose to baronial rank and played a prominent part in the politics of John's reign; Robert, son of Richard de Mucegros, who became

Queen Eleanor's seneschal in the mid thirteenth century; and Simon of Pattishall's son, Hugh, bishop of Coventry and Lichfield. One of the most striking instances of a justice's success in introducing a kinsman to the public service is Robert of Lexington's sponsorship of his brother John, who became one of Henry III's intimate counsellors.

But the sense of family extended well beyond the immediate circle to include more distant kin. One of the most evident examples is the family of Glanvill and his nephew Hubert Walter; numerous cousins and nephews of the two won royal office through their kinsmen's influence. Only Stephen of Segrave had a son who followed him onto the bench, although some succeeded in launching their sons in careers in other branches of the civil service. In fact, the tendency seems to have changed noticeably from the time of Henry II to that of John and of his son. Four of the eight lesser-ranking justices under Henry II had sons who followed them into the royal administration, but by the time of King John the sons of only two of the twelve lesser justices pursued careers in the king's service.[3] At a time when office was likely to be considered a form of property, the English monarchs and their justiciars took care to avoid any possibility of heritable places on the bench.

Critics of the royal justices' ambition were simply engaging in hyperbole when they complained of the judges' servile origins. It is true that justices were rarely drawn from distinguished old families, only 8 per cent (4/49). None of Henry II's thirteen justices and only one of Richard I's – William de Warenne of Wormegay – came from the old baronage, while two of John's justices – Master Eustace de Fauconberg and Richard de Mucegros – and only Adam fitz William among Henry III's justices came from families that traced their lineage to companions of the Conqueror. Most came from families in the middle or lower ranges of the knightly class, with kinsmen possessing enough property to get their names recorded occasionally on charters, final concords, or plea rolls. Only one or two had urban, mercantile origins: Henry of London, a member of the

---

[3] The sons of Henry II's justices William Basset, Michael Belet, Alan de Furnellis, and Roger fitz Reinfrid. Two of the eight were clerks, supposedly celibate, and the other two probably left no legitimate sons. Among John's justices, four were in major orders.

prominent London family, the Blunds, and possibly Master
Ralph of Norwich. The origins of eleven of the forty-nine (22
per cent) are so obscure that they cannot be identified definitely
with landholding families.[4] Nine of these were clerics, a fact
which calls to mind Walter Map's charge that clerics among the
royal justices were so ambitious and avaricious because they
were sons of villeins.[5] It is highly unlikely, however, that any of
the justices came from the ranks of the non-free peasantry.

The charge of sycophancy against the justices is an elusive
one, but it may imply resentment against the whole system of
clients and patrons. Anyone who sought advancement needed
the protection of powerful friends, and excesses in fawning
behaviour toward patrons are not hard to find in the few surviving letters from the period. Anyone without friends in high
places felt vulnerable. The justices were obviously caught in a
web of patronage, owing their posts to ties to the justiciar in
most cases. Early ties of several justices to Glanvill, Hubert
Walter, or Geoffrey fitz Peter drawing them to the Exchequer
and the Bench can be traced easily. A new monarch's coronation
brought little change in the composition of the judiciary; the
major changes in its make-up came rather in the midst of reigns,
1194 or 1208–9. A significant change did occur with the revival
of the *curia regis* following the civil war, 1215–17, but that may be
an indication of changes in the character of the justiciarship.
The justices in their turn were patrons, and they had to be on the
watch for rewards for their clients, most easily seen in the search
for presentations to churches for their clerks. By the time of
Henry III justices' clerks could rise into the judiciary themselves, as the Pattishall-Raleigh-Bracton succession shows.

While sycophancy is a difficult quality to assess, one aspect of
it is the professional judges' eagerness to please their royal master. Although they were not directly dependent upon the king as
patron, they recognized themselves as his servants in no sense
set apart from other royal officials, and they were responsive to
the royal will. Royal justices shared the concern expressed in the
Dialogus de Scaccario, *Glanvill*, and *Bracton* for safeguarding the

---

[4] Clerics: Richard of Ilchester, Richard Barre, William de Sainte-Mère-Eglise,
Thomas of Hurstbourne, Ralph of Stokes, Martin of Pattishall, Ralph of
Norwich, Robert of Shardlow, and William of York. Laymen: Walter of
Creeping and James of Potterne.   [5] *De nugis cur.*, i. 10.

king's interests. In their eagerness to protect the king's interest, they showed little awareness of the concept of the royal prerogative, separating the king's personal and private interests from special privileges designed to protect the resources which enabled him to preserve the common good.

More easily measurable is the influence of *avaritia* upon the courts, whether the king's avarice or that of his justices. Many twelfth and thirteenth-century writers felt that greed was getting worse in their days.[6] The profits of justice were an important source of income for the Angevin kings, and their judges were aware of this, as William of York's letter indicates. A difficult question is: to what extent were the costs of justice for suitors caused by corrupt judges, and to what extent were they due not to their personal greed, but due to excessive zeal in exercising their responsibility to safeguard the king's interest?

Fees for writs, fines to expedite proceedings, and amercements were simply part of the judicial system of that day. Large sums, or falcons and warhorses, were accepted by the king and his justices in return for special favours. Usually such fines were offered to the king, but in 1200 a Somerset man seeking his inheritance offered King John sixty marks and a palfrey, and another palfrey to William Briwerre. At Lincoln in 1201 a fine to have a jury was offered to King John, the justiciar, and to Hugh Bardolf, one of the justices present with them.[7] Those who offered fines usually sought to speed the resolution of a case or to secure some special procedure, not to influence actual judgment. John eagerly sought such offerings, especially after 1207. Henry III's government also saw the profits of justice as a means of increasing revenues, particularly after 1238.[8]

Amercement was a possibility for anyone involved in an action at the *curia regis*, not only plaintiffs and tenants but jurors as well. As Maitland wrote, 'Any litigant who hoped to get to the end of his suit without an amercement must have been a sanguine man.'[9] Judges had an interest in amercements, for the

---

[6] Murray, *Reason and Society*, pp. 80–3.
[7] *Rot. de Obl. et Fin.*, p. 95, offer by Henry son of Richard la Robe in 1200. *C.R.R.*, 1: 444, Lincoln 1201; since Hugh was also sheriff of Lincs, that is possibly the reason he was singled out for the offering.
[8] *Intro. to C.R.R.*, pp. 480, 495, 496; Meekings, *Crown Pleas of Wilts eyre*, p. 8; Turner, *King and his Courts*, pp. 274–5.   [9] Pollock and Maitland, 2: 519.

expenses of justices on eyre were often paid out of the sums they collected. Yet the justices did sometimes take pity on poor litigants, as we have seen. William of York on his 1228 eyre to the bishopric of Durham was moved by the poor, who 'cried out in a lamentable way that they were fleeced and afflicted enough . . . without my coming to ruin them completely'.[10] During the minority of Henry III especially, pardons of amercements 'on account of poverty' appear often on the plea rolls.[11]

Were additional profits from justice, beyond what went into the royal coffers, available to the justices? As we have seen, royal judges did not think it unseemly to accept pensions, grants of land, or presentation to churches from magnates or religious houses in return for their legal advice. Neither did they find it unfitting to accept the hospitality of leading county families or great religious foundations when they made their eyres, even when their hosts had suits pending before them. They readily accepted gifts from suitors, either in cash or in kind, but custom may have dictated which gifts were acceptable and which were unacceptable. Such gifts cannot be labelled bribes unless their aim was to purchase favourable judgments. The purpose may have been much like the oblations offered the king: to secure some special procedure or to speed up the case, not to pervert judgment on the main point at issue. We cannot allow our distaste at the thought of judges openly taking presents from litigants make us apply our own standard to medieval royal justices. Neither gift-givers nor takers thought themselves engaging in bribery.

Yet there can be no doubt that the justices profited from their posts. The laymen among them increased their landholdings, even if only slightly in some instances. The rapid rise of others seems to validate the charge of greed levelled against them. Men of little substance were able to secure leases, custodies, or permanent grants that raised them into the ranks of substantial landholders. An early example is Osbert fitz Hervey, condemned in the 'Vision of Thurkill.' This East Anglian knight had at his death an income of over £240, more than the £202 average annual income of a baron at the beginning of the thirteenth cen-

---

[10] Meekings, *Studies*, article 5: 503, no. vi.
[11] Turner, *King and his Courts*, pp. 155–6.

tury. Judges in clerical orders also found it easy to accumulate wealth, since their patrons could reward them with benefices, or sometimes even bishoprics. Nearly all were pluralists. Martin of Pattishall had ecclesiastical preferment valued at 1600 marks at the time of his death, and William of York had benefices worth £800 when he became senior justice *coram rege*.[12]

Yet the justices' activities must be put into context. Most professional justices managed to climb a rung or two higher on the social ladder, but their ascent was hardly dizzying. Although eleven clerics among the justices became bishops, all but three had other claims on the king's favour. Not until the time of Henry III could judicial activity alone earn a bishop's mitre.[13] Those judges who climbed highest did not limit their work to the judicial sphere, but were *curiales* with membership in the king's innermost councils. Representatives of this group are Geoffrey fitz Peter and William Briwerre, who began their careers as minor forest officers and ended them as two of the most powerful barons in all England, and among the half-dozen or so most influential royal counsellors. Resentment at their rapid rise fuelled resentment of all royal servants.

While monastic writers accuse the justices of double-dealing, the monasteries were most prominent among those seeking to influence judges with gifts. We hear nothing of complaints by modest laymen, who leave little mark on the historical records. One heavy trace of them does survive, however, in sheer numbers of cases recorded on the plea rolls. Despite some complaints about sale of justice, ordinary freemen were flocking to the royal courts with their suits. The increased number of feet of fines from the beginning of the thirteenth century offers evidence; during the 1198 eyre, over 200 final concords were made in one county alone.[14]

No doubt, many royal justices were ambitious, sycophantic, and greedy, but most Englishmen found their standard of public service acceptable. Certainly the standard they found in the courts of the Angevin kings was no lower than that of the ecclesiastical courts, including the papal *curia* at Rome. Many

---

[12] Meekings, *Studies*, article 10: 236.
[13] A possible exception is Godfrey de Lucy, named bishop of Winchester at the beginning of Richard I's reign.
[14] Norfolk, cited in *English Justice*, pp. 52, 92.

English litigants might have echoed the plaintiff in a 1220 plea who said, 'He well believes that the justices were so wise that they would not do anything that ought not be done.'[15] Complaints about justices' incompetence or ignorance of the law cannot be found easily, not even in the writings of such hostile witnesses as Matthew Paris. Chroniclers and moralists painted a distorted picture of English royal justices for their own purposes, a lofty one in the case of John of Salisbury, one of petty vindictiveness in the case of Matthew Paris. Whatever their purpose in condemning the judges, they were demanding an impossible standard given the inadequate provision for payment of royal officers and the willingness of petitioners to offer them presents. It was a standard that not even the medieval Church could meet.

[15] *C.R.R.*, 9: 110. He was seeking to have a plea in county court quashed on grounds that the matter had already been decided in the royal court. He succeeded!.

APPENDIX: ROYAL JUSTICES, c. 1176–1239

	Active as justice	Family background	Early career	Highest rank attained
Hugh Bardolf (d. 1203)	1185–1203	Knightly	Local admin.	Baronial rank
Richard Barre (d. 1202/13)	1194–1200	Knightly?	Chancery clerk	Archdeacon of Lisieux, c. 1173–90; archdeacon of Ely, 1190–
William Basset (d. 1185)	1168–85	Baronial/admin.	Local admin.	Knight
Michael Belet, Sr (d. 1201)	1176–1201	Knightly/admin.	*Pincerna*	Knight
William Briwerre (d. 1226)	1188–1215	Knightly/admin.	Local admin.	Baronial rank
Walter of Creeping (d. 1217/23)	1200–09	Knightly?	Local admin.	Knight
Master Eustace de Fauconberg (d. 1228)	1199–1209, 1218–19	Baronial	Justice's clerk	Bishop of London, 1221–8; treasurer, 1217–28
Osbert fitz Hervey (d. 1206)	1191–1206	Knightly/admin.	Local admin.	Knight
Richard fitz Neal (d. 1198)	1179–96	Episcopal/admin.	Treasurer (1159)	Bishop of London, 1189–98; treasurer, 1159–96
Geoffrey fitz Peter (d. 1213)	1188–1213	Knightly/admin.	Chief forester	Earl of Essex, 1199; Justiciar, 1198–1213
Roger fitz Reinfrid (d. c. 1196)	1176–92	Knightly?	Local admin.	Knight
Adam fitz William (d. 1238)	1232–8	Knightly	Local admin.	Knight
Ralf Foliot (d. 1198–9)	1187–97	Episcopal	Chancery clerk	Archdeacon of Hereford, 1182–93/9.
Alan de Furnellis (d. c. 1189)	1179–86	Knightly	Local admin.	Knight

	Active as justice	Family background	Early career	Highest rank attained
Ranulf de Glanvill (d. 1190)	1175–89	Knightly	Local admin.	Baronial rank, Justiciar, 1180–9
John of Guestling (d. c. 1220)	1197–1209; 1218–20	Knightly/admin.	Local Admin.	Knight
Ralf Hareng (d. 1230)	1208 (?); 1218–23	Knightly/admin.	Estate steward	Knight
Richard of Herriard (d. 1208)	1194–1204	Knightly	Local admin.	Knight
Thomas of Heydon (d. 1235)	1219–27	Priest's son	Chancery clerk	Acting vice-chancellor for Richard I
Hubert Walter (d. 1205)	1185–98	Knightly/admin.	Justiciar's clerk	Archbishop of Canterbury, 1193–1205; Justiciar, 1193–8; chancellor, 1199–1205
Master Thomas of Hurstbourne (d. 1200/1)	1185–99	?	Exchequer clerk	
Roger Huscarl (d. c. 1230)	1210–15, 1218–19; Ireland, 1222–4/30	Knightly	Professional lawyer?	Knight
Richard of Ilchester (d. 1188)	1168–84	?	Chancery clerk	Bishop of Winchester, 1173–88
Master Godfrey de Insula (d. after 1215)	1194; 1198–1205	Knightly?	Justiciar's clerk	
William de Insula (d. 1239)	1227–37	Knightly	Marshal of Exchequer	Knight

C	Jocelin (d. 1202/3)	1185–90; 1195	Episcopal	Chancery clerk	Archdeacon of Lewes (Chichester)
C	Robert of Lexington (d. 1250)	1218; 1220–44	Knightly/admin.	Chamber or Exchequer clerk	
C	Henry of London (d. 1228)	1199; 1205–9	Urban/admin.	Royal clerk	Archbishop of Dublin 1213–28; Justiciar of Ireland, 1213–15, 1221–4
	Godfrey de Lucy (d. 1204)	1179–99	Baronial/admin.		Bishop of Winchester, 1189–1204
	Richard de Mucegros (d. 1237)	1205–11	Semi-baronial/admin.	Local admin.	Knight
	Thomas of Moulton (d. 1240)	1224–36	Knightly	Local admin.	Baron of Burgh by Sands, Cumberland
M C	Master Ralph of Norwich (d. 1258–9)	1230–7	Urban?	Exchequer clerk	Chancellor of Ireland, 1249–56
C	John of Oxford (d. 1200)	1179–89	Knightly/admin.	Chancery clerk	Bishop of Norwich, 1175–1200
C	Martin of Pattishall (d. 1229)	1218–29	?	Justice's clerk	Archdeacon of Norfolk, 1225–8; Dean of St Paul's, 1228–9
	Simon of Pattishall (d. 1216/17)	1190–1215	Knightly	Local admin.	Knight
	Henry de Pont Audemar (d. 1223?)	1207–15	Knightly	Local admin. (Normandy)	Knight
	James of Potterne (d. c. 1220)	1198–1215; 1218, 1222	Knightly?	Local admin.	Knight
C	William of Raleigh (d. 1250)	1229–39	Knightly	Justice's clerk	Bishop of Norwich, 1239–43; Bishop of Winchester, 1243–50

	Active as justice	Family background	Early career	Highest rank attained
Geoffrey Ridel (d. 1189)	1179–89	Baronial/admin.?	Chancery clerk	Bishop of Ely, 1173–89; Acting Chancellor, 1162–73
William Ruffus (d. after 1194)	1180–94	Knightly/admin.	*Dapifer*	Knight
William de Ste-Mère-Eglise (d. 1224)	1194–1201	?	Chamber clerk	Bishop of London, 1198–1221
Geoffrey le Sauvage (d. 1230)	1223–6	Knightly/admin.	Estate steward	Knight
Stephen of Segrave (d. 1241)	1218–32; 1239–41	Knightly/admin.	Local admin.	Baronial rank, justiciar in 1234
Master Robert of Shardlow (d. 1253)	1229–32; 1245	Knightly?	Chancery clerk	Senior justice in Ireland, 1245–53
Master Ralf of Stokes (d. 1219/24)	1199–1206	?/admin.	Justiciar's clerk	
William de Warenne (d. 1209)	1193–1200	Baronial/admin.	Local admin.	Baron of Wormegay
Robert of Wheatfield (d. 1193/4)	1179–92	Knightly		Knight
Henry of Whiston (d. after 1209)	1190; 1199–1201	Knightly	Exchequer clerk	Clerk in minor orders
William of York (d. 1256)	1231–47	Knightly?	Chancery clerk at the Bench	Bishop of Salisbury, 1246–56

MANUSCRIPT SOURCES

All Souls College, Oxford, MS.DD.c.218
British Library, London
  Additional MSS. 8167; 9822; 14,847; 24,005; 29,436; 46,353
  Cotton Charter XI.52
  Cotton MSS: Claudius D.iii
            Julius D.ii
            Tiberius C.ix
            Vespasian E.xvii; E.xxv
  Egerton MS.3031
  Harleian Charters 43.c.26; 45.c.9
  Harleian MSS.325, 391, 645, 746, 3255, 4748
  Landsdowne MS.415
Caius College, Cambridge, MS.205
Cambridge University Library, MSS.Ff.2.33; Ii.vi.3; Mm.19.4
  Diocesan Registry, Ely, Liber M
Corpus Christi College, Cambridge, MS.297
Lambeth Palace, MSS.105, 241, 1212
National Library of Wales, MS. Peniarth 390c
Norfolk and Norwich Record Office, Norwich, SUN/8
Pembroke College, Cambridge, MS.72
Public Record Office, London
  CP.25(1)/172/24; 172/26; 173/28
  DL.36/2; 42/2; 42/5
  E.159/1; 163/1; 164/19; 164/21; 368/4
  JUST.1/869
  KB.26/90
  SC.1/1; 1/4; 1/6
Walters Art Gallery, Baltimore, MS.15
Westminster Abbey, Muniment Book 11

Clerks 22/45 = 45%

Masters 6/44 = 12%

INDEX

Accounting, treatises on, 228–9
Ada de Morevill, wife of Thomas of
   Moulton, 224, 225, 242, 247,
   253, 255
Adam fitz William, justice, 8n., 196,
   203, 206, 219, 229, 240, 248,
   263, 293
Advowson, *see* churches, presentation
   to
Aids, feudal, 18, 208, 244
Alan de Furnellis, justice, 19, 22, 26,
   27, 31, 40, 41, 60, 63, 64, 74
Alan de Neville, 18
Alan de Wassand, 215, 217
Alconbury, Hunts, manor of, 246,
   247n.
Alexander de Barentin, 115
Alexander of St Vaast, 118
Alice, countess of Eu, 249
Alice de Lucy, wife of Alan of
   Moulton, 253–4, 283
Alice Murdak, wife of Ralph Hareng
   III, 253
Alice de Rumilly, 253–4, 283
Almshoe, Herts, 206
Alrewas, Staffs, 183n., church of,
   177
Alstonfield, Cheshire, 212
Ambassador, *procurator*, 43, 44, 46,
   48, 51, 101, 103, 132, 148n.,
   154, 157, 188, 213, 227, 232–3
Amercements, 13n., 64, 67, 86, 121,
   155–6, 163, 170–1, 223, 246,
   249, 268, 295–6; forest, 42;
   pardons of, 262
Amounderness, Lancs, wapentake
   of, 119
Andrew Blund, 187
Anglo-Norman language and litera-
   ture, 33, 122
Archdeacons, 29, 40, 44, 98, 109–10,
   see also Canterbury, Chichester,

Derby, Ely, Hereford, Lisieux,
   Norfolk, Oxford, Poitiers, Richmond, Rouen, Stafford
Arnulf, bishop of Lisieux, 103
Ars dictaminis, 35, 230
Ars notaria, 99, 229–30
Arthur of Brittany, 160
Arundel, earl of, *see* William
   d'Aubigny
Ashbury, Berks, church of, 102,
   110n.
Assizes, Grand assize, 21, 167, 273,
   279; possessory assizes, 41, 129,
   135, 138, 167, 184, 198–9, 204,
   267, 287, 288; darrein present-
   ment, 134, 268, novel disseisin,
   17, 164, 167, 198, 260, 274; *see
   also* Clarendon, Northampton
Attorneys, advocates, 31, 35, 59,
   152–4, 211, 221, 222, 228–31,
   238–9, 254
Aubrey de Vere, earl of Oxford,
   143–4
Aumale, count of, *see* William de Forz;
   countess, *see* Hawise
Austin canons, 263–4
Avelina, second wife of Geoffrey fitz
   Peter, 184
Aylesbury, Bucks, manor of, 172,
   183n.

Bacon, Sir Francis, 285
Badburgham, church of, 110
Baginton, War., manor of, 209
Bampton, barony of, 111–12
Barbota, wife of John of Guestling,
   178
Baronical household, 185–6; chaplain,
   33
Bartholomew, bishop of Exeter, 31,
   38
Bartholomew Blund, 142

305